2 Vols

2

29-1-1896

1-12-62

A HISTORY OF EGYPT

VOLUME I

AGENTS

AMERICA .	THE MACMILLAN COMPANY 60 FIFTH AVENUE, NEW YORK
AUSTRALASIA	OXFORD UNIVERSITY PRESS 205 FLINDERS LANE, MELBOURNE
CANADA	THE MACMILLAN COMPANY OF CANADA, LTD. ST. MARTIN'S HOUSE, 70 BOND STREET, TORONTO, 2
INDIA	MACMILLAN & COMPANY, LTD. 276 HORNBY ROAD, BOMBAY 294 BOW BAZAR STREET, CALCUTTA NORTH BEACH ROAD, MADRAS

PLATE I

A MIDDLE KINGDOM PHARAOH
Possibly Amenemhat III
From Sir Wallis Budge's "Egyptian Sculptures in the British Museum'

A
HISTORY OF EGYPT

FROM THE EARLIEST TIMES TO THE END OF THE XVIIIᵗʰ DYNASTY

BY

JAMES BAIKIE, D.D., F.R.A.S.

AUTHOR OF "THE STORY OF THE PHARAOHS"
"THE AMARNA AGE," ETC.

IN TWO VOLUMES

VOL. I

CONTAINING TWENTY-FOUR FULL-PAGE ILLUSTRATIONS
FROM PHOTOGRAPHS

A. & C. BLACK, LTD.
4, 5 & 6 SOHO SQUARE, LONDON, W.1
1929

Printed in Great Britain

PREFACE

IN the following chapters I have endeavoured to accomplish on a more extended scale, and with greater fulness of detail, what was attempted in outline in a previous volume, *The Story of the Pharaohs*, namely, to offer to the general reader an account of the history of the most interesting race of the Ancient East which shall be readable and, to the extent of the writer's capacity, accurate.

With this end in view, the narrative has been kept, so far as possible, a narrative, and not a discussion of the opposing views of different and differing scholars, which are no less numerous in connection with the story of Egypt than elsewhere. Where it has been necessary to introduce such controversial matter, I have not hesitated to indicate with which side my preference lies; but in the main I have gone on the principle that what people want to know, and should know, about Ancient Egypt is not all the windings and intricacies of disputed and uncertain successions, but the plain course and trend of events, no matter which Pharaoh might for the moment be sitting on the throne, and some idea of how life was being lived, and what people were thinking and saying in particular periods.

Accordingly, considerable prominence has been given to the principle of letting the Egyptians themselves tell their own story, wherever the material available made such a course possible to any extent. Egypt is fortunate above the other races of the Ancient East in that her tomb-inscriptions and the survivals of her literature offer a con-

v

siderable amount of absolutely first-hand information as to events, thoughts, and beliefs. Would that the amount were vastly greater than it is! but, such as it is, no other country of the old world freely presents to us such materials for a direct insight into its past. In matters of plain historical fact, for example, what other nation can offer us such admirable filling for the outline of history as the personal narratives of Aahmes, son of Abana, or Amenemhab? while from a more literary point of view, the Story of Sinuhe offers us more insight into the mind of the Egyptian of the Middle Kingdom and his attitude towards foreign peoples than can be derived from all the grave disquisitions in the world.

To let the Egyptians speak for themselves, therefore, has been my aim to the utmost possible extent. That this has been possible in so great a degree is due largely to the labours of others; and I have especially to record my gratitude to Professor James H. Breasted and the Press of the University of Chicago for the kind permission granted to me to make such liberal use of the translation of Egyptian documents in Professor Breasted's *Ancient Records*, and to Dr. Aylward Blackman for kindly authorising me to use his translation of Professor Erman's versions of Egyptian literature, published in English under the title *The Literature of the Ancient Egyptians*. To Sir Flinders Petrie and the astonishing collection of historical material gathered with such care in his *History of Egypt* and his many other works, I owe a great debt; while I wish once more to acknowledge his great kindness in granting me again the free use of his photographs for purposes of illustration. In the present instance I owe to him the following plates: Vol. I., Plates XIX., XXI., XXIII.; Vol. II., Plate XIV. To the courtesy of Sir Alan Cobham I owe the two air views of the Gizeh Pyramid Field and of Karnak (Vol. I., Plate VIII., and Vol. II., Plate

VI.), and to the Rev. P. B. Fraser, M.A., New Zealand, Plate IV. (a), Vol. II.

The illustrations have been chosen with the double object of presenting some of the outstanding historical personages of the various periods dealt with, and some of the most notable results of the arts and crafts of each period. Inevitably, therefore, they include some of the great masterpieces, which, however familiar, can never be excluded from a representative gathering of Egyptian works of art; but recourse has also been had to work less familiar to the general public, and Dr. Howard Carter has given permission for the use of his photographs of the diadem and the golden coffin of Tutankhamen; while I have also used a number of the photographs of Messrs. Gaddis and Seif of Luxor to illustrate Egyptian relief-work and painting as shown in the Theban tombs, and, in respect of sculpture, the remarkable head of Akhenaten, discovered recently at Karnak.

The narrative has not been encumbered by references to notes at the foot of the page or elsewhere, as these are usually more of a nuisance than a help to the general reader, while the scholar does not need them; but in each case of quotation from an ancient authority the name of the person who was responsible for the inscription has been given in the text, and the inscription can easily be identified thereby in *Ancient Records* or elsewhere. A short bibliographical note of works likely to be useful to the reader has been given at the end of Vol. II., and a chronological list, giving both the longer and shorter systems of dating, has been added, instead of sprinkling dates over the text. At present the narrative is carried down to the close of the XVIIIth Dynasty and the collapse which followed upon Akhenaten's effort to impose a new form of religion upon Egypt; but it is hoped to complete it at a future date by carrying it up to the Persian Conquest.

CONTENTS

CHAP.   PAGE

' I. THE LAND: ITS PHYSICAL FEATURES, CLIMATE, AND
     CHARACTERISTICS 3

·II. THE BEGINNINGS OF LIFE IN EGYPT 22

BOOK I. THE OLD KINGDOM

III. THE "DEAD DEMI-GODS", AND THE UNIFICATION OF EGYPT 52

IV. UNITED EGYPT AND ITS EARLIEST ROYAL LINE . . 62

V. MENA'S SUCCESSORS OF THE FIRST DYNASTY . . 76

VI. "COME LIKE SHADOWS, SO DEPART!" . . . 88

VII. THE PYRAMID-BUILDERS 114

VIII. THE CHILDREN OF THE SUN-GOD 139

IX. THE SIXTH DYNASTY, AND THE CLOSE OF THE OLD
    KINGDOM 156

X. THE OLD KINGDOM; SOCIAL ORGANISATION, LITERA-
   TURE AND ART 187

XI. THE FIRST INTERMEDIATE DARK PERIOD . . . 217

BOOK II. THE MIDDLE KINGDOM

XII. THE RISE OF THEBES UNDER THE ELEVENTH DYNASTY . 245

XIII. THE RISE OF THE TWELFTH DYNASTY AND THE GOLDEN
     AGE OF EGYPT 266

XIV. THE REIGN OF SENUSERT I. AND THE STORY OF SINUHE 281

XV. TWO UNDISTINGUISHED REIGNS 303

XVI. THE CULMINATION OF THE MIDDLE KINGDOM . . 316

CHAP.   PAGE
XVII. The Middle Kingdom: Society, Foreign Relations,
        Literature and Art 346
XVIII. The Second Intermediate Period and the Hyksos
        Domination 383
  XIX. The War of Independence 413

CONTENTS OF VOLUME II

BOOK III. THE NEW EMPIRE

    XX. The Rise of the Eighteenth Dynasty . . 3
   XXI. Thothmes I. and the Great Asiatic Adventure . 24
  XXII. An Interlude; the Reign of Thothmes II. . . 45
 XXIII. The Reign and Work of the Woman-Pharaoh . 55
  XXIV. Thothmes III. and the Conquest of Asia . . 92
   XXV. Thothmes III. and the Egyptian Empire . . 122
  XXVI. A Pause on the Summit; Amenhotep II. and Thoth-
        mes IV. 152
 XXVII. The Golden Emperor; Amenhotep III. . . 172
XXVIII. The Reign of Akhenaten, and his Religious Re-
        volution 227
  XXIX. The City of the Horizon 259
   XXX. The Collapse of Egypt's Asiatic Empire . . 286
  XXXI. The Reaction, and the Close of the Eighteenth
        Dynasty 319
 XXXII. Art and Religion in the Amarna Period . . 336

        Chronological List of Egyptian Dynasties and
        Kings 381
        Bibliographical Note 389
        Index 393

LIST OF ILLUSTRATIONS

PLATE

I. A Middle Kingdom Pharaoh . . *Frontispiece*

FACING PAGE

II. Rapids at the First Cataract 6
A Nubian Landscape

III. A Pre-Dynastic Grave 33
Pre-Dynastic Pottery

IV. Palette of Narmer 48

V. Semerkhet Smites a Bedawy Chief . . . 85
Prehistoric Ships

VI. Statuette of Kha-Sekhemui. 92

VII. The "Step" Pyramid 113
The Great Pyramid

VIII. The Gizeh Pyramid Field from the Air . . . 128

IX. Diorite Statue of Khafra 145
The Sphinx

X. Copper Statue of Prince Merenra 160
Copper Statue of Pepy I.

XI. Old Kingdom Reliefs. Tomb of Tiy . . . 177

XII. Old Kingdom Sculpture. Statues of Rahotep and Nefert 192

XIII. Head of Tiy 197
Head of Ranefer

XIV. An Old Kingdom Wood Carving. Portrait of Hesi . 204

XV. Relief of Cranes 225
Relief of Gazelles. Tomb of Methen

xi

PLATE   FACING PAGE

XVI. Old Kingdom Stele of Rahotep   240
     Middle Kingdom Stele of Antef

XVII. Grey Granite Statue of Senusert III.   .   .   . 305

XVIII. An Old Kingdom Tomb-Chapel   .   .   . 320
     Tomb Chamber of Ameny, Beni Hasan

XIX. Stele of Hor-ur-ra, Sinai   341
     Miners' Workings and Huts, Sinai

XX. Statue of Amenemhat III. 348

XXI. Hand-Mirror in Silver, Obsidian, and Gold   .   . 369
     Canopic Jars of Princess Sat-hathor-ant

XXII. Statue of Sekhem-suaz-tauira   384

XXIII. Twelfth Dynasty Pectorals 389
     Gold Diadem of Princess Sat-hathor-ant

XXIV. Coronet of Princess Khnumit   396
     Pectoral of Amenemhat III.
     Pectoral of Senusert II.

Map of Egypt at end of book.

BOOK I
THE OLD KINGDOM

ANCIENT EGYPT

CHAPTER I

THE LAND: ITS PHYSICAL FEATURES, CLIMATE, AND CHARACTERISTICS

THE Land of Egypt, the home of that wonderful ancient culture which, at the very least, must rank as one of the two most ancient and fruitful civilisations of the world, might almost seem to have been created and set apart by Nature for the home and the nursery of the arts and crafts in which its people were destined to be the pioneers of the human race. Within its own limits, its natural features were such as to promote and, indeed, to necessitate the early and thorough organisation of human industry, and to familiarise the race, at a date when most of the peoples of the ancient world had scarcely awakened to the consciousness of their powers, with the great problems of engineering and construction, in the solution of which they attained a skill and facility which have seldom been equalled and never surpassed. At the same time, these limits themselves, while never such as to raise any impassable barrier against the natural spirit of curiosity and adventure, were yet such as to offer a decided check to the incursion of alien and hostile races from without. The check was never an absolute one, as the history of the land abundantly shows; yet it was always so far operative as to limit and delay such incursions as did from time to time occur, and to secure that the native race and the genius of the land had time to absorb the intruding element and to stamp it with the characteristic seal of the Nilotic culture. Instead of infiltration and conquest on the part of alien races resulting, as in less favoured lands, in the imposition of an external culture on that already existing, the result of such intrusions was merely the enrichment of the traditional civilisation of the Nile Valley, which itself remained essentially unchanged. The natural features of the land which determined this result are very broad and simple, and are responsible, not only for the restraints already described, but also for much that was most characteristic in the internal development of Egyptian culture.

The Nile Valley, which is the true Land of Egypt, and which for our purposes extends from the First Cataract at Aswan to the Mediterranean Sea, with occasional extensions into Nubia, has been described as a tube which can only be entered at its two ends; and the figure, while not more absolutely accurate than such figures usually are, is sufficiently so to need only minor modification. But the Nile Valley is only a small fraction of the area embraced within the territorial limits of the Land of Egypt; and the determining features which settled, first, that there should be such a valley, and next, that it should possess such marked individuality as it does, belong to the whole area. The Land of Egypt, in the widest sense, consists, then, of a great inclined plane of roughly rectangular shape, whose longer measurement lies north and south, and whose breadth from east to west is, roughly speaking, somewhat less than a half and more than a third of its length. The southern limit of this plane is marked by the rise of the land from a point somewhat above Wady Halfa, and its northern, of course, by the Mediterranean; though, strictly speaking, the last 100 miles northwards (the Delta) do not belong to the original land plane, but are a comparatively modern formation. The eastern limit is the Red Sea, and the western is the deep bottom, marked by the line of the oases, from whose western side the great mass of continental Africa begins to rise again.

The main inclination of this great plane, however, is not, as one might imagine, from south to north, but from east to west. Its eastern edge rises sharply and steeply from the margin of the Red Sea, the seaward slope being so narrow and steep as to represent merely, so to speak, the thickness of the tilted plane. The upper edge of the plane is the long ridge of steep volcanic hills, capped with a jagged crest of sedimentary rocks, which runs approximately parallel with the Red Sea, reaching at some points an elevation of from 4000 to 6000 feet. From this ridge the plane falls away westwards, ribbed at intervals by horizontal swells running east and west, until at its extreme westward limit along the line of the oases it falls below sea-level.

This general east to west inclination of the land, however, is far from being the feature which most immediately impresses itself upon the mind. On the contrary, the most obvious feature is that of the great trench which is dug through the middle of the east-west slope in a south to north direction, and whose remarkable characteristics have given to the land and its people their opportunity, and determined their bent. "This plane", says the late Dr. Hogarth, "is bisected by the valley of a single mighty stream, which derives neither its origin nor any of its waters from it, but, itself an alien, has laid down a ribbon of alien soil and fenced the sea from the northern edge of the plane with a large deltaic tract". The great plane which is nominally the Land of Egypt has indeed had its own share in the making of the destiny of the race which inhabited the narrow thread of cultivable soil which bisects it; but its function was more or less simply that of providing bounds and barriers within which the nation's destiny might be accomplished with less risk of interruption and opposition; it was within the great bisecting trench, and with the help of the agencies of the river which had created it, that the destiny was wrought out.

"Egypt", as Herodotus says (ii. 5) in words which have been perhaps oftener quoted than those of any other historian, "is acquired land, and the gift of the river". It would be impossible to find a sentence which should describe more aptly or more tersely the essential fact about the country. For, of the soil on which the Egyptians lived, from which they drew their nurture, and on which (with notable exceptions to be described hereafter) they wrought their great works, not one atom belongs originally to the land which it has made fruitful and habitable, but all has been carried and deposited within the Nile trench by the great river which both literally and metaphorically has been the making of Egypt.

Rising in the great lake basin of Equatorial Africa, the Nile, whose four thousand miles make it one of the longest rivers of the world, has already accomplished three-fourths of its course before it approaches the land of which it is the life. At Khartum, the White Nile, the main stream, has received its great tributary, the Blue Nile, which brings down from the Abyssinian hills the suspended detritus which from time immemorial has been creating, and which continually enriches and renews, the habitable land of the Egyptian valley. Throughout the rest of its course to the sea the river receives only one more tributary, the Atbara, a mountain torrent of similar character to the Blue Nile, which also contributes its quota of alluvium to the treasure which is being borne northwards. From the junction of the Atbara, it flows to the sea, as has been said, "a mid-African stranger", receiving nothing from the land through which it passes, and giving nothing to it until it has passed the last of its six cataracts.

These long sloping stairs by which it descends from its equatorial level begin with the Sixth Cataract between Khartum and Meroë. The Fifth Cataract lies between the mouth of the Atbara and the great westward bend of the river at Abu Hamed; the Fourth is between the latter spot and the ancient Napata, in the land which the Egyptians used to call "Karoy", and which marked the southern limit of their empire; the Third extends between the islands of Arko and Tombos, some distance south of the ancient Soleb; and the Second extends from the ancient strongholds of Semneh and Kummeh which marked the limits of Egyptian power during the Middle Kingdom to the modern Wady Halfa. But the most famous of all the cataracts is the First, whose foaming barrier at Aswan was long held by the Egyptian imagination to mark the spot where the Nile emerged from its mysterious underground sources. At this point the great river during the course of unnumbered centuries has cut its way through the bar of

PLATE II

1. RAPIDS AT THE FIRST CATARACT
2. A NUBIAN LANDSCAPE
Showing the two temples of Abu Simbel

crystalline rocks which crossed its path, and which in historic times yielded to the Pharaohs the beautiful granite of their obelisks and shrines.

Hitherto the river, with the energy gathered in its descent of the series of cataracts, has cut its trench so deeply into the limestone and Nubian sandstone over which it flows as to confine its own waters within its channel. But after its conquest of the granite barrier at Aswan, it is able to spread more widely, and when it has passed Gebel Silsileh, some forty miles further north, where the close approach of the sandstone hills on either side suggests that there was once another cataract, the valley gradually broadens out. From this point, for a matter of 400 miles as the crow flies (about 550 following the curves of the river), the rock which underlies the stream is limestone, sometimes of a harder quality as at Erment, where the valley narrows to a gut. From the apex of the Delta, immediately north of Cairo, the alluvial soil with which the river has filled the ancient fan-shaped bay of the Mediterranean extends to the sea, from Alexandria to Port Said.

Now, within the area of this great tilted plane which the Nile bisects on its way to the Mediterranean, there is practically no fertile or habitable land except along the line of the trench which the river has cut for itself. The seaward slope (the thickness of the edge of the plane, so to speak) facing the Red Sea is almost entirely destitute of streams or springs, and depends upon surface water gathered in cisterns. The mountain line above the seaward slope is desolate and barren to a degree. "No water survives above ground twenty-four hours after the rare rainstorms that fall in this region, except high up on the slope in fissures of the rock; and there are but very few wells in the depths of the wadis, and still fewer palm-oases on the lower ground." The hills, indeed, possess valuable stores of hard stone, which the Egyptians well knew how to prize and utilise, and emeralds and gold have at different periods been worked among them; but for all other purposes the whole eastern half of the plane is useless, and has never supported anything but the scantiest population of wandering tribes.

Beyond the Nile trench, on the western side, the same dreary condition of things is resumed, and, with the one exception of the great sunk basin of the Fayum and the unhealthy and sour soil of the oases, the western half of the plane is as desert as the eastern half. Thus it would seem that there are few portions of the world's surface less promising as a sphere for human effort and a nursery of civilisation than the north-eastern corner of Africa. But for one thing which has sufficed to make this wilderness rejoice and blossom as the rose, wherever its beneficent influence has come.

The great trench of the Nile Valley extends from the First Cataract to the head of the Delta, with a maximum width of about thirty miles, and an average width of from ten to fifteen miles. During the greater part of the year the river occupies but a small fraction of this bed ; but for two months it occupies the whole Valley, and, as it gradually shrinks again to its normal limits, it leaves the land which it has thus temporarily covered coated with a fresh deposit of alluvial soil. By the continual and immemorial repetition of this process, the area of the Valley, up to the limits of the river's rise, has been gradually covered with a stratum of fertile soil which reaches a depth of about thirty feet. The phenomenon of the inundation which has produced this result is one which, though it is faintly paralleled in several other lands, is really unique in its scale and its regularity.

The main agent in its production is the heavy rain which falls annually from June to September on the Abyssinian tableland, and which causes the Blue Nile and the Atbara to rise rapidly, carrying down with their flood vast quantities of suspended silt. The volume of this descending water, particularly that of the Blue Nile, which sometimes exceeds 350,000 cubic feet per second at Khartum, holds back the White Nile, so that the main agent of the inundation, in its first stages, at all events, is the lesser stream, which bears the life-giving soil. At Aswan the Nile begins to rise in the early part of June; the rise begins to reach Cairo between the 17th and the 20th of the month. The river at the First Cataract reaches in flood a height fifty feet above its minimum level, while at Cairo the rise is about half that amount. In September the flood begins to fall; but it is resumed again for a short time, and sometimes lasts into November. As it recedes it leaves on the surface of the land a deposit of the loam which it has brought down from the Abyssinian hills; and it is this perpetually renewed alluvium which has made the Land of Egypt— the Black Land, as its inhabitants called it, to distinguish it from the red desert, infertile and lifeless, which bordered it on either side, and was perpetually seeking to encroach upon it.

Thus, then, the real Egypt, within which men lived and wrought, was merely the narrow ribbon of black soil which extends on either side of the great river from Aswan to north of Cairo, where it gives place to the wider Delta deposit. Its area, therefore, was comparatively small. Including the deserts, Egypt has an area of about 400,000 square miles; but its habitable land does not exceed 13,000 square miles in area, and of this only about 10,000 square miles are cultivable. It is, therefore, comparable in size to Belgium among European states. The population maintained by this small area, however, has always been very large, amounting, according to tradition, in ancient times to seven millions, and at present to thirteen millions. The density of population is, therefore, much greater than that of any European country.

The fact which makes possible the maintenance of so great an aggregation of human beings within an area so small is, of course, the extraordinary fertility of the long narrow ribbon of alluvial soil annually renewed by the inundation. Apart from the dense concentration along the line of the Nile Valley, the population of the rest of the land is almost negligible; but few areas on the world's surface are capable of the constant productivity which the Valley has steadily maintained for many thousands of years under the many different systems of government to which it has been subject. The contrast between the barren desert which surrounds it on every side, and the amazing richness of the Valley, has never failed to impress the beholder with wonder. "The prospect of the valley of the lower

Nile," says Dr. Hogarth, "affects one who comes out of this waste (of the eastern desert) to the brink of the trough at a precipitous point with the strongest emotion that contrast can occasion. Perhaps no living thing has been seen outside the caravan and no green blade for many hours' march, and lo! sheer below, defined as sharply as with a graver, this verdure without limit to north or south, this panorama of man's handiwork and his myriad settlements." Egypt has always been more or less the granary of the surrounding lands, and when famine prevailed elsewhere it was but seldom that there failed to be "corn in Egypt". At the present time three or four crops are raised off the same land each year, while instances have been known in which seven crops were gathered in fifteen months from a single plot of ground.

Practically the whole of this extraordinary productivity is due to the life-giving agency of the river; for rain, while not unknown, is a comparative rarity even on the coastal strip, and progressively diminishes in quantity southwards. "The rainfall even on the coastal strip, from Port Said to Alexandria, is only about 4 to 8 inches per annum. In the Delta it tapers off, till at Cairo it is only about an inch. At Luxor it has fallen to vanishing point, and we enter a belt which is as nearly rainless as any in the world. The result is that Egypt simply would not exist if it were not for the Nile." "It is no exaggeration to say that if a hostile power in the Sudan were to divert the waters of the Nile (and the idea is not so utterly impossible as it may seem), there would not be a blade of corn or a human being left alive in Egypt after one summer."

Thus the Nile, which made the habitable land of Egypt in the beginning, is the sole agent of its maintenance in being; and fortunately its life-giving power seems as inexhaustible now, after so many millenniums of constant expenditure, as it was in the beginning. "Its fertilising power," says Professor Todd, "is astonishing; a little of it will really make the desert blossom as the rose. Spill a bucket of water on the desert and it will grow green things for months afterwards." But the influence of the great river is not confined to its fertilising agencies. It has always been the great high-

way which has linked together the furthest extremities of
the long straggling country through which it passes. Egypt
is the nearest approach on earth to a living illustration of
what is meant by length without breadth. Her towns and
villages are strung out for seven hundred and fifty miles
along the slender thread of the river valley with practically
no lateral extension at all, save in the Fayum depression.
Consequently transport is bound to be difficult and costly
under normal conditions. But the conditions have never
been normal throughout all the long history of the land.
The river has always offered the cheapest and most convenient of all forms of transport, and from time immemorial the Egyptians have utilised to the fullest extent
the facilities which it presents. From the gilded barge of
the Pharaoh or of his god, down to the huge pontoons
which carried the granite blocks for obelisk or colossal
statue, and the light skiffs of the fisherman or the messenger,
the constant procession has gone on ever since there was
history in the land, just as it goes on to-day.

The full utilisation of the great waterway is facilitated
amazingly by another of the characteristic features of the
long river valley. One of the most striking features of Nile
scenery is the sight of the procession of boats stemming
the full current of the river on their southward journey
under full sail, while the boats travelling downstream drift
and row slowly with the current against the wind, and with
lowered masts. For more than three-quarters of the year
this steady north wind blows almost without intermission,
neutralising, for upstream traffic, the opposition of the
current, and immensely simplifying the whole problem of
transport. The existence of such a wind is due in its turn
once more to the river. How it comes about is so admirably
expressed by Dr. Hogarth that it is best to quote his words:

"The Nile Valley is a funnel set contrary to the two sea
avenues from the south. Its mouth opens nearly where the
Red Sea funnel ends, and admits northerly climatic influences to the south. Leading far inland between vast
areas of heated sands, the Valley sucks an almost continuous draught of polar air towards the vacua of the African
deserts; and therefore the north wind blows up its stream

all the summer long and for a great part of the winter, and indeed in the whole year stands to southerly airs in the ratio of six to one. The only serious interruption occurs in the spring, or rather early summer (for spring there hardly is in Egypt), when, equilibrium having been gradually established by the winter chill on the sands, there ensues an intermittent reaction against the normal current in the form of south-westerly sand-laden and highly electric airs, which Europeans know as the Khamsin—the winds of fifty days."

Students of Egyptian literature will remember how highly the "cooling of the north wind" is appreciated, and how often it is referred to. Even the Middle Kingdom misanthrope, to whom Death seems the sweetest thing on earth, turns to the cooling breeze as the fittest image of what he is seeking. "Death is before me to-day as the odour of myrrh, as when one sitteth under the sail on a windy day." But, quite apart from its comfort and its pleasing mitigation of the summer heats, the influence of the steady air-current as an agent in all the activities of the land must have been immense, as it still is; and this agency was and is directly the result of the secular work of the river in creating the channel through which it blows.

Thus, then, Egypt owes everything more or less directly to her river—the creation of the land on which alone within her borders men can live and work—the existence of the waterway which neutralises the disadvantages of her inordinate extension, and the creation of the air-current, which makes the waterway available upstream, as the water-current helps it downstream—most of all, the annual fertilisation, without which all the rest would finally go for nothing. Egypt and the Nile—the Nile and Egypt—synonymous terms, one might almost say. Little wonder that the Egyptians deified their great life-giver, and that if one of the dominant facts of their religion has always been the solar light and heat, the other has equally been the life-giving river.

At the same time, it would be wrong to ignore, in our survey of the land, the part which the barren and desolate deserts on either side of the Valley have played in the history of the country and its people. Lifeless, or next to lifeless themselves, they may have contributed nothing to the actual life of the nation; but it would be difficult to exaggerate the part which they played in safeguarding and warding the life of the people and the growth of their civilisation. Let it be remembered that it is a total misconception to think of the Egyptian race as an aggressive and militaristic one. There were, indeed, times in the national history when, under special inspirations and in specially favourable circumstances, the Egyptian became for a while a conqueror; but the race was essentially pacific and unaggressive, as it is at the present day. There can be little doubt that if the Nile Valley had been as easily accessible as some of the other lands of the ancient world, that wonderful thing, so essentially a thing by itself, which we know as Egyptian culture, would never have been developed, but would have been lost or overlaid by the influences of fiercer and more warlike races.

But it was here that the deserts sheltered and guarded the growing plant in the future interest of the whole world. It is incorrect to call Egypt impregnable or inaccessible. The country has been conquered, not once, but many times; but at least the deserts have always made it difficult to attack and easy to defend; and in ancient times, when transport was slow-moving in the extreme, and even the pace of an army was that of marching and weary infantry, the possession of these barren wastes on either side was one of Egypt's greatest securities. The motive had to be very strong which drew an ancient army to face the risks and terrors of the long desert march from the maritime plain of Palestine across the barren bridge of the Isthmus. It was on that point that the danger mostly arose, for the approach from the south was easily controlled, and the loose aggregates of the western tribes were seldom dangerous until far on in Egypt's decline; and though the Isthmus was forced once and again, the narrow pathway was so defensible that long stretches of time lay between the various attempts, and in these quiet intervals the plant grew unchecked, until no storm could uproot it. The debt which the whole world owes to the ancient

Egyptian is not conditioned by his valley and his river alone, but in no small degree also by his guardian deserts.

Further, it was to the grim hills of his eastern boundary that the Egyptian owed much of the noble material which he used in his work. As a builder, he habitually and wisely used the rocks which underlay his own immediate abode, and built with limestone, as in the case of the Pyramids, or with sandstone, as at Karnak; but for the purposes of adornment, when special beauty or durability was desired, he turned to the granites of Aswan and his eastern hills, or to the porphyries, breccias and diorite of the Arabian range. Thence, too, came many of the semi-precious stones which he knew so well how to use for colour-decoration. The bulk of the gold which made the kings of the east look to Egypt with such envious eyes ("for in my brother's land gold is as common as dust") came, no doubt, from Nubia; but a certain proportion of it, at all events, came also from the eastern hills, however little the unlucky miners who were employed in that "land of perdition" enjoyed working it.

Most of all, perhaps, the desert was precious to the ancient Egyptian, as it has in these insatiably inquisitive days again become precious to us, because it was the "eternal habitation" of his dead. The alluvium of the valley was too much needed by the living for it to be spared, in general, for the dead; nor would the alluvium have served that great purpose of age-long preservation of the body which was the main object that was sought in accordance with the Egyptian crave for immortality. Consequently, while his great cities and many of his great temples grew up along the line of the river and on the alien soil which the river had deposited, the evidences of what kind of life the Egyptian lived, what he believed, what he could accomplish in the arts and crafts, and what he produced as a thinker, a poet, or a novelist, are, in ninety-nine cases out of a hundred, to be sought in the desert where he was buried, rather than on the cultivated land where he lived. War, with its destruction, and the ceaseless succession of the generations, with their ever-changing needs, have wiped out most of the record of

Egyptian life from the spots where it was actually lived;
but the desert has known few changes, and its sands have
proved the most matchless of preservatives, so that the
record of the land of the dead and its testimony to the
work of the past survive as in no other land. Deduct from
our knowledge of ancient Egypt and its inhabitants all
that we have learned from its tombs, and the residuum
will be singularly small. More or less, the tale of the culture
and life of any ancient land must be learned from its
tombs, because it is only in the abodes of the dead that
change is comparatively inoperative; but in no other land
does the proportion of our information derived from the
tombs reach so high a level. The contrast in this respect
between Egypt and the other great riverine lands,
Babylonia and Assyria, is remarkable, and is mainly due
to Egypt's desert surroundings.

The combination of the long Valley, with its prevalent
north wind, and the desert margins on either side of it,
"vast reservoirs of saline dryness", as they have been
called, produces in Egypt the natural results of an almost
constantly clear sky and a keen and invigorating air. The
rarity of rain, especially in the Upper Valley, has been
already noted. A heavy fall of rain is in southern Egypt a
phenomenon to be remarked, occurring only once perhaps
in three years. When it does occur, however, its results
are marked. The disintegrated and powdered soil is cut
up by the rainstorm in an extraordinary fashion, producing
such an appearance of denudation as would in northern
lands be attributed to frequent and long-continued rains.
The dryness of the climate hinders the sometimes considerable range of temperatures from being so trying as
would otherwise be the case. The mean temperature at
Cairo in January is 54 degrees Fahrenheit, at Luxor 60,
and at Aswan almost the same. In July the corresponding
figures are, for Cairo 83·5, for Luxor 89·5, and for Aswan
96·5; but even with a maximum of well over 100 degrees,
the dry heat is by no means so oppressive as a similar
temperature in more humid atmospheres.

The climate of Egypt has been for long regarded as
an almost ideal one, "devoid of the harshness of a northern

winter, but at the same time sufficiently cool to escape those enervating influences inherent in tropical conditions"; and the multitudes of health-seekers who visit the land from Europe and America each winter testify to the continuance of faith in its healthiness. On the other hand, it has been suggested that the character of the climate is such as to impart temporary exhilaration at the expense of the body's reserves of energy, and that nerves are kept at a tension which in the end produces an abnormally early failure of vital force. It has been pointed out that longevity is rare in Egypt, and that infant mortality is unusually high, and that apart from zymotic disease; but how much of this is due to the conditions of life among the larger part of the population, rather than to climatic influences, is another question. The prayer of the ancient Egyptian was that he might attain a happy existence of 110 years. It was sometimes answered; but we have no evidence that this patriarchal longevity was a common feature of Egyptian life, any more than it is of our own.

The home of the native Egyptian, then, was one of a very pronounced character, and, on the whole, marked by conditions highly favourable to his preparation for the great work which he was destined to accomplish. His landscape was one of singular uniformity—even of monotony—one long ribbon of brown, green, or yellow, according to the season of the year, stretching out endlessly between two barren margins, whose only variety was the gaunt shapes of the Libyan cliffs on the western, and the jagged peaks of the Arabian range on the eastern side. The modern view, with one or two incidental variations, is the same as that on which the fellah of the time of Thothmes or of Mena must have gazed—"as it was in the beginning, is now, and ever shall be". "The long line of a curving dyke, carrying beside a canal a cultivation road or a railway, cuts the horizon. The angles of white sails or a smoky funnel indicate the river; the chimney of a sugar factory is a landmark for miles. The rest is one flat stretch of varying hues, brown, green, red or yellow, according to the season, or is for two months a burnished sheet of inundation, now wider, now narrower, now defined by high cliffs, now melting into an easy gradient of desert, now more to east, anon more to west of the central stream. And the Delta is at first only the same view expanded, with larger and more numerous human settlements, more waterways and general evidence of civilised man's labour in roads, railways, bridges, pumping stations, long alignments of trees."

The modern elements of such a picture are merely superficial. The other elements—desert, river, alluvium, and sun—are unchanged since the first human being looked upon them; and the picture will scarcely vary when the last human being succeeds his distant ancestor. It is a world of extraordinary monotony, yet also of startling contrasts. Nowhere is the line "that just divides the Desert from the Sown" so narrow, or so sharply drawn, as in Egypt. On the edge of the cultivation you can stand with one foot in luxuriant herbage and the other in barrenness which never has borne and never will bear a living thing. There are none of the modifications and half-tones by which our northern landscapes shade away out of the richness of the lowland plains into the stern barrenness of the mountain moors and peaks. The contrasts are like those of a lunar landscape, only in different colours. The Egyptian's world had just two divisions. He lived on the Black Land; he was environed by the Red Land; and between these two there was perpetual warfare—Set, the Red Fiend, against Osiris, the beneficent master of the Black Soil and the growing corn.

With a world whose main elements were so few and so simple, with so little shading in their interrelations, the Egyptian's religion almost inevitably took on a character of somewhat sombre matter-of-factness. It was in a land of mountains and valleys, of brooks and forest-glades, and arms of the sea, where clouds and mists gave glamour and mystery, and the clear sunshine after rain an endlessly changing gamut of colour, that the beautiful mythology of Greece grew up. Such play of fancy and such wealth of invention are not to be looked for in a land where the lines are drawn so sharply and with such remorseless clearness as in Egypt. Here were no forest-glades and fountains to people with dryads and oreads, but only sun and river, fertile soil and barren desert; and the result was, naturally, a religion without half-tones, in which light and darkness, life and death, good and evil are as sharply contrasted as in surrounding Nature. There is plenty of imagination in Egyptian religion—of a kind; but it is generally grim and weird, often grotesque, sometimes even repulsive in its uncompromising realism. Broadly, the main elements of the Egyptian's religion were determined by the outstanding features of his world. "As we examine Egyptian religion in its earliest surviving documents," says Professor Breasted, "it is evident that two great phenomena of nature had made the most profound impression upon the Nile-dwellers, and that the gods discerned in these two phenomena dominated religious and intellectual development from the earliest times. These are the sun and the Nile. In the sun-god, Re, Atum, Horus, Khepri, and in the Nile, Osiris, we find the great gods of Egyptian life and thought, who almost from the beginning entered upon a rivalry for the highest place in the religion of Egypt —a rivalry which ceased only with the annihilation of Egyptian religion at the close of the fifth century of the Christian era. He who knows the essentials of the story of this long rivalry will know the main course of the history of Egyptian religion, not to say one of the most important chapters in the history of the early East."

It was perhaps the other great feature of the Egyptian world—the desert—which first wakened in the soul of the dweller in the Nile Valley that craving which has distinguished him above all other men—the passion for immortality. He can scarcely have failed at an early stage in his history to recognise how wonderfully the desert soil in which he buried his dead preserved for long stretches of time the outward semblance of the human form, and thus, no doubt, the idea of immortality was coupled in his mind with that idea of the preservation of the actual bodily frame, as a condition of the continuous endurance of the personality, which found expression at last, and during almost all the historic period, in the practice of mummification.

So far it would almost appear as if the influence of the land upon its people operated in the direction of producing a sombre and gloomy type of character, and indeed such was the impression which was produced upon the minds of the Greek observers, such as Herodotus, through whose eyes the rest of the world was so long content to view the strange people in whom the Father of History took so lively an interest. The unchanging routine of the life of the common people, coupled with the depth of their interest in the hereafter, was bound to suggest such a conception. All the same, it was a fundamentally erroneous one. Certainly the life of the toiling masses of the population can never have been one of ease, for the other idea of Egypt as a land where Nature does nearly all the work, and the peasant has but to "tickle the land with a hoe, and it laughs to him with a harvest", is just as false. Great as is the boon which the inundation bestows in the shape of a constantly fertile soil, its full advantages are not gained without continuous and toilsome work in the form of irrigation; and the fellah always has been what he is to-day, "probably the most patient and industrious labourer in any semi-tropical country in the world". The ancient pictures and reliefs show him to us as industrious at the hard work of the *shaduf* and the canal five thousand years ago as he is now.

But, on the other hand, if his labour was hard and continuous during a great part of the year, its results were, on the whole, much more certain than in any other land; and its returns were so abundant as to yield an ample supply to meet his simple needs. "So fruitful is the soil, yielding three or four crops per annum . . . that one acre of good land is enough to maintain the fellah and his wife, or even wives, and household in comfort." Nor was even the forced labour which the Pharaohs exacted for the erection of the gigantic structures in which they delighted the business of tears and despair which we have often been invited to compassionate. The forced labour was exacted, in all probability, only during the three months of the inundation, when field-work was normally at a standstill; and while the toil, no doubt, was heavy, the labourers were

maintained at the royal charges during the period of their
service, and so were tided over the blank season when they
had nothing else to depend upon. Thus there was no unemployment question in Egypt under normally prosperous
and efficient Pharaohs, and the glory of the king served
also the interests of his subjects. There was "no detriment
to the country in employing a small proportion of the
population at a season when they were all idle by the
compulsion of natural causes. The training and skill which
they would acquire by such work would be a great benefit
to the national character."

Thus, while the native Egyptian was a hard worker
both in his own interests and those of his king, he was by
no means the down-trodden slave who is so often pictured
to us. His national art shows him as very much the reverse,
and his national literature corroborates his art. There was
pleasure and merriment in his toil, and the simple songs
which have come down to us, and which he sang in the
harvest-field or at the threshing-floor, or as he waded
through the marshes after fish, are the index of a happy
and contented nature. If we are to judge of a nation, as we
surely should do, by its own conceptions of its lot, then
we must pronounce the Egyptian race to have been one of
the most cheerful and attractive of the races of the ancient
world. Certainly the Nilote makes a much more cheerful
and favourable impression than his secular rival, the grim
and bitter Semite of the great river-lands of the north.

Finally, it was not the least of his advantages that the
feature of his country which was so great an agent in the
securing of a constant livelihood to him was also the most
imperious and urgent of masters, imposing upon him from
the earliest days of the nation's history the double necessity
of national organisation for a national purpose, and of
studying the great problems of construction and engineering, without mastering which he would have been its
helpless victim. The inundation must at first have been the
ever-threatening terror of the Egyptian; but it speedily
taught him that which converted terror into blessing. Its
command was "Organise, and learn the laws of my coming
and my work, or perish"; and under this beneficent com-

pulsion the Egyptian, in the very earliest stages of his history, gradually became what he is when he is revealed to us at the beginning of the historic period—the most efficient unit of a great organisation, the finest builder, and the finest hydraulic engineer that the ancient world ever knew. It is no disadvantage for a race to have a land which is not only a bounteous nursing-mother, but also an exacting taskmistress.

CHAPTER II

THE BEGINNINGS OF LIFE IN EGYPT

WHEN we first come into touch with indications of the presence of man in what is now the Nile Valley, the land and its conditions differed totally from its present state. In place of the deep valley, with the river flowing through it, we have to picture to ourselves a series of long narrow lakes, fed partly by the upper Nile, but also receiving tribute from streams which drained the plateau above the gulf, and washed down beds of gravel to the lower level. These gravel deposits contain the first evidences of man's presence upon the plateau above in the shape of rudely chipped flint tools—"eoliths"—which exist also upon the plateau, which must then have been the only possible home of the hunters who used the implements. Later there came a period of silting, in which the lakes were wiped out by beds of deposit which still overlie the lateral gravel beds to a considerable height above the present flood-level of the Nile. During this period implements of the "Chellean" type were used by the hunters of the plateau. A warm spell, corresponding to one of the warm intervals of the glacial period of Europe, put an end to this depositing of silt, and the Nile now began to cut through the deposits the trough which was to become the present valley; and man began to recognise the advantage of the valley over the wind-swept plateau by descending and living along the line of the filled-up lakes, through whose filling the river was now cutting its way. Chellean implements still indicate his presence on the terraces on either side of the Nile gorge. Then came a second descent of the ice in Central and Northern Europe, whose counterpart in the warmer Nile gorge was a second rainy period, which deposited a fresh

22

series of gravel beds, this time to a lesser height than their predecessors, as they only reach to from 90 to 100 feet above flood-level, as against twice this height for the earlier deposits. The advance of man is once more indicated by the fact that throughout the second warm interval which succeeded this rainy period the implements which he left behind him on these new gravel beds through which the river was again cutting its way are of the more highly developed "Acheulean" type.

The third or "Riss" ice period of Europe had once more its counterpart in a third rainy age in the Egyptian valley; but the diminishing intensity of the visitation is marked, and its resultant gravels stand only about 30 feet above the present flood-level. Man, as before, followed the falling levels, and left his tools and weapons in these deposits as he had done in those that preceded them, so soon as the warm interval which followed allowed of his exploitation of the new domain. The "Wurm" or fourth ice period tallied with a less intense rainy period in the Nile Valley; and now the Nile gorge, cut by the river to a depth of 60 feet below present flood-level, begins to accumulate the alluvium which, in the course of millennia, was to raise the habitable land of Egypt to its present height. The deposit of the alluvium took place before the immediately pre-historic period in three stages, each of which may have lasted for thousands of years, and in each of which the traces of human occupation of the alluvial ground can be observed. Even in the earliest stage, and at a depth of over 50 feet below the present surface, not only flint implements, but also fragments of rude pottery and the bones of some of the animals which were subsequently, if not even at that stage, domesticated, have been found, showing that man was beginning to come into his kingdom, and to attain the stage of culture at which we find him in what is called the pre-dynastic period. By the end of this period (so far as it can be said to have an end, for the deposit of alluvium has gone on continuously, and is still going on) the surfaces of the land were roughly as they are to-day, though there was probably a considerably greater amount of marshy ground, which played a great part in the life and sport of even the dynastic Egyptian, as is shown by the Old-Kingdom reliefs.

Thus we see, though only in the rudest of outlines, something of the course of events and of the stages of human occupation in the land with which we have to deal, previous to the time at which records of a kind, which, if not written as yet, are more or less continuous and intelligible, begin. Occupation of the plateau above the Nile gorge on either side, either for purposes of settled habitation or at least for those of hunting, must have been continuous, for flint implements of all the stages referred to occur indiscriminately upon the desert surface; but as the level of the habitable land within the gorge fell with each successive stage of the geological development, we see that man systematically took advantage of the change, and occupied each level as it became habitable. And this, little as it is, is practically all that can be said of man in the Nile Valley until such time as he begins to leave behind him the unmistakable evidences of his growth in civilisation which we have next to consider.

Till within the last few years our knowledge of the earliest settled culture in Egypt has been scanty to a degree at the very point where we would most desire to have it full and complete—the point at which the hunting life of the nomads who left their flints on the desert plateau above the Nile Valley and on the successive terraces within the Valley began to pass into the settled life of an agricultural community, with herds of more or less domesticated animals, and depending for its sustenance not so much on hunting and fishing, though these would still be practised, as on the rearing of wheat and barley. In 1924–25, however, two discoveries were made —one at Badari, near Qau, above Assiut, by Mr. Brunton and Sir Flinders Petrie; the other in the Fayum, by Miss Caton Thompson—which have thrown a considerable amount of new light on the whole problem of the earlier stages of the pre-dynastic civilisation of man in Egypt. We have seen that the palaeolithic hunters were venturing down into the Valley during the successive periods which laid down the gravel terraces, and leaving their flints there to tell us of their presence. They can be traced practically down to the end of the age, as a branch of the Capsian industry has lately been recognised in the Valley. Now, as conditions gradually became drier in the North African belt, these nomads were faced with the alternative of either continuing their nomad life under less favourable conditions, or of entering upon the life of cultivation to which the conditions of the Valley were so well suited.

At this stage, in spite of the increasing dryness, rain was still falling regularly in the Valley at least as far up as Assiut. There was a fairly abundant vegetation in the wadis leading down from the plateau into the Valley, and, among the plants and grasses, wild barley and emmer wheat were apparently found; while there was also a fair amount of timber in the shape of tall trees, whose roots have still survived among the remains of the establishments of the prehistoric villagers. The ever-renewed alluvium furnished by the inundation offered an ideal soil for experiments with the seeds of the food-producing plants; and, in short, everything tended to tempt the nomad down permanently from his wind-swept plateau, which was rapidly becoming too dry, to the more settled life of the Valley and the farm. The natural result was such a settlement as Brunton and Petrie found at Badari; one out of many along the course of the Valley, no doubt.

The Badarians, the first cultivators, so far as we know in the meantime, of a land where cultivation has since been more continuous, perhaps, than anywhere else in the world, were a short and slender race, with heads of the dolichocephalic type. Apparently their descendants, the Egyptians of the present day, still bear a considerable physical resemblance to them; but there was some affinity to the negroid type in the Badarian structure, and the closest resemblance was to some of the still surviving specimens of the older races of India and Ceylon, the Dravidians and Veddahs. Their culture has made a remarkable advance upon that of the latest Capsians; so much so as to suggest that an earlier transition stage has yet to be discovered. The people already live in villages, cultivate barley and emmer wheat, and apparently keep domestic animals—among them the dog. Part of their dress still consists of goatskins; but the habit of wearing linen, which was to mark the Egyptian all through his history, has already begun, so that we must attribute to the Badarian at this stage the cultivation of flax and the beginning of a weaving industry.

Trade of a kind, though only in its infancy, must have been well-established, and two of its main routes are plain. Intercourse with the Red Sea coast furnished theBadarians with the shells which were worn for ornament, and, for the malachite which was in use for eye-paint (a hygienic as well as a decorative use), they must have established connections, even at this early stage, with the Sinai Peninsula. Malachite almost inevitably brought in its train, as we shall see, the discovery of how to produce copper; and accordingly copper beads are found, though so far there is no appearance of the use of the precious metal for either tools or weapons. Our first civilised Egyptian, however, had made a beginning in an art in which his descendants were destined to excel, and could already glaze beads for the adornment of himself and his womankind. His command of timber, in which he was more fortunate than the men of later ages, had led him to the production of stone tools suitable for the working of wood, and he ground pebbles to a sharp edge, producing axes and adzes of polished stone, adapted for cutting and splitting wood. His other work in flint included finely-shaped arrow-heads of a mitre shape. Bone was used for harpoons, and a curious curved bone, with a perforation in the end of one of its limbs, may have served as a fish-hook. Wooden throw-sticks, resembling those which are depicted in dynastic reliefs and paintings, were in use.

But the most striking production of the Badarian was his pottery. Even in this earliest known stage of settled life, when the potter's art might have been expected to be in its rudest infancy, there is no trace of anything tentative or clumsy in his work. "The pottery vessels," says Professor Gordon Childe, "especially those designed for funerary use, illustrate a perfection of ceramic technique never excelled in the Nile Valley." Several types of ware, differing in quality as well as in style, were produced. The walls of the finer grades of vases are extremely thin, and, before firing, the artist decorated his pots with a beautiful ripple marking, produced apparently by the use of a comb. The vessels were then fired inverted, so that the exposure of the lower part to the air resulted in the oxidation of the ferrous wash with which they had been painted, giving a red colour. The shoulder and rim of the vase, with the inside, being preserved from oxidation, were blackened by the action of the fire, the result being a charming black-topped red ware, delicately rippled. Besides this type, the Badarian potter turned out a fine black ware, decorated with zones of white lines or chevrons. Of this ware, only a single specimen has so far been found—a particularly graceful tulip-shaped beaker. These fine wares were re-served, of course, for special uses, largely funerary. For ordinary use, a coarse and poorly fired ware was common; though even in this ruder fabric the shapes favoured by the potter were elaborate and often graceful. Of this coarser ware there seems to have been abundance; but one curious fact shows that pottery was still regarded with sufficient reverence to be treated, when disaster overtook it, with a care somewhat similar to that with which our grandmothers used to deal with their fine china when it came to grief. Some of the Badarian vases, and particularly the finer ones, have been carefully bored on either side of any crack which began to show itself in the fabric, and grass rivets have been passed through the holes.

Our knowledge of these earliest settled Egyptians has largely come, of course, from their graves. The grave, at this stage of its development, was a shallow trench, in which the body was laid in the contracted or embryonic posture, with the knees drawn up. The dead were wrapped either in a mat or in goatskins, and were often laid on a kind of bier covered with twigs. In the grave were some-times laid little figurines, modelled in clay or carved out of ivory. These represent a female, who may either be a goddess or, perhaps, more probably a substitute for the dead man's wife—the Egyptian's disinclination to the usual slaughter of dependents, which was to show itself

in such remarkable and useful forms at later stages, perhaps
already beginning to appear. Decorated ivory combs were
in common use, and pins of the same material were seemingly used to fasten garments. Tubular beads of copper
and glazed beads of quartz and other stones were worn
for ornaments, while Red Sea shells were used for girdles
and bracelets and for necklaces. The presence of slate
palettes for grinding malachite shows that the habit of eye
and face painting was in use for comfort and decoration.
Altogether, the first civilised Egyptian, as we see him at
Badari, has reached a stage at which he is capable of considerable refinement in his utensils and adornments, and
is very far removed from the late Capsian hunter who
appears to be his nearest relative whom we can trace in
the meantime.

Very much about the same time as Sir Flinders Petrie
and Mr. Brunton were dealing with the traces of early
man at Badari, Miss Caton Thompson was finding the
relics of a somewhat similar community in the Fayum.
This great depression to the west of the Nile gorge, some
fifty-six miles above Cairo, was then to a great extent
filled by a lake much larger than the present Birket-
Qarun, and 200 feet above the present lake-level. The
shores of this lake offered attractions to a community
which had not yet left off its habits of fishing and hunting,
though it had adopted agriculture. The men of the Fayum,
like their contemporaries at Badari, cultivated barley and
emmer, and, in addition, pastured herds of oxen, goats,
sheep and swine. On the whole, there was considerable
similarity between their mode of life and that of the
Badarians; but several noticeable omissions in the list of
their effects may be due either to variation of the local
conditions or to our defective knowledge, for it should be
remembered that no graves have as yet been found at the
Fayum. The absence of copper beads may be due to the
fact that the connections of the Fayum tribe appear to
have been more with the Mediterranean littoral than with
the Red Sea or with Sinai—a fact which is hinted at by the
presence of Mediterranean shells, though those from the
Red Sea also occur. The glazed beads of Badari are also

lacking, or, perhaps it would be safer to say, have not yet been found. The greatest gap in the list of Fayum accomplishments is the lack of the fine Badarian type of pottery, though in this connection the fact that no graves have yet been explored should be kept in mind. Coarse pottery, however, is common.

What was the origin of these Badarian and Fayum communities? Sir Flinders Petrie has expressed the view that they originally came from the Caucasus. Messrs. Peake and Fleure suppose them to have been a nomadic people, who drifted across south-west Asia, picking up various elements of culture on their way, and arriving in the Nile Valley somewhere about 5000 B.C. Gordon Childe, on the other hand, follows Brunton, Miss Caton Thompson and others in the view that this earliest Egyptian civilisation was not an importation, but grew up in the Nile Valley itself, and that it originated with a tribe having Nubian affinities, whose state of culture somewhat resembled, to begin with, that which such tribes as the Hadendowa exhibited as late as last century. On the whole, it seems that this is the likeliest source from which to derive our Badarians, though it should be remembered that the arguments for an Asiatic origin are by no means to be disregarded.

All through her history, Egypt was subject to periodical incursions of the Libyan tribes from the western side of the Delta, who were repeatedly a menace to the very existence of the kingdom, and actually, in the XXIst Dynasty, succeeded in seating their own chiefs on the ancient throne of the Pharaohs. It was apparently the earliest of such incursions, or perhaps rather of such drifts, which was responsible for the modification of the Badarian stock and culture which resulted in the establishment of the next stage of Egyptian civilisation, known as the first predynastic culture. The drift eastwards of the Getulan semi-nomadic hunters of North Africa was, no doubt, the result of the increasing dryness which had originally driven the Badarians down from the plateau into the Nile Valley proper. As the drought continued and grew worse, it became less and less possible for the Libyan hunters to find a living on their old hunting-grounds, and the Nile Valley must have seemed the only possible outlet from the hopeless conditions in which they were beginning to find themselves. There was not, as yet, the dense population in the valley which at a later stage rendered such incursions things to be resisted by force of arms, and doubtless the Libyans drifted in by degrees in a more or less peaceable manner. At all events, we find that the Egyptian of the next stage (first pre-dynastic) has lost the negroid traits which characterised his Badarian predecessors, and has become more of the type which may still be seen to-day among the Beja tribesmen of the Eastern Sudan. He is still small, averaging about 5 feet 3 in height, slender and lithe, with a small skull of the long type, and small features. It is with this first pre-dynastic Egyptian that we perhaps begin to see the first step in the direction of the grouping of the inhabitants of various districts into clans, each with its own totem, which is used as the clan-ensign or symbol. There is as yet, however, no sign of any chieftainship or kingship, so far as such a distinction could be inferred from the favoured individual being accorded a grave distinguished from that of his fellows by greater richness or size. The graves, to the description of which we shall have to pay attention shortly, are so far very much on a par.

Variations from the type of culture favoured by the Badarians are sufficiently conspicuous. The disappearance of the polished stone axes and adzes which were characteristic of the Badarians warns us that, with the increasing dryness of the climate, timber is becoming scarce in Egypt, as it continued to be during all the historic period. Copper, however, is coming into more frequent use, and is found in the form of harpoons, and pins for fastening garments, as well as in the shape of beads. The most notable of all the variations is the appearance, on some of the white figured pottery of the period, of the earliest known type of ship or boat. The first Egyptian ship is already quite a workmanlike structure, made of bundles of papyrus stems bound together—a type of construction to which the Egyptian shipwright was faithful all through his long history—and propelled by several pairs of oars. The question of whether it had as yet managed to acquire a sail is still one to which no certain answer can be given, though before long we shall find the sail in common use. Two square cabins rise amidships, so that the vessel must have been more than a mere skiff; and the steersman is sheltered by something, apparently the green bough of a tree, which curves over his head—a form which eventually gives rise to the beautiful sweeping curve of the lotus bloom which decorates the stern of the Egyptian ship of the historic periods. With the evolution of the ship has come a greater development of external trade. Copper and malachite come in from Sinai, as before; but we now begin to meet with Syrian woods, with obsidian and lapis lazuli from Western Asia, and even with emery, which may have been brought from Naxos. In some of the graves of this first pre-dynastic culture we find models of water-bearers and of cattle appearing—a continuation and extension of that process of substituting such things for the actual slaves or animals formerly slain at the tomb which we have already noticed in connection with the Badarian figurines.

The pottery is good, though not so good as that of the Badarians; the black-topped ware which continues the Badarian tradition, though without the ripple ornament, is of fine fabric and design. Now, however, we begin to find the first traces of an art which was to remain to the end of Egyptian history one of the most illuminative characteristics of Egyptian taste. Some of the tombs have preserved for us examples of the painted vases, which, in the pre-dynastic age, supplied the place which was later filled by the carved and painted walls of the tomb. In the simple trench or pit of the earliest tombs there was no room for painting; but the vases in some measure made up for this lack, and are to be regarded as the first forerunners of those scenes of Egyptian life which, depicted on scores of tombs of all the historic periods, have taught us so much of the ancient Egyptian's way of life.

After a time we become conscious of a change in the type of culture, which points to the introduction of a new element into the population, differing very markedly from the Libyan infusion which had produced the first pre-

dynastic civilisation. The chief points of change are in
armament and dress. The disc-macehead of the First culture goes out and is replaced by the well-known pear-
shaped mace; the forms of lance-heads and knives (flint)
change; the old mitre-shaped arrow-heads disappear; and
the character of the pottery undergoes a radical change.
In dress, one of the most noticeable changes is the disappearance of the long-toothed ivory comb, and its re-
placement by a short-toothed article. Weapons become
rarer in the tombs, and the funerary furniture has often
been deliberately broken before being deposited in the
grave. The ships represented on the painted vases now
bear an ensign on a pole in front of their fore-cabins.
These ensigns correspond to the standards of the later
nomes, and, when several ships are represented on a single
vase, their standards are always those of contiguous nomes.
Hence it appears that the clan system is now fairly
established; and, with few exceptions, the clans which now
appear are those which constituted the nomes of the historic period. An idea of the appearance of the prehistoric
house of this period is given by a model house found at
El Amrah. It shows a building of wattle and daub,
roughly rectangular, with a wood-framed doorway near
the end of one of its longer sides. The area of the house
may have been about 25 feet by 18.

In the crafts, the working of the fine vases in hard
stone now reaches great perfection. Copper remains comparatively uncommon, but chisels and adzes, knives and
razors, pins, needles and tweezers of this precious metal
appear, and we meet with metal daggers of which one
shows a definitely metallic type, with a strengthening mid-
rib, as in later forms. Already the curious and not very
satisfactory Egyptian method of hafting a blade which
prevails at all later dates shows itself in the hafting of these
copper daggers, whose triangular blades are enveloped by
crescent-shaped arms projecting from the hilt, and the
whole hilt is fastened to the blade by rivets. In spite of the
slowly growing use of copper, the art of the flint-worker
now reaches its highest point, and some of the wonderful
flaked knives of this period are not only things admirably

PLATE III

1. A PRE-DYNASTIC GRAVE (*p.* 37)

2. PRE-DYNASTIC POTTERY

From Ayrton and Loat's " Pre-dynastic Cemetery at El Mahasna"
(Egypt Exploration Fund)

adapted to the use for which they were made, but are also beautiful in themselves.

Perhaps the most remarkable feature of this period is the development of the first beginnings of the painted tomb, of which one remarkable instance occurs at Hierakonpolis. The tomb in question measured 4·5 metres by 2 by 1·5, and its mud-coated walls had been washed over with a coat of yellow ochre to serve as a ground for the paintings. These represent, in red, black and white, scenes of war and the chase, and ceremonial dances. The work is, of course, very crude; but it is nevertheless of supreme interest as being the direct ancestor of the magnificent frescoes of the historic period, and the connecting link between them and the painted pots of the first pre-dynastic culture.

Whence is the new element which supplied the differentiating features to this middle pre-dynastic culture to be derived? As the earlier change was due to the Libyan infusion, so this later modification appears to have been caused by the arrival of a new people, possibly from Syria, almost certainly, in any case, from Asia, who established themselves primarily in the western Delta, and gradually spread thence up the Valley into Upper Egypt, but never penetrated into Nubia, as their predecessors had done. Messrs. Peake and Fleure have attempted to connect their arrival with a period during which the land of the Delta is supposed to have been subjected to a process of upheaval which changed its swamps into a fertile alluvial plain. The carved ivory handle of the knife from Gebel el-Arak, which represents among other things a combat between two peoples of different types, whose ships also differ in style, has been interpreted as an indication that the establishment of the new people in the land was not accomplished without an armed struggle. The rudiments of a script had now been devised; but whether it was the incomers who brought this accomplishment with them, or whether it arose on native soil, is still uncertain.

The painted tomb at Hierakonpolis marks for us the fact that we have now reached a stage at which social distinctions have begun to arise, and when chieftainship has made its appearance. "No private clansman rested in that sumptuous sepulchre," says Professor Gordon Childe, "but at least a chief; out of the equalitarian squalor chieftainship has arisen, preparing the way for the unification of the land under a king." Accordingly the late predynastic period is the period of transition in which the land is gradually prepared for that unification of its clans into a nation which was accomplished by the early dynasts.

As to the positive dates which are to be assigned to the successive developments of civilisation in this earliest period in Egypt, we must be content with the very vaguest of suggestions in the meantime. The upper end of the age goes back into the mists in which a thousand years is no more than an appreciable, but far from an extraordinary, unit of time; the lower end, unfortunately, is involved in that great and bitter controversy which makes all Egyptian dates prior to 1580 B.C. matters of doubt and vigorous dispute. Sir Flinders Petrie puts the Badarians at anything from 10,000 to 13,000 B.C., while various other authorities have brought them down to about 5000 B.C., by which time, according to Petrie's system of dating, the Ist Dynasty had run its course, and the IInd was well advanced. The approximate date of the rise of the middle predynastic culture has been placed by some authorities about 4475 B.C.; but it cannot be too clearly kept in mind that all such dates are for the present little better than guesswork. Some idea of the confusion with regard to dating, even in the dynastic period, may be gained from a brief summary of recent datings offered by modern scholars. Sir Flinders Petrie dates the rise of the Ist Dynasty, and consequently the beginning of Egyptian History, strictly so-called, at 5546 B.C. Dr. H. R. Hall puts it, with a query, at 3500 B.C., while Breasted contends for a century and Mayer for two centuries later. This would seem to be confusion enough; but now comes in Mr. Weigall to tell us that all the Egyptologists (with one exception) are wrong, and that King Menes established the Ist Dynasty precisely in 3407 B.C. In itself this does not seem a great departure from Hall's date, and next to none from that of Breasted; but in the same breath Mr. Weigall tells us that on the one point on which there has been a moderate amount of agreement—the establishment of the calendar in B.C. 4241—the experts have been hopelessly wrong, and that the calendar was really established by Menes seven years after his accession, or in 3400 B.C. To make up, however, for thus depriving us of nearly a thousand years of the calendar, he offers us a list of other dynasties preceding the Ist, and carrying us back to 5507 B.C., which brings the wheel round again to a fairly close approximation to Petrie's date for the Ist Dynasty.

If it were not a matter of serious history, the situation would not be without its humorous aspects. As it is, all that can be said is that certainly the pre-dynastic period had come to a close, or was coming to a close, round about 3500 B.C., and that possibly it ended two thousand years earlier. Such a statement may offer but cold comfort to the seeker after exactness; but it is the best that can be done in the meantime, until the experts have composed their little differences.

While, however, it is not possible to assign precise dates for either the beginning or the ending of the pre-dynastic period, it is possible to trace the sequence of different stages within the period itself. This possibility has arisen in consequence of Sir Flinders Petrie's tracing, at Diospolis Parva, of a certain sequence in the types of pottery which were revealed by his excavations. A certain type of pottery vessel was found to undergo a regular process of degeneration, the ridge which originally served the purpose of a handle gradually fading away until it became nothing more than a meaningless wavy line around the neck of the vessel; and this degeneration was accompanied *pari passu* by a similar degeneration in the general form of the vessel. It was thus found possible to establish the chronological succession of the whole range of such pots; and this stage once reached, similar stages of variation were found to exist in other objects which accompanied these type vases. A framework of time intervals was established, of which spaces 1-29 in the series were left blank to allow for the possible discovery of still earlier graves, while the remaining intervals, 30-100, represent the pre-dynastic and early dynastic periods. The various stages of the type series of pottery could then be fitted into the successive intervals, with the result that, when a pre-dynastic tomb is discovered, while it is still impossible to assign to it an absolute date, its position in the historical sequence is at once established by the comparison of its pottery with the corresponding stage of the type pottery.

This system of sequence-dating, as it is called, has proved of the utmost value as an instrument for settling the succession of remains within the pre-dynastic period. Obviously, it cannot give us equal intervals of time in each stage, and one stage may be far longer or shorter than its next neighbour; but at least it can be determined what preceded and what followed in an approximation to the real order of events. The pre-dynastic period, under this system, falls into three sub-periods—Early Pre-dynastic, whose sequence dates are 30-40; Middle Pre-dynastic, 40-60; and Late Pre-dynastic, 60-78, at which point begins the Early Dynastic Period, with the rise of the Ist Dynasty.

The general characteristics of the Egyptian race and of their civilisation in the pre-dynastic period have been learned entirely, or almost entirely, as one would expect, from their tombs. The qualification is necessary, because in certain cases, at Ballas, Abydos and Mahasna, traces of the settlements of the living Egyptians have been found in the shape of scanty remains of mud-brick houses, sockets which may have held the corner poles or beams of houses, hearths for domestic fires, with heaps of wood-ash and rows of large open-mouthed jars supported upon what appear to be clay fire-bars, the whole construction being apparently designed for the drying of corn, masses of wheat being found along with these primitive kilns. The last feature points to a civilisation which had made progress by no means negligible in the arts of life. With these exceptions, however, our knowledge of the period rests practically entirely on the discoveries made in the pre-dynastic cemeteries, numbers of which have been discovered and excavated during the last thirty years.

The main features of the pre-dynastic tomb are pretty much the same everywhere, though variations, the natural

result of progress, exist in the shape and construction of
the tombs. The essential feature is a comparatively shallow
pit either dug in the sand or cut in the soft rock beneath.
The earliest types, with the exception of the Badarian
tombs, are mostly circular; but at a later stage of development the circular pit is discarded in favour of what Sir
Walter Scott, in *Ivanhoe*, curiously describes as "an oblong
square, rounded at the corners". Within this pit, circular
or oblong, lies the body, doubled up into a very contracted
position, so that the knees almost touch the chin, while the
hands are brought up before the face by the acute bending
of the elbows. It was laid upon a reed-mat, or sometimes
upon a reed-mat and a skin, which were then folded
round it and brought together as a covering for it above,
some of the tomb furniture being also brought under the
covering in some instances. Occasional variations have
been observed in the shape of a hurdle of twigs lashed
together, upon which the body is laid, and there are also
instances of a wooden bier, cut out of a single piece of
wood, being employed.

The usual depth of the round graves is only three to
four feet, and they are only large enough to hold the
crouched-up body and the scanty provision of funerary
furniture which is buried along with it. The type objects
to accompany the dead are vessels for food and drink, tools
and weapons of flint or copper in the case of a man;
necklaces, armlets, and other ornaments of flint, slate, or
ivory in the case of a woman, together with a supply of
malachite for face-paint, often tied up in a little leather
bag, and a slate palette on which to grind down the
malachite by means of the pebble which is supplied to
complete the outfit. The amount of this simple provision
for the needs of the dead in the Underworld, however,
varies considerably, though the types remain always the
same. The man of means wished to be well provided for in
death as he had been in life, and soon the simple round pit,
with the few vessels and weapons, ceased to satisfy his
ideas.

The next stage is the oblong tomb, small at first, but
growing larger as the interments were richer. A typical

tomb of this type at El Amrah contained no fewer than twenty-one large pots ranged on ledges round three sides of the pit; while a still wealthier neighbour of this pre-historic capitalist rejoiced in even greater splendour, having a score of big jars in two rows along one side of his tomb, while he had also twelve other jars, one of them of polished red pottery, at the two ends. This early aristocrat also possessed, not a coffin, but a rudimentary attempt at one, in the shape of a wooden fence, made of planks tied together with cord, which enclosed his body, rising twenty inches above the floor of the grave; while his last resting-place was roofed over with sticks plastered with mud—altogether a notable example of prehistoric class-distinction.

The next stage was a natural development from this. As the funerary offerings grew more numerous, the ledges which held the offerings in these two graves developed into a shelf which broadened until the owner of the tomb was in danger of anticipating, even in death, the Solomonic doom of the rich man—"the abundance of the rich will not suffer him to sleep." Accordingly, as there was no longer room in the original tomb for its owner, because of the abundance of his furniture, a recess was cut for him on the opposite side to the ledge, so that, like the bishop in Saint Praxed's Church, he could lie through the long centuries and contemplate his splendours... Some of these luxurious tombs had the personal niche divided off from the rest of the grave by means of a wattle fence, of which the remains still survive; and in the later pre-dynastic period the custom of lining them with mud-brick came in. Roofed or unroofed, there was nothing above ground to mark where the dead were sleeping—perhaps a wise precaution, having regard to the plundering to which almost all Egyptian tombs have been subjected. One quaint later custom was the placing of the body beneath a huge inverted pot.

In his grave the dead man, rich or poor, lay in his doubled-up position almost invariably on his left side, though there are exceptions to the rule, as at El Amrah, where for some obscure local reason the right side was preferred. Usually the bodies lie roughly north and south, or rather in the direction parallel to the flow of the river at the particular place in question. Oftenest the head is to the south, though there are more exceptions to this rule than to that of the orientation of the body. In both cases we are quite in the dark as to the reason which determined the practice or its exceptions. The contracted position has been explained as being merely the natural position of the body in sleep, though it may be hoped that most of us do not rest in quite such a constrained posture; and again a more scientific or, at least, a more apparently scientific cast has been given to the position by calling it embryonic. Possibly both explanations may have something of the truth in them; though it seems somewhat unlikely that the pre-dynastic Egyptian bothered very much about "embryonic" attitudes when he laid his dead in the grave for their long sleep.

Some curious features which have been found in certain tombs are to be noted. Mummification was as yet unknown; but in quite a number of instances the bones of the skeleton lay not in their natural order, though the grave otherwise gave no hint of having been disturbed. Various conclusions have been drawn from the observed facts. It has been inferred that the bodies thus found were dismembered after death and before burial, that they were subjected to a process of exposure and secondary burial such as still prevails in Tibet and elsewhere, and even that cannibalism prevailed or was at least occasional among the early Egyptians. All these suggestions have been hotly contested by various Egyptologists, who seem to think it impossible that so nice a people as the Egyptians can ever have been given to such barbarous customs. It is certain, however, that even the nicest of races must have had a beginning sometime, and that some of the practices of primitive man in his earliest stages have never been marked by conspicuous delicacy. Moreover, the occurrence at Deshasheh in early dynastic tombs of quite undisturbed burials, in which the bodies had been dismembered and subsequently wrapped in linen which had not been interfered with at any later period, indicates at least the possibility that dismemberment was practised in the ruder pre-dynastic age—whatever may have been the case with regard to cannibalism. It ought to be remembered that a considerable degree of advancement in the arts and crafts of civilised life has repeatedly been proved to be no barrier to the existence along with itself of customs which to us are frankly barbarous.

Perhaps the quaintest of all the revelations of these pre-dynastic cemeteries is the fact that a surprisingly large proportion of the early population of Egypt had fractures of the forearm. Professor Elliot Smith regards this curious feature as merely an indication that the early Egyptian, like his descendant of the present day, was fond of playing at a kind of single-stick or quarter-staff with the *naboot*, and that he played it with realistic violence. But the curious thing is that in some cemeteries a large proportion of the women have their left forearm broken too. The obvious explanation is that the early Egyptian used his *naboot* not only to defend himself, but also to correct the wife of his bosom, and that the good lady got her arm broken in trying to ward off the blows. Mrs. Quibell remarks that "one hesitates to attribute such unpleasant conduct to people who could make such delightful pottery", but the artistic temperament has never been a safeguard against the outbreaks of a hot temper—quite the opposite. Benvenuto Cellini made delightful bronzes and other beautiful things; but he has left on record his methods of correcting the ladies whom he favoured with his smiles, to say nothing of his other somewhat violent habits. It is possible, perhaps, that there may have been a ritual reason for the fractures; if so, what it was remains in the meantime obscure.

The level of culture attested by the results of excavation in these pre-dynastic cemeteries is singularly high, even when the lowest possible dates are adopted. The pre-dynastic Egyptian was very far indeed from being in a barbarous stage, no matter at what period we sample his works, but had reached a level which can be distinctly classed as civilised. He was, as we have seen, and as his ancestors had obviously been for untold ages, the most skilful and artistic of all flint workers. The knives and other implements from the earliest tombs are most admirably wrought, the face of the weapon or tool being most beautifully ripple-flaked, while the edges were minutely serrated with deeply cut teeth of almost microscopic fineness by a method which is beyond our knowledge. Another favourite weapon was the mace of hard stone, porphyry and other beautiful stones being used as the material, first for disc-shaped mace-heads, and later for the pear-shaped variety, which succeeded the disc mace in favour. Some of these maces are exquisitely wrought, and not only must have been quite satisfactory weapons, but are in themselves things of beauty. The most wonderful product of prehistoric stonework, however, is the vase of hard stone. Such vases are comparatively rare in the earliest predynastic period, but rapidly increase in number as the age goes on, very possibly in consequence of the discovery of copper for tools. Even so, the working of the diorites, porphyries, and breccias in which the Egyptian craftsman delighted must have been a business in which time was no object, and patience to the nth degree the normal virtue of the workman.

The results, however, were worthy of the pains employed. The forms of the vases were obviously derived from the contemporary work of the potter, and as Egyptian pottery was never more beautiful in its shapes than at this period, when the potter's wheel was indeed yet unknown, but the hand-shaped vessels were amazingly satisfactory in shape and accuracy, the stone vases which copied them were correspondingly pleasing in their form. In addition, the natural beauty and colour of the stones employed were shown to the best advantage by the fine surface which the workman succeeded in imparting, while the hard stone was often wrought to such thinness as to be translucent. Altogether these stone vases are perhaps the most beautiful things that have survived from earliest Egypt, and speak eloquently of the artistic skill and taste of the race which produced them. They were never bettered, and seldom equalled in subsequent periods.

To the pottery, we have just alluded. The Egyptian potter had already learned how to levigate his clay, how to

obviate risks of disaster in firing by the introduction of
small quantities of quartz or limestone grains among his
paste, and how to produce at will, by the addition of
powdered haematite and the admission or exclusion of air
in the firing, the fine black-topped red ware which is so
characteristic of the period. He knew also the secret of a
white pigment which would stand firing, and so was able
to produce vases decorated with designs in white. "Last,
but not least," says Professor Peet, "he belonged to one of
those rare and happy periods when the craftsman seems
incapable of an error of taste, and, in consequence, almost
every form that leaves his hands is a thing of beauty."

Ivory was in common use, and was freely employed
both for weapons, for vases, and for articles of personal
adornment, such as the combs of the women. Bone was also
employed for such purposes. One of the most remarkable
exercises of the decorative instinct of the early Egyptian
was his discovery and use of a process of glazing, which he
employed to coat articles of stone or siliceous paste with
beautiful blue and green surfaces by means of fusing under
high temperatures. The glaze was used largely upon figures
and beads. Figures painted upon pottery show that ships
were in common use. The characteristic sheer of the
Egyptian ship to a high-curving bow and stern is in evidence,
and the vessels have a square cabin or cabins amidships, and
a single bank of oars. These are manifestly more than mere
river craft or fishing boats, and Petrie has suggested that
the use of emery in this period points to the establishment
of sea-borne trade with the southern coast of Asia Minor.

But the outstanding feature of the pre-dynastic equipment is the presence of metal, chiefly in the shape of
copper, though gold and silver (the latter very rarely) are
also found, and even hammered iron makes its appearance
in the shape of tubular beads, and was so much prized
as to be threaded along with gold beads. "Copper is king",
however, at this stage; and the question is, where did it
come from and how was it first found out? Probably the
greatest discovery ever made by man was that of fire, and
how to produce it—so much so that it is little wonder that
the fable of Prometheus and his theft of it from the gods

came into existence to account for so great a triumph over the material elements of human environment. But only second to the discovery of fire is that of metal; and the probability is that the two discoveries were linked together and that the second came through the first.

It seems likely that we owe the discovery of copper, and the first use of it, to the pre-dynastic Egyptian; and the probable circumstances of the discovery are not inconceivable, though two eminent Egyptologists have supplied us with theories on the subject differing somewhat in detail. It is only in detail, however, that Professor Breasted and Professor Elliot Smith differ from each other; the main elements of their reconstruction of this momentous event are similar. In both cases, the prime cause of the discovery was the Early Egyptian's use of malachite, which, as we have seen, is an article almost invariably found in pre-dynastic tombs, together with the palette for grinding it upon and the pebble used as a grinder. It was used as a face-paint; but we are not to imagine it as being merely an ancient ancestor of rouge and the lip-stick. Doubtless the Egyptian lady used it as an adornment; but it served also a much more practical purpose for both sexes, and was used as a germicide, and as a protection for the eyes against the glare of the desert.

Professor Breasted has given us a vivid picture of the Egyptian miner getting malachite in the barren wastes of the Sinai Peninsula, and happening to bed his camp-fire on lumps of the copper ore which lay about. In the morning, when he rakes out the ashes, his eye catches the glitter of a few shining globules of metal, which have resulted from the fusing of the ore under the heat of the fire. The great discovery has been made, and man has learned for the first time how to win the substance which is to make possible all his great triumphs of manufacture and engineering. Professor Elliot Smith is more gallant, and ascribes the discovery to the miner's wife. The malachite has been brought home from Sinai, and the miner's lady is using a lump of it, or some of the paste ground down from it, for purposes of personal beautification, when it drops from her hand, most luckily, into the house fire, which, also most luckily, is too hot for any rescue of the precious treasure. Next morning, when the ashes are raked out for the lighting of the fire to cook breakfast, the lump of malachite has disappeared; but in its place the sorrowing housewife finds some metal beads of beautiful reddish hue, which make her forget her loss in the new joy of possibilities of adornment.

The reader can choose between Breasted's wanderer and Elliot Smith's variant on Charles Lamb's theory of the discovery of roast pork. One way or the other, the discovery was made; and whether it was the miner's wife who made it or not, at least she was the first to profit by it. For the first use, apart from that of beads, was in the shape of pins to fasten together the scanty linen skirts or skin cloaks which were worn by the women, though when the material was plentiful her husband might get enough to make a harpoon head or a chisel blade. It was only to be expected that, once such a priceless discovery was made, the use of the metal would rapidly extend. Accordingly, we soon find tools of all sorts—chisels, adzes, needles, harpoons, and daggers—in use, the earlier examples being manifest imitations of their flint prototypes. As the metal-worker learns the advantages and possibilities of his new material, the forms of his implements change, and instead of copying the forms of stone tools and weapons, he works out genuinely metallic types, showing his appreciation of the capabilities of his new medium. The first step has been taken in the process which raised mankind out of what has been somewhat ungratefully called "the slough of the Stone Age".

So far, nothing that can with any confidence be called the beginning of a system of writing has been discovered in connection with the pre-dynastic Egyptian. In face, however, of the fact that the earliest dynastic remains show the existence of a primitive but still fully developed form of hieroglyphic writing, it is difficult to believe that a race so far advanced in other respects had not at least begun to evolve some system of written communication. A race which, as we learn from some of the royal tombs of the ist Dynasty at Abydos, had by that time not only evolved a hieroglyphic system, but had also adopted a modified form of it—an early hieratic—which was written in ink, must have been for long periods busy at the task. Fortunately, however, we are not left to such scanty evidence as that of the slate palette which Mr. Randall MacIver discovered at El Amrah, with its problematical signs, as our only proof of the intellectual attainments of the Egyptians at this stage of their history. Perhaps the most conclusive proof of the high standard to which they had attained is one that is often simply mentioned as a matter of course.

I refer to the establishment of the calendar. Unless Mr. Weigall is right and all the rest of the Egyptologists wrong, the Egyptians had adopted their calendar by 4241 B.C. To the average mind, accustomed to the succession of months and weeks and their apportionment on the printed sheet which can never be found when it is wanted, this may seem a feat that is not worth mentioning; in reality, it involves faculties both of observation and reasoning which are by no means possessed by everybody, even in our own days. The Egyptian calendar, but for one slight fault, was actually a very much more convenient arrangement than our own cumbrous modified (and spoiled) Julian calendar, with its long and short months. Their calendar had simply twelve months, each of thirty days, with five days added (the so-called "Epagomenal Days") to make up for the deficiency which they knew to exist under such a system. Had they only realised the further fact that the five days did not quite make up the gap, and added a sixth day every fourth year, they would have had a system which would have been almost an ideal one. Now, how did they arrive at the fact that the year consisted, roughly speaking, of 360 + 5 days? They did so by observing what is known as "the heliacal rising" of the star Sothis, which is our own familiar Sirius. The heliacal rising of a star is the latest visible rising of it before sunrise, or, to put it otherwise and more simply, the time when it first appears on the eastern horizon at sunrise. The day when that phenomenon was observed in the case of Sothis, or Sirius, was the first day of the first month in the Egyptian year; and the number of days in the year was computed by reckoning up the number of days which intervened before Sothis was exactly in such a position again.

But the observation of such a delicate point as the exact day on which a star rises exactly at sunrise is by no means so easy a matter as it may seem, and only those who are accustomed to the difficulties of astronomical observation can appreciate thoroughly the skill with which these prehistoric observers must have carried out their task. How exactly they accomplished their object is seen in the fact that they were able to fix the length of the year with so close an approximation to accuracy. True, they failed to appreciate the fact that they were a quarter of a day out every year, and in consequence their New Year's Day shifted by a full day every four years, and so passed right round through the year in 1460 years, thus providing a magnificent bone of contention for future students of Egyptian chronology; but the skill which, without instruments of any sort, reached even so close as that to the truth, and the reasoning power which built up the calendar on its observations, must both have been of a high order. The Egyptian of 4241 B.C. was not unworthy to stand in the direct line of succession which leads to Copernicus and Newton.

And now, having seen somewhat of the stage of civilisation to which the Egyptian of the Chalcolithic Age, before the dynastic period, had attained, we have to ask the question—What manner of man was he who thus built up so advanced a culture at such an almost incredibly early date? In this respect, the characteristics of the land which he inhabited have done for the primitive Egyptian what no other land has ever done for its earliest inhabitants, so that the facilities for studying not only his skeletal structure, but other aspects of his bodily frame, are unique, and have been taken advantage of with great thoroughness during the last quarter of a century.

"The hot, dry sands of Egypt", says Professor Elliot Smith, "have preserved through a span of more than sixty centuries the remains of the countless multitudes of the earliest people known to have dwelt in the Nile Valley; and not the mere bones only, but also the skin and hair, the muscles and organs of the body; and even such delicate tissues as the nerves and brain, and, most marvellous of all, the lens of the eye, are available for examination to-day. Thus we are able to form a very precise idea of the structure of the body of the proto-Egyptian."

Mummification was, as we have seen, unknown, or, at all events, was not practised in these primitive days, but the dryness of the soil in which the dead were buried secured a sort of natural mummification which, as has been suggested, may have been the first hint of the possibility of a more effective preservation from natural corruption. Perhaps the most extraordinary thing about this preservation is a matter which in itself is far from pleasant to think of, and which has yet been of very great value in telling us the unmistakable facts about the very diet of these men of six thousand years ago. It has been found possible to recover from the stomachs of many of these ancient folk the actual materials of the last meals which they partook of before death. These have been subjected to prolonged investigation, with the result that we know not only what the prehistoric Egyptian ate, but also to some extent how he prepared his food. Barley and millet were found in many cases—barley especially in almost every case. Root-tubers of the plant known as *Cyperus esculentes* were found in the bodies, and also in the vessels laid beside them in the tomb. Remains of fish-scales and bones, which the early Egyptians, like other more advanced folk, sometimes reprehensibly swallowed, showed that they varied their vegetable diet; indeed, the very fish which was used for these primitive fish-suppers has been identified, and anyone who is curious may know that its name is *Tilapia Nilotica*. Moreover, the Egyptian, however much nearer to primitive innocency than ourselves he may have been, was certainly not a vegetarian, even apart from his predilection for fish; for fragments of mammalian bone have been found in his stomach, suggesting a horrid habit of bolting his food.

Perhaps the strangest thing of all is that in the stomachs of a number of children the remains of the bodies of mice were found. The fact that the little animal had not been accidentally swallowed was plain from its having been skinned before it was eaten. The reason, of course, was that for thousands of years the mouse used to be a standard article of the Egyptian pharmacopoeia, and was regularly prescribed for children *in extremis*. Erman is not polite to ancient medicine when he remarks that "it was . . . necessary that the ingredients should be rare, and also if possible disgusting"; but he is telling the truth. If skinned mouse does not come under the first category, it certainly comes under the second. However we need not plume ourselves too much on our superiority to the men of 4000 B.C. when we remember that the best that the best skill of the Faculty in London could do for the dying Charles II. less than 250 years ago was to force into his mouth "a loathsome volatile salt, extracted from human skulls". Compared with that, the harmless mouse of the Egyptian Dr. Sangrado of six thousand years ago seems mild.

Meanwhile, however, our prehistoric Egyptian is waiting to be taken notice of. The proto-Egyptian, then, was by no means the giant that the works of his immediate descendants might lead us to imagine, but, on the contrary, a man of rather small stature and of slight build. He averaged about 5 feet 5 inches in height, as against the 5 feet 6 inches of the Egyptian fellah of the present day. Muscular development was not pronounced, to all appearance, for the bones are unusually free from the roughnesses and projecting bosses which are generally held to indicate powerful muscularity. "In fact," says Dr. Elliot Smith, "there is a suggestion of effeminate grace and frailty about his bones, which is lacking in the more rugged outlines of the skeletons of his more virile successors"— a fact which, as we may see later, may be explained by subsequent admixture of a race of rougher and hardier physique with the more delicate native strain.

On the other hand, the bones show certain peculiarities usually supposed to go along with, and to indicate, great muscular strength—"lateral flattening of the tibia (platycnemia) and *pilastre* of the femur, as well as flattening of

PLATE IV

PALETTE OF NARMER (*p.* 64)

the upper end of its shaft, platymeria". These peculiarities, however, have been explained as being caused by a life of constant activity spent on bootless feet—in which connection it is interesting to notice that the atrophy of the bones of the little toe, often ascribed to the habit of wearing tight boots, was as common among the bootless Egyptians of 4000 B.C. as it is to-day.

The head of this small and slender man was long and narrow—dolichocephalic, to use the necessary jargon of the anthropologist, so that, when you look from above, a typical proto-Egyptian skull presents a long and narrow approximately pentagonal appearance—rather, in fact, like the shape of a coffin. The face must have been a long oval, with pointed and slender chin and narrow jaw. Later, towards the end of the pre-dynastic period, this slender type, which is very strikingly represented still in Egyptian country villages, was mixed with and modified by the intrusion of a stronger and heavier type, with a much broader skull and more sturdy bones—the Gizeh race—whose standard of stature was even somewhat less than that of the primitive type, whose features seem to have been more pronounced, and whose brain capacity was distinctly larger—by as much, in fact, as 100 cubic centimetres. Petrie has suggested that the intruding element which modified the bony structure of the Egyptian frame and reduced the average stature, while giving an element of greater bodily, if not necessarily mental, strength, may have come from Elam, and may have been responsible for the impetus which was given to the progress of civilisation at the beginning of the dynastic period.

The proto-Egyptian was brunet, with black or dark-brown hair, which was generally straight, sometimes wavy or even curly, but never woolly like that of the negro. In fact there is no appearance, save in the Badarian stage, of the negroid type. The hair of the face was scanty, and often worn simply as a thin pointed beard without a moustache. The prevalence of this type of beard in the beginnings of Egyptian history is no doubt the reason of the fact that the dynastic Egyptian is so often represented, in spite of his habit of clean shaving, with a noble chin-beard, and that with Pharaoh himself the artificial chin-beard is almost as essential a feature of royalty as the sacred uræus on the Double Crown. Pointed chin-beards had been the thing in the beginning, and to the conservative Egyptian that was sufficient reason for their continuing to be the thing to the end. So far as can be seen, therefore, the proto-Egyptian belonged in the main to that famous branch of the human race which we have learned to recognise as the Mediterranean race—the race to which also that other brilliant people of antiquity, the ancient Cretan, belonged. The kinship between these two gifted peoples would help in that early intercourse of the great civilisation of the Nile Valley with that of the island kingdom of which the evidences are coming more and more to light. The Mediterranean type, however, must be recognised as having been considerably modified by successive infusions of other elements, Negroid, Libyan, and Asiatic. Indeed, Professor Petrie believes that he can trace upon the early sculptures five different races older than the dynastic people of Egypt: (i) the Aquiline race of Libyo-Amorite type, which is responsible for the bulk of the prehistoric remains; (ii) a race with curly hair and plaited beards, resembling the later type found in the Hittite region; (iii) a people with pointed noses and long pigtails, warmly clothed, and probably mountaineers from near the Red Sea; (iv) a race with a short nose, "tip-tilted like a flower", whose habitat seems to have been Middle Egypt; (v) a similar race, but with a longer nose and projecting beard, who may belong to the Delta. All this in addition to the Badarian race, which precedes any of these. Finally came in what was eventually to prove the dominant race—vigorous and capable in appearance and physique, with a straight-bridged nose. The original habitat of this invading race, the dynastic ruling stock of historic Egypt, he believes to have been Elam, whence they brought many of the elements which gave the impulse to early dynastic Egypt.

On the whole, we do not appear to be markedly nearer the solution of the great enigma of the original source of the Egyptian culture than we were before, though the discovery of the Badarian culture has undoubtedly cleared up several questions as to the earliest period of the prehistoric age. For the present, perhaps, the best summary of matters is that offered in a single sentence by Professor Peet: "Almost every object of any importance dating from these early times in Egypt merely serves to convince us, if we are wise, of the extent of our ignorance." In the future, perhaps, excavation may give us evidence which will either confirm or confute the existing theories, or possibly provide us with a new explanation of the origin of the Egyptian and of the sources of his culture. Where the explanation is to come from does not seem obvious, as no amount of mere repetition of information derived from sources similar to the existing ones can do much to help. But there is no limit to the possibilities of Egyptian excavation; and meanwhile the Egyptian himself is a very solid fact, apart altogether from any explanations of his origin; and his culture, whencesoever derived or originated, is one of the most wonderful and interesting things in the story of human development.

CHAPTER III

THE "DEAD DEMI-GODS", AND THE UNIFICATION OF EGYPT

LESS than half a century ago our knowledge of Egyptian history practically began with the great Pyramid-building kings of the IVth Dynasty. We knew that, according to Manetho, the historian-priest of Sebennytus, who in the reign of Ptolemy Philadelphus (283-247 B.C.) compiled that series of annals of Egypt into whose framework of thirty dynasties all our knowledge of Egyptian history has since been fitted, the Pyramid-builders were by no means the primitives among Egyptian kings, but were the successors of three other dynasties of kings, of whom Menes or Mena, the first king of the Ist Dynasty, was held to have been the Unifier of Egypt. But Manetho's accounts of those far-off days were themselves so misty and so mingled with what appeared to be obviously impossible legend that little reliance could be placed upon his statements. It was interesting, no doubt, to be told that "Binothris reigned forty-seven years, and in his time it was determined that women might hold the imperial government"; but a little solid information would have been more to the point than this romance of women's rights. And if Manetho himself was not quite sure about the Nile having flowed with honey during eleven days in the reign of King Nephercheres, he could scarcely expect other people to believe in such an unusual and uncomfortable phenomenon. Altogether the ante-Pyramid days of Egyptian history were a shadowy land into which a responsible historian ventured at his own proper peril, and with not much likelihood of being believed in such statements as he might make.

Then came the discoveries of the actual remains of the

civilisation associated with these shadowy kings at Abydos, Hierakonpolis, and elsewhere; and views as to early Egyptian history had to adjust themselves as speedily as might be to the new and unquestionable fact that the first three dynasties were as solid realities as the fourth, and that if their culture was not so grandiose as that of their great successor, it was at least quite as elaborate. But that was just the point which made it manifest that we had no more reached finality, or, rather, the fountain-head of Egyptian civilisation, at the tomb of Mena than at the pyramid of Khufu. It was not in the least a primitive civilisation which was revealed by the discoveries of the Royal Tombs. On the contrary, it was a civilisation already far advanced in almost all respects, highly sophisticated, and so far removed from being unorganised that it seems, to our minds, almost stiff with organisation. Mena's courtiers may have worn considerably less than the gorgeous lords and ladies of the court of the *Roi Soleil*; but the etiquette of the court was no less thoroughly regulated. Abydos has opened a door into the past; but, instead of looking out through it upon a landscape where the first pioneer of civilisation has just pitched his tent, you find yourself gazing, very much dazzled and puzzled, into the hall of a great palace, where the gay whirl of highly cultured life changes its colours and shapes before your eyes, only to offer another circle of new effects and equal brilliancy as you gaze.

Mr. Weigall has put the state of affairs so aptly in present-day terms that one cannot do better than to quote his picturesque summing up of the situation. The archæologist, he says, "is like a man who has come late to the play, and beholds before him the great spectacle of the second act, but does not know what has gone before, except in so far as the bald and brief statements upon his programme can serve to enlighten him". The only exception that can be taken to such a way of putting it is that it is not even the second act that we are looking upon when we see the relics of Ist Dynasty splendour, but the third at least, possibly the fourth or fifth, of a play which is not limited by the restrictions that affect the modern stage. We were to get back to the beginnings, to the very dawn of civilisation, when we reached the Ist Dynasty; now we have reached it, the beginnings seem almost as far away as ever, and what we imagined to be the dawn actually proves to be well on in the forenoon. This civilisation is not young, though it has the abundant vigour of youth; it is already old, though still in the full richness and power of maturity. So the journey has to begin all over again; and the pilgrim in search of the Fountain of Youth and the Beginnings has to admit that, even if he has got "a day's march nearer home", he has still more stages to travel than he ever at first imagined possible. It is the way of other things besides the study of ancient origins.

In this strait, the despised Manetho comes to our aid with a suggestion which may prove in the end more helpful than it looks at first. According to him, the First Dynasty of his own list of human rulers was not the first of the actual dynasties of those who held sway over Egypt. There were at least two dynasties which went before the coming of Mena and his race. The First was that of the Gods, and, as one would expect, they allowed themselves a somewhat liberal allowance in respect of time. The longest reign in the dynasty amounted to 9000 years, while the shortest only reached the ridiculously short total of 359 years—scarcely worth calling a reign, in fact—the total for the six reigns being 11,985 years. The odd five years are especially comforting by reason of the appearance of minute accuracy which they give to the whole.

The Second Dynasty was that of νέκυες οἱ ἡμίθεοι, "The Dead Demi-Gods", nine of whom, according to Manetho, reigned for a period of 856 years, an unknown and unnamed tenth having reigned for a brief two years, which brings the total up to 858. Now at first sight nothing would seem likely to be less helpful than a scheme like this, which appears to be just about as substantial as moonshine. But it is never safe to rule out any suggestion unless absolute evidence exists to prove it an impossible one; and it would be a hard thing to say that Manetho's contribution is impossible, however ridiculous it may appear. Doubtless we have to give up his Dynasty of Gods, particularly the lucky Hephaistos (Ptah), with his reign of 9000 years; but it is hard to tell how much of the 11,985 years which he allots to it we shall find ourselves needing before the story of the prehistoric civilisation is fully told. As for his "Dead Demi-Gods", there need not be much difficulty about allowing to them the 858 years which he assigns to them; for the most cautious and niggardly of chronologists would doubtless admit that eight and a half centuries, or even a millennium, would be by no means too long a period to grant for the slow developments of neolithic and chalcolithic man of which we find the scanty relics from Sequence Date 30 onwards.

But who were these Dead Demi-Gods—this ghostly dynasty which defiles across the stage like the crowned shadows in *Macbeth*? Shadowy enough they were, even to Manetho, or he would never have called them by such a name; and probably long before his time, and even in the days of the Old Kingdom, the mists had wrapped them about, and through the cloud their descendants could see them only "as trees walking", beings of a stature and nature more than human. It is the process that happens in the early days of every people, that made the enlightened Athenians of the Kimonian period seek and find the giant bones at Skyros, and hail them as those of Theseus, and that, nearer home, gives us a King Arthur who would be least of all recognisable to the men of his own time.

They were the "strong men" who "lived before Agamemnon"; the men who sowed the seed of which Mena and his line reaped the harvest. Some of them were known by another name to the Egyptians of later days. These were the legendary "Followers of Horus", who followed the banner of the Falcon-god, Horus, of Upper Egypt, and around whose struggle with the Deltaic followers of Set there grew up an immense wealth of legend. They correspond, in actual fact, to one of the great lines which led the various sections of the divided land of Egypt, and eventually prepared it for its unification. Of these there were, in the main, three; though other less prominent, though perhaps scarcely less influential, sections appear along with them, either in combination or in controversy.

Probably the most ancient of all the shadowy lines was

that which reigned over Lower Egypt, sometimes from the city of Buto, sometimes from that of Sais, both in theDelta. The very title by which the kings of this line were known infers its origin in a primitive community. The King of Lower Egypt was the *Bya* or *Byati*—the "Bee-man" or "Honey-man." His emblem was the figure of a Bee or a Hornet; and you are left to imagine whether his title was assumed in the beginning because he was the leader of his people in the productive arts of peace, or because he was as deadly to his enemies as the venomous sting of the hornet. Very probably both meanings were combined, and the king was Bee-man to his subjects, to make their land flow with milk and honey, and Hornet-man to his foes, to sting and drive them before him.

The Bee-king alreadywore a crown which was destined to be very famous in later Egyptian history—the Red Crown of Lower Egypt. No one has ever seen an actual specimen of either of the two crowns which in combination made the great Double Crown of the Pharaohs; and one of the disappointments of Tutankamen's Tomb was that it contained no trace of the long-looked-for emblem of the oldest sovereignty in the world; but we know its shape and colour, everything, in short, but its material, from innumerable pictures and carvings. The Red Crown was a kind of mitre, of bright red, and probably soft material— possibly stiffened linen, or soft leather. In shape it was curiously like the official cap of a Venetian Doge; so much so that if you can imagine the white and gold of the Ducal cap on the head of Bellini's Leonardo Loredano in the National Gallery changed to red, you will have quite a good idea of the Red Crown which adorned the head of another and earlier ruler of a race of marsh-dwellers. You will have to add to the Doge's cap, however, a curved projection, probably of gold wire, which comes from the back and curls up over the front. Red was the royal colour of Lower Egypt, and even the royal treasury was "The Red House". The papyrus plant, which abounded in the marshes of the Delta, was the cognisance of the Northern kingdom, and its symbol in hieroglyphic writing. The kingdom of Lower Egypt lay opener to outside influences than any other part of Egypt. In the Western Delta, there was always pressure from the Libyan tribes to the west; in the Eastern, there was intercourse or incursion from the Isthmus; to the North, the Mediterranean offered a path to Crete, where already a great kindred culture was growing up among a people who possessed elements of kinship with the Mediterranean element of the Egyptian race. Resemblances, in some cases identities, of religious belief and practice, which are only now being traced between Crete and the Delta cults, point to the relationship having been original and close.

The Red-king's sovereignty did not extend far south of the Delta. About 70 miles south of the modern Cairo, on the western bank of the Nile, stood the ancient city of Eheninsi, which we know better by the Greek name of Herakleopolis, which was given to it in later ages. Eheninsi, or Het-insi, is "The House of the Insi"; and the Insi was the title of the king or rather the line of kings who corresponded to another lot of Manetho's Dead Demi-Gods. Insi means "Reed", and the reed was the cognisance of this kingdom of Middle Egypt as the papyrus was that of the North. The king of it was "The Reed-man", as his brother rival of the North was the Bee-man; the simplicity of the beginnings of things apparent in both titles. The Reed-king's crown was a tall pointed white cap, somewhat resembling a hock bottle in shape. His royal colour was white, and his treasury was "The White House". Later in the story, but still sufficiently early, the capital of the Reed-kings was shifted to Nekhen, far to the south, which we know better as Hierakonpolis, and Nekhen remains as characteristic of the Southern Kingdom as Buto of the Northern; but this change probably did not take place until the intrusion and dominance of a third element had shifted the balance of power southwards.

Thus, then, we have two sets of kings reigning in Egypt in these remote days of the Dead Demi-Gods, the Bee-man of the Delta and the Reed-man of Middle Egypt. These two titles were to survive unchanged, with their emblems, all down through the long history of the conservative Egyptian. Erman has said of him that "he could forget nothing". It is equally true that he found it impossible ever to make up his mind to scrap anything. Northern Egypt and Middle Egypt gradually were united, and both were finally conquered by still another Egyptian kingdom, that of the South, of which we shall hear directly. Perhaps it would be more strictly correct to say that the younger Southern kingdom absorbed Middle Egypt, and later completed the process by absorbing the North also. But though the kingdom was thus thoroughly unified, the Egyptian never forgot, and did not wish to forget, that there had once been a time, before the unifiers had been heard of, when Egypt was two kingdoms, the Red Kingdom and the White Kingdom, and when the king of the one was the Bee-man and of the other the Reed-man. Still more curiously, the unifiers, the conquerors themselves, did not wish to have this forgotten, but adopted the titles for their own, and put the blazons of the Bee and the Reed upon their royal titulary. To the end of time, Pharaoh is *Insi-Bya*, "Reed and Bee" or "Reed and Hornet", to his subjects. He has other names, "Son of the Sun", with the goose and the solar disc for his blazon. Above all, he is the Hawk-king, with the Golden Hawk of Horus above the banner which holds his personal Horus name; and his Hawk name always stands first, because it was as Hawk-king he won Egypt to unity. But the Bee and the Reed had been honourable in the beginning, and he honoured them to the end. In such an instance, the inborn Egyptian conservatism may seem a valuable and engaging trait. Actually the Hawk-kings may have had nothing to do originally with the Double Crown of Egypt, which belonged in its parts to the lines which they conquered; but the Double Crown is the most characteristic thing of Egyptian history, more characteristic, indeed, than the Pyramids.

The element which finally came to be dominant in the Demi-God period was probably the latest of the great three to arise; for civilisation seems to have had its spring earlier in the north, and to have spread gradually southwards, reversing the order which conquest was soon to take. Roughly, it is true that as you ascend the Nile you descend the stream of Egyptian history; though, like all such figures, this one has its exceptions. If the south had been late in awakening, she speedily made amends for her inaction, once she was aroused; and the very emblem of her royal race, the Falcon, seemed to prophesy of restless and aggressive strength such as were scarcely suggested by the Bee and the Reed. The kings of the Hawk line held their royal seat at Nekhen, the Greek Hierakonpolis, afterwards, as we have seen, to be known as the typical city of the White Kingdom. Hierakonpolis stands on the west bank of the Nile, near the famous temple of Edfu, between Luxor and Aswan. Its Hawk-king bore the name of Horus before his own personal name, and was regarded as an incarnation of the god Horus. In spite of his soaring emblem and title, his original realm was probably only the comparatively small province later known as the Hawk Province. This is inferred from the fact that whereas local princes of mostly all the other provinces are known, none is known for the Hawk Province; the inference being that Pharaoh always retained the princeship of his family's original domain for himself, just as the Plantagenet Kings of England did with some of their French estates. If so, it is another instance of what, in such cases, is the valuable Egyptian conservatism.

From its situation, the Hawk Kingdom doubtless had affinities with the south—almost certainly with Nubia, very possibly also with that distant land of Punt, to which Egyptian tradition consistently ascribed the origin of its ruling race. Its culture was doubtless backward, compared with that of the White Kingdom to the north of it, and still more with that of the Red Kingdom of the Delta; but there was evidently an abundant store of energy in the kings of the younger line, and, as the event showed, also abundant capacity for the assimilation of whatever of good the kindred cultures of the north had to offer to the conquerors.

These were the three outstanding elements whose varied history, first as isolated and independent communities, then gradually with more and more close approximation to unity, made up the succession of what

Manetho called the Dynasty of the Dead Demi-Gods. The names of some of these all but unchronicled heroes have been preserved by a strange chance to remind us that they were not mere "shadows of a dream", but living men who did a notable day's work in their day. Most of them belong to the Red Bee-kings of the Delta. They are "primitive" in type; such as a child, or a child-like people, might give— Tiu, Thesh, Hzekiu, Neheb, Uazonz, Emkhet. From the south come two, even more childish, of which one, even at that, is doubtful, Ka-Ap and Ro. No names of the early Reed-kings have survived; but below a break in the Palermo Stone occurs a sign of a king wearing the White Crown of the *Insi*. That is all; "stat magni nominis umbra".

It is likely that as this constructive period began to draw towards its close, there was a gradual process of consolidation going on. So far as one can judge, it took the form of a northwards movement from the south on the part of the Hawk-kings. Quite possible their neighbours of the White Kingdom to the north were beginning to become unified with them by a time of which we can only say that it must have been from half a century to a century before the establishment of a united Egypt. How the unification of the two lines and the two kingdoms of the Hawk and the Reed was brought about, whether by conquest from the south, or by a marriage through which the Hawk-king acquired a legitimate claim to the White Crown and the *Insi* title, we have not the slightest idea. What seems to be conclusive is that Petrie found at Tarkhan, somewhat north of Medum, a cylinder jar bearing the name of the Hawk-king Ka-Ap, mentioned above, so that his dominion evidently extended as far north as this point, slightly north of the Fayum.

It seems that this conqueror or unifier is the same as the "Scorpion"-king, so named, not necessarily from any specially dangerous qualities, but from the hieroglyphic which represents him. The Scorpion-king, Ka-Ap, or Ip, goes by both of the royal titles of the South and Middle Kingdoms. He is both Horus and *Insi*. His kingdom evidently may be regarded as reaching from the southern limit of archaic Egypt, possibly about Silsileh, practically to the apex of the Delta. The whole of Upper Egypt, therefore, was now a unity, and the Bee-king of the Delta was probably beginning to feel somewhat uncomfortable at the near presence of such competent and aggressive rulers as the Hawk-kings had shown themselves to be. Now that they had taken to themselves the Reed title, the White Crown, and all the resources of the former Middle Kingdom, the Bee-king was no doubt shaking in his shoes, and wondering when his turn to be eaten up was going to come. He had not very long to wait; for the Scorpion's successor was a still greater man, the redoubtable Narmer, whose great slate palette from Hierakonpolis, one of the most famous relics of this ancient world, shows him wearing not only the White Crown of the *Insi* king, but also the Red Crown of the *Bya*. But Narmer really is more the first of the true dynastic monarchs than the last of the Dead Demi-Gods, and it will be best to give him his true place at the head of the line of the Ist Dynasty, with which we have now to do.

CHAPTER IV

UNITED EGYPT AND ITS EARLIEST ROYAL LINE

SOME of the most remarkable relics of the kings who accomplished the unification of Egypt have been found in the course of Mr. Quibell's excavations at Hierakonpolis, far up the Nile, the town which, as we have seen, was the seat of the Hawk-kings in the days when they were only kings of the Hawk Province, and the conquest of Middle, let alone Lower Egypt, was still in the dim future. Their ancient capital, from which they had started on their career of conquest, remained sacred to them, and proofs of their great deeds were sent to it in the shape of ceremonial carvings representing various aspects of their new glories, which in due course have come to light once more to bear witness to the work of the fathers of the Egyptian nation.

Thus, for the beginning of the movement we have the great ceremonial mace-head from Hierakonpolis which testifies to the activities, both warlike and beneficent, of the Scorpion. Round the top of the mace runs a row of standards, representing the nomes of the south, one series running half round the mace, and being faced by another series which runs round the other half. From these standards, there hang by the neck wretched crested birds —*rekhyut*—the symbol for the peoples who have been conquered by the south. In the scene below, the king performs the great public function of breaking ground for a new irrigation canal. He wears the White Crown, now the symbol of united Upper Egypt. The hoe is in his hands, and in front of him a man stands with a basket to catch the earth as the king cuts the first sod, while there are traces of the figure of another man bearing ears of corn in token of the fertility which is to be the result of the royal labours. Immediately in front of the king's face, with a curious suggestion of an anticipation of Pisanello's style, is a rosette, and beneath it the scorpion with writhed tail—the hieroglyphic for His Majesty's name. Behind him two fan-bearers hold the great feather fans familiar in all pictures of Egyptian royalty; while in the background we have open country with flowering plants, and the end of a festal scene, with a row of figures in palanquins, and, beneath, a line of long-haired women dancing. Beyond the king's hieroglyphic stand the standard-bearers of the army.

Here, then, is one of the most remarkable relics of these ancient days. It is remarkable, first of all, for its artistic quality, which is of a really high order. The designer of the Scorpion's mace-head had a distinct gift for the arrangement of a design which should satisfactorily fill the awkwardly-shaped space with which he had to deal; while he knew how to use low relief with wonderful skill for the production of a really dignified royal figure. The artistic interest of the piece, however, must yield to its value as an historical document, which commemorates the first step towards the unification of the land, and shows us that conquest was accompanied by peaceful triumphs, in which the conquered shared with their conquerors.

The Scorpion's relics are, however, outdone in importance by those which his successor Narmer has also left at Hierakonpolis. Of these, the first is also a great ceremonial mace-head, carved in low relief like that of the Scorpion. It represents King Narmer in the act of celebrating the *Sed* Festival, one of the most fundamental of Egyptian religious ceremonies. In it the monarch was supposed to be forcibly put to death at the end of the thirtieth year of his reign, doubtless with the object of securing what was a manifest necessity in primitive times —namely, that the king should always be a man in the full vigour of life, and capable of personally leading his armies in the field. Even by so early a time as that of Narmer, however, the slaying had become merely a ceremonial one; and indeed one imagines that the man who wanted to carry out the rite literally upon Narmer would not have his sorrows to seek. The *Sed* Festival has become merely a Jubilee Festival, as it continued to be during Egyptian history. King Narmer sits enthroned in a shrine with the traditional canopy over it, and above him hovers the Vulture Goddess of the South with outstretched wings —henceforward to be a permanent motive in Egyptian art. Before him are standards, offerings, and bearded prisoners; beneath him are his two fan-bearers; behind him are the hieroglyphic symbols of his name, crowned by the Hawk, and beneath them two rows of officials, one of them bearing the king's sandals. But now the king wears, not the White Crown of Upper Egypt, but the Red Crown of Lower Egypt. The poor Bee-king's premonitions of coming trouble had been fulfilled, and Egypt had become one from end to end of her long straggling Valley. That the unification had been by no means a peaceful one is evidenced by the fact that the mace-head records "captives 120,000"; and of captive animals, "oxen 400,000, goats 1,422,000"—a record which shows, incidentally, that the Egyptian system of reckoning was already fully developed.

Still more important than the mace-head is the great slate palette. This is a magnified specimen of the common slate palette regularly found in the pre-dynastic graves, and used for grinding malachite for face-paint. In this case, however, though the central cavity for holding the malachite still survives, the palette is obviously not for use, but for dedication in the temple as a memorial. On one side the palette is crowned with two heads of the goddess Hathor, between which appears the hieroglyphic writing of the king's name. Beneath this comes the main action of the piece. The king, a colossal figure, wearing the White Crown, the standard artificial Pharaonic beard, and a short kilt with the lion's tail, grips with his left hand the forelock of a crouching enemy, who is labelled "Harpoon-marsh", and therefore represents the Harpoon Nome in the North-west Delta, while with his right hand he clubs him. Over the doomed chief's head the Falcon of Horus, standing on six papyrus plants, holds a human head by a rope passed through its nose—an obvious symbol of the north. Behind the king comes his inevitable sandal- and cup-bearer; while beneath his feet two figures are running for their lives, looking back in terror all the time, to seek "fortress-protection", so the inscription says.

On the reverse side, the Hathor heads and the royal name occur as before. Beneath them, the king, wearing the Red Crown this time, goes to inspect the dead bodies of ten slain foes—a representative selection, doubtless— who are nicely laid out for his gratification, each man with his head tidily disposed between his feet. The Egyptians were always an orderly people, who hated a mess. Before Narmer walks his vizier, labelled *zati*, "the man", to distinguish him from Pharaoh, the god; and in front of the vizier four standard-bearers hold aloft the standards of the gods. In the background comes once more the sandal-bearer. Below this procession, two men holding halters restrain two wonderful monsters, which seem to represent a kind of combination of leopard and giraffe seen in a nightmare. The intertwined necks of the creatures form the cavity for the face-paint—a very ingenious decorative use of a monstrosity. In the bottom register, a mightily horned bull, representing the king, tramples a poor northerner under foot, while at the same time he breaks into a fortified enclosure.

I have described the great palette in some detail, because it is, as Sir Flinders Petrie has said, "the most complete, and perhaps the most important, record of the times before Mena". It is by far the most complete record we possess of one of the most important events of ancient history, the accomplishment of the unification of Egypt; for, though Narmer can scarcely be held to have quite completed the process, and doubtless the final administrative union was accomplished by his successor, the fact of his wearing the Red as well as the White Crown in these representations of his triumphs shows that the conquests of his predecessor and himself had brought the sceptre of the whole land into the grasp of a single hand.

Other palettes, or fragments of palettes, though not of the same importance as the great Hierakonpolis palette, show scenes more or less clearly indicating a connection with these times of conquest. On the *verso* of a fragment at Cairo, the royal triumph is quaintly depicted under the guise of various creatures, probably animal emblems of the king, who are industriously picking to pieces with hoes the fortifications of various towns, some of whose names have survived—"Owl-town", "Ghost-town". Another fragment at the Louvre shows on its *recto* the royal bull goring a northerner; while below, the standards of five southern gods, Anubis, Upuat, Thoth, Horus, and Min, grasp with a hand a rope which drags along another captive whose body has been broken off. On the *verso* the scene of the bull is repeated; while below, the royal lion, looking uncommonly like a stout puppy-dog with a curly tail, has apparently broken into another fortified town. All these representations go to evidence the important position which the conquest of the north occupied in contemporary Egyptian opinion.

It is scarcely necessary to do more than mention the theory recently put forward that Narmer, for this purpose identified with Menes or Mena, is the same king as the Manium or Mannu-dannu of Magan, who is mentioned by Naram-sin of Babylonia as having been defeated by him. Such a supposition can only be accepted if the modern system of dating for Babylonia be discarded, and a return made to the figures of poor derided Nabonidus, which have for long been declared impossibly high, and from this point of view the suggestion would have a decidedly humorous effect. But it is scarcely necessary to contemplate so drastic a measure, or to accept the theory of such a humiliation having been inflicted on the redoubtable Narmer. Naram-sin was, no doubt, a famous warrior; but Narmer's record in this respect seems quite as good as that of the Semite; nor is there the slightest trace in Egypt of any repercussions such as could scarcely have failed to follow upon such an event as the defeat at the hands of an outside power of the king who was only accomplishing unity within his own land by conquest. Narmer, to all appearance, handed down his sceptre, with unbroken prestige and power, to the man who succeeded him, and who formed the third of the great triumvirate that made Egypt a nation. "After the Dead Demi-Gods," says Manetho, "the first dynasty consisted of eight kings, of whom the first was Menes the Thinite; he reigned 62 years, and perished by a wound received from a hippopotamus." Narmer had been primarily a warrior, as indeed his circumstances and those of the nation demanded. Mena, who may possibly have been his son, did some fighting, which seems to have been confined to the conquest of the district between Silsileh and Aswan, thus rounding off the kingdom on the extreme south as Narmer had completed it on the north, so that the whole Nile Valley and Delta, from the First Cataract to the sea, was held in the grasp of a single hand. But the tradition which attaches to the name of Mena is not so much that of a soldier as of an administrator. Conquest may be necessary as a preliminary stage in the making of a unity out of a complex of local kingdoms; but firm and wise administration is no less necessary than conquest, if the process of unification is to be completed.

Accordingly we find that the account which was given of Menes to Herodotus was that of a man who gave Egypt a new capital, suited to the needs of a great kingdom, to which the former local capitals, in far corners of the united realm, would not have sufficed, and who also bestowed attention, as we have already seen the Scorpion doing, upon matters of irrigation. "The priests informed me", says Herodotus, "that Menes, who first ruled over Egypt, in the first place protected Memphis by a mound; for the whole river formerly ran close to the sandy mountain on the side of Libya; but Menes, beginning about a hundred stades above Memphis, filled in the elbow towards the south, dried up the old channel, and conducted the river into a canal, so as to make it flow between the mountains. . . . When the part cut off had been made firm land by this Menes, who was first king, he in the first place built on it the city that is now called Memphis; for Memphis is situate in the narrow part of Egypt; and outside of it he excavated a lake from the river towards the north and west; for the Nile itself bounds it towards the east. In the next place, *they relate* that he built in it the temple of Vulcan (Ptah), which is vast and well worthy of mention." One may be persuaded that Herodotus's conception of the "temple of Vulcan" which Menes built was very different from the reality; for the days of the great builder Pharaohs, who used huge blocks of stone as other kings used brick, lay still in the future; but the general impression which he gives is quite unmistakable, and in all probability correct in the main.

Now the king Aha Mena, who apparently succeeded Narmer, answers to all these elements of the traditional conception of Menes, though it is probable that his two predecessors, the Scorpion and Narmer, have both contributed elements to the building up of the tradition of a great first king who was the beginning of all things in unified Egypt. His second *Nebti* name, Meni or Mena, means "The Established", and may seem a fitting title for one whose work was that of consolidating what his predecessors had won by the sword (although Petrie suggests that Men was also the personal name of Narmer). He married the lady Neit-hetep; and as Neit was the goddess of Sais in the Delta, it is likely that Neit-hetep was a princess of the old Delta line of the Bee, and that with this marriage the two lines of the Hawk and the Bee were at last peacefully united. Further, he assumed a new title, to which his *Nebti* name belongs, which was henceforth to be the most honoured of Egyptian royal titles. He became "Lord of the Vulture and the Cobra"; and this double title, just as much as the Double Crown, was a symbol of the accomplishment of national unity. For the Vulture is the goddess Nekhebt, the patroness of the old Hawk capital of Nekhen (Hierakonpolis), whom we have seen already spreading her wings over King Narmer on his great mace-head at Hierakonpolis; and the Cobra is the goddess Utho, patroness of Buto, the ancient capital of the Delta, whose erected head and writhing coils were henceforth to adorn the front of the head-dress of every Egyptian royalty as long as the kingdom endured.

As significant as any of these things is the change of capital attributed to him by the tradition which describes

him as the founder of Memphis. It was doubtless manifest
that it would be quite impossible for a king who was now
master of the whole Nile Valley and Delta to rule his long
straggling kingdom from a capital which was near the one
end of the long thin line. Hierakonpolis was out of the
question, and even Thinis, the native place of the king,
though considerably nearer the centre of gravity of the
kingdom, was too far south to be a possible place from
which to control the north. The natural thing was to seek
a new capital which should be near enough to the Delta
both to propitiate and control it, and yet placed with regard to the Upper Nile so as to be in a position to deal
with its needs also. Memphis, only twenty-four miles
from the fork of the Delta, was admirably placed for both
these purposes, as the fact that Cairo, the modern centre
of gravity of Egypt, stands so near the ancient site still
shows. The name of the new city came to be Men-nefer,
"The Well-Established", from the Greek corruption of
which its general name of Memphis is derived; but it is not
quite certain whether it got that name from its founder,
whose own name forms part of it, or whether the title of
the Well-Established-City was given to it later in the time
of the VIth Dynasty. In view of the connection between
the name of the city and that of its founder, it may seem
more likely that the name belongs to the earlier period.

In shifting his capital to Memphis, Mena was not
creating a new city any more than the Emperor Con-
stantine did when he made Byzantium into Constanti-
nople. The City of the White Wall had for long played an
important part in the history of the *Insi* kingdom of Middle
Egypt as the frontier fortress of the White Kingdom
against the Red Kingdom of the Delta; and for long after
Mena had made it his capital the picturesque old name
clung to the great city which had outgrown, under his
fostering care, its narrow ancient limits as a border
stronghold. Doubtless Herodotus's tradition that Mena
built the great temple of Ptah at Memphis is only part of
the truth, for the cult of Ptah, the Artificer-god, goes very
far back in Egyptian history, and the legend of how Ptah
in the beginning shaped the egg out of which the Sun-god

issued is one of the original myths of the land; but the fact of the king's having greatly added to the ancient shrine, and laid a new emphasis on its worship, need not be questioned, and, indeed, agrees well with that other ancient tradition which depicts Mena as being both the establisher of an orderly ritual and the instructor of his people in the more luxurious crafts. Diodorus tells us that Mena taught his people "how to adorn their couches and tables with rich cloths and coverings, and was the first that brought in an elegant and sumptuous way of living". Excavation has shown us that the Egyptian civilisation, even before the days of Mena, was already capable of producing objects of beauty and luxury which may fairly be called sumptuous; but the development of a natural taste for beauty and richness is merely what one would naturally expect in a reign which brought settled government and order to crown the external unity achieved by conquest. Nothing is more natural than that a powerful and prudent king placed in the favourable position which Mena enjoyed should have been remembered as a great fosterer of the arts and crafts of civilised life; and all the evidence goes to show that he had apt scholars.

With King Mena we are now brought into touch with the actual and unquestionable evidence of the royal tombs as one of our great sources of information; a source of whose first-hand information we shall only be deprived at infrequent, though deplorable, intervals throughout the rest of the history. It was in the closing years of the nine-teenth century that Petrie, following up the somewhat slap-dash and unsystematic excavations of Amélineau, who had left his concession at Abydos with the remark that "tous les fellahs savent qu'elle est épuisée", undertook that systematic clearance of the royal cemetery of the earliest dynastic kings of Egypt which has perhaps done more than any other work of the kind towards the establishment of our knowledge of early historic Egypt and its culture on a sound basis.

The selection of Abydos as the royal burying-place of Egypt was probably determined by two reasons, one dynastic and one religious. The dynastic reason is to be found in the fact that the First Dynasty, as Manetho informs us, came from the city of Thinis or This, an obscure place quite close to Abydos; and the fact that the kings of the Second Dynasty were also Thinites would help to establish the tradition of a burial-place nearer to the natal city of the two royal lines. In all probability, however, the main reason for the selection of Abydos was the religious one connected with the legend of Osiris, the Egyptian God of the Resurrection. According to the legend, the body of Osiris, which had been recovered by his wife Isis after his slaying by Set, was dismembered by Set, who scattered its severed members over the whole land. The indefatigable Isis, however, travelled throughout the land seeking the fragments of her husband's body; and wherever she found a fragment she buried it, so that there came to be some fourteen burial places of Osiris in the country. The head of the dead god she found and buried at Abydos, which therefore acquired a special sanctity as being above all other places the secret city, the Holy of Holies of Egyptian religion. Thus a tradition was very early established, linking blessedness in the after-life with union with Osiris; and this implied the desirability of physical nearness to the burial-place of the dead god. In later days this idea possessed such a power that pilgrimage to Abydos was held to be one of the most desirable of things. If the pilgrimage could not be accomplished by the living man, it was often accomplished by his mummy; while, if even this was impossible, it was always feasible to send a votive offering of pottery, which might be laid upon the tomb of Osiris, or as near to it as possible. From this custom, observed for many centuries, has grown up the fact that part of the royal cemetery at Abydos is littered with masses of pottery, and is known as "The Mother of Pots" to-day. The most of this tradition of pilgrimage and votive offering is of later date than the early dynastic period; but there can be no doubt that a powerful religious attraction already existed when the great kings of the First Dynasty elected to make this desert spot their resting-place.

"Abydos", says Sir Flinders Petrie, "is by its situation one of the remarkable sites of Egypt. . . . The cliffs, about

800 feet high, come forward and form a bay about four miles across, which is nowhere more than a couple of miles deep from the cultivation. . . . Along the edge of this bay stand the temples and the cemeteries of Abydos; while back in the circle of the hills lies the great cemetery of the founders of Egyptian history, the kings of the Ist Dynasty. The site selected for the royal tombs was on a low spur from the hills, slightly raised above the plain, and with a deep drainage ravine on the west of it, so that it could never be flooded. . . . The situation is wild and silent; close round it the hills rise high on two sides, a ravine running up into the plateau from the corner where the lines meet. Far away, and below us, stretches the long green valley of the Nile, beyond which for dozens of miles the eastern cliffs recede far into the dim distance."

Here, then, tomb after tomb of the kings of the earliest dynasties was excavated, planned, and catalogued, with results which have been of the utmost importance for our knowledge of the earliest stages of historic Egypt. The estimation of the evidence discovered as to the stage of civilisation reached in this period must be left until we come to deal with the culture of the early dynasties; meanwhile it is enough to note what relics of the great kings who unified Egypt were found. The tomb of the Scorpion was not found, and his chief relic is still the great mace-head from Hierakonpolis. That of Narmer is doubtful, some authorities believing that it has not been discovered, while Petrie himself is of opinion that it is probably the first of the larger tombs at Abydos—a brick-lined pit, 26 feet long by 16 feet broad. A large alabaster jar of the king was found near at hand, together with many sealings bearing his name. For Narmer also, however, the main evidence is still from the great deposit at Hierakonpolis.

The case is different when we come to Aha-Mena. His tomb (or his cenotaph) is unquestionably at Abydos—another large brick-lined pit, 26 feet by 17, which had upright posts along its sides to support a lining of wood. Two smaller tombs close to it seem to have been those of members of the king's family ; while thirty-four graves are ranged in three rows to the east, and appear to have all held members of the royal establishment, as no name save that of Mena was found on their jar-sealings. Petrie's identification of one of the family tombs with the name of a princess which he reads as "Bener-ab" ("Sweetheart"), a possible daughter of the great king, has been questioned by Weigall, who reads the title as "Benrit" ("Date-wine"), and brings us down to the unromantic suggestion that the inscription merely refers to offerings of date-wine for the spirit of the deceased. As Petrie, however, states that the name occurs upon ten ivory toilet objects, it is difficult to see how Weigall's interpretation can be accepted. Of the king himself, we have an ebony label, showing the king offering for the fourth time a bowl of electrum (gold-silver alloy), while other ebony labels show the first known use of hieroglyphics for continuous writing. Of unexplained significance is the bar of gold bearing the royal name, which at least shows the use of gold for purposes other than those of the jeweller. The mention of the term "cenotaph" in connection with the tomb of Aha arises from the fact that another great tomb, in which objects bearing his name have been found, exists at Nakada, a few miles further up the Nile, and a little below Thebes. As we shall see at a later stage, it was a common practice for Pharaoh to have two tombs, of which one was for his personal use, and the other for that of his "Ka" or double. It is possible, therefore, that one or other of the tombs at Abydos and Nakada may be only the *Ka*-tomb, and it has been suggested that the large and important brick tomb at Nakada is the real tomb of King Aha, while that at Abydos is only that of his *Ka*. The size or importance of a royal tomb, however, by no means indicates that it is the personal tomb of the Pharaoh in question. Sneferu's pyramid at Dahshur is one of the very largest of existing pyramids, being, indeed, little inferior in size to the Great Pyramid at Gizeh; but there is no doubt that his real tomb was the much smaller pyramid of Medum. Further, the name of the Queen Neit-hetep frequently occurs on objects found at Nakada; so that, on the whole, the presumption is in favour of the tomb at Abydos being the real tomb of Aha, and not merely his cenotaph, while that at Nakada may have served the double purpose of the tomb of Neit-hetep and the cenotaph of her husband.

The length of Aha-Mena's reign is doubtful. Manetho, as we have seen, allots 62 years to him; but he also tells us that the king was slain by a hippopotamus, and it is scarcely apparent what a man of over eighty years was doing meddling with hippopotami. Weigall accepts Manetho's figure without hesitation as fitting into his own chronological scheme. Others, however, are less liberal, and Petrie, for instance, only allows about 47 years to the reign. The difference is not of vital importance. In either case the reign was of sufficient length for the accomplishment of the great task of stabilising the new institutions of united Egypt, so that the sceptre of a well-settled kingdom was handed on to the second king of the line, King Zer, to whom, as we shall see, a strange destiny was reserved.

Such, then, were the first three kings who emerge as real historical figures on the stage of the ancient Egyptian kingdom. What we know about them, after all, is comparatively little; but, little as it may be, it is solid and actual, and sufficient to remove them out of the category of insubstantial shadows. The Scorpion, Narmer, Aha-Mena—they are more than names to us now. We can look upon and handle actual objects which have been in physical touch with these mighty men of old, on which they bestowed care and thought, and to which they committed the story of some of their achievements and aspirations. There are many historical figures, much nearer to our own time, of which you cannot say as much. However dim our conception of them as individuals may be, these three men did a great work for their country; and it is due to them, in the main, that Egypt survived to become one of the great powers of the ancient world, and one of the main factors in moulding the destiny of civilised man. We have given them, in the telling of their story, their individual names; but it seems likely that to later ages in their own country, and to the tradition which was related to men of other races, the individuality of the three was ere long lost in the creation of a great, dim, gigantic figure, the "Menes" of Manetho and Herodotus, to whom were attributed the great deeds of all the three, whether warlike or administrative. The separate conquests of the Scorpion and of Narmer, and the triumphs of consolidation of Aha-Mena, were no longer remembered as acts of this king or that. They all contributed something to that *aura* of glory in which dwelt the mighty impersonal figure of the legendary king who united Egypt and made her great. The modern student takes this "conflate" embodiment of national beginnings, and analyses him into his component parts, giving to each of the three the credit which he justly earned. One hopes that it may be a satisfaction to the Scorpion and to Narmer, wherever they may be in the spirit-world, to receive this tardy acknowledgment of their greatness, though the satisfaction to Aha-Mena may be less; yet perhaps it was not unfitting that they should be united into one great figure in the reverent recollection of the nation which they made one.

CHAPTER V

MENA'S SUCCESSORS OF THE FIRST DYNASTY

THE kingdom thus established by the work of its three great founders was apparently handed down in peaceful succession to the second king of the Ist Dynasty. According to Manetho, his name was Athothis, and he was the son of Menes. "Athothis, his son," says the old historian, "reigned 57 years; he built the palaces at Memphis, and left the anatomical books, for he was a physician." The ordinary name by which he is known is Zer, though it is maintained by some that this name ought rather to be read Khent; his name as Lord of Thinis was Atoti, which accounts satisfactorily for Manetho's version Athothis. He was not the son of Queen Neit-hetep, but of "the Lady of the Harem, Hap or Hept", one of the king's secondary wives; but in spite of the fact that he was not of royal blood on both sides of the house, the throne seems to have been too firmly established for any serious attempt being made to dispute his claim.

If we are to judge of his power by the magnificence of his tomb (and at this early stage there is very little else to judge by), he must have more than maintained the standard set by his predecessor; for the tomb of Zer at Abydos, or rather the complex of tombs associated with his name, is much more important than that of Aha-Mena. The actual wooden tomb-chamber itself was about 28 feet square. It was set within a brick chamber measuring about 43 by 38 feet, and deeply recessed. The recesses, which were coloured red, may have been of the nature of little offering chapels round about the wooden shrine containing the body of the dead king. But the actual royal tomb is only a part of the whole. Around it there are no fewer than seven

76

rows of tombs of his household, numbering in all 334 graves. From these graves there came seventy steles of private persons, nearly all women, who were probably members of the royal harem. So extraordinary an aggregation of private tombs round that of the king suggests rather forcibly that these people did not all die in the ordinary course of nature, but that there was a great slaying, at the king's burial, of such of his household as were chosen to accompany their lord through the Underworld. Such a practice seems a crude and barbaric thing to suggest of a people so far advanced in the arts of civilised life; but to account for the observed facts on any other supposition is extremely difficult. Traces of such a practice continue to a much later period in Egyptian history; and after all, we have to remember that the Egyptians, with all their skill in the arts and refinement of taste, were still, as much of the thought of the Pyramid Texts shows, at a stage not so far removed from the crude and barbaric ideas of primitive man. If in the Vth and VIth Dynasties Pharaoh, using, no doubt, an ancient formula, could still contemplate the idea of lassoing and devouring the gods with the very crudest details of the process, there is no extravagance in supposing that his ancestor, a couple of centuries earlier, should have had his burial celebrated by the slaughter of favourites of the harem and court officials, that he might enter the Elysian Fields with a train befitting his rank.

The tomb of Zer, however, had other things to show besides this rather ghastly suggestion of barbaric survivals in the thought of the cultured Egyptian. Manetho has told us that Zer was a physician who left behind him anatomical writings; and the famous Ebers Medical Papyrus so far bears out this statement that it includes a prescription said to be due to his queen Shesh, so that the love of medicine apparently was not confined to Pharaoh himself. The prescription is for a hair-restorer, which was to be compounded of the claw of a dog, the hoof of a donkey, and some boiled dates. One tries to imagine the hairdressers of Memphis advertising the infallible remedy, "from a prescription used by Her Majesty the Queen". Unfortunately, like most such concoctions, Queen Shesh's hair-restorer was not infallible, for Petrie's quaint discovery in the royal tomb of a fringe of false curls and a switch of false hair shows that even the royal household had to resort to supposititious aids in this respect, spite of the wonderful nostrum.

Other discoveries suggest rather a pleasant side to the court-life of this learnedly-inclined king. A wooden label shows a palace called "Qed-hetep"—"Making Peace"— which brings to the mind the "Sans-Souci" of Frederick the Great. An ivory tablet shows the king seated upon his throne with a figure which seems to be that of his wife seated upon his knee. Akhenaten did the same thing in his portraits, and it has been commented upon as one of the things which tended to break down the awful reverence with which the royal office was surrounded in Egypt; but if the interpretation of this tablet is right, he was only following a precedent which was two thousand years old, and dated almost from the foundation of dynastic rule. Another piece shows the king spearing a crocodile, one of the earliest examples of that love of open-air sport of which Egyptian art has left us so many illustrations.

Most remarkable of all was the discovery of the piece of a severed arm which had probably been that of Zer's queen, with four bracelets of gold, turquoise, lapis lazuli, and amethyst. These wonderful examples of the art of the Old Kingdom will have to be noticed later in dealing with the civilisation of the period. Their survival through all the vicissitudes to which the most frequented of all sites in Egypt was exposed is one of the romances of history. Petrie thus describes the chances through which these most remarkable memorials came into the hands of one who could prize them aright. "When the tomb was cleared out for building the Osiris shrine in the time of Amenhotep III. . . . then probably the body of the queen was found and broken up. One workman hastily put this forearm in the hole in the wall, and then either got so much more plunder that he ran away, or else perished in a squabble. This hole never seems to have been disturbed when building the staircase close by it; and for more than a thousand years offerings continued to be made here, and visitors passed within a few feet of the arm without looking at it. The Copts then destroyed the shrine and all that they could find, but never touched the arm. The *Mission Amélineau* cleared the tomb, but still the arm lay in the hole in the wall. Lastly, my men eyed the gold, and preserved it with all care; and these bracelets will now be preserved in the Cairo Museum until some future convulsion, when they may share the fate which denies more than a few centuries of existence to any known treasure."

Petrie's mention of the offerings which were made for more than a thousand years at the tomb of Zer, and the visitors who frequented it, calls our attention to the extraordinary fate which attended this monarch after his death, of being identified with the great god Osiris of Abydos, so that his tomb became to all Egyptians later than the Middle Kingdom the actual burial-place of the dead god, and was visited by countless thousands of pilgrims. The story of how this came about belongs rather to the history of the national religion. Probably about the time of the Middle Kingdom (*c.* 2000 B.C.) the king's name began to be read as Khenti or Khent, instead of Zer or Ther, the reading which is preferred by most modern Egyptologists. From this to identifying him with the god Khenti-amenti, "The Chief of the Westerners", was an easy step. Khenti-amenti was an ancient god of the Abydos necropolis, whose place had been usurped by Osiris; and consequently, to identify Zer or Khent with Khenti-amenti meant to identify him with Osiris. By the time of Amenhotep III., in the middle of the XVIIIth Dynasty, the business of pilgrimage to and offering at the tomb of him who was now held to be the actual Osiris was in full swing. Later, a staircase was introduced into the tomb for the convenience of offering; and some time between the XXth and XXVIth Dynasty the shrine was completed by the introduction of a grey granite lion bier with a figure of the dead god, wearing the white crown of Upper Egypt, and holding the crook and the whip, the usual emblems of sovereignty. Thus the process was completed by which the dead king was transformed, for his people in later days, into the god of the Dead and of the Resurrection.

It was this mistake of the Egyptian people themselves which led Amélineau into the belief that when, on the 2nd of January 1898, he found the granite bier in the tomb and also a skull lacking the lower jaw, he had actually found the tomb of the god and the divine head, which, as we have seen, was traditionally buried at Abydos. Indeed it has recently been maintained (Weigall, *History of the Pharaohs*, i. 111 sq.) that Amélineau was right, that the king whom history has known as Zer was actually he whom the Egyptians worshipped as Osiris, and that the whole story of the murder of Osiris is strictly historical, the murder being the sequel to a rising of the Set-worshipping tribes against their good king. The slaying took place, according to Weigall's theory, about January 12, 3289 B.C., which is surely as exact as we have any reason to expect. If such a view could be proved correct, it would be obviously the most interesting and important of events, alike from an historical and a religious point of view, as enabling us to assist, so to speak, at the birth of a great religion. Nevertheless opinion in general continues to hold the more commonplace belief as to the shrine already explained.

The fragments of the Palermo Stone give us, among several scarcely intelligible mentions of events which may have happened either in the reign of King Zer or in that of his successor, one reference, under Year 5, to "The Design(?) of the House, Mighty-of-the-Gods", which from its wording would appear to suggest the building of a temple. This, with one or two references to the Worship of Horus, the Birth of Min and of Anubis, the Feast of Sokar and the Feast of Zet, all evidently religious ceremonies, constitute the whole written record of the reign.

Fragmentary as are the records of Zer's reign, those of his successor are still more so. His tomb at Abydos was a wooden chamber, about 29 feet by 19, placed within a brick-lined pit, 31 feet by 40, with recessed sides. Around the tomb were rows of graves to the number of 174, so that the king was either not so exigent as his predecessor, or had not the power to command that so great a slaughter should be made for him. Little of importance came from the tomb; but the king's stele or tombstone, bearing a hawk in relief above the panelled tablet or door which displays the hieroglyphic of his name, is a fine piece of workmanship. His name is generally given as Zet or Zet-Ata. Probably, however, it was Uazet, as his hieroglyphic is the Serpent, the emblem of Uazet, the goddess of Buto in the Delta. It is quite possible that the large mastaba, surrounded by smaller graves, which was discovered at Gizeh, may also have belonged to him, as the king's name occurs upon fragments found in it, and the vases discovered in the mastaba are of workmanship and material so similar to those found in the tomb at Abydos as to prove that they belong to the same time, and possibly even to the same craftsman. One or other of these two tombs, therefore, probably that at Gizeh, would be the *Ka*-tomb of the king, the other being the real place of burial.

Behind the tomb of Zet at Abydos lies a much more finely built brick tomb about 21 by 30 feet, which belonged to a queen, Merneit, or Henneit, by name. Who she was, whether the wife of Zet, or an independent queen—the first example in Egyptian history of the "monstrous regiment of women"—we do not know, and are never likely to know; for though her tomb is "by far the most carefully built of all, both in the symmetric planning of it and the regular construction", it is also, unfortunately, the poorest in its equipment of funerary furniture. It seems unlikely that so important a tomb would have been provided for one who was not actually a reigning sovereign; and the lists of nomes and the titles of officials which occur seem to indicate an actual reign; but that is all that can be said, and it is useless to speculate on Queen Merneit having possibly been the Queen of the South, Aso, who, according to Plutarch's story, was one of the conspirators who compassed the slaying of Osiris.

On the other hand, the occurrence in the queen's name of the title of the goddess Neit of Sais, along with the fact of the adoption by King Zet of the serpent of Buto to express his name, seems to signify the consistent attempt, traceable also in later reigns, to conciliate Lower Egypt by the use of titles which gave the northern section of the kingdom a place of honour in the royal titularies. It was quite natural that an attempt of this kind should be made, in view of the fact that the conquest of the north was so recent, and that the northerners might, not unnaturally, feel sore at the loss of their independence and the suppression of their own royal house and court.

With the king who succeeded Zet and Merneit a considerable stride forward is made in construction, and we are faced with the beginnings of that passion and genius for great work in stone which in the end made the Egyptian the greatest master-builder of the ancient world. The king in question was named Semti—"Two Deserts", which somewhat curious appellation was misread by later copyists as Hsapti—"Two Nomes", from which misreading Manetho derived his version of the name, Usaphais. He took the Horus name of Den, sometimes read Udimu; but the distinguishing feature of his titulary was that he was the first of the Pharaohs to assume the double title "Insi-Bya", and thus to establish a precedent, which was followed by all his successors, of uniting the two ancient titles of the kings of the two older kingdoms of the Reed and the Bee in the royal nomenclature. His predecessors, as we have seen, had been depicted as wearing either the White Crown or the Red; but now the establishment of a settled and unified dominion is absolutely vouched for by this combination of titles in the style of the king of the whole land. This acknowledgment of the ancient kingdoms must have gone, along with the other attentions shown to the Delta, to make submission to the new order easier; but it was not for some time yet that discontent in the north was finally allayed after a new conquest and marriage alliance by Khasekhem, the first king of the IIIrd Dynasty.

Semti's tomb at Abydos is the main source of information with regard to the events of the reign and the state of civilisation and society. It is a great brick-lined pit, measuring 28 by 50 feet, and has a staircase 78 feet long leading down into it. But the new feature is its pavement,

which consists of blocks of granite—the first appearance
of the material of which the Egyptian builder was to make
such splendid use for decorative purposes at a later date.
Here its presence is somewhat phenomenal, as, apart from
this, no other stone building is known until the reign of
Khasekhem, nearly three centuries later. The tomb was
surrounded by graves of courtiers and ladies of the harem
to the number of 137. The store of small ivory and ebony
labels, of the type familiar from other royal tombs, helps
us to construct a chronicle of the events of various years.
There is, for instance, a record of a river expedition to the
north, resulting in the capture of a fortified place; while
the same tablet states that in this year "The Falcon
(*i.e.* the Pharaoh) seized the abodes of the Libyans", and
also makes mention of the viceroy of the north, Hemaka,
who appears to have been the big man and Pharaoh's
alter ego of the reign. Hemaka's name occurs on many
wine-sealings, and there are six different seals of Super-
intendents of the Inundation, so that a special administrative department already existed, whose function was to
deal with and regulate this most important factor in the
national prosperity.

Perhaps the most remarkable relic from the tomb is
the lid of the ivory box in which the king kept the golden
seal with which he stamped the records of his judgments.
It bears the inscription, "Golden Seal of Judgment of
King Den", and the British Museum now possesses this
earliest record of the establishment of a regular judicial
system. Besides the records of the tablets from the tomb,
the Palermo Stone gives us some information as to the
chief events of certain years of the reign. Thus, one of the
first references is to "The smiting of the Intiu", who are
the Beduin tribes of the Eastern Deserts; and this same
event is depicted on an ivory tablet, formerly in the Mac-
Gregor Collection, where the king smites with his mace
a bearded Easterner, who has fallen on one knee before
him. Another evidence of the desire to conciliate northern
favour is offered in this picture by the fact that the king
here, for the first known time, wears on the front of his
head-dress the royal cobra, which, though it was eventually

to become the essential emblem of royalty, had so far been the emblem of the north alone. In the next year comes the record of the celebration of the Sed Festival, which, according to theory, should be held on the attainment of thirty years on the throne (or since nomination as heir). In the same year comes what may have been a kind of anniversary of the coronation, held in connection with the Sed Festival; and it is recorded as the "Appearance of the *Insi*" and "Appearance of the *Bya*", so that the two titles were evidently being diligently kept before the nation.

In the following year we have the "Numbering of all people of the nomes of the west, north, and east", apparently the first recorded census. Two years later occurs the "Design of the House"—"Thrones of the Gods", possibly a palace, or, perhaps more likely, a temple. This is followed next year by the "Stretching of the Cord for the House" —"Thrones of the Gods", by the priest of the Goddess Sefkhet"—the first occurrence of one of the most familiar of Egyptian ceremonies, corresponding to our laying of the foundation stone of a building. Next year, the "Thrones of the Gods" was apparently finished, for the record tells of the opening of its ornamental (or sacred) lake, apparently with a grand hippopotamus hunt. Another year tells us of a "Voyage to Sahseteni", an unidentified piece of exploration, and of the "Hacking up of Werka", also unidentified. The last incident of interest comes two years later—"First occurrence of 'Running of Apis'"—a ceremony which must obviously mean the hunt which, as we know, always took place after the death of an Apis bull, for another bull with "all the good marks" to replace the lost emblem of divinity. Manetho tells us that it was in the reign of King Kaiechos of the IInd Dynasty that "the bulls, Apis in Memphis, and Mnevis in Heliopolis, and the Mendesian goat, were appointed to be gods"; but the Palermo Stone reveals the fact that the beginning of animal worship, or at least of the use of animals as emblems of divinity, is of earlier date.

Altogether the impression derived from the frag-mentary records of the reign of Semti is one of a king

PLATE V

1. SEMERKHET SMITES A BEDAWY CHIEF. SINAI
2. PREHISTORIC SHIPS. HIERAKONPOLIS (*p.* 33)
By permission of Sir Flinders Petrie

characterised by force and initiative, who worthily maintains the traditions of vigour and efficiency handed down by the three great founders of United Egypt. The same can scarcely be said, however, of his successor, Merpeba, whose personal name was Enezib, or Azab. His tomb at Abydos is the poorest of the whole dynasty, and the graves which surround it are both few in numbers (64 in all) and of rough construction. Merpeba's only distinction is that he is the first king to be recognised by the Saqqara List, which is highly northern in its sympathies, as the genuine king of Lower Egypt. His father's policy had evidently borne fruit, and was probably helped by the association of the young prince with Semti during the last years of his reign. Apart from this recognition, for which, doubtless, the credit is due rather to Semti than to his son, the reign is entirely undistinguished. By his marriage with the lady Tarset, however, Merpeba left Egypt a king who was destined to start the land on the career of expansion which, though essentially alien to the genius of the race, was yet to produce such remarkable results.

The new king's name was Semerkhet, whose personal name was probably in his own time read as Nekhti or Hui, "The Strong" or "The Striker", but by an easy misapprehension of its hieroglyphic was read by the annalists of Seti I. in the XIXth Dynasty as Shemsu, "The Follower". Both strong and striker he proved to be, in any case. We have seen how, even in prehistoric times, Egyptian miners were probably busy in the Sinai Peninsula, working the malachite which was in such demand in their own country; but Semerkhet appears to have been the first Pharaoh to organise this industry, and make a national business of what had previously been a private adventure. The Pharaoh in person led an armed force to the mountain solitudes of the Wady Maghara in support of a mining venture, which was no doubt on a greater scale than any that had preceded it. His expedition met with opposition, and on the rock 400 feet above the wild valley he has left a record, admirably carved, of his triumph over the Mentiu, the Beduin who opposed him. He appears thrice;

first wearing the White Crown and striking down with his mace a Beduin chief who crouches before him, next as wearing the Red Crown, while in the third case he wears the White Crown again. In the latter two scenes he is immobile. Before the third royal figure marches "the chief and general of the soldiers", who carries a bow and arrows, and who, no doubt, did most of the fighting of which His Majesty got the credit. Semerkhet's Maghara tablet is the first of the long series which was to be carved there during many centuries, and which by their inclusions or omissions almost serve as a barometer of Egyptian prosperity and aggressiveness or their opposites.

Beyond the fact of this first assertion of Egyptian power beyond the bounds of the land, next to nothing is known of Semerkhet's reign. His tomb is of fair size, 25 by 44 feet, and is surrounded by about 72 graves, a slight advance on his predecessor's death train; and his large tombstone of hard black quartzose sandstone has survived, and is now in the Cairo Museum. With his successor, Ka-Sen, the dynasty closes, and the evidence of his tomb seems to point to a decline of the power of the throne, as the king is only accompanied by 24 of his nobles, the smallest number of any of his line. His ivory labels, however, are of interest as naming four high officials of the court—the First Peer, the Royal Constructor, the Follower of the King (perhaps the royal secretary), and the "Doer of Things", or Master of Ceremonies. The complete organisation of the court circle is thus indicated. An ivory gaming-reed shows the figure of a Libyan captive, and is of interest from the artistic point of view. In spite of his apparent insignificance, the memory of King Ka-Sen was apparently kept in remembrance for five centuries, and the names of five priests of his funerary chapel are known.

The Ist Dynasty, which thus, like so many other famous lines, came to a somewhat undistinguished end, had lasted, roughly speaking, for about 250 to 300 years. Its great work had been the unification of Egypt, and though the consolidation of the united kingdom was not perfectly accomplished, and some of the work had to be repeated under later monarchs, yet the basis of the Double

Kingdom had been established with such solidity as to endure for a longer period than any similar work in the ancient world. From this time to the end of Egyptian national history, the Pharaoh bears the title which his earliest ancestors had won in the beginning of things, and is "Lord of the Two Lands".

CHAPTER VI

"COME LIKE SHADOWS, SO DEPART!"

ONE might almost add to the quotation the stage-direction which follows it in *Macbeth*, "A show of eight Kings"; for the kings of the IInd Dynasty are little more than the shadows of names to us, and if Khasekhemui be reckoned, as the *Cambridge Ancient History* reckons him, as the first of the IIIrd Dynasty, instead of the last of the IInd, these insubstantial shades are eight in number. Hotepsekhemui, the first of the shadows, scarcely emerges at all as a reality. Even his tomb is not known, though the name of it, *Sa-ha-ka* is, as also that of his palace, *Akhut en neter*; and both of these titles we owe to stone vases which were found in the tombs of other kings. Manetho tells us of him (under the name Boethos, a Greek rendering of one of his names, Bezau), that he reigned for 38 years, and that "during his reign a chasm of the earth opened near Bubastis, and many persons perished". But this reference to an earthquake, if it be that, is all that tradition records, and as excavation has been able to supplement it with so little, the first king of the new line departs as he came, a shadow still.

Nor does his successor, Raneb Kakau fare any better. Manetho tells us that it was in his reign that "the bulls, Apis in Memphis, and Meneus (Mnevis) in Heliopolis, and the Mendesian goat, were appointed to be gods"; but as the Palermo Stone has already told us that the "First Running of Apis", or search for a new Apis to replace one which had died, took place under Semti of the Ist Dynasty, the old historian must have got his facts mixed up to some extent. It is possible, of course, that Manetho's reference may mean that the cult of the divine animals increased in this reign, which, like the others of the dynasty, seems to have been mainly spent in the north, and to have been marked by northern sympathies, though the dynasty is of Thinite origin. Kakau's tomb, and that of his predecessor, may possibly have been at Saqqara, as clay sealings of both kings have been found there. The excavations at present being conducted there by Mr. Firth may give us more light, where it is badly needed, on these reigns, as they are doing with regard to the great figure of the next dynasty; meanwhile we must wait, and dismiss the second shadow after the first.

Neneter, the third of the line, claims a moment's attention by reason of his name, which means "possessing a god"—a claim which the Pharaohs were destined to maintain in later days as one of the prerogatives of royalty. But perhaps the chief interest of the reign lies in Manetho's statement that "In his time it was decided that women might hold the imperial government". There is, of course, no means of checking such a statement. We know that the Ist Dynasty rule was "father to son"; and we know that women did eventually succeed to the throne in Egypt on more occasions than one—Hatshepsut being the outstanding example. Manetho says that it was now that such an unusual arrangement was legalised. It may have been so; and that is all we can say. Weigall has attempted to link Neneter (Bineter or Binothr of his list) with the famous myth of Horus and his destruction of the Set worshippers, as recorded on the wall of the Temple of Edfu, and to show that the story is merely a glorification of the actual happenings in the course of the suppression of a rebellion of the Set worshippers which took place in this reign. It is, of course, possible that he may be right; but it seems as yet somewhat risky to assume, as in this and the other case of the Osiris legend, that every myth must necessarily have nothing more behind it than a more or less commonplace historical fact. Beyond this somewhat problematical association and brief references on the Palermo Stone to the "Hacking up of the city Shem-Re", and the "Hacking up of the city 'House of the North'", Neneter's reign is as much a blank to us as that of the two kings who went before him.

Of the remaining kings of the dynasty, Sekhemib

Perabsen (Uaznes), Senedi, "The Terrible", Neferkara, Neferkasokar, and Kara, next to nothing is known. Perabsen's tomb at Abydos, very different in style from those of the Ist Dynasty, and devoid of surrounding courtier graves, has yielded two steles of dark grey syenite, bearing the king's Set-name in relief. Of Senedi nothing survives to justify his awe-inspiring name. If Neferkasokar be the "Sesochris" of Manetho, he was a giant of between seven and eight feet in height with a chest measurement of 52 inches—possibly a great king in the sense in which Carlyle's "August the Physically Strong" was a great king. Neferkara's sole memorial is also a statement of Manetho, that in the time of Nephercheres "it is said that the Nile flowed with honey during eleven days"; and even Manetho guards himself against the supposition of his maintaining this rather unlikely thesis as a truth. Kara has left even less trace of his passing than that friend of Johnson of whom it is solely recorded that "he lived in London, and hung loose upon society".

Like the Lady of Shalott, we are "half sick of shadows"; and the appearance of a real and unquestionable king in the person of Khasekhemui is a relief. The new king, to whom for a time we may give the name Khasekhem, which appears to have been his original one, manifests himself at once as a man of his hands, the true successor to such great nation-builders as Narmer and Aha-Mena. With him we come for the first time into touch with the physical presentment of a Pharaoh, first of all that long and wonderful line of portrait statues which has come down to us from thirty centuries of kingship, and has made the appearance of the kings of Egypt more familiar to us than that of any race of kings in the whole history of the world. He is sometimes regarded as the last king of the IInd Dynasty and sometimes as the first of the IIIrd. Whether he be the one or the other matters little; for it is evident that with him there begins a new order of things in Egypt, or rather, we might say, the renewal of the old order of Narmer and Mena, which had been decaying and vanishing away under the feeble rule of the shadow kings whom he now succeeded.

Khasekhem is obviously a southerner. His tomb is at Abydos, the greatest and most remarkable of any there up to his time. His chief relics, apart from those of the tomb, are at the old Vulture City of Nekhen or Hierakonpolis, the ancient centre of southern organisation; and the inscriptions which he has left all record the triumph of the south over the north. It was during Mr. Quibell's excavations at Hierakonpolis, which have yielded so many interesting and beautiful things, that the portrait statues, or rather statuettes, to which we have already alluded, came to light. There are two of them—one of hard limestone, the other of slate. Both, unfortunately, have been much defaced. The body of the limestone figure has been destroyed, leaving only the legs and the throne, with the head detached, but almost uninjured, save for part of the nose; the figure of the slate statue, on the other hand, is practically uninjured, but the head has been much defaced, though a good deal of the modelling remains intact. Thus the one statuette more or less supplements the other, and helps to make good its deficiencies. The face of the king is strong and vivacious, though somewhat coarse; and though this is the earliest example of a royal Egyptian portrait in the round, there is no evidence of immaturity or uncertainty in the characterisation of the features. Sculpture was already, to a great extent, master of its materials when these figures were hewn. "The art of these figures", says Petrie, "shows a complete mastery of sculpture, the face being more delicately modelled than almost any later work."

Their artistic quality apart, the main interest of the statuettes attaches to their inscriptions, which are the same in both cases. Round the base of each there is a row of slain enemies, and in front is the grim inscripton, "Northern Enemies, 47,209". Whatever the reference may be to, evidently there had been a great killing of the foes of King Khasekhem. Manetho tells us of the first king, Necherophes, of his IIIrd Dynasty: "In his time the Libyans revolted from the Egyptians; but on account of an unexpected increase of the moon, they surrendered themselves for fear." Manetho's astronomy is somewhat obscure, and Khasekhem's own inscription makes it plain that, if the events referred to are the same, it was something more than an increase of the moon which made the king's enemies surrender; but it is possible that the confused recollection of a great victory over the northerners, among whom there may have been Libyans enough, survives in Manetho's tradition.

From Hierakonpolis also came three great stone vases, one of alabaster, one of granite, and one merely a fragment of a larger alabaster pan. The inscription on each is the same: "The year of fighting the northern enemy, within the city of Nekheb the Goddess Nekheb presents the rebels and unites Egypt before the Horus Khasekhem." Here again we have evidence of war in the north; and it seems probable, in view of the change which took place in the king's name, apparently after this triumph, that the fighting was not merely against Libyan raiders but was a genuine reconquest of Lower Egypt, by which Khasekhem did over again the work of the great unifiers of Egypt, and knit the two halves of the land together once more. His original Horus name, Khasekhem, means "Appearance of the Power". His new name, Khasekhemui, means "Appearance of the Two Powers", and a change so significant is surely meant to symbolise the restored domination of the Pharaoh over both the Upper and the Lower Valley. Khasekhemui is now "Lord of the Two Lands" once more, as the great kings of the days of long ago had been. The name is a token as well as a title.

Khasekhemui's great tomb at Abydos is a very remarkable structure. It is very much larger than that of any of the earlier kings, and is also very much more complex in its arrangements. The total length of the tomb is no less than 323 feet, while at its broadest part it measures 54 feet across. Entering it from the north, one finds first a triple row of chambers for offerings, thirty-three in all; the central part of the tomb is a sunken chamber with three chambers on either hand at a higher level; last of all are seven chambers on either hand, leading to the south entrance. On the whole, the most interesting object found in this complicated structure among the store of vases of

PLATE VI

STATUETTE OF KHA-SEKHEMUI

From Fechheimer's "Kleinplastik der Ägypter" (Cassirer)

stone and copper, tools of flint and copper, great pottery jars and basket work, was the wreck of what had once been the royal sceptre. Its foundation was a rod of copper, on which were threaded cylinders of polished sard, which were encircled at every fourth cylinder with double bands of thick gold, while the staff was capped with a golden end. In its original state it must have been an object of great richness and beauty and a fitting emblem of royal dignity for the Lord of the Two Lands. The decoration of the sceptre reminds one of that of some of the articles found in the tomb of Tutankhamen, and shows how early the Egyptian tradition in this sort began to establish itself.

The most remarkable thing about the tomb of Khasekhemui, however, is not any of the treasures which were found in it, but the construction of the central sunken chamber. This measures slightly over 17 feet by 10, and is built of stone, the faces of the blocks being in some cases the natural cleavage faces of the stones, in other cases genuine hewn stone, wrought by hammer and adze. Here, then, we have the first known stone building in the world. We have already seen that Semti of the Ist Dynasty had the floor of his tomb paved with blocks of granite; but the burial chamber of Khasekhemui is a regularly built structure, and as such it marks the beginning of a new era in human development and the first example of a craft in which the Egyptians were destined to be the masters of the world. The stone-work of the tomb goes along with the evidence of temple-building afforded by the great doorjamb of grey granite found by Quibell at Hierakonpolis, and bearing Khasekhemui's name surmounted by Horus and Set, to show that the king is to be ranked as the first of the long line of great builder Pharaohs, and the man who gave the impetus to the movement towards great construction in stone which developed with such amazing rapidity during the next few generations.

Khasekhemui's queen was Nemaathap or Hapenmaat. What her origin may have been, and whether she may have been the real heiress of the IInd Dynasty, through whom, as so often in Egyptian history, the succession descended, are obscure points; but she was evidently a lady of great importance, who ranked with her husband as having an equal share in the founding of the IIIrd Dynasty. One of the seals of the reign is that of "the sealer, constructor of the *king-bearing mother* Nemaathap, who orders all things that are done for her"; and this singular descriptive epithet was used as a standing title of this great lady, for even at the close of the dynasty an inscription dealing with her worship refers to the offering of "a hundred loaves daily in the *Ka*-house of the king-bearing mother Nemaathap". Quite conceivably part of her importance may have arisen from the fact that it seems likely that two at all events of the first kings of the new dynasty were her sons.

The order of the earlier reigns of the line which Khasekhemui had succeeded in establishing is somewhat obscure, and is differently given by different historians; but after all, whether Sa-nekht preceded Zeser (Petrie) or followed him (Hall in *Cambridge Ancient History*), and whether Zeser preceded Neb-ka-ra (Weigall) or followed him (Petrie), are not matters of any great moment. The important matter is that with these early kings of the IIIrd Dynasty there comes evidently a strenuous following up of the impetus which had been given by Khasekhemui, which within a remarkably short time leads to a stage in which Egyptian civilisation reveals itself as unmistakably mature, and reaches a point which in many respects it never surpassed. Only four kings of the dynasty, Zeser, Sa-nekht, Neb-ka-ra (if indeed these two are distinct kings), and Sneferu, are historically important in the present state of knowledge; the others are as shadowy as their shadowy predecessors of the IInd Dynasty. The order of the four here followed is Sa-nekht, Zeser, Neb-ka-ra, Sneferu, and the reason for following it is not that any certainty on the points involved is claimed, but simply that the structure of Sa-nekht's tomb seems less elaborate, and therefore possibly earlier than that of Zeser's great buildings, while again the conception of Nebkara's gigantic unfinished tomb at Zawiyet el-Aryan seems even more advanced than that of Zeser's pyramid, though this idea may have to be modified in view of the results of Mr. Firth's excavations at Saqqara.

Of Sa-nekht we know little. His tomb is at Bet Khal-

laf, which is also the place of his brother Zeser's secondary
tomb. It is a large brick mastaba over 200 feet by 80. Two
descending stairways lead to two groups of chambers cut
in the gravel, and the main group has a horizontal passage
below it, with three small stone chambers on either side.
The main interest of the reign lies in the fact that the king
has left in the Wady Maghara another tablet to continue
the series which Semerkhet of the Ist Dynasty had begun.
It means that Egypt is once more feeling the instinct
for expansion and adventure which had been temporarily
checked in the more sluggish days of the later IInd Dynasty. Henceforward the Sinai tablets and inscriptions at
Wady Maghara or Serabit el-Khadem are, as it were, a
kind of barometer by which one may determine the pressure of Egyptian national spirit and enterprise. The Sinai
records are always sensitive to the condition of affairs at
home, and a busy Sinai is almost the sure index of a prosperous and spirited Egypt.

Sa-nekht's reign, probably a comparatively short one,
was followed by one of the most important and significant
reigns of Egyptian history. Zeser, whose Horus name was
Neterkhet, and who is the Tosorthros of Manetho, appears to have been the brother of his predecessor, as the
name of "The Queen-Mother Nemaathap" occurs in his
secondary tomb at Bet-Khallaf. His names savour strongly
of piety, for Zeser means "The Holy", while Neterkhet
signifies "God in the Flesh"; but consecration to spiritual
things, if such a thing be implied in his titles, did not mean
in his case, as it has so often disastrously meant in the case
of other royal saints, inefficiency in the discharge of the
mundane duties for which Providence had made him king.
His reign was not a long one, though it was longer than that
of his brother; but in his 29 (or 19) years he succeeded
in making upon the consciousness of the Egyptian nation
a singularly profound impression. A statue in the Berlin
Museum shows one of the greatest of Egyptian Pharaohs,
Senusert II, of the brilliant XIIth Dynasty, in the act of
worshipping him; priests of his spirit still carried on his
worship in the XXVIth Dynasty, and even in the Persian
Period the "Chief of the workmen Khnum-ab-ra" records

his genealogy from the time of Zeser, as who should say, "We came over with the Conqueror", though a pedigree dating from the Conqueror's time seems but a paltry thing compared with one that goes back through twenty-five centuries. A Pharaoh who succeeded in getting himself worshipped and dated from for two and a half millenniums must have written his name and fame deep on the Egyptian heart.

Zeser's fame is that of a man of knowledge, a student, a mighty builder, and a lover of literature. "Tosorthros", says the invaluable Manetho, "reigned 29 years. He is called Asklepios by the Egyptians, for his medical knowledge. He built a house of hewn stones, and greatly patronised writing." An honourable record, which seems to have the additional merit, not always found in the records of famous kings, of being strictly true; for the relics of himself which he has left us are amply sufficient to substantiate the claim which Manetho makes for him in at least the only particular which Time has left it in our power to judge. Of his medical knowledge we can no more form an estimate than we could of that of King Zer, though it is curious how such a tradition persistently clings to the memory of some of the most famous Pharaohs; nor have we any evidence to go upon as to his literature; but the man who is commemorated by the first of the Pyramids must have had some elements of greatness in him, apart from the greatness of mere position.

How much of his fame is justly his own, and how much of it is really due to Imhotep, the wise man whom he took as his guide, councillor, and architect, it is impossible to say. Great kings have the knack of finding and keeping great servants, as little kings, to the world's misfortune, seem infallibly to attract to themselves advisers as foolish as themselves; and it is surely not to the discredit of any king that he was wise enough to know a good man when he saw him, and steadfast enough to keep him at his side throughout his reign. Imhotep was the first of an honourable succession of such great servants of the Crown whose names are famous in Egyptian history, and are not the least favourable indication of the general soundness of a state which could produce such men, and which had the wit to use them in their day.

Zeser's great servant had an even more distinguished destiny than his renowned master. The Pharaoh was worshipped; but in the end his councillor was actually deified. Age by age the reputation of the great architect and statesman grew. By the time of the rise of the Middle Kingdom his words were being quoted in songs as the ultimate expression of human wisdom; he became the typical wise man, philosopher, scribe, coiner of wise sayings, and physician; the scribe caste of Egypt looked up to him as its patron saint, and the scribe poured out a libation to Imhotep before beginning any piece of writing. A temple was reared in his honour near the Serapeum at Saqqara, not far from the site of his greatest achievement, the pyramid of King Zeser. Finally the process of making a man into a god was accomplished by the acceptance of the Memphite belief that he was indeed the Son of God, being the offspring of Ptah, the Creator-God of Memphis, by a mortal mother. One of the commonest types of Egyptian bronze statue is the compact little figure of the divine wise Man, gravely perusing the roll of papyrus which lies upon his knees. When the priests of Edfu, in the Ptolemaic period, thirty centuries after his death, were describing the origin of the great temple which is the most complete extant example of an Egyptian house of God, they believed that they could give it no higher recommendation than to say that the building was a reproduction of the plan which "descended to Imhotep from heaven to the north of Memphis" in the days of King Zeser. The Greeks, who cherished a kind of awed reverence for the mysterious sort of impracticable wisdom which they imagined they discerned in the teaching of ancient Egypt, took over Imhotep with the rest, calling him Imouthes, and identified him, as his master had been identified, with Asklepios, as the patron god of learning. Stranger destiny has been reserved for no man than for this faithful servant of a great king.

An inscription of Zeser in Sinai shows that he was active, as one would have expected, beyond the borders of

Egypt; but the real evidence of his greatness, and of the extent to which the energies of the Egyptian state had already been organised under centralised control, is the huge tomb which he reared for himself, or Imhotep reared for him, in the shape of the first of Egyptian pyramids. The Step Pyramid at Saqqara is by no means one of the largest of pyramids. It measures along the base on the east and west sides 396 feet in length, and on the north and south sides 352 feet; while its height is about 195 feet. Thus it is fairly comparable with the pyramid of Menkaura, the Third Pyramid of Gizeh, which measures 350 feet along the base, while its height is 210 feet. But the significance of the building does not lie in its size, though even so it is at least of the larger order of Egyptian structures, but in the fact that with it the craft of the Egyptian master builder takes a step forward unexampled in the history of the world. It was only the other day, so to speak, that the fact of the tomb-chamber of his father Khasekhemui being built with stone was recorded as a marvel; now, at one bound, Egyptian building reaches a height at which it can produce structures which, judged by any canon, are great and splendid. Was the advance so completely *per saltum* as it seems, or were there intermediate steps of which the existence has been forgotten and the evidence lost?

The probability is that we shall never know, though it would be rash to prophesy what surprises the soil of Saqqara may or may not have in store for us, in view of the wonders which it is revealing from this very reign at the present moment. But it is almost impossible to believe that Egyptian architecture, even in the hands of a man of unexampled genius, rose at a single impulse to the conception and the accomplishment of a work like the Step Pyramid. If it was so, then Imhotep amply deserved all the honour in which he was held in after days, and his deification may plead in its favour that he had indeed something of the divine in him. The father does an unprecedented thing in the erection of a stone chamber 10 feet by 17; the son rears a hill of stone 390 feet by nearly 200. Nor is this the real measure of the change, for the excavations that are being conducted at the present time on the spot are revealing that Zeser's Pyramid was surrounded with all the complex religious arrangement of temple and offering chapels, temenos wall and subsidiary tombs, which characterises the fully developed pyramid type of Gizeh; while the artistic work disclosed shows that development had not taken place in a single craft only, but all along the line. It has often been remarked that one of the most wonderful things in the history of human progress is that within a hundred and fifty years of the building of Khasekhemui's little tomb-chamber, perhaps within a century, the Great Pyramid was being built; but the more marvellous step is that between Khasekhemui's work and that of his son. For Zeser and Imhotep were the pioneers, and it was easier for Khufu to follow than for them to lead; while they had that mastery of resources which can coordinate them and apply a whole group of crafts to subserve one great end.

After all, it is curious to think that with all this wonderful structure before us, and slowly revealing its complexity and beauty, we do not even know whether it served the purpose for which it was apparently designed, and covered the body of King Zeser after his death. For he, like so many of his predecessors and successors, had another tomb; and it is still uncertain whether the Step Pyramid or the great mastaba at Bet-Khallaf is the true resting-place of the great king. The mastaba is itself a notable structure, nearly 300 feet long by 150 wide, and over 30 feet high. It masks a long descending passage, barred by five huge portcullis blocks of stone, which leads to a dozen chambers fifty feet underground. Of the many alabaster vases which it contained, not one was inscribed; so that the fact that the building belonged to Zeser was only proved by the clay sealings which were found. For a long time it has been maintained by several scholars that the mastaba must have been the real tomb of the king, and the pyramid only that of his *Ka*; but in view of the results of Mr. Firth's excavations, it is becoming increasingly difficult to resist the belief that the pyramid is the real burial-place, and the mastaba only the secondary tomb.

One of the most curious testimonies to the reverence

with which the great name of King Zeser was regarded, even thirty centuries after his death, is afforded by the fact that in Ptolemaic times two rival sets of priests deemed it worth while to coin two different versions of a legend about him to support their conflicting claims to a piece of territory. The main legend is that inscribed on the rocks of the island of Sehel, at the First Cataract, which states that in a time of great famine Zeser wrote to Medir, his Governor of the South, to consult him as to what should be done to relieve the distress and as to what god he should apply for aid. Medir explained to the king that good and bad Niles were controlled by the god Khnum, one of the Egyptian Creator-Gods who sent forth the waters of the river from his temple at Elephantine. The king came south to interview Khnum, who explained that it was because he had been neglected that the bad seasons had come, but that he would grant good harvests if his interests were properly attended to. Zeser thereupon issued a decree endowing the temple of Khnum with the land on both sides of the Nile from Sehel to the Isle of Takompso, near Dakkeh in Nubia—in other words, the tract which was known in later days as the Dodekaschoinoi—a tract of between 80 and 90 miles in length. So far, good; but as the priests of Isis, at Philae, offer us another inscription stating that King Zeser endowed them with precisely the same tract of country, one is left in doubt as to which set of legend-mongers is telling the truth. The probability is that both were lying, though the priests of Khnum, as belonging to the cult which was the earlier in the district, may have had the better claim—if there was any better in the matter, which is unlikely.

While there is no interest to us in the question of which of two sets of mendacious land-grabbers told the more plausible lie, the fact that they both appealed to King Zeser, as to one whose hallowed memory could sanctify their grabbing, is perhaps the best possible testimony to the impression which he had made upon the Egyptian nation. It is also, perhaps, indirect evidence in favour of the belief that he may have extended the boundaries of Egypt to the south; for obviously the priests who described him as making a grant of this district of Nubia must have believed that he had it in his possession. But at best this is evidence of a very indirect and doubtful kind; and it is possibly safest to conclude that what the priests said, like what the soldier said, "is not evidence". A priest speaking for himself is one thing; but a priest making a claim for his temple is quite another story.

Of Nebkara, who may have succeeded Zeser, we have next to no historical information, save the interesting fact that in his unfinished tomb his name is given with the title "Lord of the Two Lands", a style which now begins to form part of the regular titulary of the Pharaohs, and is one of the best known parts of it. His reign seems to have been short, and this is suggested not only by the Turin papyrus, but by the fact that his tomb was unfinished at his death. Incomplete as it is, there exists in Egypt no more impressive testimony to the greatness of conception and the magnificence of execution which characterised the men of this period. What remains is simply the underground cutting for what was probably intended to be a great pyramid—a great oblong space, 82 feet by 46, and 73 feet in depth. It is approached by a stupendous descending stairway, 28 feet broad and 360 feet long; the floor of the underground cutting is paved with great granite blocks averaging 9 tons in weight; while the central block weighs about 45 tons. Sunk into this superb pavement is an oval sarcophagus, which had a lid of polished granite cemented on to it. Apparently the Pharaoh died before the substructure, with its chambers, for which stores of granite blocks were lying ready, could be got ready; he was therefore buried elsewhere, where has not been found out, and the granite blocks were piled into the cutting, and the unfinished tomb left as it stood.

On the whole, it is fortunate that it is so; though we may have been deprived of the sight of another pyramid, the richness of whose substructures makes us wonder whether the finished building might not have rivalled or surpassed Khufu's mighty tomb. Here you catch, as it were, the Egyptian master-builder in the midst of the working out of his great plans; and the sight is amazingly impressive and even awe-inspiring. Maspero speaks of its "almost brutal strength"; but there is nothing brutal about such a piece of work, and to say "almost superhuman" would be nearer the truth than to talk of brutality in such a connection. The men who conceived such a stupendous plan, and whose thoughts were such as found expression in such terms as the unfinished pyramid of Zawiyet el-Aryan, were great men in every sense of the term.

Between Nebkara and Snefru, with whom the dynasty closes, the lists of kings are hopelessly confused, and indeed there is little or nothing which can be associated with any of the names which they give. The one exception is the Neferkara Huni, who has left an inscription at Sinai, and a mastaba at Bet Khallaf; but as Petrie identifies him with his Sa-nekht, while Hall hesitatingly associates him with the builder of the unfinished pyramid at Zawiyet el-Aryan, there is obviously not much certainty to be associated with him. An interesting specimen of the Wisdom literature of the Egyptians, *The Instruction for Kagemni*, found in a Paris papyrus of the Middle Kingdom, claims to be a record of the wisdom of a vizier of Huni's day, retailed for the benefit of his children, among whom, as Erman interprets it, was the future vizier Kagemni of King Snefru. Other interpreters attribute the maxims to Kagemni himself, believing that he may have been vizier to both Huni and Snefru. Kagemni's association with the work is rather more than doubtful. There was a vizier of the name several centuries later, and the probability is that a vague remembrance of his name inspired the attribution to his older namesake.

The instruction of Kagemni is of the usual canny and practical Egyptian type: "Be not boastful of thy strength in the midst of those of thine own age. One knoweth not what may chance, what God doeth when He punisheth." Weigall translates more epigrammatically: "Do not be pugnacious because (it chances that) you are muscular. No man knows what is going to happen, or what God will do when *He* hits out"; but one may question if the old vizier put it quite so neatly as all that. The conclusion of the book carries us into the next reign—one of the pivotal reigns of Egyptian history: "The majesty of King Huni came to port (a euphemism for 'died') and the majesty of King Snefru was raised up as beneficent king in this whole land. Then was Kagemni appointed superintendent of the capital and vizier."

With the advent of Snefru as Pharaoh, we are brought, so to speak, into sight of land, historically. We have no longer to grope our way dimly by the light of a few odds and ends of personal relics, a scrap of a defaced inscription, or the sealings of a few wine-jars, among perhapses and possibilities; the facts which are presented to us—not very numerous, certainly—are yet solid and indubitable, and the essential features of the reign are clear. The king himself occupies, as between the IIIrd and IVth Dynasties, somewhat of the same position which Khasekhemui occupied between the IInd and IIIrd; that is to say, that he nominally belongs to the earlier line, but is actually in spirit and accomplishment more akin to the later. Khasekhemui was the herald of the approach of a mature Egyptian civilisation; Snefru is the herald of its actual arrival. By the time that he had finished his work, Egypt stood forth before the world of the ancient East manifestly the first of powers and the leader of the human race. "Egypt", says Dr. H. R. Hall, "now stepped into the position of the most highly civilised nation of the world, for the Babylonian culture, though a near competitor, was not yet really the equal of Egyptian civilisation. Egypt's kings were mighty monarchs who succeeded each other in an august array. Their names are no longer to be deciphered painfully from primitive scrawls on pots or weird symbols on mace-heads and 'palettes', but can be read in clear hieroglyphs on the walls of the tombs of the great men of their times, as dispensers of favour to their subjects and as benefactors to the gods."

Our first source of information for the reign of Snefru is found in the personal inscriptions of the king. These are in the Sinai Peninsula, where the presence or absence of an Egyptian mining expedition with its commemorative tablets is, as we have seen, practically the index of the nation's prosperity or adversity. Snefru has left two tablets in the

Wady Maghara. One of them is rather primitive in style, the plain rock-surface being left, without modelling, for the figures, while the background is dressed away by hammering, so as to leave the figures in very low relief. The king, wearing the White Crown of Upper Egypt, smites with his mace a Beduin chieftain whom he holds by the hair. Beneath this group stand two smaller figures of Snefru, wearing in one case the Red and in the other the White Crown. The other tablet is more elaborate, and is admirably carved in low relief. Snefru, wearing this time the *Atef* Crown, with two tall plumes and a pair of horns, smites the Beduin chieftain as in the other scene. The royal titulary is very fully given: King of Upper and Lower Egypt; Favourite of the Two Goddesses; Lord of Truth; Golden Horus; Snefru, Great God, who is given Satisfaction, Stability, Life, Health, all Joy forever; Horus, Lord of Truth; Smiter of Barbarians."

At Serabit el-Khadem, further north in the Peninsula, the Miner's Temple of Hathor, "The Lady of Turquoise", was apparently founded by him, for the figure of a hawk in grey marble, bearing his cartouche in contemporary hieroglyphics, was found there by Petrie. Indeed his work at Sinai made such an impression that in later days he was regarded as a sort of patron saint of the mining district. In the XIIth Dynasty we learn from the Tale of Sinuhe that a district in the eastern Delta, on the road to Sinai, was named after him. In other inscriptions of the same period we find him named along with Sopd and Hathor, as one of the local gods of Sinai; and the stock phrase for the commander of a mining expedition to use in describing an unusually successful venture is: "Never had the like been done since the time of the King of Upper and Lower Egypt, Snefru, triumphant (*i.e.* deceased)."

Nor were the king's activities confined to Sinai. Snefru was evidently one of the earliest of converts to the doctrine of the importance of sea-power. One of the first records of the reign on the Palermo Stone is: "Building of 100-cubit *dewatowe* ships of *meru* wood, and of 60 sixteen barges (probably galleys of 8 or of 16 oars a side), for the king." Apparently the first use made of this new fleet,

headed by the royal 170-foot Dreadnought, was southern
conquest, for the record continues: "Hacking up of the
land of the Negro. Bringing of 7000 living prisoners, and
200,000 large and small cattle." But Egypt was to show her
flag on the sea as well as on the Upper Nile; for in the
same year we read of the "bringing of 40 ships filled with
cedar wood", which is evidently the record of a voyage to
the Syrian coast for timber from the Lebanon. Snefru
thus led the way in a trade which was to continue active
throughout Egypt's history, and which produced in its
course such literary treasures as the story of the adventures of Wenamon. The first Dreadnought evidently
proved enough of a success to warrant the laying down of
others of the same type, for in the following year we are
informed of the "building of a 100-cubit *dewatowe* ship of
cedar wood, and two 100-cubit ships of *meru* wood; so that
Snefru had a squadron of four ships of 170 feet each in
length. This is far in advance of anything that any other
nation of the world was doing or was to do for many centuries yet; and indeed when we remember that the *Royal
George*, Hawke's flagship at Quiberon, and the ill-fated
Kempenfelt's at Spithead measured only 143 feet 5½
inches on the keel and 178 feet on the gun-deck, while
the corresponding measurements of Nelson's *Victory* are
151 feet 3 inches and 186 feet, we realise that Snefru's
achievement was actually a remarkable thing. Tonnage, of
course, is another story, and it is not for a moment suggested that Snefru's comparatively shallow galleys were
comparable in this respect with the more modern warships; still, Egyptian ship-designing and Egyptian ship-
wrights, five thousand years ago, were evidently deserving
of the highest respect, to say the least of it.

The royal domain and city of Snefru were situated
near Medum, about forty miles south of Cairo, and the
Palermo Stone tells us that he used some of the cargoes
of cedar which his forty ships had brought back from
Syria in "making the doors of the king's palace of cedar
wood". In spite of this splendour, however, we are not to
imagine that the palace of Snefru was comparable to the
huge edifices which Assyrian and Babylonian kings reared

for themselves. Egyptian kings had more sense, and were content with the attainment of comfort, accompanied with good taste in decoration and furnishing, without requiring to have everything as massy and gorgeous as would suit the taste of a modern profiteer. Snefru's palace, like those of all his successors, was doubtless of mud brick, however large it may have been and however beautifully furnished. It bore evidence to the curious sensitiveness of Egyptian sentiment to the past history of the land. Egypt was by now a completely united country, whose interests were one and indivisible; but the fact was never forgotten that the time had been when it was not so, and when Lower and Upper Egypt were separate and independent kingdoms. It was proclaimed in the Double Crown of state which the Pharaoh wore, in the name of his two-fold Treasury department, and in his own titulary. Now, Snefru acknowledged it again in the design of his palace, which had two great gates, one facing north, the other south, and each called by its own significant name. The Palermo Stone records the names of the gates for us: "Erection of 'Exalted-is-the-White-Crown-of-Snefru-upon-the-Southern-Gate', 'Exalted-is-the-Red-Crown-of-Snefru-upon-the-Northern-Gate'." This careful attention to the claims of local pride and sentiment was doubtless one of the factors which for so long maintained the unity of a long and straggling land, in which Nature seemed to have combined with tradition to produce a tendency to division.

With regard to his tomb, Snefru followed what seems to have been a not uncommon practice among the kings of this early period, in having a couple of mausoleums erected—one for his own personal accommodation, the other for his *Ka*. At Dahshur, a little south of Saqqara, he erected a stupendous pyramid, which, though little known or visited, is but a little inferior in size to the Great Pyramid, being over 700 feet in length along the base of each side and 326 feet in height, figures to which about 20 feet must be added in each case to obtain the original height of the pyramid. Thus, this building which, together with Snefru's other pyramid, must rank as the first of the real pyramids of Egypt (Zeser's Step Pyramid being only a mastaba enlarged by successive additions) represents the transitional stage between Zeser's tentative construction and the fully developed ideal realised in the Great Pyramid; and we see that Khufu's great tomb is not the abnormal thing which it is often represented to be, but the culminating step in a regular progression, which, however, was extremely rapid.

In spite of its greatness, it appears that the pyramid of Dahshur was only the cenotaph of Snefru, dedicated to his *Ka*, for he built for himself another pyramid at Medum, still further to the south, near the modern Wasta. This curious tower-looking structure, known by the Arabs as *El Haram el-Kaddab* (*the False Pyramid*), is of the utmost interest, because the stages of its development can be traced, owing to its ruined condition, in a fashion which is impossible in the case of a perfect pyramid. The pyramid of Medum began with a great square mastaba, a flat-topped rectangular mass of masonry, with sides sloping inwards at an angle of about 75 degrees. This mass was enlarged by an outside coating of masonry, and another stage was added above it. The process was repeated seven times; and the final result was a building in the shape of a stage tower, somewhat reminiscent of a Babylonian Ziggurat. The resemblance ceased, however, with the completion of the work, for a smooth casing of limestone was added, covering all the stages, and giving the whole a truly pyramidal outline. The building having been robbed of its outer casing, the tower-like structure which is now seen resulted.

Only three of the original seven stages of the tower survive, the lowest being by far the largest, and the uppermost a mere fragment. Even in its ruined condition, Snefru's pyramid rises to a height of 124 feet, and all visitors concur in recording the profound impression created by its desolate splendour. "To my mind," says Weigall, " . . . the most imposing of all these ancient structures." The peculiar character of the pyramid of Medum, and its evidently gradual enlargement by successive accretions, has led to the idea that all pyramids were built in somewhat similar fashion. A comparatively small pyramid, on this theory, was begun by a Pharaoh immediately on his accession. If he survived for some time, it was gradually added to, until at last, at the close of a long reign, it might assume the colossal proportions of the Great Pyramid. It should be remembered, however, that the pyramid of Medum, being the first of true pyramids, was necessarily of the nature of an experiment, and that it is dangerous to argue from a particular instance, which in the circumstances was probably quite exceptional, to a general rule. Sir Flinders Petrie has consistently argued that the interior arrangements of some of the large pyramids prove that the full size was planned from the very first; the comparative shortness of the reign of Khufu, the builder of the greatest of all pyramids, reveals the weakness of the case for the accretion theory; and it seems probable that while Snefru, in the experimental stage of pyramid-building, proceeded at Medum by such a process of accretions as we have seen, his successors, with the pyramid conception fully developed, faced at once the grand idea of the complete structure from the very laying of its foundations.

Excavating at Medum, Petrie discovered on the east side of the pyramid a complete temple such as subsequent work has taught us to expect in the case of every pyramid. At Medum, however, where everything was in the experimental stage, the temple was very small and of extreme simplicity, consisting merely of a courtyard with offering chambers, and a couple of tall steles standing in the open court. These, and the whole of the rest of the building, were absolutely plain and uninscribed; and indeed the fact that pyramid and temple were Snefru's was only found from the fact that tourists in the days of ancient Egypt had precisely the same evil habits as their successors of to-day, and left their scribbles upon the buildings which they visited just as if they had been 'Arry and M'riar of our own time. "Graffiti" is the euphemistic title by which these ancient vulgarities are diplomatically described; and five of those on the walls of the little temple mention Snefru as the king to whom the pyramid complex belonged.

Even tourists, it appears, may, by the mere lapse of centuries, come to have their uses.

Round the king's pyramid at Medum were grouped the tombs of several members of the royal family, in pursuance of a custom which was more largely developed in the succeeding reigns, and which may, indeed, have been a development of the old barbarous custom of the slaying of the king's household at his death. Two of these tombs, those of the king's son Rahotep, with his wife Nefert, and of the other royal prince Nefermaat, with his wife Atet, have yielded some of the most precious art-treasures of the period. The statues of Rahotep and Nefert will have to be alluded to at a later stage. The king seems to have been a somewhat much married man. His most important wife seems to have been the lady Mertitiotis, who may well have been of royal blood, as her title, "Uniter of the Lordships of the Vulture and the Cobra", suggests. It may have been that this was another of those marriages contracted for reasons of state of which we have already had instances. The lineaments of Mertitiotis are well known to us from the statue at Leiden; and, on the whole, one is not surprised that King Snefru sought consolation elsewhere, though perhaps this is unjust to the queen, whose aspect of wide- and sad-eyed depression may have been due to the limitations of the primitive sculptor. Mertitiotis shared a destiny which was not uncommon in Egypt, being taken over, along with the rest of the harem, no doubt, by her stepson, King Khufu, when he succeeded to the kingdom. We learn from an inscription that she was "great in the favour of king Snefru, great in the favour of king Khufu, and honoured under king Khafra"; so that she had a sufficiently eventful career.

According to a custom which was not repugnant to Egyptian sentiment as it is to ours, the king was also married to his own daughter Nefert-kau, and the Prince Nefermaat, already mentioned, was the son of this union. A third wife was the lady Mery.s.ankh, who is mentioned on a graffito at Medum. Apparently, however, the most important wife of all was one of whose existence we were only made aware as the result of Dr. Reisner's excavations at Gizeh. This was the lady Hetepheres, from whose union with Snefru was born the son who was destined to be, of all Egyptian monarchs, the most widely known—the Pharaoh Khufu (Cheops), builder of the Great Pyramid. The tomb of this otherwise unknown princess was excavated in 1927 by Dr. Reisner. It lay under the shadow of the Great Pyramid; Queen Hetepheres, who must have survived her husband, as did at least two of his other wives, having been buried near her great son, instead of beside her husband. The burial chamber lay at the foot of a great 90-foot shaft on the eastern side of Khufu's pyramid. It contained a fine alabaster sarcophagus, covered with a gilded mat, which bore the name of King Snefru, and also a mass of furniture of gilded wood, terribly decayed. The sarcophagus, on being opened, was found to be empty.

The most interesting document of the reign is the biography of Methen, one of the high officials of the Delta Administration. It comes from the chamber of his mastaba at Saqqara, where he is buried beside the Step Pyramid of Zeser; for though he was an official of Snefru, and died during that king's reign, all his family connections were with the earlier part of the dynasty. Methen is an instance of the typical Egyptian official, coming of the official caste, and rising from a comparatively obscure position to one or rather to several (for he is a confirmed pluralist) of great importance. His narrative is the first example of those biographies of prominent officials, of which we have fortunately so many, and which have added so much life and interest to the story of Egypt.

Methen begins by telling of his succession to the inheritance of his father. "There were presented to him the things of his father, the judge and scribe Anubisemonekh; there was no grain or anything of the house, there were people (serfs) and small cattle." His own official position was nothing great to begin with. "He was made chief scribe of the provision magazine, and overseer of the things of the provision magazine"; but with true official acquisitiveness he soon added to these small appointments others better worth having. Perhaps it would be fairer to say that diligence was rewarded by the bestowal of the higher

offices. "He was made (   ), becoming local governor of
Xois, and inferior field-judge of Xois"; and so on up the
official stairway, until we see him at last as a bloated pluralist
to the following extent: "Ruler of Southern Perked; Ruler
of Perwersah; Ruler and local governor of the stronghold,
Hesen, in the Harpoon nome; Palace-ruler and local governor in Sekhemu of Xois; Palace-ruler and local governor in
Dep (Buto); Palace-ruler and local governor in Miper of
the Saite nome; Palace-ruler and local governor in Two
Hounds, of the Mendesian nome; Palace-ruler in Heswer;
Ruler of fields in the west of the Saitic nome; Palace-ruler
of the Cow-stronghold, local governor in the desert, and
master of the hunt; Ruler of fields, deputy and local
governor in the Sekhemite nome; Nomarch administrator
and deputy in the eastern Fayum; Field-judge, palace-
ruler of the west of the Saitic nome, leader of (   )."

There was not much doing in the Delta neighbourhood,
evidently, that Methen did not have his fingers into and
get his pickings out of. Let us hope that his merits as an
administrator, and "Master of the Hunt", were in proportion to his emoluments. It is truly touching and satisfactory, from the permanent official's point of view, to
read of the personal benefits which a grateful sovereign
conferred upon this good and faithful servant. "There
were conveyed to him as a reward 200 *stat* of lands by
numerous royal (decrees); a mortuary offering of 100
loaves every day from the mortuary temple of the mother
of the king's children Nemaathap (Zeser's wife); a house
200 cubits wide and 200 cubits long, built and equipped;
fine trees were set out, a very large lake was made therein,
figs and vines were set out. . . . Very plentiful trees and
vines were set out, and a great quantity of wine was made
therein. . . ." Evidently it was worth while being a
persona grata in the official world in Snefru's day. Nor
were "unconsidered trifles" from his family connections
considered too insignificant to be worth the great man's
acquiring and recording. "There were conveyed to him
50 *stat* of land by his mother Nebsent; she made a will
thereof to her children; it was placed in their possession by
the king's writings in every place."

So we may leave Methen to grow stout and complacent on his 200 *stat* of land, with his fine house and pretty garden, with the ornamental water that the Egyptian always loved, and a comfortable provision of wine to gladden his heart, thanking him for the glimpse which he has given us of a state as well organised as our own, and an official world whose unchanging affinities are quite recognisable. His type is one of the most familiar things in Egypt, ever since the day when Mariette's workmen unearthed the wooden statue at Saqqara, and unanimously called it "Sheikhel-Beled"—"The Headman of the Village"; so little does officialism change its outward features through the centuries.

A solitary story has come down to us in the Westcar Papyrus about Snefru himself. It occurs in the interesting series of Tales of the Magicians which are told, according to the manuscript, before King Khufu by his sons, to pass the time one day when His Majesty is bored. Prince Baufra, who tells the story to his father, says that on one occasion King Snefru also was plunged in deep depression and bored to death. He called his chief wise man Zazamankh to him, and requested a remedy. Zazamankh's prescription was attractive but unusual. It was that the royal barge should be prepared, and manned by twenty of the prettiest girls of the harem, who were to be clothed for the occasion in fishing nets. "Then will the heart of Thy Majesty be diverted, when thou shalt see how they row to and fro." This suggestion produced an immediate change in His Majesty's mood. "I will go boating," he cried, and immediately gave orders for Zazamankh's prescription to be dispensed. "And it was done according to all that His Majesty commanded. And they rowed to and fro, and the heart of His Majesty was glad when he beheld how they rowed." Then follows the famous incident of the falling of the malachite pendant from the head of the steerswoman into the water, and its recovery by the wisdom of Zazamankh, who adopts the simple expedient of making one half of the water of the lake to stand up on the other half, so that the bed becomes dry, and the pendant is descried lying on a potsherd. The water then obediently returns to

PLATE VII

1. THE "STEP" PYRAMID
2. THE GREAT PYRAMID

its former level; "and His Majesty spent the whole day in merriment with the entire palace, and he rewarded the chief-kerheb Zazamankh with all good things."

The value of the tale for history is, of course, nothing, save to demonstrate that the standing trouble of kingship has been the same in all ages, and that a wise medicine-man even five thousand years ago knew that the best way to minister to a mind diseased is not by the exhibition of drugs.

Snefru, though reckoned as the last king of the IIIrd Dynasty, is actually the founder of the IVth, with which the glory and splendour of the Old Kingdom culminates, and to which we must next turn.

CHAPTER VII

THE PYRAMID-BUILDERS

WITH the rise of the IVth Dynasty (3100–2965 B.C., *Cambridge Anct. Hist.;* 4777–4493 B.C., Petrie), the glory and achievement of the Old Egyptian Kingdom rises to its culmination. The duration of the dynasty was not long, probably not over 150 years (Weigall allows it only 73 years), and the last two kings are entirely insignificant; but the burst of splendour with which the dynasty opens has seldom been equalled and certainly never surpassed by anything in the history of any other nation of the ancient world. An almost unknown Pharaoh, Shaaru, the Soris of Manetho, appears to reign for a short time at the beginning of the dynasty, though his place there is somewhat uncertain, and some historians prefer to place him further down the line; then the most famous monarch of the Old Kingdom takes his place, and in a few years Egypt proceeds to the accomplishment of the series of gigantic works which have ever since left an impression on the imagination of the world such as is produced by no other works of man.

Shaaru is only known by a solitary monument of little importance, and nothing is known as to his parentage, though it is almost certain that he must have been a son of Snefru, as otherwise he would never have been able to thrust his obscure reign between the masterful Snefru and the still more masterful Khufu. Khufu, who succeeded him, was certainly the son of Snefru, by the lady Hetepheres, who, save for her untenanted tomb at Gizeh, is otherwise unknown. How it was, indeed, that some of the other sons of Snefru, say by a more outstanding wife, such as Mertitiotis, were not preferred, is not known; but the fact that Khufu was not brought up at court, but at a comparatively obscure place in Middle Egypt, which afterwards bore the name of "Menat-Khufu", in commemoration of its privilege of rearing the future monarch, seems to point to court jealousies and rivalries, which the young prince, when he came to maturity, was able to overcome. At all events, whether by his father's favour or by his own irresistible energy, Khufu finally asserted himself, and that so conclusively that there is no trace of any dissension in the land over his accession. The name of Khnum-Khuf is associated with that of Khufu in several inscriptions, notably at Sinai, among the pyramid quarry marks, and in the quarry of Hat-nub, near Tell el-Amarna; and it has been supposed that Khnum-Khuf may have been a co-regent, who died before Khufu. Khnum, however, was the patron-god of the district in which Khufu was brought up, and it is probable that he used the compound name at first, but afterwards dropped it in the plenitude of his power.

The only thing that we know of the reign of this vigorous and powerful king, apart from the one achievement which has preserved his fame, is that he, like his father, made an expedition to Sinai. He left there the usual tablet in the Wady Maghara, which, one is ashamed to say, was brutally smashed up some years ago by an English commercial company in its search for turquoises. The tablet, of course, was worth far more than all the turquoises that were ever got out of Sinai; but such an idea was quite beyond the comprehension of these Vandals. It appears to be quite needless to question, as has been done, the fact of Khufu's presence at Sinai, on the ground of his preoccupation with the vast home interest of his pyramid. Notoriously it is always the man who is doing most who is able to do more; and the energy which organised the colossal enterprise of the Great Pyramid must have been ample to afford an overflow into the Sinai expedition, which the king would undoubtedly consider necessary to the prestige of his reign, seeing that his father had made such an expedition before him. At the same time the pyramid is undoubtedly the supreme interest of the reign, overshadowing everything else, so that the one thing which is remembered of what must surely have been a strenuous reign is this vast evidence of other-worldliness.

Indeed so much does the Great Pyramid dominate everything else in the reign of Khufu that it has done serious injury to his reputation in history. "Suphis" (Cheops, Khufu), says Manetho, "reigned 63 years. He built the largest pyramid. He was also called Peroptes and was translated to the gods, and wrote the sacred book." There is no great suggestion of impiety here, though another reading, "arrogant to the gods," perhaps gives us the origin of the evil tradition. It was full-blown even in the time of Herodotus, who gives it with great wealth of detail. "Now they told me," he says, "that to the reign of Rhampsinitus there was a perfect distribution of justice, and that all Egypt was in a high state of prosperity; but that after him Cheops, coming to reign over them, plunged into every kind of wickedness. For that, having shut up all the temples, he first of all forbade them to offer sacrifice, and afterwards he ordered all the Egyptians to work for himself; some, accordingly, were appointed to draw stones from the quarries in the Arabian mountain down to the Nile, others he ordered to receive the stones when transported in vessels across the river, and to drag them to the mountain called the Libyan." After a few more flights of imagination, in which Khafra, Khufu's successor, comes into the same condemnation, Herodotus concludes his lamentable tale : "Thus one hundred and six years are reckoned, during which the Egyptians suffered all kinds of calamities, and for this length of time the temples were closed and never opened. From the hatred they bear them (Khufu and Khafra), the Egyptians are not very willing to mention their names; but call the pyramids after Philition, a shepherd, who at that time kept his cattle in those parts."

In this sad story, Herodotus, who is obviously leading up, with his innate instinct for effect, to his description of the Great Pyramid and his romance of Mykerinos (Menkaura), has been guilty, either of himself or through too ready acceptance of the tales which were told him, of libel upon two great kings—libel which has been accepted for truth so long that it seems almost hopeless to attempt to dispel the cloud of detraction which has surrounded the names of the two greatest builders of the earth. Yet there is not a trace of any such impiety as the historian attributes to the two kings; on the contrary, the Great Pyramid itself, with its companion, far from being merely a monument to the vainglory of a proud king, is actually the expression of one of the deepest-rooted religious instincts of the Egyptian mind. It may have been strictly personal and even selfish piety which caused Khufu to build his monstrous pyramid; but it was piety all the same. Nor did the Egyptians of his own time, or of the generations immediately following him, regard Khufu as being in the least the impious oppressor of Herodotus's romance. Khufu was worshipped steadily during his own and the succeeding dynasty, during which period no fewer than twenty priests of his memory are known; and no more than a century before the Greek historian passed into the other world to find out the truth about the matter himself, the worship of his impious tyrant was being revived under the kings of the XXVIth Dynasty. With all Herodotus's acuteness and occasional scepticism, one has the suspicion now and again that he fell a victim to the leg-pulling instincts of the Egyptian priests, or perhaps to the results of their jealousies; and it may well be that his informant in this case was one of a priestly clique which had a quarrel with the priests of the Khufu clique. Perhaps the explanation is still simpler, and the unjust tradition merely represents the traditional dislike of the native Egyptian for the hard work of which he has had to do so much throughout the ages, and for the memory of the man who made the race work harder than it ever did before or since.

One may pretty safely relegate to the dust-heap all the pictures of monstrous tyranny which have grouped themselves around the building of the Great Pyramid— the miserable throngs of sweating and straining wretches, driven beyond the limits of human strength by the whips of their brutal overseers and the butts of the spears of Pharaoh's guardsmen, toiling until flesh and heart could toil no more, and they dropped and died where they stood. In point of fact that was never the Egyptian's way of working. He faced the most gigantic tasks, as he faces a big job to-day, with amazingly cheerful energy, once he knew that he was in for it; and the work of transporting the most gigantic masses of stone went along with a song and a heave, as our sailors used to send round the capstan-bars. The Egyptian was never work-hungry, any more than any other type of man has been; but once in the collar, he was the cheerfullest of workers, whether as overseer or subordinate. "Give us an order," said one of a gang of modern Egyptian workmen to one of our excavators, "and we will build you a pyramid." The instinct for such work was in the race then, as it is still; Khufu simply knew how to get the utmost out of it—that was all. Tyranny and merciless driving could only have resulted in disaster on a task of such gigantic magnitude. What presided over the erection of the Great Pyramid was not brute force, but organised ability, magnificently trained to use to the best advantage the strength of a race of fine workers. No doubt there was plenty of hard work at the building of the pyramid, more in all probability than anywhere else in the world at that time; no doubt, also, there were accidents and loss of life and maiming of limbs, as in every big piece of human work in all ages: but the place was not a shambles where slaves were driven till they died, but a hive of willing and skilled labour, in which men were proud to be able to say in after days that they had wrought.

How big the work was, everybody knows. The Great Pyramid measures 755 feet along the base-line of each side. It is 451 feet in height, and in its present stripped condition it consists of more than 2,300,000 blocks of stone, weighing, on an average, 2½ tons apiece, so that its total weight is about 5,750,000 tons. It has been calculated that the houses of a town to hold 120,000 people could be built out of the materials of the pyramid, and that if its stones were divided up into blocks a foot square, and these were laid end to end, they would reach two-thirds round the circumference of the earth at the Equator. Perhaps the best idea of the astonishing magnitude of this huge tomb is afforded by a comparison of its area with that of a few famous buildings. The area of the base of the Great Pyra-

mid is 570,996 feet. That of St. Peter's, Rome, is 227,000
feet; that of the Cathedral of Milan, 108,277; that of St.
Paul's, 84,311; and that of Westminster, 61,729. In other
words, the area of the base of the Great Pyramid is two
and a half times as great as that of St. Peter's, about five
and a quarter times as great as that of Milan, six and three-
quarters as great as that of St. Paul's, and more than nine
times as great as that of Westminster Abbey. The whole
of these four great cathedrals could be grouped within the
area of the base of the pyramid, leaving room over for the
accommodation of the Duomo of Florence or the Cathedral of Cologne, as might be found convenient.

No such building was ever reared on earth before its
completion; none such has ever been reared since, nor is it
likely that such another will ever be reared. Yet, as we
have already seen, the difference between it and the pyramid of Snefru, at Dahshur, to which few people ever pay
any attention, is comparatively small; and the fact that
this is so renders it almost a certainty that the Great Pyramid was not begun on a small scale, and then gradually enlarged during a long reign. Khufu was not likely to be content with a pyramid that was not larger than that of his
father's *Ka*; nor did his comparatively short reign admit of
the slow progress of accretion which Borchardt's theory requires. In addition, there is the evidence of the internal
passages. "That it could not have been designed of any
much smaller size", says Petrie, " is shown conclusively by
the internal passages. The entrance to these would have
been quite impracticable in design on any size of building
not much over two-thirds of the present base."

The workmanship of the great mass is, in general, as
remarkable as its size. The pyramid was built of nummu-
litic limestone (not of granite, as is sometimes ludicrously
stated), which was brought, as Herodotus quite correctly
states, from the quarries on the eastern side of the Nile,
as no such stone exists on the western bank. When complete, it was cased from pyramidion to base with a sheath
of the same fine limestone. No granite was used, so far as
is known, on its exterior work; and in this respect it differed
from the Second pyramid, which had a single row of granite

casing along its base, and from the Third, which was cased in granite for sixteen courses above the base. Supreme skill and curious inaccuracy, carefulness and carelessness, are strangely conjoined in the work. "On the one hand," says Petrie, "most brilliant workmanship was disclosed, while on the other it was intermingled with some astonishing carelessness and clumsiness. The laying out of the base of the Great Pyramid of Khufu is a triumph of skill; its errors, both in length and in angles, could be covered by placing one's thumb on them. . . . The work of the casing stones which remain is of the same class; the faces are so straight and so truly square that when the stones were built together the film of mortar left between them is on an average not thicker than one's thumb-nail, though the joint is a couple of yards long; and the levelling of them over long distances has not any larger errors. . . . Side by side with this splendid work are the strangest mistakes. After having levelled the casing so finely, the builders made a hundred times the error in levelling the shorter length of the King's chamber, so that they might have done it far better by just looking at the horizon. . . . And the kernel of the whole, the sarcophagus, has much worse work in it than in the building, or than in other sarcophagi of the same period."

Petrie accounts for this mixture of good and bad work by the supposition that the architect who was the supreme directing mind of the whole construction must have died during the progress of the building, leaving a man of inferior powers to complete the work; and this suggestion is perhaps as likely as any that can be made. The Great Pyramid, as is well known, has for long been the playground of cranks and paradoxers, whose chief diversion has been to suggest, or rather to aver with consummate assurance, that it contains the revelation of the will of the Almighty and of His future purposes, to say nothing of other by-products of Divine revelation, so to speak. Why the human instruments who were entrusted with the carrying out of the Divine will in this respect were allowed to make such extraordinary bungles in the midst of the otherwise admirable work which they did is one of these matters which seem to indicate that it is rather a risky and indeed irreverent thing to call in the Divine element to account for what, after all, is a perfectly explicable piece of human handiwork.

Herodotus, whose interest in the Great Pyramid was evidently keen, and whose information about it is, on the whole, wonderfully accurate, tells us that the building of the great tomb was carried on by one hundred thousand men at a time, each party working during three months. Ten years, according to him, were spent in making the great causeway leading up from the plain to the pyramid plateau and in excavating the subterranean chambers, and twenty years in the completion of the pyramid itself. The ten and the twenty years in all probability ran concurrently for the first half of the work, so that we may believe the whole to have been finished in twenty years, or inside the shortest of the various periods which are allowed to the reign of Khufu. The Greek historian's story of the body of Cheops being laid in a subterranean island within the pyramid, from which access was cut off by an artificial moat supplied with water from the Nile, is, of course, merely a variant of the usual tale of subterranean passages which is told to the tourist in connection with every ancient building, and is accepted with unquestioning faith to-day as it was twenty-three centuries ago.

Petrie's simple interpretation of the seemingly huge figures of Herodotus as to the staff of workmen employed has brought the whole matter into a reasonable and comprehensible shape. He suggests that the statement as to the hundred thousand men, each party working for three months at a time, means that the full strength was only employed during the three months of the inundation, when the land was under water and agricultural work was suspended. Thus no injury was done to the country by any diversion of the workers' energies, as they would have been idle anyway; and no injury was done to the workers themselves, but, on the contrary, a benefit was conferred upon them, as they were maintained at the expense of the state during a time when they would otherwise have been earning nothing, and would have been dependent on their own resources. In other words, Khufu's gigantic scheme was not only a selfish attempt to secure immortality for himself, but incidentally proved to be the first unemployment relief scheme on record. The suggestion is not only an attractive but also an eminently reasonable one, replacing the lurid visions of tyrannical strain and misery which have been so long associated with the building of the Great Pyramid. After all, the Egyptians were one of the most reasonable and sane of ancient peoples, and if a reasonable way is apparent towards the accomplishment of an end, it is only common-sense to assume that they took that in preference to an unreasonable way. Khufu, we may be sure, knew well enough that his land must live, even while his great mausoleum was being built; and if a way could be found which conserved the energies of the nation, and minimised the drain upon its resources, we must surely credit him with sense enough to adopt it. Weigall, who has gone at some length into the detail of how the labour may have been distributed on the work, comes to the conclusion that the staff allowed by Herodotus was amply sufficient, on Petrie's supposition, to accomplish the task in the twenty years, and that the pyramid rose, not to the sound of groans and sighs, but to that of the cheerful songs with which Egyptian workmen in all ages have been accustomed to lighten their burdens.

The completion of the pyramid by no means meant the completion of the great scheme by means of which immortality was to be secured for the king. A temple, in which offerings might be made for his spirit, rose against the pyramid on its eastern side; while a long causeway, which had already served for the transport of the stones used in the building, led down to the level ground beneath the plateau, where it terminated in a portico-temple, with a quay to which the boats of the priests could come during the inundation season. Around the sacred enclosure of the pyramid, members of the royal house, and prominent courtiers, were allowed to make their tombs, so that the king might have company in the spirit-world. Three small pyramids of the royal family still stand at the south-east corner of the enclosure, while beyond these lies a perfect town of the dead, consisting of five streets of mastabas, several of them belonging to royal princes or princesses, while the rest are those of great courtiers, either of the time of Khufu or of a later period. Between two of the small pyramids, Dr. Reisner's excavations revealed the existence of the boat-pit of one of Khufu's queens, which once contained the funerary barge in which she would be transported across the rivers or lakes of the Underworld. The pit for Pharaoh's own barge lay beside the causeway.

The Great Pyramid, whose religious significance we shall have to discuss later, is practically the sole monument of Khufu's reign, which is almost devoid of contemporary inscriptions. We know that the king opened up the famous alabaster quarries at Hatnub, near Tell el-Amarna, and that he executed some great building work at Bubastis, of which one granite block bearing his *Ka*-name still survives; beyond that there is nothing to tell us of the work which so energetic a king cannot have failed to do. A late inscription on what is known as the Inventory Stele states that he "built his pyramid beside the temple of this goddess (Isis) and he built a pyramid for the king's daughter Henutsen beside this temple". This is likely enough, as Henutsen is known from other sources, but no dependence can be placed on the other statements of the stele, some of which, in fact, are demonstrably false. Merit. s. ankh, another of Khufu's daughters, was married to Khafra, the builder of the Second Pyramid; and five sons are known, besides two, Baufra and Hordadef, who are mentioned in the Westcar Papyrus and the Book of the Dead, but nowhere else.

One of the curiosities of survival is that while Khafra, the builder of the second pyramid, is represented by quite a number of fine statues, and especially by the magnificent one in diorite which is one of the marvels of ancient art, and makes the king live before us, Khufu, his greater predecessor, has left not one single statue by which we may judge of the appearance of the greatest builder of the world. The solitary likeness of him that we possess is a tiny ivory statuette, discovered by Petrie at Abydos. The diminutive scale of the little ivory figure makes the strangest of contrasts with the vastness of the pyramid by which he is remembered; but fortunately the skill of the early artist who carved the portrait has been equal to the delineation of character even within such narrow limits. The head of the figure is admirably executed, and, even after so many centuries, still suggests the vigour and fiery energy which urged on and brought to completion the greatest of the works of man.

The order of succession after Khufu is a little doubtful. Manetho gives a second Suphis, who must correspond to Khafra, and to whom is attributed a long reign like that which the historian attributes to Khufu; but the lists of Saqqara and Abydos give, between Khufu and Khafra, a king Radedef, with a short reign of eight years. Radedef is evidently the Ratoises of Manetho, and is placed by him after Menkaura, with a reign of 25 years. Whether he comes before or after the other two of the Gizeh Pyramid group is a matter of small importance, for his relics indicate a reign of little moment. Radedef departed from the example set by Khufu, and built his pyramid at Abu Roash on the edge of the western desert, some 15 miles north of Memphis. The pyramid of Abu Roash is much smaller than that of Khufu, being only 320 feet square—a fact which may account for Radedef's selection of a site where his modest tomb would not invite comparison with Khufu's vast pile. Possibly Radedef aimed more at sumptuousness than at size in his work, for the pyramid of Abu Roash seems to have been cased in granite, and to have been a very magnificent structure. Another of the whimsicalities of survival is seen in the fact that the likeness of this otherwise almost unknown king has come down to us in the shape of a remarkably fine head in red sandstone which is now in the Louvre. In other respects the reign is practically a blank, nor is there any evidence of any great work, apart from that of his pyramid, having been done in his time. The suggestion has been made that Radedef should be identified with the royal prince Hordadef, son of Khufu, who figures in the magical tales of the Westcar Papyrus, and who is mentioned in one of the rubrics to the 64th chapter of the Book of the

Dead as travelling through the land to inspect the temples. For this identification, however, no evidence exists, though there is no evidence which renders it impossible. Incidentally, it may be pointed out that if Hordadef, who appears, from the Westcar Papyrus, to have been a man interested in learning, was appointed to inspect the temples throughout the land, it seems unlikely that Herodotus's story of Khufu's impiety is more than a fairy tale.

Khafra, the next occupant of the throne, is a very different figure from the shadowy Radedef, and hardly any Pharaoh, certainly no other early Pharaoh, is so well known to us so far as his outward presentment goes. This, of course, is due to the magnificent portrait statue of the king in diorite, which Mariette unearthed from a subterranean chamber in connection with the so-called Temple of the Sphinx. His relationship to Khufu is not quite certain, but there seems no reason to doubt the Westcar Papyrus in its naming of him as the first of the sons of the great Pharaoh. He was evidently a worthy successor to his father in energy, and had, like him, the full control of a perfectly organised kingdom, whose resources were once more turned towards the completion of a great funerary establishment which should rival that of Khufu. Indeed in some respects, the work of Khafra at Gizeh is even more interesting than that of his father, embracing, as it does, not only the Second Pyramid, but also the so-called Temple of the Sphinx, and, in all probability, the Sphinx itself.

Khafra's pyramid is somewhat smaller than his father's. Its original height was 472 feet, as against the original 481 of the Great Pyramid, and the length of its base was only 706 feet, against the 755 of the larger building. The workmanship of the pyramid also is inferior to that of its rival. On the other hand, the pyramid stands on slightly higher ground than the earlier structure, and thus gains the appearance of being actually higher; while the lowest course of its casing was of granite, which does not appear on the casing of the Great Pyramid. It is possible that Khafra may have intended to cover his whole pyramid with granite, as Radedef had done with his smaller tomb, and so to outrival Khufu in splendour, if not in size; but if this intention was ever cherished, it was soon abandoned, and the rest of the pyramid was cased in limestone. Part of the casing still remains on the upper part of the pyramid, making its ascent and descent somewhat of an athletic feat, which is, however, regularly performed by Arabs, and occasionally by tourists. The Second Pyramid was penetrated in 1818 by Belzoni, as the Great Pyramid had been by Caviglia a little earlier. In neither case was any trace of the Pharaoh found. The granite sarcophagus of Khafra, when Belzoni found it, was sunk into the floor, and its lid, which had been fastened down by copper bolts and secured by resin, had been displaced by the robbers who had rifled the tomb, doubtless in antiquity, and had destroyed the body of the king.

From the pyramid the usual causeway led down to the valley level, terminating there in a building which, though now beneath the level of the surrounding desert, was then a free-standing temple. It is usually known to-day as "The Temple of the Sphinx"; but it has nothing to do with the Sphinx, save that it is a work of the same king who created that enigmatical statue. It is really the portico-temple of the Second Pyramid, from which the processions of priests and relatives began their progress up the causeway to the Pyramid Temple on the east side of Khafra's tomb on the days when the king's memory was celebrated. Simple and devoid of all ornamentation as it is, this small temple, with its great monolithic pillars of red granite and its wall surfaces of translucent alabaster, is perhaps the best extant evidence of the power and taste of the builders of the IVth Dynasty. The simplicity is that of richness, and the great monoliths of squared granite testify to the unsurpassed ability of the Egyptian of the time in the handling of stone.

Not far from this temple stands or crouches the Sphinx, which, along with the group of pyramids beside it, may be taken as the most typically Egyptian relic in existence, as it is the most famous. The Sphinx was originally a promontory of the Libyan rock of the plateau on which the pyramids stand. Possibly some rude resemblance to a crouching figure in the great mass of rock attracted the attention of the Pharaoh, or of his master of works, and started the idea of completing what Nature had begun, and fashioning the monster who now keeps watch over the pyramid plateau. Anyhow, the rock was hewn into the likeness of a couchant lion, with outspread paws and human head, the latter being adorned with the usual linen head-dress of the Pharaoh, while the face was probably designed as a likeness of the reigning king. Between the paws, which in places had to be made up with masonry, a temple and altar were set up; and the whole was dedicated to the sun-god in his fourfold aspects as Harmakhis, the rising sun, Khepri, the Creator-sun, Ra, the sun of the zenith, and Atum, the sun at the setting. In ancient times the Egyptians called the great monster simply "HU", the "hewn thing"; later it is often called "Hu-n-Harmakhu", the Hewn Figure of Harmakhis; while Thothmes IV., who has left an inscription between its paws, calls it Khepri. Roughly speaking, it represents the Sun-god as king, though its face may have been a portrait of the Pharaoh who caused it to be hewn.

Who, then, was this Pharaoh? The inscription of Thothmes IV., mentioned above, tells us that in his time (1420 B.C.), the Sphinx was already ancient, and it also mentions King Khafra, though in a mutilated part of the inscription from which no conclusions can be drawn. On the other hand, there is a tomb-shaft in the middle of the monster's back; and none of the tomb-shafts in this part of the Gizeh cemetery is older than the reign of Khafra. Obviously the tomb-shaft cannot have been sunk after the sacred figure was carved, as such an act would have been sacrilege. It seems, therefore, to follow that the Sphinx belongs to the reign of Khafra, but to the latter part of the reign; but while such a conclusion seems probable, it ought to be held with reserve, as certainty is far from having been reached on the point.

The great figure is 70 feet in height from the pavement at its feet to the crown of its head; while its length is about 150 feet. From time immemorial it has been exposed to the drifting sand of the desert, and has had to be cleared repeatedly. The clearance which Thothmes IV. celebrated in his inscription is the earliest on record. Since then the process has had to be repeated on several occasions, the last being the clearing by M. Baraize, of the Egyptian Service of Antiquities, which was only accomplished recently, and has been the most thorough to which Harmakhis has been subjected, revealing details of his structure which had been unknown before. The face of the god, 14 feet across, was originally painted a bright red, which remained fresh until A.D. 1200, when Abd el-Latif describes it as being "as brilliant as if it were new". It suffered sorely in 1380 from the fanatical attempts of a Mohammedan devotee to destroy such a colossal contravention of the law against the making of graven images; but in spite of its battered condition, perhaps, to some extent, because of it, the Sphinx remains still one of the most impressive of the relics of a land which possesses more abundance of impressive monuments than any other country in the world.

For us, the reign of Khafra means the Second Pyramid, the Temple of the Sphinx, and the Sphinx itself. He did other work on a great scale near Memphis, and in the Delta; but the traces of it which have survived are so scanty as to leave us no clue to the character of his accomplishment in these places. Beyond the borders of his own land he has left no trace—an unusual thing for a king who had so complete a command of the resources of Egypt as he appears to have had. Herodotus, in his fairy tale of the impious pyramid-builders, brings Khafra (Chephren) into the same condemnation as Khufu (Cheops), as having continued his father's persecution of the gods and their worship; but no one who has seen the actual lineaments of the great king, as his Egyptian master-sculptor portrayed them in his great diorite statue, will ever believe that Khafra was the impious tyrant of the Greek historian's story. Petrie talks of the expression of this noble piece of work "combining what a man should be to win our feelings and what a king should be to command our regard", and this is much more to the point than the Greek's scrap of two-thousand-year-old scandal.

PLATE VIII

THE GIZEH PYRAMID FIELD FROM THE AIR
Showing Mastabas behind the Great Pyramid
By permission of Sir Alan Cobham

THE PYRAMID-BUILDERS

One of Khafra's sons, the Prince Nekura, has le
will, which fortunately has survived to our time, and p
of an elaborate testamentary enactment, establishing th
endowment of the tomb of an unknown official of the
reign, has also come down. Both of these documents bear
witness to a thoroughly stable and highly organised state
of society, in which legal forms, and also the many ways in
which they can be evaded, were as fully understood as they
are in our own country at the present time.

With the two reigns of Khufu and Khafra, it may be
said that the civilisation of Egypt under the Old Kingdom
reaches its highest point. There are, indeed, a few points of
detail in which the VIth Dynasty may have surpassed the
IVth; but the general impression which is given of solid
and stable attainment under the two great pyramid-
builders is far in advance of anything suggested by even
the ablest reigns of the later line. The two IVth Dynasty
kings were obviously masters of their land as none of their
successors ever was. Indeed it would almost appear that
the declension from the height to which Khufu and Khafra
had brought the Egyptian efficiency began practically as
soon as the latter was laid in his grave. The history of all
human attainment is ever the same, nor has any human
culture ever proved able to continue in one stay.

> Nativity, once in the main of light,
>   Crawls to maturity, wherewith being crowned
> Crooked eclipses 'gainst his glory fight,
>   And Time that gave doth now his gift confound.

Menkaura, the Mykerinos of the Greeks and the
Mencheres of Manetho, who succeeded Khafra, and was
probably his brother, was obviously a favourite of Herodotus, or of the priests from whom he drew his information. "They said that after him (Khafra), Mykerinos, son of
Cheops, reigned over Egypt; that the conduct of his father
was displeasing to him; and that he opened the temples,
and permitted the people, who were worn down to the last
extremity, to return to their employments, and to sacrifices;
and that he made the most just decisions of all their kings.
On this account, of all the kings that ever reigned in Egypt,

they praise him most, for he both judged well in other respects, and moreover, when any man complained of his decision, he used to make him some present out of his own treasury, and pacify his anger." So that, if this account be true, as Khufu must be regarded as the originator of unemployment relief work, so Menkaura must be held to be the originator of the dole system, and one would imagine that appeals against his judgments would be frequent, when litigants learned that by appealing they could always secure a dole from the royal treasury. The probability is, however, that Menkaura was not quite such a fool as Herodotus makes him out to be.

Upon this foundation of benignant feebleness, Herodotus proceeds to build his famous romance of the good king who, being visited with all sorts of undeserved misfortunes, and finally informed that his reign was to be cut short, and that he was to live only for six years longer, at last rebelled against the injustice of heaven, and spent the six years in one continual and colossal spree, which lasted day and night, and by which he hoped to convict the gods of falsehood, and to turn his six years into twelve. One must admit that the supposed action is quite in keeping with the character whom Herodotus depicts, and that the king who was fool enough to pay each disappointed litigant for his disappointment was just the kind of fool who would carry out the piece of silliness which the Greek historian has related with all gravity, and to which Matthew Arnold has attempted, with somewhat doubtful success, to lend a semblance of dignity.

> So six long years he revell'd, night and day,
> And when the mirth wax'd loudest, with dull sound
> Sometimes from the grove's centre echoes came,
> To tell his wondering people of their king;
> In the still night, across the steaming flats,
> Mix'd with the murmur of the moving Nile.

One touch of Herodotus's little romance has not lost its pathos even now—the story of Menkaura's dying daughter, who begged her father to let her see the sun once a year after her death, and whom her sorrowing father thereupon entombed in the hollow image of a Hathor cow, which would be carried in solemn procession annually, and would thus fulfil the wish of the dying girl. But even this rather pretty story is manifestly, as the historian himself in a moment of candour admits, a "trifling fable"; and the bulk of his information about Menkaura's reign is of no higher authenticity.

In spite of the historian's partiality for this king, there can be little doubt that his reign marks a decided falling off from the level of attainment which had been reached by his predecessors. The fact that his pyramid is so much smaller than those of Khufu and Khafra has been generously accounted for by Weigall on the supposition that "he had the strength of mind not only to be satisfied with a pyramid conceived and executed on a much smaller scale, but also to place it so close to those of his father and uncle (or brother) that comparison can hardly be avoided", and that he "combined with a notorious mildness of disposition and love of good-living a sufficient degree of common sense to restrain him from exhausting the resources of the nation in building a third pyramid on the vast scale of the other two." This, however, is scarcely convincing, especially in view of the fact that a few pages before the author argues at some length that there was no exhaustion of the national resources in building the Great Pyramid; and it is much more likely that Menkaura built a small pyramid, not because he chose to do so of his own free will, but because he was unable to build a big one. The remaining reigns of the dynasty subsequent to his reign show the decline unmistakably. It must have begun somewhere; and where can the beginning be more certainly placed than in a reign whose public works, though still imposing, are manifestly inferior to those of the preceding reigns? Menkaura was doubtless still a great and, if his portraits may be trusted, a good king; but he had not the same complete control of the resources of his country as was held by his more resolute predecessors.

The Third Pyramid is not only inferior to the other two of the great trinity in size, but also in accuracy of construction. The length of each side at the base is only 356 feet, as against the 755 feet of Khufu's pyramid, and the

706 feet of Khafra's; the height is 219 feet against the original 481 of Khufu's and the 472 of Khafra's. Still, although it is dwarfed by its mighty neighbours, it is all the same a remarkable structure, and in another situation would attract much more attention than it does at present. The statement of Diodorus that "it far excelled the others in its ingenuity of structure" is not true; but he came nearer the truth in his remark that "for fifteen tiers the sides were made of black marble, the remainder being of the same stone as that of the other pyramids." It is true that the lower casing of Menkaura's pyramid is not of black marble, but of red granite, and that it continues for sixteen courses instead of fifteen; but at least Diodorus had some idea of the differences between this and the other pyramids, and modern conceptions of accuracy in description are not to be expected from an ancient tourist.

The inner chambers and entrance passages of the pyramid show obvious traces of an alteration having taken place in the plans during the progress of the building; but there is no trace of Diodorus's "ingenuity of structure". Entrance into Menkaura's resting-place was effected in A.D. 1226 by treasure-hunters. "After passing through various passages, a room was reached wherein was found a long blue vessel (the sarcophagus) quite empty. . . . They found in this basin, after they had broken the covering of it, the decayed remains of a man, but no treasures, excepting some golden tablets inscribed with characters of a language which nobody could understand." Menkaura's pyramid, like its greater neighbours, had evidently been rifled long before this attempt, probably, indeed, not very long after it was built, or at all events not later than during the disturbances which marked the fall of the Old Kingdom.

In 1837, Colonel Howard Vyse succeeded in forcing an entrance into the chambers. In the upper chamber he found portions of a wooden coffin purporting to be that of "the King of the North and South, Men-kau-Ra, living for ever", together with the remains of a man wrapped in a coarse woollen cloth of a yellow colour. Vyse also found, in the lower chamber, the fine basalt sarcophagus, whose emptiness had disappointed the thieves of 1226. The wooden coffin and the remains were duly conveyed to England, and are now in the British Museum; the basalt sarcophagus was shipped for the same destination in 1838. The ship bearing it left Leghorn on October 12, 1838, and has never since been heard of. A few bits of wreckage were picked up off Carthagena, and it may be concluded that Menkaura's great sarcophagus rests somewhere at the bottom of the Mediterranean.

Better fortune has attended the excavations of Dr. Reisner, whose work at Gizeh has given us some remarkable portrait statues and statuettes of the king. It is impossible to doubt that these are faithful likenesses of a man who was both a good and worthy king, but who cannot have been, in any sense of the word, a great one. Honesty and kindliness are written very plainly on his face; and together with them a certain simplicity which may have been very attractive, but would not make for efficiency. "Farmer George" is written all over all the statues; only there is nothing of the stubbornness which marked our own wearer of the title. Compare the Reisner statues, which are wonderfully consistent in their versions of the king's face, with the strength and self-possession of the Khafra head, and the difference between a great king and one who is merely respectable becomes manifest. Menkaura was what a Scot would call a "decent, canny body", and he succeeded one who, whatever his character may have been otherwise, was plainly a master of men; there is no need to seek further for the reasons of the decline which begins with him, and goes on with inevitable acceleration throughout the remaining reigns of the dynasty.

The rubric of the 64th chapter of the Book of the Dead, already mentioned, calls the Prince Hordadef, who is said to have discovered the chapter, the son of Menkaura, or at least attributes the discovery by Hordadef to the reign of Menkaura. In view of the other evidence which exists to show that Hordadef was actually the son of Khufu, it is safer to regard this famous wise man, whose dark sayings were found so difficult by Egyptians of a later date, as being Menkaura's brother, and not his son. In fact, there is no evidence as to the existence of any sons of Menkaura, though it is possible that his successor, Shepseskaf, may have been his son.

One of the officials of the reign, Febhen by name, has left us an account of how His Majesty graciously detailed fifty men to build a tomb for his faithful servant—a compliment which, however whimsical it may seem to us, was the greatest which Pharaoh could pay to a man who had served him well. The orders were given on an occasion "when His Majesty was upon the road beside the pyramid *Her*, in order to inspect the work upon the pyramid *Neter*". *Neter*, "The Divine", is the name of the third pyramid of Gizeh, the recognised pyramid of Menkaura. *Her*, therefore, must have been another pyramid connected with Menkaura in some way; and it has been conjectured that Menkaura, like some of his predecessors, had two tombs, of which the pyramid *Her* may have been for his *Ka*. This, however, is uncertain, as the pyramid *Her* may have been that of some other member of the royal family.

Shepseskaf, who succeeded Menkaura, again offers to us little more than the shadow of a name. Almost the only information that we have about him comes from the autobiography of his son-in-law Ptahshepses, a singularly perfect and complete specimen of the Egyptian bureaucrat. With that tenacious hold upon life which seems to be so characteristic of official gentlemen who have attained to a comfortable post with equally comfortable emoluments, Ptahshepses proved himself to be surely the most permanent of all permanent officials, for he lasted through at least eight reigns, and was still holding office in the ninth. On one calculation of the duration of these reigns, he must have been somewhere about 130 when he reluctantly laid down office and its perquisites; and even on a less liberal allowance there seems no possiblity of admitting less than eighty years of royal favour and bounty. In either case, Ptahshepses, before his untimely cutting off, must have been what journalists are in the habit of calling with reverence "the *doyen*" of the Egyptian bureaucracy, and what others with less reverence call "the oldest inhabitant, who never remembers anything". Along with tenacious vitality went, as one would expect, conspicuous elasticity. Like Russell Lowell's candidate, Ptahshepses didn't believe in Principle, but oh! he did in Interest; and though he was bound by the closest ties to the IVth Dynasty, he had not the least objection to becoming the servant of the kings of the Vth, which displaced, probably with violence, its predecessor. As husband of the King Shepseskaf's eldest daughter, he might himself have asserted a perfectly valid claim to the throne; but, like a wise and cautious man, he took no risks, and preferred to draw a good salary under "whatsoever king might reign".

The life-story of this early Egyptian Vicar of Bray belongs, of course, mainly to the period of the half-dozen kings of the Vth Dynasty whom he served; but as the first steps in his rise to fortune were made under the IVth, and the interest of his narrative is purely personal, and adds nothing to our general knowledge of the later period, it may be as well to let him tell his tale at this point. He does so with such dithyrambic fervour as is seldom found in the annals of bureaucracy, as who should say "Breathes there the man with soul so dead" as not to acknowledge with praise the advantages of an official standing! The narrative falls into almost poetic form, and each strophe closes with his own greatly blessed name, as follows:

(Who was born) in the time of Menkaura; whom he (*i.e.* Menkaura) educated among the king's children, in the royal harem; who was honoured more before the king than any child; PTAHSHEPSES.

―― in the time of Shepseskaf; whom he (*i.e.* Shepseskaf) educated among the king's children, in the palace of the king, in the privy chamber, in the royal harem; who was more honoured before the king than any youth; PTAHSHEPSES.

His Majesty gave to him the king's eldest daughter, Maatkha, as his wife, for His Majesty desired that she should be with him more than with anyone; PTAHSHEPSES.

(Attached to Userkaf, High Priest of Memphis), more honoured by the king than any servant. He descended into every ship of the court; he entered upon the ways of the southern palace at all the Feasts-of-the-Coronation; PTAHSHEPSES.

(Attached to Sahura, more honoured by the king than) any servant, as privy councillor of every work which His Majesty desired to do; who pleased the heart of his lord every day; PTAHSHEPSES.

(Attached to Neferarkara, more honoured by the king than) any servant; when His Majesty praised him for a thing, His Majesty permitted that he should kiss his foot, and His Majesty did not permit that he should kiss the ground; PTAHSHEPSES.

(Attached to Neferefra, more honoured by the king than) any servant; he descended into the sacred barge at all Feasts-of-the-Appearance; beloved of his lord; PTAHSHEPSES.

—— attached to the heart of his lord (Ra-en-user or Nusserra), beloved of his lord, revered of Ptah, doing that which the god desires of him, pleasing every artificer under the king; PTAHSHEPSES!

It must be acknowledged that Ptahshepses was a singularly fortunate man, if felicity lies in the signs of royal favour which he recounts with such pride and awed reverence. Apart from his matrimonial honours, which may have proved more of a danger than anything else, when the change of dynasty happened, one has to endeavour to realise the almost unspeakable privilege which was conferred upon him when King Neferarkara granted to him to kiss the royal foot instead of "smelling the ground", or, as the common phrase more crudely put the prostration, "lying on his belly in the presence of His Majesty". Indeed, the supreme value of the little autobiography of Ptahshepses is that, at this early stage, it shows us the Egyptian bureaucrat already fully developed, and possessed of all the engaging qualities and convictions which mark his class all through the history of the land. There was far more receptivity in the make-up of the ancient Egyptian than is generally acknowledged, and Egypt was by no means the changeless land of sinister mystery of the popular novelist; but there was at least one thing in Egypt which never changed, and that was the attitude of the official class towards the desirability of office, and its scorn of everything unofficial. Ptahshepses wrote his tale of heroic constancy to place and profit at an early stage of the tradition; but there was never an official throughout all the thirty centuries which followed who would not have said with unction, "Let me die the death of Ptahshepses, and let my last end be like his". It is one of the most prominent and also one of the least pleasing features of a national life which has much that is pleasing in it.

The tradition which Herodotus relates as to King Asychis, who corresponds to the Shepseskaf of the native records, having built his pyramid of brick is quite possibly true, though the inscription on the brick pyramid, as he gives it, was certainly never written by an Egyptian, and may be disregarded. Brick pyramids are by no means unknown in Egypt, and though we have no knowledge of such a fabric at this period, it is possible that a king such as Shepseskaf, whose power over the resources of his land was diminishing, might choose to make his tomb of the humbler material. There is no trace left of the magnificent gate to the temple of Ptah at Memphis, which was built, according to the Greek historian, by this king, and "which in size and beauty far surpasses the other three gates"; but this is no proof of its non-existence, as work of much later times has perished quite as utterly.

Of Herodotus's blind king, Anysis, who succeeded Asychis, and fled to the fens for fifty years, during which time Egypt was conquered and ruled by Ethiopian kings, the native records know nothing. Instead, the quarries of the Wady Hammamat offer us an inscription naming at this time a king Imhotep, who must be the original of Manetho's strangely named Thamphthis, and who reigned, according to his account, for nine years. The reign may have been considerably shorter, as the Turin Papyrus seems to show room at this point for a reign of only two years; but as nothing at all is known of this Pharaoh, speculation as to the duration of his reign is obviously worthless.

With his death, or perhaps his forcible deposition, the great IVth Dynasty comes, as so many great royal lines of history have come, to a somewhat impotent conclusion. It had not lasted long as dynasties go, and only three, or perhaps, if we exclude Menkaura, only two of its monarchs had been men of marked and outstanding ability. But these two, Khufu and Khafra, had achieved what few other monarchs have been able to do. They had impressed upon their land the character by which it has largely been known ever since, so that when Egypt is named, it is the Egypt of the Pyramid-builders and of the Sphinx which rises at once to the mind. There may have been many far greater kings in the long line of Egyptian Pharaohs, and quite possibly Narmer, Aha-Mena, Khasekhemui, or Zeser were really more responsible than Khufu and Khafra for the characteristic greatness of the Old Kingdom; yet when all is said, it was these two who succeeded in striking the key-note which vibrates "Egypt" throughout the ages.

CHAPTER VIII

THE CHILDREN OF THE SUN-GOD

ONE of the most famous of Egyptian papyri, the Papyrus Westcar, already mentioned more than once, shows us King Khufu in a fit of ennui, craving to hear from his sons some tales of the old magicians. Prince Khafra tells him the story of the wise scribe Uba-aner and his faithless wife; Prince Baufra follows, with the tale of the voyage which the wizard Zazamankh planned for King Snefru, and the incident of the lost malachite pendant. "Then Prince Hordadef stood up to speak and said: 'Hitherto hast thou heard only examples of what they knew that have gone before us, and one knoweth not the truth from falsehood. But even in thine own time there is a magician' ." Khufu naturally asks who the wise man is, and Hordadef replies that he is one Dedi, who knows how to put on again a head that has been cut off, and to make a lion follow him of its free choice. Moreover, added the prince, as a special testimonial to the wisdom of Dedi, he knoweth the design of the locks of the sanctuary of Thoth. "Now the Majesty of King Khufu was always seeking for himself the locks of the sanctuary of Thoth, to make for himself the like thereof for his Horizon (his pyramid)."

Hordadef is sent to bring the wizard to court, and in the presence he joins on again the head of a goose that had been cut off, then that of a duck, and finally that of an ox. Convinced of his powers, the king presses him as to the matter in which he was really interested—the locks of the sanctuary of Thoth. Dedi admits that he knows where they are; "but," he says, "O King, my Lord, lo, it is not I that shall bring the chest to thee". "And His Majesty said: 'Who then will bring it me?' And Dedi said, 'It is the

139

eldest of the three children who are in the womb of Ruddidet that will bring it thee'. And His Majesty said: 'But I desire that thou say who she is, this Ruddidet.' And Dedi said: 'It is the wife of a priest of Ra of Sakhebu, that hath conceived three children of Ra, Lord of Sakhebu. He (Ra, the Sun-god) hath told her that they will exercise this excellent office (the kingship) in this entire land, and that the eldest of them will be high-priest in Heliopolis.'

"Then His Majesty's heart grew sad thereat. And Dedi said: 'Pray, what is this mood, O King, my Lord? Is it because of the three children? Then I say unto thee: Thy son, his son, and then one of them' "—very much in the style of a Hebrew prophet informing a king that because of his repentance the evil shall not happen in his day, but in that of a successor. Khufu, like King Herod, displays a suspicious curiosity as to the time of the birth of these three children, who are to displace his great grandson from the throne, and intimates his intention of being present when the great event takes place, doubtless with the same thought in his mind as was in Herod's, when he bade the Magi bring him word of the infant Redeemer, 'that I may come and worship him also'. "And His Majesty said, 'She (dwelleth in) the region of the Canal of the Two Fishes; I myself would set foot there; I will see the temple of Ra, Lord of Sakhebu' ."

The narrative then leaves the king and his magician, and describes the birth of the three children of the Sun-god, at which the great goddesses Isis, Nephthys, Meskhent, and Heqt are present in the guise of dancing-girls, with the god Khnum to act as their porter. The priest Ra-user offers them a measure of barley in payment of their services, and they accept it, but ask him to store it for them against their return. Then they fashion three royal crowns and hide them in the barley; and when they have departed, first Ruddidet's handmaid, and then Ruddidet herself hear sounds of music and rejoicing as for a king's coronation, proceeding from the bin where the barley is stored. Shortly after, Ruddidet quarrels with her maid and beats her; whereupon the girl goes off with the threat that she will tell King Khufu of the whereabouts of the three divine children who were to usurp his throne. Providence, however, interposes, and as the maid stoops for a drink of water from the Nile, a crocodile carries her off. Here the manuscript unfortunately breaks off; but no doubt the remainder of the story told how in due time the children exercised "this excellent office", and sat upon the throne of Egypt one after another.

Apart from its merits as literature, which are by no means negligible, and its value as a specimen of Egyptian tradition from about the Hyksos period, to which the papyrus apparently belongs, the story has great historical importance, because it represents the popular tradition of the change which took place on the crumbling of the IVth Dynasty, and which resulted in the triumph of the priestly college of Ra at Heliopolis, and the establishment upon the throne of a dynasty of kings who owed their position to priestly influence, and were in fact, though perhaps not in name, the nominees and servants of the priesthood of the Sun-god. The tale is, as Breasted has said of another such story of a later date, "folk-history, a wave mark among the people, left by the tide" which the revolution set in motion. The priests of Ra had to account to the nation at large for the possibly violent and at least irregular series of changes which displaced the last weak descendants of the great pyramid-building line from the throne of Egypt, and substituted for them the puppets of the priesthood. They did so in the convenient way which priesthoods have always had at hand as a justification for the actions which their policy requires or finds convenient. The first three kings of the Vth Dynasty, whom the Heliopolitan priests knew well enough as very mere men, even as puppets whose strings they pulled, must needs appear before the nation as divine, the actual sons begotten by Ra himself. Probably from the very beginning Pharaoh had claimed a certain divinity for himself; now it was claimed for him as a necessity of priestly policy, and the permanent ascendancy of the Sun-god was assured by the fact that henceforth every Pharaoh, no matter how poor a weakling, is Son of Ra, and bears the name as part of his royal titulary in addition to his Horus-name.

On the death, or deposition, of the shadowy Imhotep, the first of the three brothers whose accession was prophesied by the magician came to the throne. Userkaf (the name means "Mighty is his Spirit"—*i.e.* the Spirit of Ra) was already High-priest of Heliopolis at his succession, and if any weight is to be allowed to the tradition of his birth during the reign of Khufu, he must have been past middle life before he ascended the throne. As might be expected, therefore, his reign was comparatively short, probably not much more than seven years in duration, and it is almost void of any records of national importance. We learn from the Palermo Stone that he gave large endowments of land from the royal domain for the temple of Ra, and for the purpose of providing offerings on feast-days for the "spirits of Heliopolis", that he built a shrine in the temple of Horus in Buto, endowed the worship of Hathor with an estate in the Delta, built a temple to the seldom-mentioned god Sepa, and endowed it with a small domain, and, in general, behaved towards the gods with a piety which was to be expected of one who was the nominee of the priestly caste. On a cylinder-seal in the British Museum, he bears the title, "Beloved of the Gods", and he seems to have earned it by his attention to their interests. He built, like the succeeding kings of the dynasty, a Sun-temple, probably at or near Abusir; but it has vanished, like his pyramid, having in all likelihood been used as a quarry by later kings. The temple was called "Nekhen-Ra", "The Court of Offerings of Ra". A vase of white marble bearing the name of this temple was found at a place so remote as Cerigo, suggesting that intercourse of some kind was already established between Egypt and the islands of the Ægean.

The chief private document of the reign is the inscription in the tomb of Nekonekh, at Tehneh in the Delta. Nekonekh was "Steward of the Palace, Governor of the New Towns, Superior Prophet of Hathor, Mistress of Royenet, and King's Confidant"; obviously an official person of some importance, whom it was well for an usurper to keep sweet. Userkaf did so by making over to him the two offices of priest of Hathor at his own town, and of mortuary priest of the tomb of Khenuka, a great nobleman of the time of Menkaura. The two offices carried with them large endowments of land, amounting in all to 120 *stat*, and Nekonekh, who enjoyed the Oriental felicity of having his quiver full to the extent of thirteen children, makes a will dividing up the endowments between them, while they were to discharge the duties of the two offices among them. Unfortunately there were only twelve months in the year, and 120 *stat* in the endowment to divide up between the thirteen children; so eleven of them each got ten *stat*, with a month's duty to perform, and the last two got five *stat* each, with a month's duty to divide between them. Having thus done his best for his numerous offspring, the worthy priest contemplated the future with a calm mind. "It was the majesty of Userkaf who commanded that I should be priest of Hathor, Mistress of Royenet; whatsoever was paid into the temple, it was I who was priest over everything that came into the temple. Now it is these my children who shall act as priests of Hathor, Mistress of Royenet, as I myself did, while I journey to the beautiful West, as one revered (leaving ?) in charge of these my children." The opinion of the last two of the thirteen children on the arrangement is not recorded.

Sahura, who succeeded Userkaf, may have been his brother, if the legend is true, and quite probably was so, as the shortness of the reigns of the three kings whose names are associated with the story indicates that they could not have belonged to successive generations. If so, he must also have been elderly before he succeeded to the crown; but in spite of his age, he seems to have been a man of considerable energy. The usual Sinai barometer of Egyptian energy furnishes us with a record of his activity in the shape of a tablet of the king in the crown of Upper Egypt smiting the Asiatic. A graffito of the reign occurs as far south as Tomas in Nubia, indicating that Egyptian interests were extending southwards beyond the normal limit of the First Cataract, and the reliefs from the king's Sun-temple at Abusir show that he dispatched a squadron of ships to the Phœnician coast. In the latter part of the reign, the

Palermo Stone mentions an expedition to the Land of Punt (Somaliland?) which brought back 80,000 measures of myrrh, 6000 of electrum, and 2600 staves, probably of ebony. Weigall would assign this important voyage to a later king, Shepseska-Ra Assa, but the evidence seems quite insufficient to warrant us in depriving a king, whose records otherwise show him to have been energetic, of an important expedition, and assigning it to another of whose activity no other trace has survived.

At home the most important work of the reign was the building of the great Sun - temple at Abusir, near Memphis. This type of temple, which is characteristic of the priestly line of the Vth Dynasty, stood not far from the Pharaoh's pyramid, and, like the pyramid-temple, contained a type of column new to Egyptian architecture. The novelty consists in the use of palm-leaf capitals, gracefully carved on monolith columns of red granite, of twenty feet in height. Sahura's architects also introduced another novelty in the shape of the clustered papyrus column with six lobes. The architecture of the great Sun-temples will have to be dealt with in connection with the Religion of the Old Kingdom. Meanwhile we may notice the appearance of relief sculpture on the wall surfaces on a large scale. The familiar emblem of the solar disc, flanked with uraei, makes its first appearance; and the walls are adorned with scenes of offering and victory. "A new feeling and new methods burst into the earlier aims of geometrical perfection which had been the ideals of the previous dynasty."

The Palermo Stone records large endowments of various deities, of a similar kind to those of Userkaf; but the most interesting document of the reign is the inscription on the tomb stele of Nenekhsekhmet, who was chief physician to the king. The tomb of this worthy Dr. Fillgrave at Saqqara is of a very modest character, but is adorned by a finely executed false door of Turra limestone; and the reason for this is given us by the proud record of the inscription, which is so characteristic of the Egyptian attitude of mind as to be worth quoting in full: "The chief physician Nenekhsekhmet spoke before His Majesty: 'May thy Person, beloved of Ra, command that

PLATE IX

The Times

THE SPHINX

DIORITE STATUE OF KHAFRA

there be given to me a false door of stone for this my tomb of the cemetery.' His Majesty caused that there be brought for him two false doors from Turra of stone, that they be laid in the audience-hall of the house called 'Sahura-shines-with-Crowns', and that the two high priests of Memphis and the artisans of the [necropolis?] be assigned to them, that the work might be done on them in the presence of the king himself. The stone-work went on every day, there was an inspection of that which was done on them in the court daily. His Majesty had colour put on them, and had them painted blue.

"His Majesty said to the chief physician Nenekh-sekhmet: 'As these my nostrils enjoy health, as the gods love me, mayest thou depart into the cemetery at an advanced old age as one revered.' I praised the king greatly, and lauded every god for Sahura's sake, for he knows the desire of the entire suite. When anything goes forth from the mouth of His Majesty, it immediately comes to pass. For the god has given to him knowledge of things that are in the body, because he is more august than any god. If ye love Ra, ye shall praise every god for Sahura's sake, who did this for me. I was his revered one; never did I do anything evil toward any person."

The smug satisfaction and self-righteousness of the thing is typical of Egyptian officialdom, and if the good court-physician thought well of himself, he was not alone in the land. Where but in Egypt could you find a subject whose dearest desire was to gain from royal favour a tomb-stone for himself, or a king whose best wish for his faithful body physician was to see him have a good funeral? Yet both these things are thoroughly characteristic of the Egyptian mind all through its history, and this without a trace of the morbid quality which would seem to be the natural accompaniment of such a frame of mind, for the Egyptian was one of the least morbid of men, canny, practical, fond of all the good things of this life, and not least of a joke, as he understood such a thing.

After Sahura, the order of succession is a little doubt-ful; but it is much more likely that Kakau, the third of the divine triplet, succeeded at this point to his brother, than that two other reigns intervened before Ra's purpose was completely accomplished. The king, who passes more generally by his other name of Neferarkara, must, on any theory of the succession, have been well up in years before he came to the throne, and what remains of his work suggests the haste of one who judged that his time might not be long. There is no record of work at Sinai, and the king's Sun-temple at Abusir, the "Favourite-Seat-of-Ra", is of poor work compared to that of Sahura, its great court and forecourt being largely built of brick, while its columns are four-lobed instead of six-lobed, as in his brother's temple. There is the usual record of endowments for the worship of various gods, and also of what must have been some notable works of art in metal, in the shape of an electrum statue which was set up in the temple of Hathor, and copper morning and evening barks of the Sun at the royal Sun-temple.

The work of this reign, however, is probably better known than that of any of the early kings, owing to the fact that one of the great officials of Neferarkara was the "royal architect and manager of the pyramid" Tiy, whose great mastaba at Saqqara is one of the most famous of Egyptian show-places, with its extraordinarily vivid representations of all aspects of Egyptian life and work. The superb statue of Tiy, which was found in his mortuary chapel, gives us a wonderfully lifelike representation of the robust and energetic type of the Egyptian official of this period, and is a worthy companion to that of Ranefer, from which it cannot greatly differ in date.

A more intimate sidelight on the relations between the king and his servants is given by the tomb-inscription of the "Vizier, Chief Judge, and Chief Architect", Weshptah at Abusir. The tomb was not built by Weshptah himself, but by his son, who in the inscription tells us the reason for this unusual arrangement. Weshptah, obviously a busy and much overworked man, with three such offices to discharge, was superintending, in his capacity of chief architect, the erection of some important building. The Pharaoh and the royal family come one day to inspect the building, and are greatly delighted with its beauty. "They wondered greatly beyond everything, and lo! His Majesty praised him because of it." But the strain had been too much for the overtaxed man, and a sudden illness fell upon him, even as the king was speaking. "His Majesty, however, saw him that he heard not," and apparently cried out that Weshptah was ill, though the exclamation is lost from the record. "When the royal children and companions, who were of the court, heard, fear beyond everything was in their hearts."

At once the stricken architect was carried to the palace, "and His Majesty had the royal children, companions, ritual priests and chief physicians come. His Majesty had brought for him a case of writings", which was obviously a medical papyrus, for the Pharaoh had a traditional interest in medical science from the earliest days. Nothing could be done, however, for what was seemingly a case of cerebral haemorrhage arising from overwork; and the king retired to mourn and pray in private. "They said before His Majesty that he was lost. . . . The heart of His Majesty was exceeding sad beyond everything; His Majesty said that he would do everything according to his (*i.e.* the dying man's) heart's desire, and returned to the privy chamber, [where] he prayed to Ra." When the end came, "His Majesty commanded that there be made for him a coffin of ebony wood, overlaid. Never was it done for one like him before. His Majesty had him anointed by the side of His Majesty. It was his eldest son, First under the King, Advocate of the People, Mernutterseteni, who made this inscription for him, while he was in his tomb of the cemetery. One (*i.e.* the king) caused that it be put into writing upon his tomb. His Majesty praised him (the son) on account of it, and he praised the god for him (thanked the king) exceedingly." Another scrap of inscription tells us that the king did not forget his dead servant, for he established a mortuary endowment for the tomb of Weshptah, "which was by the pyramid 'The-Soul-of-Sahura-Shines' ".

In the sense of dates and hard facts, all this, of course, is not history; as a light upon the human nature of the age, and the relations of man with man five thousand years ago, it is more valuable than a bushel of dates or hard facts. The great necessity, and the great difficulty, in dealing with a past so remote, is to realise that these people, whose names echo faintly across five millenniums, were flesh and blood like ourselves, loving and hating, hoping and fearing, suffering and dying at last, like us; and whatsoever will help us, like this fragmentary memorial of the death of Pharaoh's chief architect, to feel the common humanity of kings and commoners in these ancient days is the most precious essence of history. Neferarkara stood in kindly human relationships towards his servants, spite of his own divine sonship and royal dignity; we owe him something for that, however little else he may have left us to remember him by. Perhaps it does not matter so much, either to him or to us, that his Sun-temple compares poorly with those of others of his line, and that he could only attain to brick, where Sahura and Neuserra had carven stone.

Neferarkara's two successors, Shepseskara and Neferefra or Khaneferra, are names to us, and not much more. It is possible that like the first three kings of the dynasty, they, with Neuserra, who succeeds them, were brothers, being all sons of Neferarkara; but this is by no means certain. Neuserra warred in Sinai, where he has left a tablet in the Wady Maghara, showing him smiting an Asiatic, with the inscription: "The Smiter of the Asiatics of all countries"; while his pyramid-temple at Abusir was adorned with reliefs showing his victories over Libyan and Syrian foes. He was thus something more than a mere priestly puppet, as some others of his line may have been. His greatest work in Egypt was the building of the great Sun-temple at Abusir—a building which is of the utmost importance as evidence for the architecture and ritual connected with Sun-worship at this period, and which presents manifest differences from subsequent Egyptian temples. The details of this building will have to be considered in connection with the religious development of the Old Kingdom.

Two of Neuserra's wives are known to us by name, Khenti.khou.s., and Nub; while we know also of two of his daughters, Khamerer-nebti and Mertates. But the king's greatest title to immortality lies in the possibility of his having been the father of the writer of what has been for a long time known as "the oldest book in the world"—The Instruction of Ptah-hetep. Ptah-hetep claims to have written his book, or rather spoken the material of which it consists, in the reign of King Assa, whose tutor he seems to have been; and as he also claims to have been "son of the king, of his body," he must have been descended from a previous Pharaoh, and Neuserra is the most likely of the preceding kings to have been his father. If Neuserra indeed begot the father of all book-makers, he has perhaps a glory greater than even that of the building of the great Sun-temple; he has certainly a greater responsibility. The Sun-temple was a thing finished and done with; but the book-making!

The worthy Ptahshepses, whose hymn to his own glory we have read in last chapter, closed his long and variegated career under Neuserra, and departed to become the model of successful officialdom for all time coming. Another ornament of the Egyptian Civil Service who departed to his rest in this reign was the "Judge, attached to Nekhen, and Eldest of the Hall," Hotephiryakhet, whose tomb inscription is conspicuous for the candour with which it seeks to entice the passer-by into a treaty of reciprocity. "I have made this tomb as a just possession," he says, "and never have I taken a thing belonging to any person. Whosoever shall make offering to me therein, I will do it for them; I will commend them to the god for it very greatly; I will do this for them, for bread, for beer, for clothing, for ointment, and for grain, in great quantity." One wonders if the offer of a somewhat nebulous intercession with Osiris produced much bread and beer from the practical Egyptian passer-by for the hungry and thirsty Ka of the late judge.

Hotephiryakhet makes another statement which casts a somewhat grim light upon the Egyptian practice of the time, which is also the Egyptian practice of all time, in regard to tomb-property and to property in a tomb. He finds it necessary to declare that he himself has not stolen the tomb of any other man, and equally necessary to warn off possible stealers of his own tomb, or of anything in it; as thus: "I have made this my tomb upon the western slope in a pure (*i.e.* hitherto unoccupied) place. There was no tomb of any person therein, in order that the possession of him who had gone to his *Ka* might be protected. As for any people who shall enter into this tomb as their mortuary property, or shall do any evil thing to it, judgment shall be had with them for it, by the great God. I have made this tomb as my shelter; I was honoured by the king, who brought for me a sarcophagus." Egyptian mortuary morality was evidently not of a conspicuously high standard under the Vth Dynasty; nor did it improve in the least as time went on.

Of the short reign of Menkauhor, who succeeded Neuserra, almost nothing is known. He sent an expedition to Sinai, where a damaged inscription of his still survives on the rocks of the Wady Maghara. No relief remains; it may have scaled or cracked off. The inscription reads: "Horus: Menkhu; King of Upper and Lower Egypt: Menkauhor, who is given life, stability . . . Commission of the King, which——executed." Unfortunately the name of the commander, which was originally cut in the blank, has vanished; so that we do not know who was the first Egyptian officer who ventured to carve his own name alongside that of his master, and so to claim a share in the glory which previous Pharaohs had reserved for themselves. After this the practice becomes regular, and two inscriptions of the next reign at Sinai name the leader of the expedition, though in one case the name has become effaced. Yet one would fain have known the name of the first captain who took the unprecedented risk of putting in for a share of the credit which he had won for his king. "Nox alta premit," as Scott's Abbotsford windows put it. The Louvre has a single finely carved relief of Menkauhor, which was built into a wall of the Serapeum, and was probably stolen from his pyramid-temple, which, with his pyramid, is now unknown.

Dadkara Assa, who succeeded, seems to have been a king of some vigour. No fewer than four of his inscriptions

have been found in the Wady Maghara, one of which gives
the title "Son of Ra," now beginning to come into general
use. Assa also sent an expedition into Nubia, as is evident
from the fact that a graffito has been found on the rocks at
Tomas; and an inscription in the Wady Hammamat names
the king. One of the Sinai inscriptions is of interest. It runs
as follows: "Year after the fourth occurrence of the numbering of all large and small cattle, when the god caused
that costly stone be found in the secret mine—a stele with
writing of the god himself; Horus Dedkhu; King of Upper
and Lower Egypt, Favourite of the two Goddesses; Dedkhu; Golden Horus; Dad; Dadkara Assa, living forever.
Royal commission sent with the ship-captain, Nenekh-
Khentikhet, to the terrace the name of which is 'Malachite'." The sea-captain, Nenekh Khentikhet, is thus the
first commoner whose name has survived on the rocks of
the Wady Maghara; but Weigall (*History of the Pharaohs*,
i. 208-9) has suggested a very different importance for this
tablet. His idea is that it commemorates the finding of the
block of stone which was used for the carving of the Annals
of the early kings of Egypt—a fragment of which is known
as the Palermo Stone. He suggests, in this connection,
that one of the royal letters which Senezemab, the king's
architect, inscribes on the walls of his tomb refers to the
erection of a building to hold the precious block. The idea
is an interesting one; but it should be remembered that it
is pure speculation, and that there is absolutely no means
of proving it. Indeed Breasted points out that the phrase
in the Sinai inscription, "A stele with writing of the god
himself," is a stock-phrase used to describe any ancient
inscription, and that its probable meaning is that an
ancient stele of some former expedition was found which
led the miners to the desired vein.

Assa's reign was signalised by one of those expeditions
into Equatorial Africa which became not uncommon in
subsequent reigns of the Old Kingdom. Our knowledge of
this expedition is not derived from any contemporary record, but from a casual mention of one of its results in the
letter which Pepy II. of the VIth Dynasty wrote, more than
a century and a quarter later, to his servant Herkhuf. Com-

mending Herkhuf for his success in securing a dwarf from
Central Africa for his master's diversion, Pepy observes
that the dwarf is "like the dwarf which the Treasurer of
the god Baurded brought from Punt in the time of Assa",
and promises the successful caravan-leader "a greater
thing than that which was done for the Treasurer of
the god Baurded in the time of Assa". Baurded is otherwise entirely unknown; but he deserves the credit which
Pepy's reference to him has fortunately enabled history
to give him as one of the first of the long line of African
explorers.

We have already seen that King Assa's tutor was that
Ptah-hetep, who in his old age dictated his "Instruction"
to prepare his son for the succession to his offices. The discussion of his book belongs to the literature of the period;
but Ptah-hetep's introduction may be quoted as a typical
example of the old man's sententious style, and the characteristic Egyptian desire to keep the good things of officialdom in the family so far as possible. "So spake he unto
the Majesty of King Assa: 'Old age hath come, and dotage
hath descended. The limbs are painful, and the state of
being old appeareth as a novelty. Strength hath perished
for weariness. The mouth is silent and speaketh not; the
eyes are shrunken and the ears deaf. The heart is forgetful,
and remembereth not yesterday. One's bones suffer in old
age, and the nose is stopped up and breatheth not. To
stand up and to sit down are alike ill. Good is become evil.
Every taste hath perished. What old age doeth to a man is
that it fareth ill with him in all things. Let therefore the
servant there (*i.e.* myself) be bidden to make him a staff of
old age; let my son be set in my place, that I may instruct
him in the discourse of them that hearken, and in the
thoughts of them that have gone before, them that have
served the ancestors in times past. May they do the like
for thee, that strife may be banished from among the people
and the Two River-banks may serve thee.'" King Assa evidently assented to the desire of his ancient sage (as who
would not, after so pathetic an exposition of the woes of
age and infirmity?), and Ptah-hetep, who, after all, was
himself a prince of the blood, was spared, we may hope, to

see his son's attainment of the chief aim of the Egyptian's ambition—a good post with a comfortable salary attached.

Another big man at the court of Assa was that Senezemab, "Chief Judge, Vizier, and Chief Architect," who has already been mentioned. His chief distinction was that His Majesty was so pleased with his servant's work as to write to him two letters with his own hand, and both of these are duly inscribed on his tomb by the delighted official. "His Majesty", writes Senezemab, "himself wrote with his own fingers, in order to praise me, because I did every work which His Majesty commanded to do well and excellently, according to the desire of His Majesty's heart towards it." Assa, it must be confessed, reveals himself in his letters as a shameless punster, and one of that disastrous type who, having got hold of a pun, and a poor one at that, cannot allow it to rest, but must needs drag it in upon every occasion. "My Majesty", writes the king, "has seen this thy letter which thou hast sent to inform me that (all is ready?) for the building called 'Beloved-of-Assa,' which is built for the palace of ——. Thou art truly Senezemab (which means 'Rejoicing the Heart'), in rejoicing the heart of Assa." One imagines His Majesty lying back in his chair and chuckling at his own ingenuity. Two lines later the wonderful joke has to come out again in a modified form, and before the letter closes the royal bore has to get it in a third time. "Every vessel in the building", he winds up, "rejoices the heart of Assa." Even Pharaoh, one sees, Son of the Sun as he was, was not free from the frailties of humanity. We can only be thankful that our own failings of a similar kind are not likely to be brought up in judgment against us five thousand years after we are in our graves!

The last Pharaoh of the line of the "Sons of the Sun" was Unas, a king who has become of singular importance, not because of any evidence we possess as to his achievements, for we have little or nothing of this sort, but because he is the first Pharaoh whose tomb contains those religious inscriptions which are known as the "Pyramid Texts", and which have proved of supreme value for the study of early Egyptian beliefs, in which connection they will have to be considered at a later stage. Apparently Unas, like so many of the early Pharaohs, possessed two tombs, one for himself and one for his *Ka*. The secondary tomb is probably the building known as the *Mastabat-el-Faraun*, at the south end of the Saqqara pyramid-field. Though of mastaba form, its arrangements are those of a pyramid, and, indeed, closely resemble those of Unas's personal pyramid. Further, one of the priests of the *manes* of Unas has two steles in his tomb, on one of which he is called "Prophet of the Unas pyramid *Nefer Asut*", which is the name of the Pyramid of Unas, while on the other he is called "Prophet of the Unas pyramid *Asut asuti*". The latter title must therefore seemingly apply to the *Mastabat-el-Faraun*.

The pyramid of Unas, *Nefer asut*, at Saqqara, is of no great importance as a pyramid, for its smallness and poverty of construction afford ample proof that the power of the dynasty and the royal control over the resources of the land were diminishing. Its importance lies in the fact that when it was opened in 1881, at the instance of Maspero, by Emil Brugsch, the walls of its chambers were found to be covered with inscriptions cut in the stone and inlaid with blue paste. Mariette had almost to the end of his life maintained that all the pyramids were devoid of inscriptions, as the great Gizeh group has proved to be; and the return of Brugsch with the information that the Vth Dynasty and VIth Dynasty pyramids were inscribed was practically the last incident of which he was conscious as he lay on his death-bed. The texts, which were first adequately interpreted by Maspero, have since been edited and commented upon by many scholars, among whom Sethe, Breasted, and Speleers may be mentioned. They consist of a long and elaborate ritual for the dead king, by means of which he was supposed to be enabled to protect himself against all the dangers of the Underworld, to overcome the resistance with which he would meet on his way to the abode of the gods in heaven, and finally to reach heaven as greatest among the gods, whom he subjects to his will and his appetite.

There is no need to say more of them at present than

this, that, while the texts present us with a considerable
amount of highly interesting and imaginative conceptions,
couched in language which is by no means devoid of a certain rude poetic fire, they quite obviously represent a state
of thought which is certainly not in keeping with the advanced state of culture to which the Egyptians of the Vth
Dynasty had attained. What we have in them is the
traditional embodiment of a range of thoughts which date
from a very much earlier and ruder state of society; and
therefore, while it is quite true that a set of texts dating
from the Vth Dynasty cannot be said to give an adequate
representation of what the primitive Egyptian beliefs may
have been, it is also true that the Pyramid Texts only
nominally date from such a period. Their real date must
be much earlier, possibly many centuries earlier; and while
their preservation and use in the latter days of the Old
Kingdom is a tribute to the innate conservatism of the
Egyptian mind, it is also a hint that we may never be likely
to get much nearer to the original religious conceptions of
the primitive Egyptian than we do here. Compared with
the date of the beginnings of civilisation in Egypt, the
Pyramid Texts are late; actually they carry us back to a
much more primitive state of things than that which is
represented by the cultured society of the Vth Dynasty, as
can be seen in a moment from a comparison of their wild
savagery with the canny wisdom of Ptah-hetep. It is possible that Unas may have warred in southern Palestine, if
the sculpture on the wall of a tomb at Deshasheh, representing with some vigour a scene of siege in a Semitic land,
belong to his reign. But the stamina of the Vth Dynasty
was obviously failing, and with his death the priestly line
closes, and the throne is occupied by a line of kings whom
Manetho derives from Memphis.

CHAPTER IX

THE SIXTH DYNASTY, AND THE CLOSE OF THE OLD KINGDOM

THE new dynasty which succeeded to that of the Children of the Sun is in some respects one of the most interesting of the many lines of Egyptian Pharaohs. It is true that there are really only two outstanding monarchs, and that the second of these appears to have reigned too long for his own reputation and the good of his country; true, also, that several of the reigns appear to have been quite ephemeral, and have left little mark upon history; while the final collapse of the dynasty leads to what is known as the First Intermediate Dark period—a time of obscurity from which we do not really emerge until the Mentuhoteps of the XIth Dynasty are preparing the way for the vigorous rule of the Senuserts and Amenemhats of the XIIth. But, granting all this, the fact remains that now we begin to get into touch with ampler evidence of royal and national activity, and especially with evidence of the spirit of adventure and curiosity as to the unknown world beyond the bounds of the Nile Valley. There are, indeed, no monuments of any of the VIth Dynasty Pharaohs which can for a moment be compared with the gigantic works of their IVth Dynasty forerunners, or even with the Suntemples of the Vth Dynasty kings; but, on the other hand, there is a greater number of monuments of one kind or another, those which exist are spread over a wider extent of territory, and there is evidence of a wider range of royal authority under the really efficient kings. Above all, during this dynasty we are fortunate enough to meet with a number of private inscriptions which enter into the most interesting details of the work which their authors carried out under the various Pharaohs whom they served, and which strike an intimate personal note which we do not meet again in any Egyptian inscriptions until we come to the autobiographies of the two Aahmes of El-Kab and that of Amenemhab, the faithful captain of Thothmes III. Even the XVIIIth Dynasty reminiscences, vivid as they are, have scarcely the freshness of the records of Herkhuf, Sebni, or Pepinakht, who were giving the world for the first time what may be regarded as the trial pieces of one of its most delightful kinds of literature. There is always a charm, to be found nowhere else, in the first crude essays at what we have come to know as a finished art:

> the season
> Of Art's spring-birth, so dim and dewy;

and this is what the reader finds in the guileless narratives of the Egyptian "Keepers of the Gate of the South". It may be a far cry from Herkhuf to the artless mastery which is the supreme art of Marbot; but Pepy's Warden of the Marches and Napoleon's cavalry captain are kinsmen in an unbroken line of descent. It is work like Herkhuf's which gives to the period of the VIth Dynasty a reality and a charm denied to other periods which may have left us far more imposing memorials. You feel that you are dealing with actual life, not with a series of historical events, and with human beings, not with a chronicler's puppets.

Of Teta, the king who heads the line of the new dynasty, we unfortunately know comparatively little. One would imagine the founder of a new line to be almost necessarily a man of force and perhaps ruthless determination (unless, indeed, he were only the stalking-horse of a faction); but if the mask found by Mr. Quibell near Teta's pyramid-temple is to be accepted as a likeness of the king, he was a man of gentle and sensitive disposition, whose care-worn expression does not suggest that he found his royal dignity a bed of roses. Manetho derives his VIth Dynasty from Memphis, apparently with justice, to this extent, at least, that whereas the main religious interests of the preceding line of kings seem to have been Heliopolitan, those of the VIth Dynasty seem to have been, for a time, at all events, Memphite. Two inscriptions survive, both emanating from High-priests of Ptah at Memphis, which indicate that King Teta interested himself in the organisation of the priesthood of Ptah, and made important changes in the constitution of the priestly college; while an important stele in the British Museum preserves a poem of this age in which the creation of all things visible and invisible is ascribed to the Memphite creator-god:

> Ptah, the great, is the mind and tongue of the gods . . .
> Ptah, from whom proceeded the power
> Of the mind, and of the tongue.
> That which comes forth from every mind,
> And from every mouth:
> Of all gods, of all people, of all cattle, of all reptiles,
> That live, thinking and commanding
> Everything that Ptah wills.

That such a philosophical conception should have been contemporary with the crude savagery and cannibalism of the Pyramid Texts is in itself curious enough, and argues for the Pyramid Texts being the survival into a much more cultured age of a primitive barbarism; but for our present purpose the point of the inscription is its assertion of the supreme position of the Memphite god.

The tomb-inscription of Sabu Ibebi, from his mastaba at Saqqara, tells us that, after having served as High-priest of Ptah under Unas, the last king of the Vth Dynasty, he was "to-day in the presence of the Son of Ra, Teta, living forever, High-priest of Ptah, more honoured by the king than any servant. . . . High-priest of Ptah, cup-bearer of the king, master of the secret things of the king in his every place". Thus the High-priest of Ptah, under the new order, held a place of very close intimacy with the sovereign which he would scarcely have been likely to hold when Heliopolitan influence was supreme. The inscription of another Sabu, Sabu Thety, who was also High-priest of Ptah, obviously in succession to Ibebi, tells us that he held "all the sacred possessions and all duties which two high priests of Ptah did", and that "the temple of 'Ptah-South-of-His-Wall' in its every place was under my charge, although there never was a single High-priest of Ptah before". The inference from the poem, with its assertion of the supremacy of Ptah, and the priestly steles, is that there may have been a reaction against the dominance of Heliopolis, and in favour of the rival god of Memphis. This is supported by the fact that in an inscription on a statue Teta calls himself "Beloved of Ptah".

Teta's pyramid at Saqqara was early rifled by robbers, and, indeed, Petrie believes that it was the one on which they "tried their prentice hands" before proceeding to the more scientific rifling of the other members of the Saqqara group. "They have burnt and broken their way through the granite portcullises, instead of cutting a way over them as elsewhere, and so gained the experience which showed them that it was useless to search thus in other pyramids." It contains a series of Pyramid Texts, of which many passages are identical with those in the pyramid of Unas, though there are variations which are "more religious, and less of a direct ritual". These texts are written in a smaller writing than those of Unas, and the diminution is carried still further in the pyramid of Pepy I. The body of the king had been smashed up by the robbers, and nothing was left but an arm and shoulder. This small fragment is stated to show evidence of hasty and inefficient embalming, and as Manetho records that this king was killed by his guards, this has been viewed as a corroboration of the statement. It seems a somewhat small foundation; but the possibility of the king's murder through some palace intrigue derives more support from the fact that the succeeding reign seems to have been short and undistinguished, as might be expected in the case of that of the puppet of a military mutiny.

To the reign of Teta belongs the beginning of the busy career of Una, a worthy of the Egyptian Civil Service of whom we shall hear more in the future. Una, who was buried at Abydos, has left us there, on the wall of his tomb, what Breasted describes as "the longest narrative inscription, and the most important historical document from the Old Kingdom". His greater distinctions were to be earned in two later reigns, in which he rose at last to be "Count, Governor of the South, chamber-attendant, attached to Nekhen, lord of Nekheb, sole companion". The reign of Teta was the day of small things for this future ornament of the bureaucracy, in which "Lowliness was young Ambition's ladder", on the lowest rungs of which he was just setting his untried feet for the long climb to the topmost round. "I was a child," he says, "who fastened on the girdle (we would say, ' was put into trousers') under the Majesty of Teta; my office was that of supervisor of ——, and I filled the office of inferior custodian of the domain of Pharaoh." There were much more luscious plums, however, awaiting the young supervisor, and we may leave him until he begins to attain them.

For knowledge of the short reign which seems to have intervened between that of Teta and the very important reign of Pepy I., we are indebted to two sources, whose connection with one another is a matter of inference. The Abydos list of kings gives here a king Userkara, of whom nothing is known otherwise. An inscription in the Wady Hammamat records the visit of an official named Ptah-en-kau, who came, with 200 archers and 200 quarrymen, to bring stone for building the pyramid of King Aty, of whom also nothing is known otherwise. As the Hammamat inscription clearly belongs to this time, it is inferred that Userkara and Aty are the two names of the same king, who may be the usurper who ascended the throne after the supposed murder of Teta. How long he may have reigned is quite uncertain, though the probability is that the reign was quite short, possibly not exceeding six years.

Pepy I., who now steps upon the stage on which he is to be the central figure for more than half a century, must be regarded as one of the great Pharaohs. Of the actual events of his reign, we have, indeed, no records comparable with those of the great monarchs of the XVIIIth Dynasty, save for the relative parts of the inscription of Una; but the number of monuments, large and small, the quarry inscriptions, the inscribed vases and other personal relics of the king show that he must have been active and energetic; while the fact that so many of his subjects adopted the royal name in one or other of its forms, and were called either Pepy or Meryra, shows his popularity in his own

PLATE X

COPPER STATUE OF PEPY I

COPPER STATUE OF PRINCE MERENRA

time. A similar phenomenon, on a far greater scale, occurs
in the case of Thothmes III.; and while Pepy's popularity,
judged by this standard, cannot for a moment be compared
with that of the later king, yet when allowance is made for
the difference in time, and the greater expansiveness of
feeling under the XVIIIth Dynasty, the evidence of the
position which Pepy held in the eyes of his subjects is
quite conclusive. He is, indeed, the outstanding king of
his line, more so even than Khufu in the IVth, or Zeser
or Snefru in the IIIrd Dynasty; for while his own son
Pepy II. reigns for nearly twice as long as his father, the
latter half of his reign, at least, must have been disastrous
for his country.

Fortunately, we have a more complete and lifelike
representation of King Pepy as he looked in life than of
almost any of these early kings, with the possible exception
of Khafra and Menkaura, and it may be questioned if the
faithfulness of his great copper statue as a personal rendering of the individual is not greater than that of the more
official portraits of the other two Pharaohs. The statue,
one of the most notable treasures which modern Egyptology has brought to light, was found by Mr. Quibell,
along with a smaller statue in the same metal, in the course
of those excavations at Hierakonpolis, which produced
also the famous statues of Khasekhemui, already mentioned, and the magnificent golden hawk, one of the greatest
artistic works of any period of Egyptian history. The two
statues arc obviously related to one another. It has becn
generally held that, while the larger one is that of King
Pepy, the smaller one, which represents a boy in the usual
costume, or rather lack of costume, of Egyptian childhood,
is that of one of his sons, either Prince Merenra, who
immediately succeeded his father, or Prince Neferkara
(Pepy II.), who succeeded at one remove, after the early
death of his elder half-brother. Sir Flinders Petrie, however, considers both of the statues to be representations
of the king himself, the youthful one being provided so
that his spirit might have the choice of either youth or
maturity when selecting its habitation in the life beyond.

Both statues are splendid specimens of the work of

the early Egyptian artist in metal. Their technique, save for minor variations, is very much that of the somewhat earlier copper statues of bulls and other animals discovered in 1919 at Tell el-Obeid by Dr. H. R. Hall. The bodies are composed of plates of what is either copper or bronze, hammered over a wooden core, to which they were fastened by nails. The heads were cast, though in a somewhat different manner from the Sumerian animal heads, and the eyes are inlaid in obsidian and white limestone. (The eyes of the Obeid bulls were inlaid also, the materials used being red jasper, white shell, and blue schist.) Pepy's head, no doubt, originally wore a golden crown, which has unfortunately disappeared, as was to be expected; and the golden kilt, which he also doubtless wore, has vanished with the crown. Apart from these losses, the figure is complete. The size is somewhat larger than life, as in its present imperfect condition the statue measures about six feet nine inches in height. The face, which in spite of incrustations is wonderfully preserved, is that of a vigorous and good-natured man in the full power of early maturity. Nothing more intimately personal and individual has survived from such ancient times, and the work testifies most conclusively to the artistic genius as well as to the technical skill of the Egyptian sculptor of the time. Those who hold, with the late Mr. March Phillipps, that "all Egyptian faces stare before them with the same blank regard which can be made to mean anything precisely because it means nothing", and that "Egyptian sculpture is a sculpture barren of intellectual insight and intellectual interest", may be advised to consider, among other items, the Pepy statue, after which operation, if they still continue in their heresy, they can only be left in the darkness which they have chosen, "prayers at the same time", as Carlyle once remarked in another connection, "being put up for them in all churches".

From a comparison of this statue with the mask, already alluded to, which is attributed to Teta, Weigall infers that Pepy was the son of the earlier king. The resemblance, however, is by no means so constraining as to amount to proof, especially in view of the fact that the attribution of the mask to Teta is still uncertain. Petrie, on the other hand, apparently believes him to have been the son of the intervening king Aty "as Queen Aput, who was the mother of Pepy I., was not the wife of Teta". The question, however it may be decided, is not of much importance. What is important is the energy evinced during this long reign by temple-building or repairing from end to end of the land. Pepy's actual work has largely disappeared owing to later rebuilding; but from Tanis and Bubastis in the Delta, to Elephantine at the southern limit of Egypt proper, fragments of his work still remain to testify of his zeal and energy; while his rock inscriptions extend as far as Lower Nubia. The chief characteristic of his building activity seems to have been the increased employment of granite as a decorative material for temples, and it is from his time that the famous granite quarries of Aswan begin to show signs of the greater output which henceforth prevailed throughout the historic period. Inscriptions at Hat-nub and in the Wady Hammamat show that the king was exploiting the stores of alabaster and breccia which characterise these two localities; while a fine stele at Wady Maghara in Sinai gives us the name of the commander who had charge of the expedition to that region: "Commission which the commander of the army Ibdu, son of the commander of the troops Merira-ankh carried out".

All the king's power and energy, however, could not save him from domestic trouble. His queen was named Amtes, which, with the fact that he had to bring her before a court specially constituted to try her, is all that we know with regard to her. We are left completely in the dark as to what her crime, if any, may have been. Possibly it may have been nothing more than the fact that she had failed to bear to her lord an heir to the crown. Again, the fact that the king was also married successively, or simultaneously, to two other ladies, who were sisters, and who both bore the same name, Meryra-ankhnes, and that each of these princesses bore a son who came to the throne in after years, may have stirred up the jealousy of Queen Amtes, and induced her to engage in a conspiracy such as made trouble in the harem of Ramses III. many centuries later. We do not know, and probably never shall. Harem troubles have never been lacking in the chequered stories of Oriental courts, such as we are apt to forget an Egyptian court to have been. In any case, the matter was entrusted to that rising young jurist Una, whose account of the affair, which we shall hear directly, is scrupulously discreet. He heard the case alone, and presented a report in writing, drawn up by himself and another judge "attached to Nekhen"; but he tells us nothing as to what his report may have been, whether the queen was acquitted or found guilty, and if the latter, what was her fate. We hear no more of either Queen Amtes or her affair, and it is generally assumed that she must have been found guilty, and that the silence concerning her means that there suddenly ceased to be any more to tell; but the truth is that there is no evidence for such an assumption any more than for the assumption of her acquittal. It is possible that Una would not have mentioned the affair if the queen had been acquitted; but it has always to be remembered that he was writing his tomb-inscription, and the things which an Egyptian would not mention in his tomb-inscription, if they redounded in the least to his glory, are singularly few. On the whole, we must leave poor Queen Amtes with the unsatisfactory Scottish verdict of "Not Proven".

The other two wives of Pepy (that we know of) were, as we have seen, sisters. They were also great ladies, daughters of the "Hereditary prince, count and priest" Khui and his wife Nebet, whose family domains were apparently at Abydos. With such a pull at court as was afforded by the marriage of two of his daughters to the reigning Pharaoh, and the birth of an heir to the throne from each of them, we need not wonder to find that the family of the hereditary prince prospered exceedingly, and that the brother of the two queens, Count Zau, was Chief Justice, Vizier, Master of the Wardrobe, Keeper of the Royal Seal, and half a dozen other high-sounding things in the reign of his little nephew Pepy II. His gratitude to the sisters by whose help he had climbed to greatness is commemorated on a stele found at Abydos, on which the two royal ladies are both named and described as "King's wife, attached to the pyramid called 'Meryra-Remains-Beautiful', very amiable, very favoured, great in possessions, companion of Horus, King's mother". The son of Meryra-ankhnes I. was the short-lived Pharaoh, Merenra; the son of her sister Meryra-ankhnes II. was Pepy II. (Neferkara), who lived to be a hundred or so, and reigned for at least 94 years. It has been conjectured that the first Meryra-ankhnes died soon after the birth of her son Merenra; and this is possible enough; but Egyptian sentiment made nothing of bars of consanguinity which seem prohibitive to us, and there is no reason known to us why Pepy I. may not have been married to both sisters at once, and lived with them both in such domestic felicity or infelicity as this arrangement might be likely to afford.

Pepy's pyramid was built at Saqqara, and was called *Men-nefer*, "The Well-established". It was larger than those of his predecessors Unas and Teta, and, like them, was inscribed with a version of the Pyramid Texts, the writing being still smaller than that in the pyramid of Teta. The chamber of the tomb in which the sarcophagus rested was of very elaborate construction, with no fewer than three roofs made of great stone cantilevers; giving a margin of strength far in excess of what the superincumbent weight demanded. In spite of all precautions, however, the tomb was early broken into, the black basalt sarcophagus destroyed, and the mummy of the great king broken up. "The spiteful destruction of this pyramid", says Petrie, "is far beyond what would be done by treasure-seekers. Every cartouche in the entrance passage is chopped out; and the black basalt sarcophagus has been elaborately wrecked, rows of grooves have been cut in it, and it has been banged to pieces, breaking through even a foot thickness of tough basalt." The vicious spite of all this we may probably ascribe to the end of the dynasty, when not even the memory of Pepy's greatness as a ruler would suffice to protect his tomb against revolutionary fury. The cruel work of the destroyers has, however, done this for our knowledge of the period, that it has left plain the methods of construction used in the erection of the pyramid. It is at once manifest that we have left behind us the days when men built like Titans. Instead of the magnificent blocks of the pyramid of Khufu, the body of the pyramid is built of walls of flakes, filled in with loose chips. The gigantic sincerity of the past was forgotten, and what was aimed at was a good appearance which might conceal poor enough interior work. The Old Kingdom might be still vigorous; but it was going steadily, if slowly, downhill.

Meanwhile the respectable Una has been waiting, with more or less patience, to be summoned again before the curtain to the stage on which he was so admirably qualified to play his part. The beauty of an Egyptian official is that in dealing with him you are never troubled with any of that modesty, mock or otherwise, which is so notoriously characteristic of our own public men. When an Egyptian thinks that he has done well and deserved credit (and he generally thinks so), he has not the least hesitation in telling us so—with emphasis. So with Una, who is the official type *in excelsis*. His narrative of events under Pepy begins with the recital of the steps of his promotion— companion and under-prophet of the king's pyramid-city, judge attached to Nekhen. "I heard (causes)", he says, "being alone with only the chief judge and vizier (one individual, probably Zau, the king's brother-in-law) in every private matter . . . in the name of the king, of the royal harem and of the six courts of justice, because the king loved me more than any official of his, more than any noble of his, more than any servant of his." What Una says three times must be true.

"Then", with a thoroughly Egyptian touch, "I besought the Majesty of the King that there be brought for me a limestone sarcophagus from Turra. The King had the treasurer of the god ferry over, together with a troop of sailors under his hand, in order to bring for me this sarcophagus from Turra; and he arrived with it, in a large ship belonging to the court, together with its lid, the false door, the setting, two . . ., and one offering tablet. Never was the like done for any servant, for I was excellent to the heart of His Majesty, for I was pleasant to the heart of His

Majesty, for His Majesty loved me." Which would be very impressive as to the unique character of Una's favour, if we had not heard others before him saying the same thing, and were not destined to hear others after him repeating it, with scarcely even a change in the wording.

Next came the great legal event of Una's life—the trial of Queen Amtes. "When legal procedure was instituted in private in the harem against the queen Amtes, His Majesty caused me to enter, in order to hear the case alone. No chief judge and vizier at all, no prince at all was there, but only I alone, because I was excellent, because I was pleasant to the heart of His Majesty, because His Majesty loved me. I alone was the one who put it in writing, together with a single judge attached to Nekhen; while my office was only that of superior custodian of the domain of Pharaoh. Never before had one like me heard the secret of the royal harem, except that the King caused me to hear it, because I was more excellent to the heart of His Majesty than any official of his, than any servant of his." Thus Una's record of a great state secret; the only thing to be deplored is that, when he unsealed his lips so far, he did not tell us a little more, instead of leaving us to infer all sorts of things about a poor lady whose only sin may have been one of omission rather than of commission—the failure to bear an heir to the crown.

But even more thrilling events awaited the upright custodian of the royal domain. The essentially unmilitary character of the Egyptian state is nowhere more clearly seen than in the way in which important military expeditions are entrusted to the care of officials whose whole previous training had been of the most pronouncedly civilian type. It was apparently considered that a man who heard cases well in the law courts was thereby qualified to succeed in the command of an army. In due course this Chinese principle was applied to our worthy friend, and Una was appointed commander-in-chief of an Egyptian Expeditionary Force. "His Majesty", says Una, "made war on the Asiatic Sand-dwellers, and His Majesty made an army of many ten thousands in the entire South, southward to Elephantine, and northward to Aphroditopolis; in the Northland on both banks in the stronghold, and among the strongholds among the Aarthet negroes, the Mazoi negroes, the Yam negroes, among the Wawat negroes, among the Kau negroes, and in the land of the Temeh." The native Egyptian, it may be seen, was no fonder of fighting then than he is now, for the personnel of Una's army is almost entirely composed of Sudanese black battalions, and what is not Sudanese appears to be Libyan; not a single native Egyptian corps is mentioned.

The whole business—plan of campaign, transport, commissariat—was left in the hands of this phoenix among officials; and, if we may believe his own statement, there never was such a complete success in the annals of eastern warfare. "I was the one who made for them the plan while my office was only that of superior custodian of the domain of Pharaoh. Not one of the army [quarrelled?] with his neighbour; not one thereof plundered dough or sandals from the wayfarer; not one thereof took bread from any city; not one thereof took any goat from any people. I dispatched them from the Northern Isle, the Gate of Aahotep, the Bend of Horus Nebmaat, Snefru. While I was of this rank [I arranged] everything, I inspected the number of these troops, although never had any servant inspected." So far Una, though doing, as we see, fairly ample justice to his own transcendent merits, has limited his soaring spirit to plain prose, though of the decorated style. Now, when he has to describe his martial feats, he spurns the earth, and bursts into verse, almost with the success of Mr. Silas Wegg:

This army returned in safety, after it had hacked up the land of the Sand-dwellers;
This army returned in safety, after it had destroyed the land of the Sand-dwellers;
This army returned in safety, after it had overturned its strongholds;
This army returned in safety, after it had cut down its figs and its vines;
This army returned in safety, after it had thrown fire in all its troops;
This army returned in safety, after it had slain troops therein in many ten thousands;
This army returned in safety, after it had carried away therefrom a great multitude as living captives.
His Majesty praised me on account of it above everything.

Having found conquest so easy, Pharaoh resolved to repeat the performance; or perhaps it would be nearer the truth to say that so soon as Una's military procession was over, and the Arabs saw the back of the last retiring Sudanese, they reverted to their old ways, so that the work had to be done all over again. As Una had proved so good an organiser, he was called to the command as a matter of course. "His Majesty sent me to dispatch this army five times, in order to traverse the land of the Sand-dwellers at each of their rebellions, with these troops. I did so that His Majesty praised me on account of it." Whether the Sand-dwellers, who so reprehensibly struck back when they were smitten, joined in the praises, and whether the Sudanese battalions behaved quite so much like lambs as Una would have us believe—these are other matters.

Yet more exciting adventures were reserved for this pearl of bureaucrats, and his next expedition was one of the earliest illustrations of the influence of sea-power upon history. The Egyptians, who were never such incompetent sailors as some would have us believe, were swift to appreciate the advantage given to an army by the power of transporting itself to any given point accessible from the sea-board, without the long and dangerous desert marches otherwise necessary; and Una was now called upon by his master to carry out a campaign in which both arms, military and naval, were to act in conjunction. "When it was said there were revolters because of a matter among these barbarians in the land of Gazelle-Nose, I crossed over in troop-ships with these troops, and I voyaged to the back of the height of the ridge on the north of the Sand-dwellers. When this army had been brought into the highway, I came and smote them all, and every revolter among them was slain." The sudden appearance of an army thus transported as if by magic so as to take their defences in the rear must have been a most unpleasant surprise to "the revolters", who, after all, were only defending their own independence; but one wishes that Una had been a little more precise in his geography. Here is the first joint military and naval expedition that history records, and we are left with only the very vaguest indication as to where it all happened. Most authorities have been content to assume that it was merely to the southern highlands of Palestine, or perhaps to the high land at Akaba, due south of the Dead Sea. But as long ago as the time of Snefru, Egypt had interests in northern Palestine and Syria, and was sending fleets to bring back cedar from the Lebanon. The mention of "the back of the height of the ridge on the north of the Sand-dwellers" almost irresistibly suggests a landing in the nook at the back of the ridge of Carmel, and there is no inherent improbability in Dr. Hall's suggestion that Una's expedition was to this point.

With this supreme adventure, on which he was doubtless most unheroically sea-sick, Una's record of service under Pepy closes. We shall meet him again, as diligent as ever, though beginning now to age, under the new king Merenra.

Pepy's elder son, who now succeeded him, was but a youth when he came to the throne, for his father's marriage to the two princesses from Abydos seems to have taken place towards the end of his long reign. His personal name was Mehti-em-saf, "The-God-Mehti-is-his-Protection", which accounts for Manetho's mention of him as "Methusuphis"; but he appears as Merenra in both the Saqqara and Abydos lists. His reign was a very short one, either of four, or at most of seven years, and he died apparently when he had not much more than entered upon his teens. His pyramid was begun, like that of every other Pharaoh, immediately he ascended the throne, and the indefatigable Una, who seems to have been a kind of Admirable Crichton, competent for any kind of task and efficient in all, was employed, as he will tell us directly, in the work of quarrying and transporting the fine stone required for it; but, with all the expedition displayed by him and his fellows, the tomb cannot have been ready much before it was needed. Merenra's body, found in the sepulchral chamber in 1880, is the earliest complete, or nearly complete, body of a Pharaoh which has survived to our times. It had been despoiled of its wrappings by the robbers who had rifled the pyramid; but it was otherwise unharmed, save that the lower jaw of the mummy was wanting. Pathetic evidence is borne by it to the youth of the king, for the side-lock which all Egyptian boys wore until they attained adolescence is still attached to the skull, showing that Merenra was still only a boy at the time of his death.

Apparently the chief preoccupation of his short reign was with the southern frontier of his dominions. Latterly his father had been concerned with northern interests, as we see from the expeditions of Una; but now both official and private records show that attention was once again turned to the south. Una, who had accomplished so much as a mere superior custodian of the royal domain, had been early appointed by the boy king to the more or less ornamental offices of Master of the Footstool of the Palace, and Royal Sandal-bearer; he was now given an office more in accordance with his merits, or his own opinion of them, being made Count and Governor of the whole of Upper Egypt. "When I was Master of the Footstool of the Palace, and Sandal-bearer," he says, "the King of Upper and Lower Egypt, Merenra, my Lord, who lives forever, made me Count and Governor of the South, southward to Elephantine, and northward to Aphroditopolis; for I was excellent to the heart of His Majesty, for I was pleasant to the heart of His Majesty, for His Majesty loved me." "I acted as Governor of the South to his satisfaction," he goes on. ". . . I accomplished all tasks; I numbered everything that belongs to the court in this South twice; all the *corvée* that is due to the court in this South twice. . . . Never before was the like done in this South. I did throughout so that His Majesty praised me for it."

It was not long before the influence of the strong hand of the new governor began to make itself felt in the Border district, where the conditions had formerly been such as to necessitate a strong convoy for any vessels bringing cargoes from Aswan. The improvement is manifest from Una's description of the work which he accomplished in bringing down granite from the Aswan quarries for the queen's tomb. "His Majesty", says the governor, "sent me to Abhat to bring the sarcophagus, 'Chest-of-the-Living', together with its lid and the costly splendid pyramidion for the pyramid, 'Merenra-Shines-and-is-Beautiful', of the queen. His Majesty sent me to Elephantine to bring a false door of granite, together with its offering-tablet, doors and settings of granite; to bring doorways and offering-tablets of granite, belonging to the upper chamber of the pyramid, 'Merenra Shines-and-is-Beautiful', of the queen. Then I sailed downstream to the pyramid, 'Merenra-Shines-and-is-Beautiful', with six cargo boats, three tow-boats, and three . . . boats to only one warship. Never had Abhat and Elephantine been visited in the time of any kings with only one warship." After another expedition to the alabaster quarries at Hatnub, to bring an offering-table, a task which he executed with his customary success, Una was ordered to go south once more to Aswan and dig five canals there, for the purpose of securing a fairway through the First Cataract—a task which may have been undertaken at this time in preparation for the royal visit which immediately followed. The energetic governor accomplished this laborious task in a single year, with the help of the chiefs of the neighbouring negro tribes, whom he seems to have been able to conciliate and interest. His own story of the work may be quoted; it is the last time, unfortunately, that we shall hear the rotund periods of the old man: "His Majesty sent me to dig five canals in the South and to make three cargo boats and four tow boats of acacia wood of Wawat. Then the negro chiefs of Aarthet, Wawat, Yam, and Mazoi drew timber therefor, and I did the whole in only one year. They were launched and laden with very large granite blocks for the pyramid, 'Merenra-Shines-and-is-Beautiful'. I then . . . for the palace in all these five canals, because I honoured, because I . . ., because I praised the fame of the King of Upper and Lower Egypt, Merenra, who lives forever, more than all gods, and because I carried out everything according to the mandate which his *Ka* commanded me."

The digging of the five canals was apparently the last piece of work which fell to the lot of Una as an official. Dr. Hall has suggested that this heavy task, carried out with such rapidity, "probably killed the old man"; but the fact that he closes his story with it does not necessarily imply that he died. He may have lived in retirement under his own vine and fig-tree to a good old age, though he did not serve under any other king; and indeed he need not have been a man of more than sixty at the outside when he retired from public service. He makes his bow of farewell in the usual style: "I was one beloved of his father, and praised of his mother; first-born—pleasant to his brothers, the Count, the real Governor of the South, revered by Osiris, Una." He is a thoroughly typical specimen of the bustling, vigorous, self-satisfied official caste, out of which the Pharaohs contrived to get such an amazing amount of good work. Whether the royal visit for which he had been preparing followed or preceded Una's retirement from office we do not know. One would prefer to imagine that the worthy old gentleman reaped the due reward of honour for his exertions, and was the dry-nurse of his boy-king on so great an occasion as a personal visit of Pharaoh to his frontiers—a task for which he strikes one as admirably fitted. In any case the visit was duly paid, and is commemorated by two inscriptions at the First Cataract. The relief shows Merenra leaning upon his staff, with the god Khnum behind him and the Nubian chiefs before him. His title reads: "King of Upper and Lower Egypt, Merenra, Beloved of Khnum, Lord of the Cataract," and the date is given: "Year 5, second month of the third season, day 28." "The coming of the King himself, appearing behind the hill-country, that he might see that which is in the hill-country, while the chiefs of Mazoi, Aarthet and Wawat did obeisance and gave great praise."

Historians are seemingly determined that this journey to the First Cataract must have proved fatal to somebody. Dr. Hall makes it kill off Una; Mr. Weigall prefers to make it dispose of Merenra himself—"it seems that the fatigues of the journey proved fatal to him". There is, of course, no evidence for such a supposition, save on the principle of *post hoc ergo propter hoc*. It may have been so; quite as likely it may not have been so, and the death of the young king may have been due to quite another cause. Nobody knows or is likely to know; nor does it much matter now either to Merenra or to us. The chief interest of his brief reign lies in the systematic exploration of the south country and development of its trade-routes which is now seen in full operation. Una's work at the First Cataract was probably part of a settled policy of development upon which the young king's councillors had entered, and even in Merenra's time the more or less peaceful penetration of Nubia was being diligently carried on. The chief agent of the work was Herkhuf, one of the barons of Elephantine whose tombs, seventeen in number, are still to be seen in the rocks opposite the island. Already, before the death of Merenra, this active servant of the crown had made three journeys into the interior; but the consideration of his record will be more conveniently postponed until we have to deal with the expedition under Pepy II., which evidently formed, in his own opinion, the crowning glory of his life.

Merenra was succeeded by his half-brother and cousin, Neferkara, or Pepy II., to give him the name by which he is more generally known. The new king, so Manetho tells us, was a boy of six when he came to the throne, and this fact is vouched for by the double consideration of his brother's youth at death, and the extraordinary duration of his own reign. Manetho states that he "reigned till he had completed his hundredth year", which would give him a reign of 94 years. Eratosthenes, however, tells us that he "is said to have reigned 100 years, with the exception of one hour"—a precision of statement for which we could not be too grateful, if we could only believe that it meant anything real. In any case his reign is one before which all other records of length seem paltry and insignificant, and the only similarity between them and this colossal example of longevity upon the throne is that it seems to have been as disastrous towards its close as other unduly long reigns have usually been.

The beginning of the reign, however, was marked by none of the disturbances which have always been common in the East under such conditions; perhaps because the chief authority in the kingdom was Zau, who besides being vizier and chief justice, was brother to both of the queens dowager, and was not likely to see his sisters' rights interfered with if he could prevent it. Seemingly the young king's mother acted at first as the figure-head and visible emblem of royal authority in the state; for in the inscription at the Wady Maghara which commemorates an expedition to the mines, the king, though mentioned by name, does not appear in the relief, while his mother does. Her titulary here emphasises her connection both with the reigning monarch, as his mother, and with Pepy I., his father: "King's mother, attached to the pyramid, 'Nefer-kara-remains-Living', King's wife, his beloved, attached to the pyramid, 'Meryra-remains-Beautiful', Ankhnes-meryra, whom all the gods love."

The policy of the exploitation of the south which had been in progress during the preceding reign went on unchanged; and the great event of the opening years of Pepy's long reign was the fourth expedition of Herkhuf to the Southland. He was already familiar with the work, and indeed bears as one of his proudest distinctions the title of "Caravan-conductor". The story of his various adventures as an explorer is told by himself so concisely and with such freshness in the inscription on his tomb, that it will be best to let him speak for himself. He begins with the usual recital of his honours and dignities, which is only conspicuous by reason of the prominence with which his connection with the south is emphasised: "Count, sole companion, ritual priest, chamber-attendant, judge attached to Nekhen, lord of Nekheb, wearer of the royal seal, caravan-conductor, privy councillor of all affairs of the South, favourite of his lord, Herkhuf, who brings the products of all the countries to his lord, who brings the tribute of the royal ornaments, governor of all countries of the South, who sets the terror of Horus among the countries, who does that which his lord praises . . . the revered by Ptah-Sokar, Herkhuf."

The three earlier journeys which he had made under Merenra are then described: "The Majesty of Merenra my Lord sent me, together with my father, the sole companion and ritual priest Iri, to Yam, in order to explore a road to this country. I did it in only seven months, and I brought all kinds of gifts from it. . . . I was greatly praised for it. His Majesty sent me a second time alone; I went forth upon the Elephantine road, and I descended from Aarthet, Mekher, Tereres, Aarthet, being an affair of eight months. When I descended, I brought gifts from this country in very great quantity. Never before was the like brought to this land. I descended from the dwelling of the chief of Sethu and Aarthet after I had explored these countries. Never had any companion or caravan-conductor who went forth to Yam before this, done it." The last statement, of course, is only the statutory declaration which every Egyptian official deems it necessary to make about his own exploits, and is by no means to be taken as literally true. As we shall see, there were other caravan-conductors in Herkhuf's own time who were doing much the same kind of work, and saying the same thing about it.

His next journey, however, was a more adventurous and eventful one, and he describes it in greater detail: "His Majesty now sent me a third time to Yam; I went forth from —— upon the Uhet road, and I found the chief of Yam going to the land of Temeh to smite Temeh as far as the western corner of heaven. I went forth after him to the land of Temeh, and I pacified him, until he praised all the gods for the king's sake. . . . Now when I had pacified that chief of Yam—below Aarthet and above Sethu, I found the chief of Aarthet, Sethu, and Wawat—I descended with 300 asses laden with incense, ebony, *heknu*, grain, panthers, ivory, throw-sticks, and every good product. Now when the chief of Aarthet, Sethu, and Wawat saw how strong and numerous was the troop of Yam which descended with me to the court, and the soldiers who had been sent with me, then this chief brought and gave to me bulls and small cattle, and conducted me to the road of the highlands of Aarthet, because I was more excellent, vigilant, and —— than any count, companion or caravan-conductor, who had been sent to Yam before. Now when the servant there (my modest self) was descending to the court, One (Pharaoh) sent the sole companion, the Master of the Bath,

PLATE XI

OLD KINGDOM RELIEFS. TOMB OF TIY (*Chapter X.*)

Huni, upstream with a vessel laden with date-wine, cakes, bread and beer." The sending of one of the courtiers to meet the returning expedition may have been either a delicate attention on the part of the king to his weary servant or the expression of a fear lest the expedition should have run out of supplies.

The fourth expedition, which was carried through in the second year of the little king Pepy II, was destined to bring the crowning glory of Herkhuf's adventurous life. He had apparently pushed far enough south through Nubia to come into contact with the pigmy races of Central Africa, and had succeeded in either capturing one of the little men, or inducing him to accompany the caravan north to the Egyptian court. Probably either capture or purchase is the explanation of the matter, having regard to the nature of the pigmy race. For some reason or other, the Egyptians in all ages attached the greatest value to these dwarfs as ornaments of the court, and were highly delighted by the acquisition of a specimen of the race. Add to this the excitement of a boy of eight, who was none the less a boy, though he lived forty-six centuries ago and was called Pharaoh, at the prospect of a new living toy to play with, and Pepy's delightful letter to his daring servant is the most natural thing in the world. Herkhuf was so proud of it that he decided, fortunately for us, to have it inscribed verbatim on his tomb; and so it has come down to us, one of the earliest documents concerning African exploration, and a real bit of human nature out of the dead past, telling us of the unchanging element in the "soaring human boy" of all time.

No apology is needed for presenting in full this most charming of ancient documents. It begins very regally: "Royal seal, year 2, third month of the first season, day 15. (His Majesty being of the mature age of eight.) Royal decree to the sole companion, the ritual priest and caravan-conductor, Herkhuf.

"I have noted the matter of this thy letter, which thou hast sent to the King, to the palace, in order that One (The Egyptian royal We) might know that thou hast descended in safety from Yam with the army which was with thee.

Thou hast said in this thy letter, that thou hast brought all great and beautiful gifts, which Hathor, Mistress of Aamu, hath given to the *Ka* of the King of Upper and Lower Egypt, Neferkara, who liveth forever and ever. Thou hast said in this thy letter, that thou hast brought a dancing dwarf of the god from the land of spirits, like the dwarf which the treasurer of the god Baurded brought from Punt in the time of Assa. Thou hast said to My Majesty: 'Never before has one like him been brought by any other who has visited Yam.'

"Each year (finds) thee doing that which thy Lord desires and praises; thou spendest day and night in doing that which thy Lord desires, praises and commands. His Majesty will make thy many excellent honours to be an ornament for the son of thy son forever, so that all people will say when they hear what My Majesty doeth for thee: Is there anything like this which was done for the sole companion, Herkhuf, when he descended from Yam, because of the vigilance which he showed, to do that which his Lord desired, praised and commanded!

"Come northward to the court immediately; thou shalt bring this dwarf with thee, which thou bringest living, prosperous and healthy from the land of spirits, for the dances of the god, to rejoice and gladden the heart of the King of Upper and Lower Egypt, Neferkara, who lives forever. When he goes down with thee into the vessel, appoint excellent people who shall be beside him on each side of the vessel; take care lest he fall into the water. When he sleeps at night, appoint excellent people, who shall sleep beside him in his tent; inspect ten times a night. My Majesty desires to see this dwarf more than the gifts of Sinai and of Punt. If thou arrivest at court, this dwarf being with thee, alive, prosperous and healthy, My Majesty will do for thee a greater thing than that which was done for the treasurer of the god Baurded, in the time of Assa, according to the desire of the heart of My Majesty to see this dwarf. Commands have been sent to the chief of the New Towns, the companion and superior prophet, to command that supplies may be requisitioned from him in every store-city and every temple, without stinting therein."

The past has not often spoken to us with a voice so authentically personal as that which speaks in every line of this ancient letter, where the boyish eagerness of the eight-year-old Pharaoh breaks irrepressibly through the stilted forms of court etiquette. Simple as the subject matter may be, this inscription from Herkhuf's tomb is of far more real importance than five out of every ten of the pompous rigmaroles in which Pharaoh after Pharaoh repeats the story of exaggerated, and sometimes mythical conquests. One does not wonder, even apart from the divinity which hedged a king in Egyptian eyes, that Herkhuf was proud of Pepy's letter; royalty has not often praised a subject so manifestly "out of the abundance of the heart".

The story of the long reign of Pepy is virtually that of the foreign expeditions, which, at least in the earlier part of the reign, are characteristic of this period. It was obviously a time when the Egyptian genius was quickening, and reaching out with a new spirit of curiosity to all the lands around. Two of the other inscriptions of the barons of Elephantine, dating from this time, are of a double interest, not only as revealing the amount of activity in exploration which was shown in spite of danger and the occasional cutting off of a pioneering party, but also because they disclose, quite incidentally, the fundamental attitude of the Egyptian mind towards death and the disposal of the dead. Exploration may be important; but it is still more important to bring home, at all costs, the dead bodies of the explorers who have met their death in the service, that they may not have their chance of immortality prejudiced by lack of proper interment, but may be buried in their native land with all due ritual. To attain this end, a special expedition will be sent out, if necessary; and the leader who succeeds in bringing back the body of a dead explorer is praised for that, and not for the nine-foot elephant tusks that he had succeeded in bringing back along with the dead man. Strange to say, in ancient Egypt piety went before profit.

The first of these inscriptions is that of Pepinakht, who was a high official, holding the usual number of pluralities which an Egyptian courtier accumulated, and was also able to call himself "Governor of Foreign Countries," whatever that may mean, but who was not "Governor of the South"—an office which was held, first by Herkhuf, then by Sebni, whom we shall meet directly, and finally by Ibi, in this reign. Evidently Wawat and Aarthet (*i.e.* Nubia) were not always so peaceful as when Herkhuf had the handling of them, for Pepinakht's first statement, after the usual recital of his titles, tells us of a punitive expedition. "The Majesty of my Lord sent me to hack up Wawat and Aarthet. I did so that my Lord praised me. I slew a great number there, consisting of chiefs' children and excellent commanders. I brought a great number of them to the court as living prisoners, while I was at the head of many mighty soldiers as a hero. The heart of my Lord was satisfied with me in every commission with which he sent me."

Things had not gone so well, however, with some other commanders. One of these, Enenkhet, had been sent with a command to the Red Sea coast, there to build a ship, and sail to the land of Punt which the Egyptians always looked to as a semi-divine land, and the source of their own nationality. While busy with his ship-building, Enenkhet had seemingly failed in vigilance, and he and his expedition had been surprised and cut off by the local Arabs, then, as now, fierce and untrustworthy. This truculence had to be punished; but above all, the bodies of Enenkhet and his men had to be brought back to Egypt; so Pepinakht was sent out again. "Now the Majesty of my Lord sent me to the country of the Asiatics to bring for him the sole companion, commander of the sailors, the caravan-conductor, Enenkhet, who was building a ship there for Punt, when the Asiatics of the Sand-dwellers slew him, together with a troop of the army which was with him. . . ." From this point the record is unfortunately imperfect, and all that we can gather is that the task was carried out: "I slew people among them, I and the troop of the army which was with me."

The task which fell to the third of the Aswan barons, Sebni, was of the same character, save that the unfortunate commander whose body he had to rescue from the

negro tribes was his own father. His inscription is mutilated
at the beginning, and the story opens abruptly with Sebni's
receipt of the news of his father's murder. The work of
caravan-conducting was evidently a hereditary business
among these energetic border magnates, and fathers
trained their sons in it, as we have already seen in the
case of Herkhuf, and themselves stuck to their task, even
after their sons were mature and skilful leaders. Mekhu,
Sebni's father, had made his last journey, and had perished
somewhere in the heart of Africa. "Then came the ship
captain, Antef, and the overseer of the (probably the black
troops of Mekhu's party) to give information that the sole
companion and ritual priest Mekhu was dead. Then I took
a troop of my estate (one remembers Abraham's 318 servants born in his house and trained to arms; these Aswan
lords evidently kept little local armies of retainers) and 100
asses with me, bearing ointment, honey, clothing, oil, and a
variety of garments, in order to make presents in these
countries, and I went out to the countries of the negroes."

One of the things that we learn incidentally from Sebni's
story is that it was necessary for a great border lord to send
word of his movements to Pharaoh before he started on any
expedition; and this Sebni now proceeds to do. "Then I
sent people who were in the Gate (some of the garrison of
the frontier, 'the Gate of the South'), and I made letters to
give information that I had gone out to bring this my
father, from Wawat and Aarthet. I pacified these countries
(and I found my father's body) in the countries of ——
the name of which is Mether. I loaded the body of this
sole companion upon an ass, and I had him carried by the
troop of my own estate. I made for him a coffin which was
prepared in order to bring him out of these countries.
Never did I send for help or ask a negro convoy. I was
greatly praised on account of this."

While the necessarily slow and melancholy journey
northward was dragging on, it was necessary to hasten pre-
parations for the embalmment and final interment of Mekhu; so, as soon as the comparatively civilised Wawat was
reached, an advance party was sent forward, and Sebni,
who like a prudent man had not failed to attend to busi-

ness as well as to filial piety on his journey, sent with it samples of the ivory and other treasures which he had gathered. "I descended to Wawat and Uthek, and I sent the royal attendant Iri, with two people of my estate, as messengers, bearing incense, clothing, and ivory 3 cubits long, one tusk, in order to give information that my best tusk was 6 cubits long; and that I had brought this my father and all kinds of gifts from these countries. When I descended in person from the Bend (the great bend of the Nile between Abu Hamed and Korosko) to give information, behold Iri came from the court as I came, to embalm the count, wearer of the royal seal, sole companion, ritual priest, this Mekhu. He brought embalmers, the chief ritual priest and other funeral priests, the mourners and all offerings of the White House (The Palace). He brought festival oil from the Double White House and secret things from the double House of Purity, linen from the Double White House, and all the burial equipment which is issued from the court, like that which was issued for the burial of the hereditary prince Meru.

"Now when this Iri arrived, he brought to me a message to praise me on account of what I had done. It was said in this message, 'I will do for thee every excellent thing, as a reward for this great deed, because of bringing thy father. Never has the like happened before.' I buried this my father in his tomb of the necropolis; never was one of his rank so buried before. I went north to Memphis, bearing the gifts which this count (poor Mekhu) had collected. I deposited before my army and the negroes every gift which my father had gathered. The servant there (I myself) was praised at the court, and the servant there gave praise to the king, because the servant there was so greatly favoured by the king. There was given to me a chest of carob wood containing vessels of ointment; there was given to me clothing; there was given to me 'the Gold of Praise' (The Egyptian equivalent to the D.S.O.); there were given to me rations, meat and fowl. There were given to me thirty *stat* of land in the North and Southland from the royal domain of the pyramid 'Neferkara-Remains-Alive', in order to honour the servant there."

One of the quaintest and most interesting records of Pepy's interminable reign is afforded by the inscriptions of the house of that Prince Zau, who, as we have seen, was the brother of the two princesses, both named Meryra-ankhnes, whom Pepy I. married. Zau himself was Pepy II.'s prime minister during part of the reign, and he left a son who, though he did not attain to the viziership, held high local rank, being first nomarch of the Cerastes Mountain nome, and then also of the Thinite nome. Finally he was appointed Governor of the South, possibly in succession to our friend Sebni. His tomb inscription tells us the usual story of his virtues—how he gave bread to the hungry and clothing to the naked. This is merely common form, of course, and would be claimed as boldly by the cruellest tyrant as by the most beneficent of rulers. Where Ibi displays real interest is in the thing that most interested every Egyptian—the uninterrupted tenancy of his tomb after death. The formula which he uses in this connection is worth quoting, though it is common enough, as an example of the national attitude of mind, and also the national pre-dilection for appropriating other people's tombs and funer-ary equipment: "The real governor of the South, Ibi; he saith; 'As for any people who shall enter into this tomb as their mortuary property, I will pounce upon them like wild-fowl; for I am an excellent equipped soul, I know every charm, and the secrets of the court which is in the nether world'."

Ibi left a son Zau-Shemai, who apparently died at a comparatively early age, as no records of his accomplish-ments are left to us. His son, another Zau, however, suc-ceeded to the family dignities, having made special peti-tion to Pharaoh in the matter, doubtless on account of his father's early death. He tells us the usual tale of the un-paralleled magnificence with which he buried his father: "I buried my father, the count Zau (Shemai) beyond the splendour of any equal of his who was in this South. I re-quested as an honour from the Majesty of my Lord, the King of Upper and Lower Egypt, Neferkara, who lives forever, that there be taken a coffin, clothing, and festival perfume for this Zau. His Majesty caused that the custodian of the royal domain should bring a coffin of wood, festival perfume, oil, linen, two hundred pieces of choice linen and of fine southern linen, taken from the Double White House of the court for this Zau. Never had it been done for another of his rank."

So far, Zau the younger says nothing but what every noble felt it to be necessary to say, without expecting, probably, that anybody would believe in the unique splendour of the funeral arrangements. But now comes an utterance of his very heart, in which he combines in the most curious manner a really pathetic expression of love for his dead father with the most unblushing and even ludicrous snobbery. Love made the worthy man sacrifice his own desire for a fine tomb for himself, and give directions that he should be buried in the same tomb with his father; but it would never do, he felt, to leave future generations to imagine that he did this because of motives of economy. He could never rest in peace if he thought that people believed that he had been too hard up to afford two tombs. So we have the following, which is certainly unique among Egyptian inscriptions of its kind, and would be hard to match anywhere: "Now I caused that I should be buried in the same tomb with this Zau, in order that I might be with him in one place; not, however, because I was not in a position to make a second tomb; but I did this in order that I might see this Zau every day, in order that I might be with him in one place." If he has any knowledge of events on this world, Zau must surely be more than gratified at the success of his little apologia; more people than he ever dreamt of know to-day that the "great lord of the nome of Cerastes-Mountain" was able to afford as many tombs as he wanted, but preferred to share one with his father for the love which he bore to him. But perhaps his point of view has changed a little by this time!

The most ironic of commentaries on all these elaborate funerary arrangements which the originators of them fondly imagined eternal is furnished by an inscription which Petrie found in the temple of Osiris at Abydos, and curiously it relates to this very same great family of the Zaus. The great Prince Zau, vizier and king's brother-in-law, had apparently set up statues of Pepy II., of himself, and of his two sisters, the queens of Pepy I., in the temple at Abydos, and, as was customary in such a case, had provided an endowment to secure offerings of milk and meat to each of the statues on festival days. The inscription, which is of a king whose name has unfortunately been destroyed, but who must have reigned not long after Pepy II., catalogues the statues and describes the amount of meat and milk provided for, and then continues: "The divine servants of their several endowment estates are discharged from this duty. . . . I have not granted that the royal larder provide (?) these things . . . to the extent of eternity." Testators' dispositions, no matter how firmly sanctioned, have still a knack of ending in ways which their originators never contemplated. This Abydos decree shows us that the uncertainty attaching to such things is an old one. The old prime minister's wrath, had he been able to realise the fate of his testamentary arrangements, would doubtless have been terrible; but probably the unknown king felt that he was pretty safe, for the line of the Zaus seemingly became extinct with the pious son who shared his father's tomb.

Apart from these records of the great nobles, we have next to nothing from the 94 years of Pepy II. It is curious to think of the bright boyishness of his early days, witnessed to by his letter to Herkhuf, and to compare it with the long, dragging, dreary years that came after. All the men who made the reign famous must have gone long before the old man finally dropped into his grave; and no doubt Pepy was as weary of his royalty as his subjects apparently were of him. The great barons of Elephantine, with their troops of retainers, were doubtless only examples of the kind of thing which was growing up over all the kingdom; and the very enterprise which had been encouraged in them during the early and energetic part of the reign would go to seed and breed anarchy when it was no longer employed upon useful objects. Pepy was certainly succeeded by another Pharaoh, Merenra Mehtiemsaf; but nothing is known of his reign, which according to Manetho lasted only for one year. Manetho tells us also that he was succeeded by a queen, Nitokris, "who was the most handsome woman of her time, of a fair complexion; she built the third pyramid, and reigned 12 years". This story of Nitokris is obviously confused to a degree, and especially in the attribution of the Third Pyramid to her; but the probability is that there was a Nitokris at this time, and that the confusion about the pyramid arises from the resemblance of her other name, Menkara, with that of the actual builder of the pyramid, Menkaura of the IVth Dynasty.

Herodotus tells us a story of how the brother of Nitokris had been murdered, and how she avenged herself upon his murderers by inviting them to the feast at the consecration of a great underground chamber which she had prepared, and then letting the Nile in upon them. He adds that she then threw herself into a room full of ashes, and so died. The story as it stands is quite too romantic and fanciful for truth; but it is by no means impossible that behind it there may lie a grain of truth about the troubled close of the VIth Dynasty, which may well enough have ended with the assassination of the reigning Pharaoh, and with a furious revenge on the part of his queen, who may, as was common enough, have been his sister, and with whom the title to the throne would rest.

One way or another, the VIth Dynasty collapsed, and before Egypt for generations there lay a time of obscurity and misery, when there was no manifest and supreme authority in the land, and when "every man did what was right in his own eyes". This period is known as the First Intermediate Dark period.

CHAPTER X

THE OLD KINGDOM; SOCIAL ORGANISATION, LITERATURE AND ART

THE period of time which elapsed between the unification of Egypt under the Scorpion, Narmer, and Aha-Mena, is usually estimated at about one thousand years (Petrie's estimate is about fifteen hundred). It may be questioned if ever in the world's history there has been a millennium fraught with more important developments, or richer in examples of man's gradual achievement of mastery over the material elements in the midst of which his life is cast. To take only a single instance, it was during this period that one of the two great methods of government by which the civilised communities of the ancient world came, practically universally, to be ruled reached its full development in Egypt. Kingship was, indeed, an old thing in Egypt, and the organisation of a court, with all its offices and formalities, had already begun to crystallise upon a fixed pattern, long before the rise of the united kingdom under the founders of the Ist Dynasty; but the principle of a single kingdom, catching up in its sweep all the powers of the half-dozen of little kingships within its bounds, and unifying all the energies of the land from the First Cataract to the sea, was established and vindicated as a satisfactory working principle during the period of the Old Kingdom from Mena to Pepy II. The world was to owe its first conception of a true kingdom, as opposed to a congeries of small states, to Egypt's experiment in unity. Meanwhile, during the same period, Babylonia, under its Sumerian rulers, was working out its solution of the problem from another angle, and producing the first examples of the city-states which have done so much for human advancement. The two ideals were destined to produce widely different results, and, while the Egyptian ideal may be said to have triumphed in the end, it would be hard to say whether its rival may not have done quite as much for the uplift of the race. If the one path led to the Roman Empire, the other led to Athens; both tracks were pioneered and well marked out before the Old Kingdom fell.

At the head of the whole complicated organism of the Egyptian state stood the Pharaoh. The very title by which he is universally known shows something of the awe and reverence which attached to one who was felt to be divine (the "Good God", as distinguished from "the Great Gods") even during his life, and still more so after his death. For Pharaoh is "Per-o", "The Great House"—a circumlocution to express a person who must not be named, save with due reverence. The term which was generally used to express royalty was the impersonal "One", while modesty forbade the subject to mention himself personally in connection with a mention of his king. Thus Herkhuf tells us that "when the servant there (himself) was descending to the court, One (Pharaoh) sent the sole companion, etc." At the same time, the Pharaoh was by no means the irresponsible despot often pictured, and perhaps realised in such monarchies of the ancient East as that of Assyria. His power was doubtless very great, both from a secular and a religious point of view; but it was by no means unlimited. Indeed, the very conditions under which the united kingdom had been formed, coupled with the innate conservatism of the Egyptian race, imposed upon him restrictions which are reflected in his royal titles, and had their repercussion in the practical affairs of government. Pharaoh was not only king of Egypt, but of a land which had once been half a dozen of separate kingdoms; and this fact he was never allowed for one moment to forget. If he was Hawk-king, in virtue of his southern royalty of Hierakonpolis, he was not less Bee-king in virtue of his northern royalty of Sais; and again, if his emblem was the Bee, it was not less the Reed of his kingship of Ehininsi, so that all down through the dynasties he is Insi-Bya, the Reed-Bee-man. His state-crown was "The Double Crown" a combination of the Red Doge's cap of Lower Egypt with the White Mitre of Upper Egypt; and the Vulture of Nekheb reared herself upon his brow side by side with the Cobra of Buto in the Delta. We may be sure that when the outward emblems of the old rights and privileges of the ancient states continued to be honoured as they were, the states were quite as insistent upon the royal observance of their rights and privileges in practice, and asserted their right to be governed according to their ancient customs. There was thus, from the beginning, a constitutional check upon the irresponsible caprice of the king.

Further, it is difficult to see how a Pharaoh of Egypt can have found the time to be the self-indulgent and self-willed despot who is generally regarded as the typical Eastern king. Though his high-priesthood of all forms of worship throughout his kingdom may have been largely nominal, and was often delegated, even in the case of the greater gods, to his sons, there was a regular daily ritual of religion which it was necessary that he should carry through in person; and if the statements which have survived of his provision for the needs of his officials in the other world are representative of general practice, he must have had a considerable burden of business to carry through from this point alone. All tomb - endowments throughout Egyptian history are "an offering which the king gives"; and while this becomes merely a formula, there can be no doubt that his supreme priesthood, both of the living and the dead, must have entailed a vast amount of often irksome ritual detail.

But his religious duties were only a fraction of his work. The early sculptures to which reference has already been made show that he was expected to look after the material welfare of his land by personal encouragement of public works such as irrigation canals, and the records show that even a king like Merenra, who was no more than a boy, was expected to show himself in person at the frontiers of his kingdom in order to confirm Egyptian authority there. The passages which have already been quoted from the tomb-inscriptions of Weshptah, of Una, and of Herkhuf, show that royal interest in and super-vision of the work of public officials was much more than nominal. If the king was head of the priesthood, he was no less head of the army. On every sculpture which records a warlike triumph, from the Narmer palette onwards, it is the king who is represented as personally smiting down the enemy with his mace; and while this also becomes merely a formula, so far as sculpture is concerned, and is repeated almost without a line of variation for thirty cen-turies, it was much more than a formula in actual fact. If Seqenenra fell under three ghastly wounds in the XVIIth Dynasty, if Thothmes III. was first man of his army through the pass of Aaruna in the XVIIIth, and Ramses II. fought hand to hand with the Hittite chariotry at Kadesh in the XIXth, we may be sure that in the more primitive days of the Old Kingdom the royal leadership of the army was a very active reality.

At a late stage of the history it is said of the Pharaoh: "He could not do any public business, condemn or punish any man to gratify his own humour or revenge, or for any other unjust cause; but was bound to do according as the laws had ordered in every particular case." That this statement is no mere fancy picture is proved by the utter-ance of Ramses III. when appointing the special commis-sion to investigate into the harem conspiracy of his reign: "What the people have said, I do not know. Hasten to investigate it. You will go and question them, and those who must die, you will cause to die by their own hand, without my knowing anything of it." This is not the language of the typical Oriental tyrant, but that of a constitutional monarch who realises that the legal arrange-ments of his realm are quite adequate to deal even with an offence against his own person without any need of his interference; and that such an attitude dates back to a very early point of Egyptian history we see from Una's statement about the trial of Queen Amtes in the reign of Pepy I. Whatever the offence of Amtes may have been, it was dealt with strictly in the course of legal procedure, and the king, though the person most directly concerned, took no part in the matter, though he may have had to give sentence in accordance with the finding of the court.

Thus it appears that the position of a Pharaoh of Egypt came much nearer, in some respects, to that of a constitutional monarch than to that of a despotic ruler. In a land so devoted to tradition, everything was ruled by precedent, and there was a precedent for every occasion. Pharaoh, however imposing his royal dignity, was pretty much tied hand and foot by the law, written or unwritten, of the past; and while he had a good deal of initiative in such matters as public works, or the appointment of officials, he had always to exercise his undoubtedly large powers within established limits. As a recompense for this limitation of his powers, he was surrounded with an inordinate amount of deference. Whether his subjects actually took his divinity as seriously as he appears to have taken it himself, or as they appear to take it in the utterances which have come down to us, we have no means of ascertaining. Certainly they were in the habit of according to him the most slavish signs of reverence and adoration. Every subject, no matter how high his official position, was expected to prostrate himself on entering the presence, to "place himself on his belly", or to "smell the ground"; and only in exceptional circumstances was this ceremony modified to a slight extent. Thus our dear friend Ptah-shepses, who was not only brought up with the king's children, but was also married to the king's daughter, records, as an instance of extreme favour, that "when His Majesty praised him for a thing, His Majesty permitted that he should kiss his foot, and His Majesty did not permit that he should kiss the ground".

The extreme deference thus paid to the king during life was followed up by the worship of him after death—a worship which, as in the case of Khufu, the builder of the Great Pyramid, was maintained from the IVth right down to the XXVIth Dynasty, considerably more than 2000 years. Devotion was shown in a grimmer and more barbaric way during the earlier stages of the Old Kingdom by the immolation of a number of courtiers and women of the royal harem at the king's grave, in order that His

Majesty might not lack for company of his most faithful
servants, and the ladies in whom he took most delight, on
his journey through the Underworld. Such a custom
seems almost too barbarous to be accepted as having
formed part of the practice of so advanced and kindly a
race as the Egyptian; but the evidence is too strong to
be resisted. Writing of the courtiers' tombs of the Ist
Dynasty, Petrie says: "The large squares of graves of royal
servants, cleared in 1922, show that in some instances they
were conscious when buried. They seem to have been
stunned—perhaps by sand-bagging—and thrown directly
into the grave and buried." Barbaric as the custom seems
and is, it lasted in Egypt and its dependencies down to the
period of the Middle Kingdom, when Hepzefa of Siut was
buried far south in Ethiopian Kerma, with 300 slaughtered
Nubians lying around him to serve him in the Underworld, and when the ladies of the harem of Mentuhotep
Neb-hapet-Ra were apparently sacrificed at the tomb of
their lord to bear him company in the spirit world. That
the living king's relationships with his servants were, however, more kindly than a custom so barbarous would lead
us to anticipate, is manifest from the incident of the sudden
sickness and death of Weshptah, already narrated, when
the anxious solicitude of the Pharaoh for his faithful vizier
and architect is pictured to us as very human and even
pathetic.

Beneath the king, the most important man in the kingdom was, of course, the vizier. In these early days he was
required to be a man of many talents and a versatile mind,
for the duties which he was expected to perform were very
various, and his competence in them was not in the least a
nominal thing. Thus in the case of Weshptah, just mentioned, we have a vizier who was also chief judge and chief
architect. The judgeship might be a position requiring
nothing more than the exercise of enlightened common-
sense and the capacity to administer a code of already
long-established laws; but the chief architectship inferred
technical knowledge of a high order, in view of the exacting
requirements of an Egyptian king, and that the position
was no sinecure is shown by the death of Weshptah in the

PLATE XII

OLD KINGDOM SCULPTURE.   STATUES OF RAHOTEP AND NEFERT

actual discharge of its duties. Imhotep, the typical wise man and king's right hand of the Old Kingdom, sets the standard of a versatility which was apparently looked for as a natural thing in the holder of the vizier's office; and right down through the history of the land the first subject of the realm was still expected, in spite of the minute sub-division of the bureaucracy, to be able to turn his hand to almost anything, from the general superintendence of the kingdom to the minutiae of the direction of Nile traffic.

A typical example of the multitude of offices which might be held by the vizier of the period is given by the list of his titles which the great local magnate, Prince Zau, whose two sisters were both queens of Pepy I., inscribes upon the stele of the two queens at Abydos. He is "Real hereditary prince, count and governor of the pyramid-city, chief justice and vizier, overseer of the king's records, prophet of the gods of Buto, prophet of the gods of Nekhen, chief ritual priest, sem-priest and master of all wardrobes, wearer of the royal seal, judge—revered by the god, Zau". At an early stage of the kingdom, the ex-pansion of its frontiers southward necessitated the ap-pointment of a "Governor of the South", an office which was held by our friend Una at a curiously late stage of his official career, and also by Sebni of Elephantine.

The development of the court was extraordinary, and had reached an advanced stage at a very early date in the dynastic history. Already on the great palette of Narmer the royal sandal-bearer appears behind his master, and so great a man as Una records his holding of the office, immediately before his appointment as Governor of the South, with great pride: "While I was master of the foot-stool and sandal-bearer, His Majesty praised me for the watchfulness and vigilance which I showed in the place of audience." The tomb of Queen Merneit of the Ist Dynasty gives us the "Royal Sealer of the Wine", and from that of Semti come six different seals of "Superintendent of the Inundation". In Semti's reign also we learn the name of the Chancellor and Viceroy of the North, Hemaka, evi-dently the most important man of the reign. Later in the same dynasty, come the First Peer, the Royal

Constructor, the Follower of the King, and the Master of Ceremonies. But besides these officials, who evidently had some important function to discharge, we have a multitude of minor officials, whose duties can scarcely have been more than nominal, and who regard their positions at court with satisfaction, not because of the weight of authority which lay upon them, but obviously because of the social standing which they entailed. Thus the nobleman who records that he was "overseer of the cosmetic box, doing in the matter of the cosmetic art to the satisfaction of his lord", can scarcely have been more unduly burdened by his duties than the Lord of the Bedchamber, whose august task it was to put the clean shirt over the royal head of Louis XIV. each morning when he rose. He had, however, so much to do that a seal for sealing "mouthwash for the royal house" exists from the reign of Semerkhet of the Ist Dynasty, and doubtless the other items of the royal cosmetic box were similarly safeguarded.

It is quite evident that many of the offices were simply sinecures which were created to give important nobles something official to hold, which would keep them about the court, and under observation, instead of allowing them to spend their time less innocently upon their local domains, where they might easily become centres of local patriotism and disaffection. The unifying of Egypt was too new a thing for this danger to be disregarded; and in all probability it was the eventual cause of the break-up of the Old Kingdom. The biography of Methen, one of the very earliest of those which have come down to us, dating from the reign of Snefru, gives us a list of the offices held by him which is absolutely appalling, and puts in the shade the pluralists of any other country. Most of these are local administrative offices, which would only be discharged by deputy; but his position as "Master of the Hunt" attached to the court a man whose local influence might easily, under other conditions, have become a dangerous thing to the throne.

The attachment of powerful nobles to the throne was secured by other means as well as by the bestowal of court sinecures. It was customary for the Pharaoh to conciliate an important man, and secure for his line a supporter in the next generation, by causing one of the sons of his powerful subject to be brought up along with the royal family in the harem, and perhaps by bestowing upon the young man the hand of one of the numerous royal princesses. This was done, with completely satisfactory results, in the case of the lyrical Ptahshepses, whose loyalty remained proof against a change of dynasty and through seven reigns, though he might conceivably have established quite a good claim to the throne for himself, in virtue of his position as husband of a royal princess.

The court, which was the centre of the administration of the whole realm, remained for a considerable part of the duration of the Old Kingdom a movable thing, devoid of a fixed habitation. This curious fact may possibly have arisen from the same desire to conciliate the old prejudices of the various states composing the realm which led to the maintenance of the different titles in the royal titulary, and to the adoption of the Double Crown. None of the ancient local capitals could consider itself prejudiced by the preference of another if the court was held at none of them. Accordingly we find that in the earlier stages, at all events, the location of the court was, roughly speaking, determined by that of the reigning king's pyramid. The frequent shifting which this involved was rendered easier by the fact that palace and city were all of the easily wrought and easily discarded mud-brick. Gradually, however, the neighbourhood of Memphis came to be regarded as the most suitable locality, alike for the pyramids and the court. The royal palace maintained the elaborate fiction of the dual monarchy. It, too, was double, or was supposed to be so; and its two gates were named, at least after the reign of Snefru, from the two sections of the kingdom. The two gates of the palace which was built during Snefru's reign were named "Exalted-is-the-White-Crown-of-Snefru-upon-the-Southern-Gate", and "Exalted-is-the-Red-Crown-of-Snefru-upon-the-Northern-Gate"; and this fiction of a double palace and court lasted until late in the New Empire.

It was carried into all departments of the administration, which were all, at least nominally, double; and it is quite probable that in the case of a country so long and straggling as Egypt the doubling of the boards of administration was not merely nominal, but an actual fact, based upon the necessities of the case. In later times there was a southern court, consisting of a council of thirty who elected their own president; while in the north a council divided into six courts was presided over by the vizier. It is likely that this reflects and continues a much earlier arrangement. Justice was administered according to a perfectly well-recognised code of laws. "The council-chamber", says Ptah-hetep, "acteth by strict rule; and every arrangement therein is in accordance with the measuring-cord." Procedure was strict, and regulated not by favour, but by definite order. "If thou standest or sittest in the council-chamber, wait quietly until thy turn cometh. Give heed to the servant that announceth; he that is called hath a broad place. . . . It is God who assigneth the foremost place; but one attaineth nothing by shoving with the elbow." At least, this was the theory of the thing; the mortuary inscription of Nezemib, apparently one of the few unofficial gentlemen of the reign of Assa, suggests that the practice was not always so impartial as the theory. "Never", he says, "was I beaten in the presence of any official since my birth." The stick, as a means of extracting the truth or cash, must plainly have been a common feature of local administration when this worthy citizen found it necessary to explain upon his tombstone that he had never tasted of it!

Under the supreme court, there was a lower court in each district, presided over by a district judge, who was assisted by a legal assessor, "the expounder of the law", much as local Justices of the Peace dispense justice by the light of the Clerk of the Court. Judges frequently bear as one of their titles, "attached to Nekhen", a title which preserves the memory of the days when Nekhen or Hierakonpolis was the capital of the Southern Kingdom. Una was attached to Nekhen as his first step of promotion on the official ladder in the early days when he was only a bright young man, "companion and inferior prophet of the royal

PLATE XIII

HEAD OF TIY   HEAD OF RANEFER

From Fechheimer's "Die Plastik der Ägypter" (Cassirer)

pyramid city", and eager enough to pick up whatever crumbs might fall from the bureaucratic table.

For administrative purposes, the land was divided into districts which the Egyptians called by the name *hesep*, and the Greeks "nomes". These, no doubt, corresponded more or less to the ancient principalities of the days when the land was divided. Roughly there were about forty of them in later days, and about twenty-five in the Old Kingdom, and they answered somewhat to our own counties. At the head of each nome was the *Nomarch*, who was usually a local magnate, and whose position corresponded to that of our Lord-Lieutenants, in the days when a Lord-Lieutenancy was a reality. The nomarch was responsible generally for the well-being of his nome, for the upkeep of its canals, for the collection of its local revenue and its contribution to the royal treasury, for the maintenance of its temples and their services, being frequently, though not invariably, high-priest of the local god, and for the commission of array or local militia of the nome, which maintained the king's peace in the district and contributed its quota to the royal army in case of a war with an external power. For the execution of all these duties, in addition to which he had also to act as local president of the courts of justice, the nomarch was provided with a staff of trained officials out of the innumerable army of scribes of all types which grew up at a very early stage of Egyptian history. He was also provided with two officials whom he could scarcely be expected to regard with much favour. These were the "Corner-men", the two royal deputies who were appointed, one for each end of the nome, by the central authority, and were supposed to keep an eye on the activities of the nomarch, and to see that his work was done as it should be, and with a due regard to the interests of his master at the capital. One can imagine that they were loved just as much as such checks upon local authority have always been loved, and were generally regarded rather as the king's spies than as helps to the administration of the nome.

As long as the central authority was strong, and the link with the royal master was made visible by the Pharaoh's occasional personal appearance in the districts, the nomarch system no doubt worked quite well, and the nomarchs were earnest and strenuous upholders of the authority of their royal master, as well as of the welfare of the nome. On the other hand, however, under a slack central administration or a sluggish king, it afforded to a powerful and ambitious noble a great opportunity for self-aggrandisement at the expense of his king. Pharaoh might be the Good God, but he was far away, at Memphis or somewhere else in the north; and the nomarch, less divine, no doubt, was the actual and visible local providence of the district, "giving", as he was not slack to remind his vassals, "bread to all the hungry, and clothes to the naked". In such a time as the long senility of Pepy II., it is not to be wondered at that the local magnates, unrestrained by the strong hand of the central power, should have got out of hand, and become a danger to the welfare of the state. It was this anarchy, when every nomarch "did what was right in his own eyes", which, with the probable additional complication of a foreign invasion, broke down finally the elaborate fabric of the Old Kingdom. The fact that the succession to honour and office, though practically hereditary in the great local families, was subject to the personal grant of the Pharaoh, as in the case of the Count Zau, nomarch of the Cerastes-Mountain, may have acted as a slight check on the ambitious nobles; but it was not sufficient to overcome the centrifugal tendencies of the end of the dynasty.

What a respectable nomarch of the Vth Dynasty, before the beginning of the break-up of the old order, held to be due to his nome and himself, may be seen in the tomb inscription of the nomarch Henku, at Der el-Gebrawi, the earliest of such inscriptions to have survived. Henku was nomarch of the Cerastes-Mountain nome, and an ancestor of the great and powerful Zau family, and he thus describes his government: "O all ye people of the Cerastes-Mountain; O ye great lords of other nomes, who shall pass by this tomb, I, Henku tell good things. . . . I gave bread to all the hungry of the Cerastes-Mountain; I clothed him who was naked therein. I filled its shores with large cattle, and its lowlands with small cattle. I satisfied the wolves of the mountain (sacred in Henku's locality) and the fowl of heaven (the hawk, also sacred) with flesh of small cattle. . . . I was lord and overseer of southern grain in this nome. . . . . I settled the feeble towns in this nome with the people of other nomes; those who had been peasant-serfs therein, I made their offices as officials. I never oppressed one in possession of his property so that he complained of me because of it to the god of my city; I spake, and told that which was good; never was there one fearing because of one stronger than he, so that he complained because of it to the god. I arose then to be ruler in the Cerastes-Mountain together with my brother, the revered, the sole companion, the ritual priest, Re-am. I was a benefactor to the nome in the folds of the cattle, in the settlements of the fowlers. I settled its every district with men and cattle. . . . . I speak no lie, for I was one beloved of his father, praised of his mother, excellent in character to his brother, and amiable to his sister."

If Henku's record is to be taken at its face value, the Cerastes-Mountain was indeed fortunate in its ruler. Of course he was merely putting down to his credit what every nomarch claimed, and there is not much more variety in the tomb-record of the average nomarch than in the various copies of Ashur-nasir-pal's Standard Inscription; but at least he shows us what it was considered right and proper that a nomarch should do in those early days—whether he did it or not.

Obviously such a system of local government afforded innumerable openings for officials of all sorts and sizes. As Pharaoh's central administration had its vast army of scribes, so each nome had its battalion of the same unlovely, though perhaps necessary class. A very considerable section of the population of the land must have been thus withdrawn from useful labour and devoted to the unprofitable business of scribbling reports, meddling with their unofficial neighbours, or spying upon their superiors. If one were to judge from the proportion of tomb-inscriptions in which the subject of the epitaph is devoid of an official title, the conclusion would be that nearly everybody in Egypt held a government office of some kind or another, and that the whole population of Egypt lived by the taking in of one another's washing—often, no doubt, of rather dirty linen. If the man is not a Real Royal Councillor, or a Sole Companion, he is a King's Confidant, or a Royal Attendant. In the absence of all else, he will at least be able to tack Ritual Priest after his name. In fact, it must have been almost as remarkable to be untitled in Old Kingdom Egypt as in pre-war Germany, or as to be a righteous man in Sodom. Nezemib, the confiding individual who told us a little while ago that he was never beaten in the presence of any official since his birth, is honourably distinguished by the fact that he actually appears to have been a private citizen; but what is he among so many! The probable explanation of this plague of official locusts is that the undistinguished majority could only rarely afford a tomb inscription, while an official, even of very ordinary standing, could always find ways and means, honest or otherwise, of getting his virtues commemorated; but at the same time, there can be no doubt that Egypt, all through her history, had far more officials than was good for her, and that the overpowering flavour of scribe which pervades her native records is one of the least agreeable features in them.

It is quite in accordance with this prominence of officialdom that practically the only specimens of what can, even by courtesy, be called literature which have come down to us from the Old Kingdom are, at least nominally, the work of great government officials, and bear, upon almost every line, the stamp of the cautious regard for self-interest which marks the scribe of all ages. The two books known as the "Instruction for Kagemni" and the "Instruction of Ptah-hetep" are of extraordinary interest as being the oldest extant examples of what we can really call a book. Both date, in their present form, only from the Middle Kingdom, the writing of the Prisse Papyrus, in which they are both found, being considered to date from the XIIth Dynasty; but both claim to belong in their original form to the Old Kingdom, the Instruction for Kagemni to the reign of King Huni of the IIIrd Dynasty, the Instruction of Ptah-hetep to that of Assa of the Vth, and there seems no reason to doubt the claim. Kagemni is merely a fragment, and even the Instruction of Ptah-hetep is by no means perfectly preserved; but there is no reason to believe that the lost portion of the older book contained anything of a different type from that which is adequately represented in the surviving fragment and in the later volume of Ptah-hetep. In the one case, the old king Huni, who died, or as the papyrus puts it, "came to port", before the accession of Snefru, seems to have commanded his unnamed vizier to put his experience into writing for the benefit of his children, among whom was numbered Kagemni, a future vizier. "The vizier had his children called after he had completed (his treatise on) the ways of mankind and on their character as experienced by him. And he said unto them: 'All that is in this book, hear it as if I spake it.'—— Then they placed themselves upon their bellies. They read it as it stood in writing, and it was better in their heart than everything that was in this entire land; they stood up and sat down in accordance therewith."

The "Instruction of Ptah-hetep" has a setting almost precisely similar. Ptah-hetep, the aged vizier of King Assa of the Vth Dynasty, complains to his master of the assaults of old age, and begs to be allowed to instruct his son in wisdom, so that he may be able to take up the duties of the viziership in due time, "that strife may be banished from among the people, and the Two River-banks may serve thee". Accordingly the "Instruction" is given: "The beautifully expressed utterances, spoken by the prince and count, the father of the god and beloved of the god, the bodily son of the king, the superintendent of the capital and vizier Ptah-hetep, while instructing the ignorant in knowledge and in the rules of elegant discourse, the weal of him that will hearken thereto, and the woe of him that shall transgress them." At the end of his discourse, the ancient statesman adds: "So act that thy lord may say concerning thee: 'How goodly was the instruction of his father!' ——It is not little that I have wrought upon earth. I have spent an hundred and ten years in life, which the king hath given me (two Egyptian ideas—the one of the perfect duration of life, the other of its royal sustenance) and with rewards beyond those of them that have gone before because

I wrought truth and justice for the King unto mine old age."

When one comes to examine the wisdom thus highly commended, one finds that its merits are not difficult to sum up. Such a thing as an ideal is totally unknown either to the IIIrd Dynasty vizier, or to Ptah-hetep, unless it be that expressed in the familiar proverb, "Look after Number One". The sole principle which the two moralists recognise as the adequate motive for action is that of self-interest. Occasionally a faint whisper of higher things is heard through the steady rumble of selfish platitude. "Be not haughty because of thy might in the midst of thy young soldiers. Beware of making strife, for one knoweth not what God will do when He smiteth." But even then, right action is recommended or wrong action avoided, not because of its rightness or wrongness, but solely for prudential reasons. One pictures Ptah-hetep as a canny, practical old gentleman, who has seen so many ups and downs in life, and come at last to the conclusion that honesty is the best policy, having tried the other way too, and found it wanting. Devoutly to be avoided is that vanity of youth which imagines that it knows everything so soon as it knows anything. "Be not arrogant because of thy knowledge, and have no confidence in that thou art a learned man. Take counsel with the ignorant as with the wise, for the limits of art cannot be reached, and no artist completely possesses his skill. A good discourse is more hidden than precious emeralds, and yet it is found among slave-girls over the mill-stones." Now and again the old man's wrinkled countenance brightens into a smile, as when he pictures the two orators and the way to deal with each. "If thou findest an orator in his moment, speaking sound sense, and better than thou, then bend thine arm, and bow thy back. But if he speaketh ill, then fail not to withstand him, in order that men may call out to him 'Thou ignorant one'." It is not precisely what one would call generous advice; but Ptah-hetep was not the only man to see the advantage of it, or to practise it.

Even five thousand years ago, wisdom had learned thoroughly modern views as to the advisability of recreation and the foolishness of mere money-grubbing. "Follow thine heart during thy lifetime; do not more than is commanded thee. Diminish not the time of following the heart; it is abhorred of the soul (*Ka*) that its time (of enjoyment) should be taken away. Shorten not the day-time more than is needful to maintain thine house. When riches are gained, follow the heart; for riches are of no avail if one be weary." The same doctrine of the happy mean between undue laboriousness and undue indulgence in pleasure is preached in another utterance: "One that reckoneth accounts all the day passeth not a happy moment. One that gladdeneth his heart all the day provideth not for his house. The bowman hitteth the mark, as the steersman reacheth land, by diversity of aim. (Can it have been possible to tack with an Old Kingdom sailing boat?) He that obeyeth his heart shall command."

If Mr. Battiscombe Gunn's translation of one passage may be accepted, one of our most modern and most exasperating difficulties was no novelty to the great households of the most ancient Egypt; but the rendering of Ptah-hetep's observations on the problem of domestic service is so pat to modern conditions that it is hard to believe that a modern flavour has not unconsciously entered into the version. Here is the passage in question: "Satisfy thine hired servants out of such things as thou hast; it is the duty of one that hath been favoured of the God. In sooth, it is hard to satisfy hired servants. For one saith, 'He is a lavish person; one knoweth not what may come from him.' But on the morrow he thinketh, 'He is a person of exactitude (parsimony), content therein.' And when favours have been shown unto servants, they say, 'We go' (a month's notice). Peace dwelleth not in that town wherein dwell servants that are wretched." What remains to be said but Solomon's old and weary truism: "That which hath been shall be, and there is nothing new under the sun."

Altogether, the impression left upon the mind by these scanty specimens of the thought and outlook of the Old Kingdom Egyptian is that, on the whole, if his practice was in any way accordant with his preaching, he ought to have been a fairly comfortable person to get on with. If in his company you need never expect to be led to great heights, or to have Pisgah sights of possible spiritual greatness, neither need you dread that your feet will be defiled with the mire of the depths. "Medio tu tutissimus ibis" and "Nothing in excess" were mottoes to which he would cheerfully have subscribed. "Be good, and you will be happy" is pretty much the highest wisdom of the Old Kingdom moralist, and goodness is not an end in itself, but only a means to the greater good of happiness. All that we know of the ancient Egyptian, not of this age only, but all through his history, suggests that his first literary representative truly reflected the national spirit and ideals. The Egyptian was one of the most amiable of ancient types; but nothing in his history suggests the spirit that breeds saints or martyrs. And when, in the person of the unfortunate Akhenaten, he was confronted with a king who actually had ideals, and tried to live up to them, his discomfort at being roused and incited to a spiritual effort was extreme. "A little leaven leaveneth the whole lump", it is true; but the story of Atenism shows that there must be a certain proportion between the size of the leaven and that of the lump which it is to permeate.

Apart from these utterances of the smug worldly wisdom of their class which Kagemni and Ptah-hetep have passed on to us, nothing of what can truly be called literature has survived from the Old Kingdom. Far more really literature, indeed, are some of the more poetic utterances of the Pyramid Texts, with their wild fire and barbarous vigour; but the religious interest of the Pyramid Texts so far overpowers their literary merits as to make it more advisable to consider them in connection with a general survey of the Religion of Ancient Egypt. The one general consideration which becomes obvious when one reads the Texts is the extreme contrast between the rude and barbarous form and spirit of them and the cultured and conventional society which adopted them as the expression of its ideals of the future life. The period to which we owe them in their present form is that of the latter part of the Vth and earlier part of the VIth Dynasty; that is to say, the period when Ptah-hetep was elaborating his cautious and

PLATE XIV

AN OLD KINGDOM WOOD CARVING.   PORTRAIT OF HESI

utterly unvisionary maxims of conventional morality; the period also when Egyptian art, if somewhat less vigorous and nervous than in the time of the first four dynasties, was still amazingly fresh, and was beginning to be touched with that spirit of refinement which is only too often the herald of over-ripeness and decay. But the Pyramid Texts only belong in name to a period such as this. Their whole outlook is that of an earlier, a fiercer, a ruder and more strenuous age, when men still saw visions, instead of having no outlook but one of profit and loss. Manifestly they are survivals; and while it may be literally correct to say that they belong to a late period of the Old Kingdom, and not to the earliest stages of the development of Egyptian religion, actually they bring us far nearer to primitive ideas and conditions than the mere date of the extant texts suggests. Religion of all types, and in all ages, is full of such survivals, fossil remains of its earlier developments, which are always of great interest, and only become harmful when they are believed to be still living and binding upon the present.

Here and there, among the tomb-reliefs which represent for us with such vivacity and truthfulness the lives of the workers of the period, occur little scraps of verse which are supposed to be sung by the persons represented in the relief. Of these, the most complete and famous is the song of the shepherd, as he drives his sheep across the muddy field left by the subsiding inundation, to tread in the seed. Miss M. A. Murray has very happily rendered it in English verse:

> O, your shepherd is a shepherd of the West!
> He will paddle in the water
> And salute the fish's daughter.
> O, your shepherd is a shepherd of the West!
> Every happiness he'll wish
> To all the little fish,
> O, your shepherd is a shepherd of the West.

It is only a scrap, and can scarcely be called literature; but it expresses an aspect of the life of the toiling masses of the Egyptian populace which deserves to be kept in mind as a corrective to ideas about it which have for too long held the field. The down-trodden serf of this ancient despotism, toiling and sweating and dying under the task-master's lash, is an old friend. Miss Murray's little verse gives us the reality, and there is not much of the down-trodden serf about it.

We come now finally, in this brief survey of Egyptian life during the Old Kingdom, to the art of the time. Here we are on ground which, if not altogether firm, is at all events much firmer than that which we have had to tread in considering any other aspect of our subject; for, while a vast deal has perished, much more has survived than in the case of the literature. In respect of two features of Egyptian art, sculpture in the round, and sculpture in low relief, helped by painting, we are at least moderately well furnished with specimens which enable a judgment to be formed as to the characteristics and merits of the artists of the Old Kingdom. In the minor arts, or artistic crafts, we are not quite so fortunate, and it is not until the Middle Kingdom that the full merit of the Egyptian craftsman is adequately revealed to us by numerous specimens of magnificent work; yet even at this early stage, there is enough surviving to justify us in anticipating the brilliance of a day which dawns so brightly. The long story of the art of ancient Egypt falls into four chapters, of which the first is that with which we have to deal at present; the second is that of the Middle Kingdom, almost as remark-able as the first in its vigour and sincerity; the third, that of the New Empire, attractive for the new element of grace and beauty which it introduces, but already showing signs of the over-elaboration of detail and substitution of pretti-ness for strength which were to prove fatal to it; while the fourth is that Saite revival of the very end of the Empire, under the XXVIth Dynasty, whose chief merit lay in the technical perfection with which it imitated, in a spirit of conscious archaism, the work of the First period. Of these, there can be no doubt that the art of the First period is alike the most interesting and the most powerful. Primitive art has always an attractiveness of its own in the freshness and naïveté of its products, and this is a characteristic of the earliest developments of Old Kingdom art; but before long the Egyptian artist passes away from the hesitations and tentative fumblings which are often even charming in primitive work, and develops a style which is characterised by anything rather than by hesitation or feeling after an uncomprehended ideal. There is nothing primitive, in any sense of the word, in the work of the great age from Snefru to the end of the IVth Dynasty. The artist knows with absolute certainty what he is aiming at, and has full confidence in his ability to attain it. The consequence is that he has attained his ideal with a perfection seldom realised in the history of art—whether we think that ideal the highest or not.

The first indications of that artistic quality which was part of the national inheritance are seen in the workmanship of the pre-dynastic Egyptian. The beautiful execution of the flint tools and weapons which he used reveals a taste for beauty as well as for efficiency; while the fine shape and tasteful colouring of the hand-wrought pottery which he produced disclose the same instinct working in a field which afforded wider room for its exercise. "Despite his ignorance of the potter's wheel," says Professor Peet, "he moulded his shapes so perfectly that its absence is never felt; and, last, but not least, he belonged to one of those rare and happy periods when the craftsman seems incapable of an error of taste, and in consequence almost every form that leaves his hand is a thing of beauty". The same sense of the beautiful is seen very notably in the forms of the vases of hard stone which he worked with such inexhaustible patience. Our admiration for the craftsmanship which produced these marvels of accuracy, and for the indomitable determination which persevered in the work with such imperfect tools until it had achieved results which the most perfect modern appliances could not surpass, ought not to blind us to the fact that the results attained are not merely wonderful, but beautiful as well. There are some feats of workmanship at which you marvel, more because of the perverted taste which wasted time and skill upon the creation of ugliness than at anything pleasing in the result of so much labour; but that qualified admiration never needs to be extended to early Egyptian stonework. If the labour was almost infinite, the beauty of the finished product justified it. To noble material was added fine taste for form, and ancient crafts-manship has produced nothing finer in its kind than the pre-dynastic stone vase.

Sir Flinders Petrie has suggested that towards the latter end of the pre-dynastic period an artistic degenera-tion set in, which he attributes to the incursion of a less cultured race, probably from the east. With the advent of the Ist Dynasty and the unification of Egypt, however, there is a renaissance of artistic feeling, and art advances steadily into new territory which it occupies with growing confidence and certainty until it reaches the culmination of its development in the mature and masterly work of the IVth Dynasty. The comparatively rude and barbaric forms of the early slate palettes pass into the carefully studied and balanced decoration of the great mace-heads of the Scorpion and Narmer, and the ceremonial palette of the latter king. Perhaps the earliest examples of Egyptian sculpture in the round are the great figures of the god Min from Koptos (now in the Ashmolean Museum); but, im-pressive as these are, the prophecy of the excellence which this form of art was to attain is given rather by some of the small work of the early time, such as the tiny ivory figure of a king, found by Petrie at Abydos, and now in the British Museum. Here, first of all, the Egyptian sculptor begins to display not only mastery of his material (that he always had), but understanding of character and the power of rendering it. This little figure with its slightly bent head, and the delicate face with its curiously mingled expression of gentleness and cunning, is already a masterpiece, despite its smallness of scale. "It is in small art of this kind", says Dr. H. R. Hall, "that we find the Egyptian artist is already showing his mastery. He is the *architech-nites*, pre-eminently the best art-craftsman of the world; his training, to be handed down from generation to generation through the millennia, is now bearing its first fruits. And when, as in the case of this figure, he is a real artist as well as craftsman, he is already hard to beat."

In fact, the Egyptian artist has already, at this early

stage of his history, unmistakably manifested the direction
in which his genius is going to lead him towards the position which he occupies among the great artists of the
world. That position must finally be determined by his
skill in two departments of his art—his sculpture in the
round, and in low relief. And of these two, the sculpture in
the round is the form in which he is unchallenged and un-
challengeable in the ancient world, until he is immeasur-
ably surpassed by the Greek in beauty of conception,
though not in rendering of character. His work in low relief is of great decorative beauty, often of wonderful delicacy of execution and fineness of feeling, and must always
have been more pleasant to live with (though almost entirely employed for the decoration of the houses of the
dead) than that of his great rival in this kind, the Assyrian
sculptor; but at the same time it would be idle to deny that
in some important aspects of such work he remains a child,
compared with the Assyrian, whose mastery, for example,
of the representation of strenuous action is a thing to which
the Egyptian never attained. On the other hand, the
Egyptian is quite as far ahead of his rival when the question
is one of the representation of the human figure in the
round. From the very beginning, he displays a sense of
what is to be done in this respect, and of the right way to
do it, to which the Assyrian sculptor never attained, even
in the most mature days of his art. To ask the Assyrian to
submit to a comparison of his best work in the round with
the best work of the Old Kingdom, such as the diorite
Khafra, the Rahotep and Nefert, or the Menkaura with
the figures of the nomes, would be ridiculous. But the
Kha-sekhem statuette in green schist, now in the Cairo
Museum, may be fairly compared with the famous statue
of Ashur-nasir-pal, now in the British Museum. The
Assyrian piece has every advantage in point of date and
condition; but primitive and battered though the Khasekhem may be, it is the work of an artist who knew what
he was aiming at, what a statue in the round should be, and
how to create it, while the Assyrian is a conscientious
stone-hewer who has not yet succeeded in visualising the
essential differences between a milestone and a man, and

gives us, in consequence, something which is not a good representation of either.

Old Kingdom sculpture never looked back, from the time of the Kha-sekhem, till it had produced its acknow-ledged masterpieces in such world-famous statues as have been mentioned a moment ago. It has suffered in general estimation, as all Egyptian art has suffered, through being judged, not by its best alone, but by the mass of common-place work which was turned out to meet a theological and not an artistic need. But when the inferior stuff is allowed to take its proper place, as of religious instead of artistic import, and the art of the early dynasties is judged, as every great art has the right to be judged, by the best which it produced, it becomes manifest at once that we are in the presence of one of the great arts of the world, which takes its place, not unworthily, as the earliest stage of the splendid development which, in the fulness of time, pro-duced the triumphs of Greek and Italian sculpture.

It should be remembered that from the beginning to the end the Egyptian sculptor was essentially a portrait sculptor. The conditions of his art forbade him to idealise or to aim at the creation of beauty, as the Greek did. Sculpture existed, almost exclusively, to meet a religious necessity. Apart from the colossal work which was used for the adornment of the later temples, the statue was created to give the artist's patron a better chance in the life after death. "The dead man would more certainly live again in the underworld if his portrait-statue were like him", or perhaps his *Ka*, which could wander at will, would find a recognisable lodging-place, when it returned to the tomb, in the statue of the dead man, even though his body should have mouldered into dust and ceased to be tenant-able. Therefore, the first necessity for Egyptian sculpture was that it should produce a life-like representation of its subject, and, above all, of that part of it by which the man was recognised in life—the face. For the rest of the body—that did not matter so much, so long as the figure gave a reasonable representation of a human body, and stood or sat in the position which convention had decreed as proper. Accordingly you have heads which are wrought with all the skill that the artist could command, both technical and interpretative; while the trunk, the limbs, and the hands and feet are often rendered in the most perfunctory manner. The degree of divergence from faithfulness may almost be said to vary in proportion as the artist gets away from the subject of his chief preoccupation—the head—and the work often degenerates after the fashion of the statue of Nebuchadnezzar's vision; the statue of a king will naturally be better finished all over than that of a commoner, as may be seen in the diorite Khafra and the statues of Menkaura, already mentioned; but in all, king or commoner alike, the concentration upon the head leaves the artist at liberty to be less strenuous in his interpretation of the body.

Thus, in the famous Ranefer of the Cairo Museum, you have a head of amazing vitality set upon a torso which is only mediocre, and which is supported upon legs of which the less said the better. The same is true of the statue of Tiy, whose head is almost more vigorous, if that be possible, than that of Ranefer. Perhaps the most attractive of all the statues of the period, as they are also the most famous, are those of Prince Rahotep and his wife, the Lady Nefert. Of these, Nefert, being a handsome woman, has somewhat overshadowed her husband's sturdy efficiency; but, apart from his attractive consort, the head of the prince is an astonishingly vivid and intelligent piece of portraiture. But here again the sculptor's conscientiousness dwindles from the head downwards, and while Rahotep's extremities perhaps do not matter, it is impossible to believe that so charming a lady as Nefert ever had such ankles as her sculptor has seen fit to bestow upon her.

Bearing in mind this fact, which is the key to the interpretation of Egyptian sculpture in all ages, and remembering also that, as the statues which have survived from the Old Kingdom are almost exclusively works which were destined to serve the purpose described, they were strictly restricted to conventional attitudes, we are in a position to appreciate the manner in which the artist carried out the ideal which was alike his inspiration and his limitation. The verdict must be that nothing more conclusive in the

way of faithfulness has ever been accomplished by a
school of sculpture. Sir Thomas Lawrence is said to have
remarked of Raeburn's portrait of The McNab that it was
"the likest thing to a man that ever was put upon canvas".
Some of these Old Kingdom heads are the likest things to
a man, and doubtless to the men for whom they were
wrought, that ever were hewn from stone; and one can
only marvel at the blindness which has pronounced that
"Egyptian sculpture is a sculpture devoid of intellectual
insight and intellectual interest". Of course, as has been
already indicated, its product is astonishingly uneven, as is
to be expected when one realises that its production was a
religious as well as an artistic necessity. Many of the
statues which occupy places in our museums, and are
gravely regarded as examples of Egyptian art, are merely
the product of the stone-hewers employed by local under-
takers in obscure towns, and have no more claim to be
called art than the average tombstone; but Egyptian art
may safely stake its reputation upon the best of the Old
Kingdom portrait-statues. Nothing better in its kind was
ever done by the Egyptian sculptor throughout all his long
history; and there is not so much first-rate work in this
sort in the world that we can afford to despise this earliest
example of genuine portrait-sculpture. "The Egyptians",
says Dr. H. R. Hall, "throughout their art-history were
the greatest masters of portraiture of the ancient world".
It is high praise; but there can be no question of its being
thoroughly well deserved.

Almost as characteristic of the period as the portrait-
sculpture is the relief work which so abundantly adorns
the tombs of the great men of the Pyramid Age and the age
immediately following. At a very early stage, the Egyptian
artist gave evidence of his predilection for this form of art.
Apart from the early relief carvings in ivory, the most
notable performance of the archaic period is the relief
work on the statues of Min from Koptos, in which the
characteristics of animals, such as the hyaena and the ox,
are caught with wonderful precision, though the work is
of the most elementary type. From this primitive stage,
relief speedily advances to the true relief work of the slate

palettes, much of which is of amazing delicacy. One of the most notable examples of the vigour and skill with which the early artist could represent natural forms is the stele of the Serpent-king Ata or Zet Ata, of the Ist Dynasty, on which the hawk is depicted in relief with extraordinary accuracy and vivacity. Narmer's great palette and mace-head, a little earlier, show considerable knowledge of anatomy, to say nothing of the study of decorative effect in the grouping of the figures.

But the great glory of the Egyptian work in this sort is to be found in the tomb-reliefs. The artist who carved the wooden panels of Hesy, especially that with the standing figure, already understood and appreciated both the advantages and the limitations of this style of work, and has left us a masterly study of the vigorous and efficient, perhaps slightly hard, official of the time. Animal form was rendered with admirable accuracy, and with a remarkable power of seizing the salient characteristics of each type. The gazelles from the tomb of Methen, the donkeys, cattle and sheep from the tombs of Tiy and Ptah-hetep, are rendered with a faithfulness which could scarcely be excelled, but which is never allowed to interfere with the decorative effect of the tableau. It would be difficult to imagine a more perfect interpretation of asinine nature than that which is offered in the relief of asses now at the Leiden Museum, or a more striking contrast of gait and nature than that given by the slab in Berlin which depicts a panther and a porcupine meeting one another face to face.

Later, the work tends somewhat to degenerate, and become overloaded with detail ; but the marsh reliefs from the tomb of Mereruka, the artificial feeding scenes from the tomb of Kagemni, and the cranes from that of Manefer are still of great interest and charm. It will be noticed that, as already remarked, the Egyptian artist succeeds most fully in scenes of rest, or at the utmost of not too strenuous motion. When, as in the great historical reliefs of the Empire, he has to represent violent and complicated effort and movement, he almost invariably fails, and the charging chariot-horses of Seti or Ramses irresistibly suggest rocking-horses. One has to go to

Assyria and the reliefs of Ashur-nasir-pal or Ashur-bani-pal to see violent motion rendered as it should be. Of course there are exceptions to this rule, and occasionally an Egyptian artist succeeds with a *tour de force* of motion, just as occasionally the Semitic artist succeeds in giving a perfect rendering of repose; but the charm of the Egyptian relief lies undoubtedly in the suggestion of peaceful life and gentle activity. He can give you, with a very pronounced sense of humour, scenes of wrangling and squabble, or a kind of lightning sketch of the contortions of a dancer ; but these things are merely his diversions, and his true strength lies elsewhere.

Artistic work in metal had reached a high state of perfection at an early stage of the period. Very little has survived in anything like perfect condition, and, after the wonderful bracelets of the queen of King Zer, we have nothing to compare with the astonishing work which Mr. O. L. Woolley has been unearthing from contemporary graves at Ur of the Chaldees. But the queen's bracelets are themselves sufficient proof that the Old Kingdom gold-smith was a master of his craft. From the VIth Dynasty we have the fine statues in copper (?) of Pepy I. and his son Prince Merenra (or of Pepy as a grown man and as a youth). To the same period must probably be referred the magnificent head of a hawk in gold, with eyes of obsidian, which was found at Hierakonpolis along with the copper statues. No finer rendering of accipitrine nature has ever been given in any period than is offered by this splendid work, which may fitly be compared with the early study on the stele of the Serpent-king as an example of how the Egyptian artist advanced to a more naturalistic rendering without losing the dignity of the earlier work.

Such specimens of the artistic crafts as have been preserved are in more or less (generally more) fragmentary condition. Enough has survived, however, to show us that the Egyptian of the early dynasties had long left behind him the barbarism of the earlier pre-historic days. He might still, in deference to ancient religious custom, have his dependents sand-bagged at his grave, or have barbaric texts suggesting ancient cannibalisms carved on the walls of his pyramid chambers; but these were fossil survivals, which always endure in religion a century or two longer than anywhere else. In point of fact, he was a highly cultured and intelligent gentleman, whose artistic tastes were ministered to daily by every article of furniture which he used, by every vessel from which he ate or drank, and by the decoration of the very tombs where he made offering to his ancestors. Indeed, it would not be doing him an injustice to say that by the time we meet him in the Ist Dynasty, he is already so far from being primitive, that "sophisticated" would be the adjective which would more exactly describe him. A society which by a curious irony has left us, out of all the thousands of relics which might have survived, a fringe and switch of false hair and a prescription for a hair restorer, is obviously very far removed from primeval innocence. At the same time, it would be manifestly unfair to suppose that because the noble Egyptian of the early dynasties lived in the midst of beauty and luxury he was either effeminate or degenerate. When a Hebrew began to live in ivory houses, ceiled with cedar and painted with vermilion, to drink wine in bowls and anoint himself with the chief ointments, while his nation was going headlong downhill, it was time for the prophet of the Lord to speak plainly; but it was a different thing when beauty and art were not ministers of vice to a degenerate profiteer, but the natural surroundings of a beauty-loving and virile race in the heyday of its youth and energy.

Of the condition of the rank and file of the people during this period of abounding energy and luxury, we have not so much evidence as might be desired; yet there is sufficient to show that the old conception of a tyrant king, backed by a heartless aristocracy trampling on the necks of a miserable people, is a mere figment of the imagination, probably derived in about equal proportions from a misapplication of the treatment of an alien race (the Hebrews), and a misinterpretation of certain statements of Herodotus. Slave labour, as Sir Flinders Petrie has pointed out, never attained large proportions in Egypt, even during the imperial stage of her history, and was comparatively a negligible element during the early period. We have seen that the great building schemes of the IVth Dynasty Pharaohs, far from being a burden on the common people, rather represented a distinct benefit to them during a period of unemployment. Such evidence as survives (scanty enough) concerning the housing of the proletariat goes to show that the working-man's house of the earliest period, while simple enough, and to our minds lacking in equipment, was adapted to the climate, and compared not unfavourably, in the amount of accommodation which it afforded, with houses of the present time. "Much nonsense has been written", says Petrie, "about the oppression of the people, their tears and groans". Unless we are to assume that all the tomb-reliefs in existence represent not the truth, but a deliberate attempt to suppress the truth on the part of the artists of ancient Egypt, we must believe that the lot of the peasant in Old Kingdom Egypt was, comparatively speaking, a bright and cheerful one, and that the relations between the classes were better than in many more modern lands. Such evidence, no doubt, is not always to be taken at its face value, and there were assuredly dark enough shadows which do not come into the picture. But, on the whole, the impression which we gain of society in the early dynastic period is one of healthy and prosperous activity, and of a sound and vigorous people, as yet unspoiled, "rejoicing as a strong man to run a race", endowed by nature with unusual faculties of self-expression, and taking delight in the exercise of them.

CHAPTER XI

THE FIRST INTERMEDIATE DARK PERIOD

WE now reach what is in some respects the most obscure and difficult period of Egyptian history—the period which lasts from the fall of the VIth Dynasty till the rise of Thebes to supremacy under the Antefs and Mentuhoteps of the XIth Dynasty. Modern historians have given us different estimates as to its length. Reckoning from the beginning of the VIIth Dynasty to the rise of the Antefs at Thebes, Petrie allows 344 years to the period; Breasted allows 315 years for the four dynasties from the VIIth to the Xth; the estimate of the *Cambridge Ancient History*, from the fall of the VIth to that of the Xth Dynasty, is 331 years, or from the fall of the VIth to the rise of the XIth Dynasty, 256 years; while Weigall reckons 255 years from the rise of the VIIth to the fall of the Xth Dynasty, and 181 years from the rise of the VIIth to that of the XIth Dynasty. It is obvious, therefore, that certainty as to the exact date of any particular monarch or event within this period is not a thing to be looked for, at least in the meantime, and until more reliable evidence is forthcoming as to matters of detail. At the same time, it is also evident that the discrepancy as to the total length of the period is not large, and when allowance is made for the slightly divergent points from which the above estimates are reached, one may come to the conclusion that a period of about three centuries, roughly speaking, fairly represents the total duration of this time of confusion.

The obscurity is rendered still more dense by the absence of contemporary monuments or records, or at least their extreme paucity, especially during the earlier part of the period. Even the great obscurity between the

Middle Kingdom and the New Empire is rendered somewhat less obscure by the presence of what, in comparison,
is almost an abundance of monumental and other evidence;
but for this earlier darkness, in its earlier stages, at all
events, next to nothing is forthcoming. Reign after reign
passes in the VIIth and VIIIth Dynasties, with practically
not a single contemporary monument to indicate that it
was more than a shadow. A few scarabs of Neferkara,
whose attribution to the period of the VIIth Dynasty is
doubtful; a green jasper cylinder of obviously Syrian
design, though of Egyptian motive, and belonging to a
Pharaoh, Khendu or Khondy, of the VIIIth Dynasty; a
seal of a king Neferkara Telulu, "Lord of the North"; a
decree of a Neferkauhor, in favour of an official whose
name, Shema, again suggests Syrian connections, and two
or three trifling remains of another king Nefersa-hor;
these, with a few more or less doubtfully attributed
scarabs, sum up the total of contemporary relics extant
from the first two dynasties of the period.

When we come to the IXth Dynasty of the Khetys of
Herakleopolis, we are somewhat better provided for, and
it is possible that a very remarkable document of this
period may be attributed to one of them, as we shall see;
while the records of the Princes of Siut eke out the otherwise still insufficient material; but the case for the Xth
Dynasty is even more lamentably undocumented than
that for the VIIth and VIIIth, and consists practically of
three scarabs of a king Shenes, otherwise unknown to fame,
whose right to a position somewhere hereabouts in the
dreary bog of uncertainties rests solely on the workmanship and style of these three trifles. Manifestly, therefore,
an attempt to construct a detailed and consecutive narrative out of these pitiful fragments of what, even at its best,
was probably only a time of shreds and patches, in which
little district puppet-kings struggled for a while to maintain themselves against the overwhelming tide of something which seems curiously like Bolshevism, only to go
under, and be succeeded by others of the same stamp,
whose heads bob up for a few seconds above the muddy
waters and then vanish again, is mere vanity and vexation

of spirit. The profit of drawing up a list of lines of kings who, at their best estate, were never much more than shadow-kings, is more than doubtful. The most that can be done, so far as that aspect of history goes which consists in a recital of a catalogue of king's names and the chief events of their reigns, is to indicate those who seem to be the chief figures of the moving shadow-show, to suggest one or two outside influences which seem to be indicated by the evidence as having been brought to bear upon Egypt during this time, and to point out the general trend of the events which obscurely and gradually lead up to that great Renaissance of Egyptian power and vigour which we know as the Middle Kingdom.

On the other hand, as regards that other aspect of history which is surely of far greater importance, the aspect which deals with the actual conditions of human life during these three centuries, we are much more fortunately placed. It is of next to no earthly importance that we should know, never so clearly, how shadow-king Khety III. of Herakleopolis offended shadow-king (not quite so shadowy) Uahankh Antef of Thebes, and got rapped over the fingers in consequence, and had the good sense to admit that he was rightly served; but it is of lasting importance that we should know how certain millions of human beings lived in Egypt for these three hundred dark years, how they regarded the state of their land, and what were their opinions as to the kind of government which had brought things into such a condition. And in this respect, very luckily and curiously, this period of muddle and misery is more amply documented than almost any other period of Egyptian history.

That "wrath makes poetry" is an ancient belief; and it is exemplified in the literary remains which have survived from this period in Egypt, to this extent, at least, that several of the most interesting pieces of Egyptian composition, which, in spite of the fragmentary condition in which they have come down to us, and the ignoble uses to which some of them had been put, have a greater claim to the name of "Literature" than nine-tenths of the mass of Egyptian writing, seem to date from this miserable age, and to reflect, from various angles and in various aspects, the abounding wretchedness of the times. From the throne (a somewhat tottery one), we have "The Instruction for King Merykara" of that shadow-king Khety III. referred to above, who gives us his impressions of things, of state-craft, and its occasional consequences, with refreshing candour and simplicity. From the point of view of a generous and clear-sighted man who sympathised with the misery of the nation, we have "The Admonitions of Ipuwer", one of the most remarkable documents of Egyptian literature, which, *longo intervallo* indeed, but yet very forcibly, reminds one both in matter and spirit of the utterances with which the Hebrew prophets were wont to expose the miseries of their people, and to rebuke the indifference of their kings. "The Prophecy of Neferrohu", though it belongs to the brighter time when the dawn was beginning to break, gives us all the more forcibly the contrast with the darkness which the advent of the beneficent ruler was about to disperse; while its almost Messianic references to the advent and work of the great founder of the XIIth Dynasty make the piece one of the most interesting remains of the religious literature of the Near East. Finally, "The Dispute with his Soul of a Man who is Tired of Life" gives, with a strange, eerie and uncanny power, the view of things which had come at last to be taken by an honest man who had "seen an end of all perfection", and was only anxious to get out of the muddle —if only he could have decent security from his soul as to what awaited him on the other side.

Altogether the literature of this dark and dreary period is remarkable—for quantity, when one remembers the paucity of remains of any other type; but still more for quality—a quality which makes what is otherwise the most barren period of Egyptian history into one of the most interesting from the point of view of our knowledge of the conditions of human living throughout the ages. Dark ages are often dumb, as well as dark; the wonderful thing is to hear so many voices speaking out of the almost unmitigated darkness of these three obscure centuries.

Over the historical outline of the VIIth and VIIIth

Dynasties, then, there is neither need nor opportunity to linger. Practically nothing is known of either of them, except what has been mentioned above. There is, however, a certain amount of evidence, scanty enough, certainly, yet still not to be despised in view of the total absence of other information, which seems to support Sir Flinders Petrie's suggestion that at the close of the VIth Dynasty the country, weakened and disorganised by the over-long senility of Pepy II., was invaded and perhaps conquered, as to Lower and part of Upper Egypt, by invaders from the north-east, Syrians, in fact, whose conquest would thus be a first draft or rehearsal of the much more famous and important invasion by the Hyksos, in the interval between the Middle Kingdom and the Empire. The main evidence is that of the "Button-Badges" which appear from the close of the VIth Dynasty, disappearing again in the IXth and Xth. This style of object has been found in Mesopotamia (Bismiya), in Cilicia, and Aleppo, as well as in Egypt. The Egyptian specimens are not of Egyptian workmanship, and though in some cases Egyptian motives are used, such as the Ankh and the Falcon, the execution of the design could never be taken for Egyptian. Besides these, there are such articles as the green jasper cylinder of Khendu, obviously also foreign in design, though again using Egyptian detail. Several names of the period, such as *Shema*, *Neby*, *Telulu*, and *Annu*, seem to be of Semitic derivation; and the scarab of a king Ra-cn-ka, has, along with Egyptian elements, the *guilloche* which is also seen on the cylinder of Khendu, and which is "entirely Asiatic". The evidence thus summed up is manifestly of the scantiest; but, taken in conjunction with the obvious disorganisation of the whole kingdom at this period, it is probably sufficient to give likelihood to Petrie's suggestion, which, indeed, is more or less generally accepted by historians.

Petrie has also suggested that early in this period another invasion of Upper Egypt took place from the South, and resulted in the establishment at Thebes of the race which afterwards gave to Egypt the two lines of kings whom we know as the XIth and XIIth Dynasties. This idea is also virtually accepted by Dr. H. R. Hall (*Cambridge Ancient History*, i. 295-6), and the presence of Nubian elements in the blood of the Mentuhoteps, Senuserts, and Amenemhats of these dynasties would to some extent account for the very strongly marked facial characteristics of these famous monarchs. Thus the kingdom was being shaken at both of its ends by foreign incursion, and the old days of division, with consequent helplessness, had returned. A third element had, however, still to be reckoned with, and succeeded for a short time in establishing a limited and shaky sovereignty over the central portion of the land, from about the mouth of the Fayum as far south as Thinis and Abydos, though these ancient and sacred seats of royalty and divinity were only held by the newcomers for a brief space.

The seat of this transient and embarrassed line of monarchs was at the town which the Greeks named Herakleopolis, and which was known to the Egyptians as Ehininsi or Hininsu; and it has been surmised that the line was of western origin (Libyan?), and invaded Egypt by way of the Fayum province. Such a line of advance would make Herakleopolis a natural capital for the invaders; but the city itself had already a very ancient claim to recognition, alike from the dynastic and the religious point of view. It was the ancient capital of the *Insi* kings of Upper Egypt, before the unification of the land; and it was also one of the most sacred sites of the kingdom. It was at Herakleopolis, according to one tradition, that Shu, the god of space, raised up the firmament from the earth, and caused the latter to become solid; it was from Herakleopolis that Ra sent forth Sekhmet to destroy mankind, in consequence of their rebellion against the ageing god; and it was at Herakleopolis that both Osiris and his son Horus were crowned; while the "Crusher-of-Bones", one of the dreaded 42 assessors before whom the dead man had to make his abjuration of sin in the Hall of Truth, came forth, as the 125th chapter of the Book of the Dead tells us, from Herakleopolis.

The founder of this Herakleopolitan dynasty (the IXth) was a certain Khety or Ekhtai. He has long enjoyed a somewhat evil reputation owing to statements in Manetho and Eratosthenes which have been attributed to him. Manetho's statement says that "of nineteen Herakleotic kings, who reigned 409 years, the first was Akhthoes, the worst of all his predecessors. He did much harm to all the inhabitants of Egypt, was seized with madness and killed by a crocodile"—a notable example of poetic justice, if Akhthoes was as black as he was painted. "The 27th of the Theban kings," says Eratosthenes, "Khuthur Taurus the tyrant, reigned 7 years, A.M. 3636"; and on the principle that you may as well hang a dog as give him a bad name, coupled with the very moderate degree of resemblance between the names Khuthur Taurus and Akhthoes, the founder of the IXth Dynasty has been saddled with the evil deeds of both the scoundrels of the two historians.

No doubt Khety or Ekhtai is the Akhthoes of Manetho; but there is no evidence, save Manetho's statement, for the lurid and ungrammatical account of his misdeeds. Founders of usurping royal lines, however, are apt to be men of their hands, and to be somewhat heedless of whose toes they may tread upon as they climb the ladder of fortune; and perhaps Khety was no better than the average. Evidently he succeeded in establishing for himself a reputation as an ill man to meddle with—which was probably precisely what he desired to do. It was a pity that some of his successors had not a little more of his terribleness and a little less of the plaster saint, as we shall see. If he be, as Petrie holds, the Neb-kau-Ra Khety of the "Complaints of the Peasant", then he had a distinct and highly peculiar vein of humour, which may have perhaps justified Manetho's estimate in the eyes of an unappreciative public. The arrangement of the four Khetys of the Herakleopolitan line, however, is uncertain, though we may provisionally accept Neb-kau-Ra Khety as the first of the line. Nothing else is known with regard to him.

The second of the line, however, was almost certainly Khety Meryabra, whom we may call Khety II. So far as is known, he reigned (for 25 years, according to Petrie; for 11, according to Weigall) in peace over his central Egyptian kingdom; but quite obviously the extremities of the land were in a state of more or less hopeless muddle, from which the thrust of the Herakleopolitans had not been sufficient to deliver it. The Delta, according to the account of things given by his successor, Khety III., to his son, afterwards Khety IV., was "in evil case", and was only reduced to some semblance of order by considerable exertion on the part of Khety III., who was here more successful than he was in his relations with the south. Beyond Thinis and Abydos, and thence to the First Cataract, the Herakleopolitan Pharaoh's authority was evidently practically non-existent, and even north of Thinis, the Siut (Assiut) district was held by a line of local princes who, though thoroughly loyal to their nominal master, were actually far more powerful than the king whom they held by force upon a tottering throne. These princes of Siut have left us invaluable material for the history of the period in their tomb-inscriptions, of which three date from this time. The order of these is not quite certain; but it appears that the prince now usually numbered as Khety II. (for the family name was the same as that of the Pharaonic house), is actually the first of the three, and is followed by Tefaba, and the present Khety I. At all events, the inscription of Khety II. contemplates with satisfaction a period of peace and plenty such as certainly did not prevail during the latter years of the dynasty.

The Prince of Siut tells us that, like some other magnates of whom we have heard, he was brought up along with the royal household, giving a curious detail of his education. "He [the king] had me instructed in swimming along with the royal children." He mentions that he maintained an army, and had a fleet of "goodly ships", which he held at the service of the king on occasion, that he did many public works for his principality, and that the land throve under his administration. "Siut was satisfied with my administration; Herakleopolis praised God for me." Altogether a notable subject of a peaceable king, who might well think, as he voyaged up-river in the ships of Siut, that it was perhaps as well that this mighty man had been taught swimming in past days along with the royal children.

PLATE XV

1. RELIEF OF CRANES
2. RELIEF OF GAZELLES.   TOMB OF METHEN

From Fechheimer's "Die Plastik der Ägypter" (Cassirer)

So far as we know, Khety II. of Herakleopolis went down to his grave in peace; but the destiny that was appointed for his successor, Khety III., Uahkara, was very different. To him was appointed a thorn in the flesh, of the most pronounced and irritating character, in the shape of his relations with another princely house of the South, which had for some time been growing in power, and was now beginning to get somewhat above itself under the vigorous leadership of its reigning prince. This was the House of the Antefs of Thebes, whose present representative was probably Prince Antef-aa (Antef the Great), son of the nomarch Prince Antef the First. Antef-aa's father was already virtual ruler of the southern part of Egypt, though he makes no claim to royal dignity. He describes himself as "The hereditary noble, ruler of the Thebaid, satisfying the desire of the king, keeper of the gate of the frontier, pillar of the South, the administrator, making his two lands to live, chief of the prophets". All this is no more than many a loyal subject had long ago claimed for himself, and there is no suspicion of disloyalty in Prince Antef's statement that he satisfied the desire of the king. But the power was there, as it was in the case of Khety II. of Siut, and perhaps there was a lack of the personal bond which kept the Prince of Siut loyal. It needed only the combination of a more ambitious successor to Antef, and a grievance as a pretext, to change indifference into hostility to the reigning but scarcely ruling house at Herakleopolis.

The more ambitious successor duly appeared in Prince Antef-aa. Hitherto Thebes had occupied in Egyptian history a place so insignificant as to contrast most forcibly with her subsequent domination and splendour; and her inhabitants were backward in culture compared with the districts to the north which had been more in touch with the great cultural movements of the Old Kingdom. All this was now to be changed, and Thebes was ere long to acquire a precedence among Egyptian cities which she never altogether lost again until the Empire was going down in disaster. Probably it was not very long after the appearance of the new Theban prince that the pretext was given which resulted in an open breach between the House of Antef and the reigning House of Khety.

The giving of the pretext was the work of Herakleopolis, and, as the Pharaoh Khety III. sorrowfully but candidly admits, he was in the wrong, though he did not know of what was happening until the mischief had been done. Our information, such as it is, comes from the curious document known as Papyrus Petersburg 1116A, or "The Instruction for King Merykara". In this very remarkable writing, which comes to us in an XVIIIth Dynasty version, an old king, who must be identified with Khety III., addresses his son Merykara, who is Khety IV., the last king of the Herakleopolitan line, and gives him the fruits of his life's experience as a guide for his own conduct on the throne. In this wonderfully candid self-revelation there are two references to what seems to have been the bone of contention between the Pharaoh and his too powerful nominal subject at Thebes. In the first it is stated: "Egypt fights in the necropolis with violating of tombs. . . . Even so did I, and even so did it occur"; and this reference to desecration of tombs must point to the sacred city of Thinis, of which the king immediately says: "I captured it like a cloudburst". A little later the king says: "Behold, a calamity happened in my time: the regions of Thinis were violated. It happened in sooth through that which I did, and I (only) knew of it after it was done. That was evil —— Take heed concerning it. A blow is rewarded with the like thereof."

What precisely had happened is obscure; but it appears as if it had been something like this. Both Khety III. and Antef-aa apparently claimed Thinis (and Abydos, which lies close to it) as belonging to their respective dominions. For Khety, or at least for his sturdy vassal Tefaba of Siut, it is "The Fortress of the Port of the South"; for Antef, it, or its neighbourhood, is "The Door of the North". Probably some squabble arose between taxing authorities or frontier-guards about the disputed district, which, both on account of its ancient association with early lines of Pharaohs, through Thinis, and with religious beliefs, through Abydos, was unspeakably sacred;

and in the fighting which arose over this boundary trouble, that disaster happened to which Khety makes such doleful reference. The sacred tombs of ancient royalty were violated, and Khety, who had sent out the troops who had committed the sacrilege, had to shoulder the responsibility for a deed of which he knew nothing until after it had happened, and of which he was heartily ashamed. No doubt the whole land was shocked, in spite of its already large experience in tomb-robbing, at this violation of the most sacred sites in Egypt; and the Theban Prince was not the man to relieve poor Khety's shoulders of the burden which the conduct of his troops had tied on them, or to lose so good an opportunity of doing with public sympathy what perhaps he half-unconsciously intended to do all along. At all events, Antef seems to have now assumed the Horus name of a Pharaoh, and calls himself the Horus Uah-ankh, Antef-aa, What was of more practical importance was that he also sailed north with a fleet, a frank and open rebel, to revenge the insult that had been offered to his dignity and to religion. His first attempt, however, was a complete failure, or, at least, so says Tefaba of Siut, who met him in defence of his overlord. "The first time that my soldiers fought with the southern nomes," says the Prince of Siut, "they smote them as far as the southern boundary. When I came to the city, I overthrew the foe —— I drove him —— as far as the Fortress of the Port of the South." A second attempt met with no better success, and ended in the ignominious downfall of Antef's commander. "There came another, like a jackal —— with another army from his confederacy. I went out against him —— I ceased not to fight to the end, making use of the south wind as well as the north wind, of the east wind as well as of the west wind —— He fell in the water, his ships ran aground, his army were like bulls when attacked by wild beasts, and running with tails to the front."

So much for the results of the first naval battle of which any account has survived, and of which the Prince of Siut was obviously, and perhaps not unreasonably, proud. Those southern barbarians only needed someone who would really face them, and they soon found their proper and lowly place! Unfortunately for Tefaba, and still more for his master, the southern barbarian most reprehensibly declined to be put in his place, even after two defeats. He came north again; and this time it is not Tefaba who tells us the story, but the other fellow. "(I made) her northern boundary," Antef says on his tomb stele, referring to his kingdom, "as far as the nome of Aphroditopolis (just north of Thinis). I drove in the mooring-stake in the sacred valley, I captured the entire Thinite nome, I opened all her fortresses, I made her the Door of the North"—in place of Tefaba's "Fortress of the Port of the South".

Khety III., still shivering in his palace at Herakleopolis at the thought of the sacrilege that a pious king like himself had been committed to, had good enough reason now to write down in his Instructions for his son—"A blow is rewarded with the like thereof"; in fact he might perhaps think that Antef had returned the blow with interest. The calamity which had befallen him had indeed a double edge, and the territorial loss, serious and shameful enough, was doubtless, to a king of his temperament, almost a small thing in comparison with the spiritual deprivation. Thinis and Abydos, the most sacred spots in Egypt, were now closed to him, and when he died he must go without the pilgrimage to the Holy Places, which was almost equivalent to a passport to heaven. This was bitterness indeed, and the saddened king, an intensely religious man, accepted it as the manifest judgment of an offended God. "A generation hath passed among men", he wrote years afterwards, "and God, who discerneth characters, hath hidden himself." Against such a dispensation of the Judge of all the earth, it was vain to make any protest, and apparently the broken king made no attempt to recover his lost frontiers.

Neither, doubtless to the intense surprise of the Prince of Siut, and perhaps to that of himself and his triumphant army, did the Horus Uahankh Antef-aa advance farther. Possibly he was one of these unusually wise men who really know that "too much is too much", and know when to stop. He had been stubbornly persevering in his determination to wipe out the insult of the violation of the tombs at Thinis, even after two defeats. Now, with almost incredible good luck, he had succeeded even beyond his utmost hopes. Better not to presume upon good luck too far. So, with a delicate appreciation of the dangers of *Hubris*, the Theban held his hand, made peace to all appearance with his beaten enemy, and even agreed, though he ceased to send the normal tribute of the days of his nominal inferiority, to allow his Herakleopolitan rival access to the granite quarries of Aswan—an act both of grace and of piety. On his side, Khety III. was apparently well pleased to make the best of a bad job, in which his own conscience was as much his enemy as was his southern rival. Henceforward he seems to have cherished a wholesome respect for the south and its redoubtable master, and he hands on to his son, much as Bismarck handed on the precept of never quarrelling with Russia, the rule of maintaining good terms with a neighbour who had shown himself capable of so much harm if provoked, but had also revealed an unexpectedly placable disposition.

Once and again he refers in his Instruction to this as a prime necessity of policy for his son, and presses into his service, to underline his warning, an old Palace saw about the matter. "Be not on ill terms with the Southern Land, for thou knowest what the Residence hath foretold concerning it, and that happeneth even as this did happen (his own defeat). . . . Be lenient concerning it; for it is good to work for the future. Stand well with the Southern Land. Then the bearers of bags (nominal tribute) come to thee with gifts. I did the same as the forefathers; 'Though it hath no corn that it may give it, yet let it be pleasing to thee, seeing that they are but weak unto thee. Satisfy thyself with thine own bread and beer' (Don't stir them up again even though their corn tribute does not come in). The red granite comes to thee also without hindrance." (Be thankful for small mercies, and for this concession on the part of the lord of Aswan.) It is curious to see the old king referring in this connection to a habit which has been the besetting sin of the Pharaohs of all ages—the habit of appropriating the fine work of a previous king's tomb or temples to eke out one's own poverty. If King Khety's gentle admonition had only been hearkened to by his successors, the difference to the study of Egyptology would have been immense. Men like Ramses II. and Merenptah ought to have bound the following sentences as a frontlet between their eyes: "Harm not the monument of another, but quarry thyself stone in Turah. Build not thy tomb out of what hath been pulled down." But Khety, wise through bitter experience, was but the voice of one crying in the wilderness, and king and commoner went gaily on with the work of spoliation as before.

Having delivered his soul with regard to the South, Khety discusses for the benefit of his son the conditions in the other parts of the realm. If he had muddled the southern business, he flattered himself that he had straightened out things in the Delta. "I pacified the entire West as far as the margins of the lake. Also on the east side of the Delta (where) matters were in evil case, it is made into districts and cities, and the authority that used to be in the hand of one is in the hand of ten (The Delta magnates had apparently been getting above themselves, and had been suppressed). Now they give a whole list of all manner of taxes, the priest is invested with fields, and tribute is paid thee as if they were a single gang. It will not come to pass that there are evil foes thereamong. Thou sufferest not from the Nile that it cometh not (inundations are good), and thou hast the products of the Delta."

The Eastern Delta, too, the old man feels, is more or less secure, thanks partly to his own precautions, and partly to the essential characteristics of Arab nature, which were exactly the same five thousand years ago as they are to-day. "Behold I drave in the mooring-post in the East. The boundary from Hebenu unto the Path-of-Horus is settled with cities, and filled with people of the best of the entire land, in order to repel the arms of the Asiatics. . . . This is said, moreover, with regard to the barbarian: 'The wretched Asiatic, evil is the land wherein he is, with bad water, inaccessible because of the many trees, and the roads thereof are evil by reason of the mountains. Never dwelleth he in a single place, and his feet wander. Since the time of Horus (from time immemorial) he fighteth and conquereth not, but likewise is he not conquered, and he

never announceth the day in fighting.'" National characteristics have seldom been more vividly or more concisely
described than in these few sentences, which depict the
Semitic nomad "as he was in the beginning, is now, and
ever shall be". A curious note is the grievance which the
king, as head of a disciplined army, which proceeds
according to rule, and after due declaration of war, feels
against the Arab raider, who "never announceth the day in
fighting". Khety IV., his father says, is not to worry
himself about the Arabs, whose limited capacity to do ill is
correctly estimated. "Trouble not thyself about him, the
Asiatic; he plundereth a lonely settlement, but he captureth
not a populous city."

After all, however, the old trouble in the south still
presents itself to the old king as the danger point. He
wisely sees that the bad example of a new southern outbreak may undo all his good work in the north, unless
precautions are taken; and his safeguard against the danger
of the north being infected by the unrest of the south is
the creation of numerous fortified towns, which will hold
the various districts in check. "If thy boundary towards
the Southern Land is in revolt, the foreigners of the North
will also begin fighting. Build (therefore) towns in the
Delta. A man's name will not be small through what he
hath done, and an inhabited city is not harmed. Build
towns!" Khety's appreciation of his difficult position,
between the Devil of the South and the Deep Sea of the
North, is obviously edged by all the force of bitter experience, and his policy was probably quite a sound one—
only his son did not get the chance to carry it out.

Perhaps the quaintest part of "good King Khety's
Testament" is that which gives his maxims of statecraft.
Again the king was in a strait betwixt two. On the one
hand there was the over-powerful vassal, whose trouble-
some claims had made mischief in the Delta before they
were firmly dealt with; on the other was the Bolshevik
agitator, whose modern representative counts himself the
latest thing in political wisdom, but is indeed only the last
avatar of an ancient nuisance. Khety had the same remedy
for both. "With regard to one whose dependants are many,

and who is pleasant in the eyes of his serfs, one that talketh much—the king's advice is: Suppress him, slay him, wipe out his name—root out the memory of him and his dependants that love him. A cause of unrest for the citizens is a quarrelsome man, one that createth two factions among the youth. If thou findest that the citizens cleave to him . . . cite him before the courtiers, suppress him; he too, is an enemy." A policy of Thorough is possibly the most immediately and momentarily satisfactory method of dealing with such problems as are presented by King-makers on the one hand, and Demagogues on the other—always on condition that one is strong enough to carry it out; but again, Khety IV. seemingly did not have time to experiment in the direction of sitting on the safety-valve.

On reflection, Khety realised that powerful subjects had their place in a well-ordered kingdom, provided they were kept in their place. A great man had not that temptation to partiality in judgment for the sake of a bribe, which has always been the curse of the East, and may be expected to tell peculiarly in the case of poor men raised to judicial positions. "Make thy counsellors great, that they may execute thy laws, for he that is rich in his house dealeth not partially, he is a possessor of substance that wanteth nought. But the poor man speaketh not according to what is right for him, and he that saith 'Would that I had' is not fair. He favoureth him that hath a payment for him. Great is a great one whose counsellors are great. Strong is a king that possesseth a court (of the right kind) —— Speak thou the truth in thine house, that the nobles who hold sway in the land may fear thee. It goeth well with a lord that is upright of heart. It is the inside of an house that inspireth the outside with fear."

Through the whole of the Instruction there runs a vein of anxious and almost tremulous piety. The one great blunder of the king's life had been the involuntary sacrilege at Thinis; and it evidently bore heavily on his conscience, and gave his religious outlook somewhat of a dark cast. "It is worth noting", says Erman, "that we meet with religious conceptions in this composition that are practi-

cally non-existent in the other works of the same class."
Khety has a strong sense of the presence and immediate
supervision of God in human affairs, and makes it the basis
of his plea for moderation. "Take heed lest thou punish
wrongfully. Slaughter not, that doth not profit thee;
punish with beatings and imprisonment (which are not
irrevocable) —— God knoweth the froward, God requiteth
his sins in blood." (Therefore the irrevocable punishment
may be left to him: "Vengeance is mine, I will repay,
saith the Lord".) A man must do all as mindful of the last
Judgment, when Thoth, the God of Wisdom, will super-
vise the trial. "The Judges who judge the oppressed (at the
Last Judgment), thou knowest that they are not lenient on
that day of judging the miserable, in the hour of carrying
out the decision. Ill fareth it when the accuser is The Wise
One! Put not thy trust in length of years; They regard a
lifetime as an hour. A man remaineth over after death, and
his deeds are placed beside him in heaps. It is for eternity
that one is there, and he is a fool that maketh light of
Them (The judges of the dead). But he that cometh
unto them without wrong-doing, he shall continue yonder
like a god, stepping boldly forward like the Lords of
Eternity."

Such is the teaching of this remarkable document, one
of the most noteworthy contributions to the understanding
of the standards and conceptions of Egyptian royalty at
this early date that we possess. It would perhaps be unfair
to regard Khety III., with his anxious and somewhat
broken-spirited piety, as representing adequately the
average Pharaoh; he was probably as much below the
average in practical efficiency as he was above it in ethical
and religious sense. All the same, this is by far the most
vivid picture of an Egyptian Pharaoh that survives; and
after all deductions on the score of the very pronounced
personality of its author, it leaves us with the feeling that
we have come nearer to the comprehension of Pharaoh as a
man, instead of an official puppet, and with the wish that
more of Khety's predecessors or successors had seen fit to
imitate his testamentary example, and to leave us a self-
portrait as vivid and convincing as that of the weary,

anxious old king, whose intentions were always so good, but with whom the world had gone rather hardly.

The pity of it all is that so far as can be judged the good advice of the old king proved of no effect, not necessarily because of any folly on the part of Khety IV., but simply because the Herakleopolitan Pharaohs occupied a position of unstable equilibrium which could not be permanently stabilised even by the loyal efforts of the princes of Siut. Almost our only information about the last reign of the IXth Dynasty comes from the tomb-inscription of the second Khety (Ist as usually numbered), son of Tefaba of Siut. The new prince duly followed in his father's steps, and the house of Siut continued to be the pillar of the throne, which needed all the support it could get. How trouble began is not quite clear from Khety's inscription; it is never far away at a change of reign in an eastern kingdom, especially if the ruling dynasty is not too securely founded. The probability is, judging from Khety of Siut's mention of conveying the king "up-river", that Uahankh Antef-aa did not feel obliged to show to the son the for-bearance which he had shown to the penitent father, and that there was some act of aggression on the part of the old Theban prince, now getting near the end of his long reign of 50 years. The dreaded trouble in the south was followed, as Khety III. had foreseen, by rebellion else-where—not in the Delta, as he had feared, but in the very heart of the realm, at Herakleopolis itself. Khety of Siut, however, remained true, and by the assistance of his local army and fleet the tottering throne was propped up for a little longer. First, the Herakleopolitan rebellion was quelled, and then the two Khetys turned their attention to the south, and went upstream to the frontier. Apparently the difficulties there were resolved for the time, and the victorious king and his vassal returned downstream, their huge fleet, as the Prince of Siut tells us with pride, stretching for many miles along the river.

"Thou hast chastised Middle Egypt", says the Siut inscription, recounting its author's great deeds, "for his (i.e. the king's) sake alone. Thou didst convey him up-stream, the heaven cleared for him, the whole land was with him, the counts of Middle Egypt, and the great ones of Herakleopolis, the district of the Queen of the land (the local goddess), who came to repel the evil-doer. The land trembled, Middle Egypt feared, all the people were in terror, the villages in panic, fear entered into their limbs. The officials of Pharaoh were a prey to fear, the favourites to the terror of Herakleopolis (Evidence of the rebellion having been even among the court magnates), the land burned in its flame. . . . Never was the van of a fleet brought into Sheshotep, while its rear was still at (?). They descended by water and landed at Herakleopolis. The city came, rejoicing over her lord, the son of her lord; women mingled with men, old men and children."

This gleam of success was, however, the last that was to shine upon the house of Herakleopolis. It was followed, apparently, by a short period of peace, during which certain public works were undertaken and carried out. At Siut a temple was built to the local god, Upuat, "The Opener of the Ways", or guide of the dead, the Egyptian equivalent of the Greek *Hermes Psychagogos*; and the Pharaoh built his pyramid at Saqqara, and set up a statue of himself of fairly creditable work. It was probably during these halcyon days that the last of the Siut princes was gathered to his fathers, mercifully taken away from the evil to come. At all events the conclusion of his tomb-inscription speaks of nothing but abounding prosperity.

"Thy city-god loves thee, Tefaba's son, Khety. . . . How beautiful is that which happens in thy time, the city is satisfied with thee. That which was concealed from the people, thou hast done it openly, in order to make gifts to Siut—by thy plan alone. Every official was at his post, there was no one fighting, nor any shooting an arrow. The child was not smitten beside his mother, nor the citizen beside his wife. There was no evil-doer in —— nor any one doing violence against his house. Thy city-god, thy father who loveth thee, leadeth thee."

Meanwhile in the South the old Theban Prince Antef-aa had also passed away, and had been succeeded by two kings whose reigns were brief, and apparently not without trouble. The next Theban king is Neb-hapt-ra

Mentuhotep II., who is once more a Pharaoh of all Egypt, and who speaks in his inscription at Gebelen of "binding the chiefs of the two lands, capturing the South and North Land, the highlands and the two regions, the Nine Bows and the Two Lands". Plainly, therefore, the catastrophe of the Herakleopolitan Pharaohs of the IXth and Xth Dynasties occurred between the death of Khety of Siut and the recognition of Mentuhotep II. of Thebes as Pharaoh of the whole land. How it came about, we have no idea. Manetho's statement that the Xth Dynasty consisted of 19 Herakleotic kings, who reigned for 185 years, is hopeless. The solitary possible trace which the Xth Dynasty has left is a group of three scarabs of a king Shenes, who may conceivably have belonged to this time. Plainly we are faced with a period when the nation was hopelessly divided against itself, and when the only cure for its ills had to be by the sharp surgery of civil war, until the strong and vigorous Theban house should assert its supremacy and introduce a stable state of things once more.

All this is reflected with poignancy and vividness in three remarkable pieces of writing which apparently belong to this time, or to the succeeding period of the XIth Dynasty, when the land was only slowly recovering from the miseries into which its divided state had plunged it. Of these, the most famous, as it is also the longest, is the well-known "Admonitions of Ipuwer". The beginning of this extraordinary document is lost, and one can only picture an Egyptian Jeremiah whose head is waters and his eyes a fountain of tears, as he weeps day and night for the miseries of his people. When we get touch with his actual words, he is already in the full tide of his catalogue of woes, in the presence of the king whom he is trying to waken to a sense of the responsibilities of his position.

"The (very) door-keepers say, 'Let us go and plunder'. The washerman refuseth to carry his load. Even the bird-catchers have to make themselves ready for battle, with shields. The confectioners and brewers are in revolt, and a man looketh upon his son as an enemy. —— The virtuous man goeth in mourning because of what hath happened in

the land —— strangers (normally despised) are become
Egyptians everywhere —— Nay, but the land is full of
troops of brigands. A man goeth to plough with his shield.
. . . Nay, but Nile is in flood, yet none plougheth for
him. Every man saith: 'We know not what hath happened
throughout the land'. Nay, but women are barren, and
there is no conception. Khnum fashioneth men no more
because of the condition of the land. Nay, but poor men
now possess fine things. He who once made for himself no
sandals now possesseth riches. . . . Nay, but many dead
men are buried in the river. The stream is a sepulchre,
and the Pure Place is become a stream. Nay, but the high-
born are full of lamentations, and the poor are full of joy.
Every town saith: 'Let us drive out the powerful from our
midst'. . . . The land turneth round as doth a potter's
wheel, and the robber possesseth riches. . . . Nay, but
the river is blood. Doth a man drink thereof, he rejecteth
it as human, (though) one thirsteth for water. . . . Nay,
but the crocodiles are glutted with what they have carried
off. Men go to them of their own accord. Nay, but gold and
lapis lazuli, silver and turquoise, carnelian and bronze,
marble and . . . are hung about the necks of slave-girls.
But noble ladies walk through the land, and mistresses of
houses say: 'Would that we had something that we might
eat' . . . Men do not sail to Byblos to-day. What can we
do to get cedars for our mummies? Priests were buried
with their produce, and princes embalmed with their
resin, as far as the land of Keftiu, and now they come no
more. . . . Nay, but laughter perisheth and is no longer
made. It is grief that walketh through the land, mingled
with lamentations. . . . Nay, but great and small say: 'I
wish I were dead!' Little children say: 'He ought never to
have caused me to live!' "

So the jeremiad goes on through four different sections
or poems, each beginning with its own distinctive word, as
the first with "Nay". In the fifth, unfortunately much
mutilated, the prophet turns upon the king, and brings the
burden of all this home to him. "Ah, but had he but
perceived their nature in the first generation; then would
he have smitten down evil; he would have stretched forth

the arm against it, and destroyed the seed thereof and their inheritance. . . . There is no pilot in their time. Where is he to-day? Doth he sleep then? Behold, his might is not seen. . . . Command, Perception, and Truth are with thee; but it is confusion that thou puttest throughout the land, together with the noise of them that contend. . . . Lies are told thee; the land is brushwood, mankind is destroyed —— all these years are confusion —— Would that thou mightest taste some of these miseries (thyself)! Then thou wouldst say——"

"This is what Ipuwer said", concludes the poem, "when he answered the Majesty of the Lord of All". Certainly he did not shrink from telling the truth even with emphasis to his royal master, and one seems to catch the true note of prophecy in the fearlessness with which he brings his message home to a king who, like so many others, was being fed on lies. The prophecy has a certain monotony, and indeed it is difficult for such an utterance, which depends for its effect upon the recital of a catalogue of woes, to be anything else but monotonous; but the cumulative effect of the rehearsal of sorrows is singularly impressive, and the "Admonitions of Ipuwer" have much more of a claim to the title of literature than the bulk of Egyptian writings.

Of less importance, but of a character similar to the work of Ipuwer, is the prophecy of Neferrohu, which, though its reference is obviously to the rise of the XIIth Dynasty under Amenemhat I., and its date is therefore somewhat later, is so plainly inspired by conditions similar to those which drew forth Ipuwer's lamentations that it may be mentioned most fitly here. The prophecy professes to be the utterance of an ancient sage called Neferrohu, who was summoned by King Snefru, of the IIIrd Dynasty, to divert His Majesty who was suffering from boredom, and who took advantage of the opportunity to lay before the king the miseries of the realm in a manner probably not quite what Snefru expected when he asked to be amused. The legend is, of course, purely a fiction, as the distinct prophecy of the coming of Amenemhat clearly shows; but Neferrohu's catalogue of woes strikes a distinct note of its

own, and is not without power. "He said: 'Up mine heart,
that thou mayest bewail this land whence thou art sprung.
Rest not! Behold, it lieth before thy face. The whole land
hath perished, there is nought left, and there surviveth not
so much as the black of a nail of what should be there! . . .
I show thee the land in lamentation and distress; that
which never happened before hath happened. Men shall
take up weapons of war, that the land may live upon
uproar. Men shall fashion weapons of copper, that they
may beg for bread with blood. Men laugh with a laughter
of disease. Men will not weep because of death, men will
not sleep hungry because of death; a man's heart followeth
after his own self. . . . I show thee the son as foeman,
and the brother as adversary, and a man murdereth his
father.'" There is distinct literary power in such a picture,
and the touch of "men laughing with the laughter of
disease" has a grim sincerity that almost vouches for the
truth of the whole.

The striking feature of the prophecy, however, is the
picture, almost Messianic in its tone, of the coming of the
Saviour-king. "A king shall come from the south, called
Ameni, the son of a woman of Nubia, and born in Upper
Egypt. He shall receive the White Crown, and wear the
Red Crown. . . . Be glad, ye people of his time! . . .
They that work mischief and devise hostility, they have
subdued their mouthings for fear of him. The Asiatics
shall fall before his carnage, and the Libyans shall fall
before his flame. The foes succumb to his onset, and the
rebels to his might. The royal serpent that is on his forehead, it pacifieth for him the rebels. . . . And Right shall
come again into its place, and Iniquity—that is cast forth.
He will rejoice who shall behold this, and who shall then
serve the king." It may be, of course, that this is merely
wisdom after the event, and glorification of an already
regnant and powerful monarch, with whom it was well to
be on good terms; but it has a singular appearance of
sincerity, in addition to its undoubted power.

What the ordinary man, who had no gift of prevision,
thought of this time of wretchedness is seen in the extraordinary "Dispute with his Soul of One who is tired of

Life", a piece which for weird fascination has no equal in Egyptian literature. "Then my soul opened its mouth to me, to answer what I had said. . . . 'Never wilt thou go forth again to behold the sun. They that builded in granite and fashioned a hall in the pyramid, that achieved goodly work—when the builders are become gods (*i.e.* when the kings are dead) then their offering-tables are empty, and they are even as the weary ones which die upon the canal-bank without a survivor; the flood hath taken its end of them, and likewise the heat of the sun, and the fish of the river-bank hold converse with them." Surely that is grim enough.

The summing up of the whole matter is in the little set of verses in praise of Death, with its characteristically Egyptian pictures of the cool north wind mitigating the sultry heat, and the cheery drinking-bout on the river-bank:

> Death is before me to-day
> As when a sick man becometh whole,
> As when one walketh abroad after sickness.

> Death is before me to-day
> As the odour of myrrh,
> As when one sitteth under the sail on a windy day.

> Death is before me to-day
> As the odour of lotus-flowers,
> As when one sitteth on the shore of drunkenness.

> Death is before me to-day
> As a well-trodden path,
> As when a man returneth from the war unto his house.

> Death is before me to-day
> As a clearing of the sky,
> As a man . . . to that which he knew not.

> Death is before me to-day
> As when a man longeth to see his house again,
> After he hath spent many years in captivity.

Such were the estimates formed of this Intermediate period by various types and classes of men who lived through its miseries. Poorly documented as it may be in respect of monumental relics, or actual records, such writings as we have been considering give us an otherwise

PLATE XVI

1. OLD KINGDOM STELE OF RAHOTEP
2. MIDDLE KINGDOM STELE OF ANTEF (*p.* 249)
To illustrate the decline of Art in the interval.
From Sir Wallis Budge's "Egyptian Sculptures in the British Museum"

unmatched vision of a period of darkness and gloom, and of a land fast reverting, as Egypt has always shown a curious tendency to do when the strong guiding hand has been removed, to anarchy and barbarism. The period has left us little in the way of material relics; but we know the essential spirit of it perhaps as well as that of the most amply illustrated period of Egyptian history—thanks to its heavily laden prophets and pessimists, from the weary Pharaoh Khety to the unknown commoner who felt that the best thing a man could do in such a time was—to die.

BOOK II

THE MIDDLE KINGDOM

CHAPTER XII

THE RISE OF THEBES UNDER THE ELEVENTH DYNASTY

In tracing the collapse of the Herakleopolitan Pharaohs, we have carried the narrative somewhat beyond the point at which the next line began, and have to take up the thread of the story, so far as it relates to the Theban princes, who now emerge as the rulers of a once more united Egypt, from a point whose exact place is difficult to determine, but which was at all events somewhere in the time of the IXth Dynasty, and before the reign of Khety III. We have seen that the founder of the new Theban line was the nomarch Antef, "the hereditary prince, count, great lord of the Theban nome, satisfying the king as keeper of the Door of the South, great pillar of him, who makes his two lands to live". The fact that he is thus described on his funerary stele indicates that up to the date of his death there had been no open breach between the Theban princes and the Herakleopolitan line of Pharaohs. We know nothing more of him beyond the fact that he was recognised in later days as the founder, not only of the XIth but also of the still more important XIIth Dynasty. Senusert I. of the latter line dedicated a statue to him at Karnak, on which he is described in terms which imply direct relationship: "The king of Upper and Lower Egypt, Kheperkara (Senusert I.) he made it as his monument for his father, the hereditary prince Antefa . . . born of Akua". The XIth and XIIth Dynasties were therefore not only both Theban, but were directly connected with one another by blood.

Prince Antef appears to have made no claim to the crown; but his son Antef-aa, as we have seen, was more ambitious, and assumed the title of the Horus Uahankh,

Son of the Sun, Antef-aa. He also called himself *Insibya*, "King of Upper and Lower Egypt", though this title did not correspond to the actual fact, as he died before the final unification of the land after the fall of the Herakleopolitan Pharaohs. There is no need to recapitulate the steps by which he succeeded in wresting from Khety III. a considerable part of his domain. A stele of one of his captains in this strife gives us a glimpse of one of the men who were winning for the Theban princes the chance which they so splendidly took of re-creating Egypt: "The prince, the sole confidential friend, the governor of the Residence, the superintendent of the granaries, Zara, says, The Horus Uahankh, the King of Upper and Lower Egypt, the Son of Ra, Antef, the creator of beauties, sent me a message, after I had fought with the house of Khety in the domain of Thinis, and messages came that the prince had given me a ship, in order that there might be protection for the land of those who belong to the South, to its whole extent, southwards from Elephantine and northwards to Aphroditopolis, because he knew my excellence. I say, I was promoted amongst the elders, I was fierce of heart on the day of smiting." The style of Captain Zara's stele, which is crude and coarse to an extreme, bears witness to the comparative lack of culture in the Theban district at this time. Separation from the great Memphite tradition of the Old Kingdom, owing to the prevailing disunion, had not improved the style of the Theban craftsmen. On the other hand, this must not be pressed too far, as the stele of Thetha, another of Antef's high officers, who lived on into the next reign, is of comparatively good style and execution.

Thetha, who describes his own merits and honours with all that shrinking modesty which is so characteristic of the Egyptian official, and so attractive, tells us that he "passed a long period of years under the Majesty of my lord Horus, Uahankh, King of Upper and Lower Egypt, Son of Ra, Antef, this land being under his authority up-river as far as Thes, and down-river as far as Thinis". "I was one", he goes on, "who was a real favourite of his lord, a great and favourite official, the coolness and warmth in the house of his lord, to whom salaam was made in presence of the grandees." Officialdom seems to have lost the secret of this lyrical fervour in describing its own merits. The portrait of this worthy man, in the British Museum, gives a good idea of the general appearance of the competent servants who were helping the Theban line to build up the new Egypt of the Middle Kingdom.

King Antef-aa, whose moderation in the day of his triumph has already predisposed us in his favour, has another claim to our regard, as having been a lover of dogs to the extent of having five of his pets depicted along with himself on the tomb stele which was placed in his unimposing brick pyramid at Qurneh, in the Theban Necropolis. Eleven hundred years after he was in his grave this amiable little trait of character was duly embalmed in the report made by the Tomb Commission which was appointed to examine into the violation of the royal tombs at Thebes in the reign of Ramses IX.: "The monument of king Sa Ra An-aa, which is at the north of the temple of Amenhotep of the terrace. This tomb is injured on the surface opposite the spot where the tablet is placed; on the tablet is the image of the king standing, having between his feet his dog named Behukaa. Examined on that day, it was found in good condition." Modern vandals have not been so kind to the memorial of this old empire-builder and dog-fancier as the tomb-robbers of ancient Thebes had been. Mariette discovered the stele in 1860, took a rough copy of it, and left it where he found it. Twenty years later it was appropriated by a fellah, who broke it up to use the stone in a *sakieh*. The fragments which could be found were rescued by Maspero and placed in the Cairo Museum, where King Antef may still be seen with four out of the original five dogs, called "The Gazelle", "The Greyhound", "The Black", and "The Firepot". Before the king were the lines of inscription telling of his conquest of Thinis, and of the great works he had done for Thebes: "I filled Amen's temple with august vases, in order to offer libations. . . . I built their temples, wrought their stairways, restored their gates, established their divine offerings to all eternity"; but perhaps we can feel more of a

kindred spirit in Antef the dog-lover, who craved for the
company of his favourites even in the other world, than in
the conqueror and temple-builder.

King Antef has yet another claim to immortality if he
be, as is likely, the king from whose tomb-chapel the
famous Song of the Harper was copied on to an XVIIIth
Dynasty papyrus. It will not surprise us, after the literary
power exhibited in such work as the " Admonitions of
Ipuwer", to find that this age of strife and confusion was
capable of producing the solemn music of "The Song
which is in the House of King Antef, the justified, which is
in front of the singer with the harp":

> How prosperous is this good prince!
> It is a goodly destiny, that the bodies diminish,
> Passing away while others remain,
> Since the time of the ancestors,
> The gods who were aforetime,
> Who rest in their pyramids,
> Nobles and the glorious departed likewise,
> Entombed in their pyramids.
> Those who built their tomb-temples,
> Their place is no more.
> Behold what is done therein.
> I have heard the words of Imhotep and Hordadef,
> Words greatly celebrated as their utterances.
> Behold the places thereof;
> Their walls are dismantled,
> Their places are no more,
> As if they had never been.

So the poem runs on to its *carpe diem* conclusion:

> Celebrate the glad day,
> Be not weary therein.
> Lo, no man taketh his goods with him.
> Yea none returneth again that is gone thither.

One may be tempted to imagine that it was the fact of
having such a moral before his eyes that persuaded the old
king to be content with so insignificant a monument when
his fifty years of prosperous struggle were drawing to a
close. More probably, however, it was the simple fact that
the comparatively rude art of the Thebaid was not equal to
anything much more imposing. In any case, Antef's true

memorial was an Egypt which his efforts had put into the way of regaining her old unity and self-respect.

The founder of the dynasty was succeeded by his son Antef, whose Hawk name was the mouth-filling one Nakht-neb-tep-nefer, or "Mighty-is-the-Lord-in-the Height-of-Good-Fortune". Thetha, whose service of Uahankh Antef we have already seen, tells us of the accession of the heir: "Horus Uahankh . . . journeyed to his horizon. Then, when his son assumed his place, even Horus, Nakht-neb-Tepnefer, King of Upper and Lower Egypt, Son of Ra, Antef (II.) . . . I followed him to all his good seats of pleasure". Antef II. must have been an elderly man when his father died, and perhaps his good seats of pleasure were more to his taste than fighting to increase their number. He continued, however, to hold the Thinite province. In all probability his reign was a short one of not much over five years.

His successor, Sankh-ab-taui Mentuhotep (I.), is named on a stele of an official called Antef, now in the British Museum, a fair example of the somewhat crude and poorly proportioned art of the time. It is useful, however, because it gives us the order of the first three kings of the dynasty, under all of whom this Antef served, and also because it mentions, between the figures of Antef's second and third wives, "the fourteenth year after the year of the revolt of Thinis". This revolt is also mentioned upon the stele of another official Henun. Two things follow: first, that King Sankh-ab-taui's reign must have lasted for over fourteen years; and second, that the new dynasty had not yet quite consolidated its hold upon the conquests of its founder. But this is all that is known of the first Mentuhotep.

With the next Pharaoh, Mentuhotep II., Neb-Hapt-Ra, however, we get into touch with a figure of genuine importance in Egyptian history, albeit the remains of his reign are of the scantiest, and his very name has been confused with that of his successor. For it was Mentuhotep II. who at last succeeded in accomplishing once more the unity of the whole land, without which Egypt was always powerless. We have already mentioned the fact that on one of the blocks from the temple at Gebelen he describes himself as "binding the chiefs of the Two Lands, capturing the South and Northland, the highlands and the two regions, the Nine Bows and the Two Lands". Here there is no attempt whatsoever to disguise the fact that he holds himself to be master of Egypt, just as much as of his foreign possessions, by right of conquest; in fact, the point is underlined by the sculpture on the same block, which represents the king smiting four enemies, of whom one is an Egyptian! There is not much show of sparing the susceptibilities of the people who, after all, were to be his subjects in the future; but there can be no doubt that the conquest, however harshly insisted upon by the conqueror, and however bitter and galling to the more cultured folk of the north, who now saw themselves subjected to the rule of one whom they must have regarded as little better than a half-breed barbarian, was a most beneficial event for Egypt at large.

Neither, in point of fact, was there any real reason for any fear of a relapse into semi-barbarism in consequence of the triumph of the south. If Mentuhotep and his rude soldiers, many of them probably Sudanese, were uncultured and ignorant, they were at least capable of appreciating culture when they were brought into contact with it, and the arts and crafts of Egypt were much more likely to flourish in the end under the firm hand of a single master, who was ready to learn what he did not know, than in the incompetent grasp of a score of feeble aspirants who, however cultured themselves, had not learned that unity makes strength and division weakness. The surviving evidence shows that the king was able to command the skill of artists, who, although their work is still somewhat angular and gawky, with a certain suggestion of immaturity about it, were yet by no means unskilful in their craft. Indeed, there is a distinct promise of better things in the comparatively thin and tentative work of the reign, which seems to be feeling after something appreciated, but as yet unattained.

The works of art which tell us so much with regard to the time are found in connection with a series of six tombs and shrines which were discovered at Der el-Bahri by Messrs. Naville and Hall during their excavation of the XIth Dynasty temple there; the coffin and sarcophagus of one of the six (the finest of the set) being subsequently discovered by Mr. Winlock.

These tombs and shrines belonged to six wives of Mentuhotep II., who were named Aashait, Henhenit, Kemsit, Kauit, Sadhe, and Mait. All these great ladies had been priestesses of Hathor, to whose worship the king seems to have been specially devoted, as his other work, at Gebelen and Dendereh, is also connected with Hathor, and at Gebelen he calls himself "Son of Hathor, Mistress of Dendereh, Mentuhotep". The whole six shrines are placed upon a platform of rock and gravel below the great cliffs of Der el-Bahri, and the range of buildings had subsequently to be incorporated into the structure of the great temple which was built here by Mentuhotep's successor, Mentuhotep III. The tombs were small rock-cut chambers, in front of each of which stood a shrine, with a statue of the dead queen. The limestone sarcophagi of the queens were carved with remarkable representations of the dead ladies in all sorts of attitudes, being fanned and perfumed at their toilettes by their maids, sniffing lotus-flowers, drinking milk warm from the cow, which is being milked a little further on in the scene, and so forth. The lady Aashait, who proved to have been "a plump little person, with bobbed hair", and whose statuette showed her dressed in a scarlet frock much resembling, both in shortness and skimpiness, the dresses of 1928, was amply provided with bed-linen all duly marked either with her husband's name, or with the words, "Fine-linen Ward-robe", and also with an abundance of amulets. Another queen, Mait, whose name, "The Cat", scarcely seems dignified enough for such an exalted personage, proved to have been a child of five years old; so that marriages of policy were evidently not unknown in the royal house of the XIth Dynasty.

Such a Henrician rate of mortality among queens as is suggested by the fact of six queens dying in a single reign has been explained as being the natural result of the

king's keeping a large harem. Quite possibly he did; but
the more likely explanation is that the six ladies were
sacrificed at the death of their lord to accompany him
through the Underworld. We know that this barbarous
custom still survived in the XIIth Dynasty, as the tomb of
Hapzefa, with its slaughtered slaves, proves. If such a
holocaust was possible at Kerma under Senusert I., we
may be pretty certain that Mentuhotep II., himself very
probably of half-Nubian blood, would not go out on his
long journey unaccompanied. If the six princesses were
thus slaughtered, poor little Mait must have bought her
momentary dignities dearly enough, in spite of the "five
charming necklaces of gold, silver, carnelian and green
felspar" which were round her neck when she was discovered.

One of the most interesting discoveries of the time is
the statement made on the funeral stele of a certain
Khnemerdu, who seems to have been what we can only
describe as the librarian of a great lady named Neferu-
kayt, who may possibly have been another of the queens of
Mentuhotep II., and who was herself of very lofty descent,
being "daughter of a king, wife of a king whom he loved",
and who was, besides, a great heiress in her own right, in
virtue of her descent from her mother Nebt, who claimed
as her own the land from Elephantine to Aphroditopolis.
Neferu-kayt was evidently a patroness of learning, as her
mother had been before her, and Khnemerdu, having had
the good fortune to attract her attention by "the excellence
of his handiwork", was taken in hand by the great dame.
"Then she placed me in Dendereh, in the great treasure-
house (?) of her mother, great in writing, eminent of
sciences, great council-chamber of the South." Like a good
librarian, Khnemerdu at once entered upon a course of
reform. "I made extensions to the collection, enriching it
with heaps of precious things, so that it did not lack in
anything to the extent of my knowledge of things. I
organised it, I made fair its arrangements with beauty
more than before, I repaired what I found decayed, I tied
up what I found loose (Papyrus-rolls), I arranged what I
found muddled." A model librarian, in short! The impor-

tant point, however, is not Khnemerdu's virtue as a librarian, but the fact that here, even in "a barbarous age", we have two great ladies who, one after the other, seek to keep the lamp of learning burning in Egypt. When two queens in succession were women of learning and patronesses of literature, we are warned that we must not attach too implicit trust to the doleful pictures of the relapse of Egypt into comparative barbarism during this time of confusion. Much was lost, no doubt, especially in the art of the time, whose gradual recovery can be traced by actual examples; but where such ladies as Neferu-kayt and her mother, both of them southern, took such an interest in learning, it must be inferred that their respective courts were not altogether without a tincture of the arts and sciences.

There are no other certain remains of Mentuhotep II., except a rock tablet at Konosso, and the length of his reign is quite uncertain. Petrie only allows him 5 years, which seems short for a reign in which such a great work was accomplished; and Weigall's 25 years seems to be based upon no very sure foundation.

The next Pharaoh was another Mentuhotep, the third of the name, which has now become the standard name for the rest of the dynasty. Mentuhotep III. is much better known to us than any of his predecessors, and it would appear that in his reign the XIth Dynasty reached the culmination of its power and achievement. His long reign of considerably over forty years was apparently marked by complete control of all the resources of the united land, though there is one tablet which has been interpreted as meaning that there had been dissension between the Mentuhotep line and the Antef section of the dynastic house, ending in the acceptance by the representative of the Antefs of a vassal status.

This tablet is carved on the sandstone rock of the valley known as Shatt-er-rigal, about four miles below Silsileh, and shows a colossal figure of Mentuhotep III. standing with his mother, the lady Aoh, "The Moon", behind him. In front of him stands the smaller figure of a king, who is named "Son of the Sun, Antef", and who is accompanied by Mentuhotep's treasurer Khety. One of the Antef side of the house, therefore, contemporary with Mentuhotep III., is obviously recognised as royal, but as of inferior rank; and the inference has been drawn that trouble in the royal house had resulted in the definite attainment of superiority by the Mentuhotep branch, and the recognition of its suzerainty over the Antef branch, which still, however, continued to be recognised as royal. It is possible that a reference to this state of affairs may be found in the statement made by Aty, an official of this dynasty, on his stele from Gebelen. In this document, after the usual averments of his superior virtue and capacity, and an allusion to a time of scarcity when there were 400 unemployed in Gebelen who had to be sustained, Aty says: "I followed my great lord, I followed my lesser lord, and nothing was lost therein". The "great lord" and "lesser lord" might be regarded as Mentuhotep III. and his vassal Antef; but the attribution of the worthy assistant-treasurer's tablet to this reign is by no means certain, so that it is hazardous to build any theory upon what may be a mere verbal coincidence.

The great evidence of the power of the new king is to be found in the now famous mortuary temple which he caused to be built for himself in the great bay of the Libyan cliffs at Der el-Bahri opposite Thebes, to the south of the still more famous temple of Queen Hatshepsut, and on the site already occupied by the tombs and shrines of the six queens of his predecessor. The ruins of this building were excavated during the years from 1903 to 1907 by Messrs. Naville and Hall, with the result of giving to the world an exceedingly interesting structure of an unusual type, which had manifestly inspired Hatshepsut's great architect Senmut, when he came to design the splendid temple of the famous queen. Indeed, so manifest is this inspiration, when the two temples are viewed side by side, that there has been of late an altogether unjust tendency to deny to Senmut any credit for his superb design, and to give it all to the unknown designer (perhaps Mertisen) of Mentuhotep's temple. "Hatshepsut's temple", says Dr. H. R. Hall in his notes to the *Cambridge Ancient History*, vol. i. of Plates, "was directly imitated from that of her predecessor, to whom and not to her or her architect Sennemut, any praise for its supposed (not real) originality of design is due". To say this is, however, to do to Senmut an injustice as great as that which was unconsciously done to the architect of Mentuhotep's building by attributing to the XVIIIth Dynasty architect all the credit for his design before we knew that the other existed. It is not denied, and indeed cannot be denied, that Senmut was influenced by the example which he had before him; but he was not influenced any more by it than Shakespeare was influenced by the various romancers from whom he derived the plots of some of his greatest plays. He knew a good idea when he saw it, took it and converted it to his own uses; but no one with any sense of true merit in an architectural design will ever put the somewhat clumsy and groping design of Mentuhotep's architect on the same plane as the extraordinarily happy work of Senmut. The Mentuhotep building contains a good idea, very imperfectly realised and carried out. Senmut saw the merits of the idea, and realised them to the full in his great work, avoiding, by an intuition quite as happy as the original idea, the demerits of the XIth Dynasty design.

So far as the original design of Mentuhotep's architect can be made out from the remains of the building, it was a curious combination of pyramid and colonnaded temple. From the edge of the cultivation, a straight avenue, about 100 yards wide, with a pavement 18 yards broad running up the middle, led up to the temple in the bay of the cliffs a mile away. It terminated at the limestone wall of the forecourt, an enclosure 200 yards long by 100 wide, planted with sycamore-fig trees. The central part of this court was faced at its upper end with a double colonnade of pillars of square section. A ramp led up the centre of this colonnade to the level of its roof, from which point a square platform extended at the same level backward towards the cliffs. On the central portion of this platform rose what appears to have been a small pyramid on a high base 60 feet square. This was surrounded by a covered-in colonnade, with three rows of columns in front and on either side, and two at the back; while the enclosing wall of this roofed-in colonnade round the pyramid was surrounded on the outside by a double colonnade of square section pillars. The six shrines of the harem ladies of Mentuhotep II. were somewhat awkwardly incorporated into the back wall of the roofed colonnade. Behind the pyramid, an open court, flanked by a pillared arcade, extended up to the face of the cliffs, and a great sloping passage was cut in the rock from a point within the court down to a subterranean chamber deep within the rock, within which stood an alabaster shrine, destined for the burial of the king. Unfortunately there was no trace of the actual burial when the chamber was opened by Messrs. Naville and Hall.

Altogether, the temple was a remarkable and striking conception, for which all credit is due to Mentuhotep's architect, who evidently appreciated, as did Senmut still more perfectly several centuries later, the difficulty of placing any building characterised by pronounced vertical lines against the soaring cliffs which form the background at Der el-Bahri, and resorted to the long horizontal lines of the colonnades to give dignity to his design. The only blot on an original conception seems to have been the stumpy little pyramid which appears to have disfigured the centre of the whole composition, and which was no doubt only inserted as a concession to the old custom of a pyramid for royalty; but it is not yet sufficiently determined that the centre was actually pyramidal for us to condemn the design on that account. Fragments of reliefs show scenes of eastern warfare against the Aamu and Mentiu, so that it is evident that the reunited Egypt was now beginning to feel her strength and to aim at foreign conquests.

It is quite likely that the architect of this interesting temple is the same Mertisen whose accomplishments in his craft as an artist have been described by himself with the usual Egyptian candour and self-appreciation. "I know", he says, "the mystery of the divine word (the secrets of art), an artist skilled in his art. I know what belongs to the dropping waters" (an allusion probably to the practice of marking out work by means of flicking a wet string with red ochre against the surface to be marked off), "the figure produced by reckoning up these measures, how to produce the forms of going forth and returning, so that the limb may go to its place. I know the walking of the image of a man, the carriage of a woman, the wing-spread of a hawk, the twelve hours of the darkness, the contemplating of the eye which sees without a fellow, the poising of the arm to bring the hippopotamus low, the going of the runner. I know the making of amulets which enable us to go without the fire giving its flame upon us, or the flood washing us away. No one succeeds in it but I alone, and the eldest son of my body. God has decreed him to excel in it, and I have seen the perfections of his hands in the work of chief artist in every kind of precious stones, of gold and silver, of ivory and ebony." Petrie has called attention to the sequence in this catalogue of artistic perfections. "First the figures in slow action, then the differences of the male and female figure, then mythological subjects, then figures in rapid action, and, lastly, the trade secrets of the potency of amulets." It is a thoroughly Egyptian trait that the modest artist evidently attaches the supreme value, not to his legitimate knowledge of anatomy, but to the hocus-pocus of amulet-making. It is also evident that there was a regular and recognised course of training through which an artist had to advance before he reached the highest grades in his profession; and, as Dr. Hall has suggested, the fact that Mertisen was so inordinately proud of his skill may indicate that in this stage of gradual recovery from a period of confusion such skill was uncommon.

The reign of Mentuhotep III. was the culminating point of the XIth Dynasty, and he was revered to a late date in Egyptian history as one of the great kingdom-builders. In the Ramesseum, for instance, he is honoured, together with Mena and Aahmes I., as one of the outstanding kings. Of his external activities, little is known beyond what has been stated; but he evidently prepared the way for the foreign activity of the succeeding dynasty.

The order of succession in the case of the two following kings, with whom the dynasty closes, is a little obscure; but it seems probable that the great Hammamat inscriptions of Amenemhat, which belong to the reign of Mentuhotep

Neb-taui-ra, are the indications of the rise to power of the Amenemhat who became the founder of the XIIth Dynasty. In that case, Neb-taui-ra will be Mentuhotep V., and Mentuhotep Sankhara, who is sometimes placed last in the dynasty, will be Mentuhotep IV.

The short reign (probably eight or nine years) of Mentuhotep IV. was marked by considerable activity, as the number of his monuments still extant shows; but the chief event seems to have been the great expedition to Punt and Hammamat, which was carried through at his command by Henu, his "overseer of the temples, overseer of the granary and White House, overseer of horn and hoof, chief of the six courts of justice", and which is recorded with great pride by that diligent official. Incidentally it may be noticed that one of Henu's titles suggests that, with all the culture of Egypt, men were not altogether out of touch with the ancient barbarism which viewed eclipses and such-like phenomena as horrible disasters to be averted by strenuous measures. Henu asserts that he was "high-voiced in proclaiming the name of the king on the day of warding off", and one seems to see the Egyptian court turning out unanimously and banging upon all the copper vessels that could be collected, while they shout defiance in the king's name to the black dragon which is devouring the sun or moon, and no doubt threatens misfortune to the royal house unless he is driven off.

Henu's story, then, runs thus: "(His Majesty, Life! Health! Strength!), sent me to dispatch a ship to Punt to bring for him fresh myrrh from the sheikhs over the Red Land (desert), by reason of the fear of him in the highlands. . . . I went forth with an army of 3000 men. I made the road a river, and the Red Land a stretch of field, for I gave a leathern bottle, a carrying pole, two jars of water and 20 loaves to each one among them every day. The asses were laden with sandals. . . . Now I made 12 wells in the bush, and two wells in Idehet, 29 square cubits in one and 31 square cubits in the other. I made another in Iheteb, 20 by 20 cubits on each side —— Then I reached the Red Sea; then I made this ship, and I dispatched it with everything when I had made for it a great oblation of cattle, bulls, and ibexes."

Henu, it will be seen, did not sail with his ship to Punt, having another commission to execute. "I returned through the (valley) of Hammamat, I brought down for him august blocks for statues belonging to the temple. Never was brought down the like thereof for the king's court; never was done the like of this by any king's confidant sent out since the time of the god. I did this for the Majesty of My Lord, because he so much loved me. . . ." Henu's protestations of the unexampled nature of his exploits will not be taken at their face-value, as we have seen and shall see too many worded almost identically. What is of interest, however, is his account of the provisioning of his 3000 men. The twenty loaves, are, of course, little round cakes of bread; but even so, the commissariat had to provide 60,000 of these fresh every day for this by no means abnormally large expedition, and did it apparently as a mere matter of course. Amenemhat's expedition in the next reign numbered 10,000 men, and if the provisioning was on the same scale (it would not be less, looking to the character of Amenemhat), it must have taken 200,000 loaves a day to keep his men going. Some other nations, who have had much wider experience of foreign expeditions than the Egyptians ever had, might with advantage have taken a leaf out of the Egyptian book in respect of the organising of such matters. We have usually preferred to expend the men; the Egyptians preferred to expend foresight, and to keep the men alive.

As the Punt expedition seems to have been the outstanding event of this reign, so that of the reign of Mentuhotep V., Neb-taui-ra, was the great expedition of Amenemhat and his 10,000 to Hammamat for fine stone. The inscriptions which record this important piece of work are not only interesting on their own account, but also because the probability is that in this prime minister, who goes out with an army of 10,000 men at his back, and records his own deeds so fully, we should see the Amenemhat who shortly succeeded in establishing a new dynasty. Egyptian officials were never bashful in proclaiming their own achievements and merits; but Amenemhat is peculiarly expansive in this direction, and his Hammamat tablets redound much more to his own glory than to that of his master. When one sees, on the one hand, a Pharaoh whose reign is a matter of not more than four years, and possibly only of two years, and on the other a "too-powerful subject", who, on his own showing, had accumulated upon his own fortunate head practically all the important posts in the kingdom (the list of his titles occupies eighteen lines of print in Breasted's *Ancient Records*), and who had at his command practically the whole force of the realm, it does not require a very powerful or fanciful imagination to forecast the end of such an unequal yoking together. Mentuhotep V. disappears, and Amenemhat I. reigns in his stead; who the Amenemhat I. was, unless the prime minister, it is difficult to see.

Meanwhile, however, the plum was not ripe, though rapidly ripening, and Amenemhat was wise enough to be faithful to his allegiance until the time should come for being otherwise. If the king chose to send so great a man to bring down the fine stone for his sarcophagus, well and good; in due time the prime minister might also arrange that the sarcophagus should be occupied by the right person.

Amenemhat's story of the Hammamat expedition begins, after the date, with the account of what must have seemed to the prime minister's quarrymen something very much like a direct interposition from heaven. "This wonder which happened to His Majesty: that the beasts of the highlands came down to him; there came a gazelle great with young, going with her face toward the people before her, while her eyes looked backward; but she did not turn back until she arrived at this august mountain, at this block (the special block which the quarrymen were cutting out for the king's sarcophagus lid), it being still in its place, and meant for this lid of this sarcophagus. She dropped her young upon it while this army of the king was looking. Then they cut off her neck before the block, and brought fire (for a sacrifice). The block descended in safety.

"Now it was the Majesty of this august god, Lord of the Desert, who gave this (sacrificial) offering to his son Nebtauira, Mentuhotep V., living forever, in order that his heart might be joyful, that he might live upon his throne forever and forever, that he might celebrate millions of Sed-jubilees. The hereditary prince, count, governor of the city and vizier, chief of all nobles of judiciary office, supervisor of that which heaven gives, the earth creates, and the Nile brings, supervisor of everything in this whole land, the vizier, Amenemhat."

The vizier's concise account of his duties suggests that he can never have lacked for occupation, as he seems to have been supervisor of everything that was in heaven above or in the earth beneath, or in the waters under the earth. His account of the miracle which consecrated the block for the sarcophagus gives us what is rare in such things—a distinct touch of direct observation of nature, together with a touch of pathos, in the picture of the poor terrified gazelle, running the one way, yet looking in terror behind her all the time; but one must regretfully admit that the Egyptians were no sportsmen. To take advantage of the poor creature's extremity in order to make their paltry sacrifice was an action quite beyond the pale. The desert god who was pleased with such an offering must have been uncommonly like the devil.

This narrative, however, is only a preliminary to the real account of the expedition. Twelve days after the occurrence of this prodigy, Amenemhat set up the official account of the purpose and scale of the expedition. His tablet begins with a statement that it is set up (really carved on a rock-wall) by authority of the king. "His Majesty commanded to erect this stele to his father Min, Lord of the Desert, in this august, primeval mountain. . . ." Then after some official verbiage, comes the statement, nominally from the lips of Mentuhotep V.: "My Majesty sent forth the hereditary prince, governor of the city and vizier, chief of works, favourite of the king, Amenemhat, with an army of 10,000 men from the southern nomes, Middle Egypt, and the —— of the Oxyrhynchus nome; to bring for me an august block of the pure costly stone which is in this mountain, whose excellent qualities Min has created; for a sarcophagus, an eternal memorial, and for monuments in the temples of Middle Egypt, according as a King over the Two Lands sends to bring for himself the desire of his heart from the desert lands of his father Min. He made it as his monument for his father Min of Koptos, Lord of the Desert, Head of the Troglodytes, in order that the king might celebrate very many Jubilees, living like Ra, forever."

So much for the king; and, as Amenemhat doubtless thought, more than enough. It remained to glorify a much more important person. Accordingly, on the same day, Amenemhat executed his own personal tablet, before whose profuse self-adulation anything that had been said for Mentuhotep V. completely pales: "Year 2, second month of the first season, day 15. Royal commission, executed by the hereditary prince, count, governor of the city, chief judge, favourite of the king, chief of works, distinguished in his office, great in his rank, with advanced place in the house of his lord, commanding the official body, chief of the six courts of justice, judging the people and the inhabitants and hearing causes; to whom the great come bowing down, and the whole land, prone upon the belly; whose offices his lord advanced; conducting for him millions of the inhabitants to do for him the desire of his heart towards his monuments, enduring upon earth; magnate of the King of Upper Egypt, great one of the King of Lower Egypt, conductor of the palace, first (?) in stretching the measuring-cord; judging without partiality, governor of the whole south, to whom is reported that which is, and that which is not; conducting the administration of the Lord of the Two Lands; zealous of heart upon a royal commission; commander of those that command, conductor of overseers; the vizier of the king at his audiences, Amenemhat, says:——"

Doubtless Amenemhat had a pretty shrewd idea that his royal master would never see this fairly ample estimate of his vizier's merits; otherwise Mentuhotep might have been tempted to remark, as did a Scottish king of an overpowerful subject—"What wants this knave that a king should have?" and to make arrangements accordingly, as James V. did with Johnnie Armstrong. So much must, of course, be written off for the usual Egyptian brag; but, with all deductions, it is pretty evident that Amenemhat was so great a power in the state that he must eventually be either greater still, or very much less. The inference from subsequent history is pretty obvious—that he, not unnaturally, chose the former alternative. At all events, Mentuhotep V. shortly ceased to reign, and an Amenemhat succeeded him. Surely there were not two Amenemhats in Egypt, at this particular juncture, who had power enough to found a new dynasty.

In the meantime, however, the vizier is waiting to continue his narrative. "My Lord, the King of Upper and Lower Egypt, Nebtauira," he goes on, "sent me, as one sends a person in whom are divine qualities (admire my modesty), to establish his monument in this land. He chose me before his city, I was preferred before his court. Now His Majesty commanded that there go forth to this sacred desert an army with me, men of the choicest of the whole land: miners, artificers, quarrymen, artists, draughtsmen, stonecutters, goldsmiths, treasurers of Pharaoh, of every department of the White House, and every office of the king's house, united behind me. I made the desert a river, and the upper valleys a waterway (commanders of such expeditions invariably do this, if we are to believe them). I brought for him a sarcophagus, an eternal memorial, an everlasting reminder. Never descended its like in this desert since the time of the god. My soldiers descended without loss; not a man perished, not a troop was missing, not an ass died, not a workman was enfeebled. This happened as a distinction for the Majesty of my Lord, which Min wrought for him because he so much loved him; that his *Ka* might endure upon the great throne in the kingdom of the two regions of Horus. . . . I am his favourite servant, who does all that he praises every day."

Even so, Min was not done with the wonders of his beneficence towards the king, not forgetting, of course, his vizier, who was so zealous. Eight days later comes another inscription, which, after the usual preliminaries, says:

"One set to work in this mountain on the lid block of the sarcophagus. The wonder was repeated, rain was made, the forms of this god appeared, his fame was shown to men, the desert was made a lake, the water ran to the margin of the stone, a well was found in the midst of the valley, 10 cubits by 10 cubits on its every side, filled with fresh water to its edge, undefiled, kept pure and cleansed from gazelles, concealed from Beduin barbarians. Soldiers of old, and kings who had lived aforetime, went out and returned by its side, (yet) no eye had seen it, the face of man had not fallen upon it, (but) to His Majesty (to say nothing of his humble servant Amenemhat!) it was revealed. . . . Those who were in Egypt heard it, the people who were in Egypt, South and Northland, they bowed their heads to the ground, they praised the goodness of His Majesty forever and ever."

To conclude the story of this wonderful expedition, the following docket is added to the official account, five days later than this last effusion: "Day 28. The lid of this sarcophagus descended, being a block 4 cubits by 8 cubits by 2 cubits, coming forth from the quarry. Cattle were slaughtered, goats were slain, incense was put on the fire. Behold an army of 3000 sailors of the nomes of the Northland followed it in safety to Egypt." Which seems to show that the sailors of Egypt, as of Britain, were the handy men of their time, who could be relied upon for any matter requiring skilled pulling and hauling. Amenemhat's expedition has been allowed to describe itself at such length because its importance is much greater than that of the mere getting out of a sarcophagus lid of 4 cubits by 8 cubits by 2 cubits. It is our evidence of the growth of a power behind the throne, which, to all appearance, was soon to become the power upon the throne.

Amenemhat, however, was not the only official who made expeditions into the desert during the brief reign of Mentuhotep V. A far more intimate personal appeal is made by the comparatively insignificant inscription of Senekh, a worthy official of lesser degree, who tells us with a real touch of personal feeling that he went into the desert, though he was a man of 60 years, and had 70 grandchildren, all descendants of himself and his one wife. "Happy is the man that hath his quiver full of them!" If so, Senekh's felicity must have been unbounded. Here is his little story, which contrasts forcibly with the magniloquence of Amenemhat: "Nebtauira, living forever. Commander of troops in the desert, steward in Egypt, captain of the fleet on the river, Senekh says: 'I was commander of the troops of this entire land in this desert, equipped with water skins, with baskets, with bread, beer, and every fresh vegetable of the South. I made its valleys green, and its heights pools of water (the beneficence of these Egyptian officials!), settled with children throughout, southward to Zau, and northward to Menat-Khufu. I went forth to the Red Sea, I hunted adults, I hunted cattle. I went forth to this desert, though I was 60 years of age, with 70 grandchildren of the children of one woman. I did all correctly for Nebtauira, living forever."

"Living forever" was, however, to be, as so often, merely an irony in the case of Mentuhotep V. How long it was before the sarcophagus whose lid was brought out with such expenditure of energy and eloquence was actually occupied we do not know; but certainly the reign was short, and with its close came also the close of the XIth Dynasty. The line of the XIIth which succeeded was of kindred blood to its predecessor; but the fact that its accession had to be justified by the fabrication of the Prophecy of Neferrohu (as the accession of the Vth Dynasty was justified by the legend of Ruddidet's children by the Sun-god) seems to show that there was a forcible dispossession of the older branch of the family. The line of the Antefs had done good work for Egypt, and the glory of the re-unification of the land must always belong to them; but they had now to give place to a still more forceful stock, whose two centuries of dominion were among the most glorious years that Egypt ever knew. When the curtain rises again, Amenemhat I., whether our eloquent vizier from Hammamat, or another extremely like him, is on the throne.

CHAPTER XIII

THE RISE OF THE TWELFTH DYNASTY AND THE GOLDEN AGE OF EGYPT

ONE of the curious features of modern study of Ancient Egypt is the change which within living memory has come over the perspective in which the history of the country is viewed. Half a century ago or less, the supreme figure of Egyptian story, overshadowing everything and everybody else, was Ramses II. of the XIXth Dynasty, whose innumerable monuments, or usurpations of the monuments of better men, had imposed him upon the imagination of the world as the typical example of a great Pharaoh. Then came the gradual realisation of the fact that much of the work which seemed to testify to the greatness of Ramses was really that of other men, upon which he had laid nefarious hands, and that the impression of the greatness of Ramses was largely the creation of the skilful use of a royal publicity propaganda which needed to learn nothing from modern methods; while the historical events of his reign, instead of witnessing to the glory of his reign, as was skilfully suggested, testified rather to his own incompetency, and to the gradual decline of his country as a world-power.

Ramses was succeeded, as a candidate for the position of leading figure among the Pharaohs, by sundry monarchs of the preceding dynasty, the XVIIIth. Foremost among these were the famous Queen Hatshepsut, whose sex served her interests where her achievements might scarcely have done so; her nephew, possible husband, and rival, Thothmes III.; and of late days the unfortunate Akhenaten, the enigma of whose religious adventure has made him a figure of romance, in spite of the prosaic fact of the serious decline of Egyptian power during his short but momentous reign. But the tendency of historians of Egypt has of late years been more and more in the direction of setting aside even the great XVIIIth Dynasty as the expression of the genius of Ancient Egypt, and of setting up in its place the period of that XIIth Dynasty with which the Middle Kingdom culminated, and may almost be said to have closed, as the true Golden Age of Egypt, when in every respect the land and the people most fully attained to the consummation of Egyptian ideals, alike in national development, in literature, and in art.

On the whole, this modification of our ideas with regard to the relative importance of the different periods of Egyptian history seems to be in the right direction. But the supremacy of the XIIth Dynasty as the exponent of the real greatness of Egypt cannot be simply accepted without qualification and limitation. Though the great monarchs of the dynasty were by no means pacifically inclined, and did in fact accomplish a good deal of fighting, their warlike ambitions were of an entirely limited character compared with those which inspired the soldier Pharaohs of the XVIIIth Dynasty—Thothmes I., Thothmes III., and Amenhotep II. Great rulers as the Amenemhats and Senuserts undoubtedly were, their problem was a simple one compared with that of the later Pharaohs, because the conception of an Egyptian Empire, and of Egypt as a world-power, had not dawned upon them. Empire for the XIIth Dynasty Pharaohs meant the pushing of a fluctuating southern frontier as far as the Third Cataract, and the occasional repulse of the Nubian or negro tribes who tried to break the frontier line, together with one or two *razzias* into Palestine, which accomplished little even at the moment, and certainly produced no permanent effect. Empire for their XVIIIth Dynasty successors meant the creation and maintenance of Egyptian supremacy over practically the whole of the land between the great bend of the Euphrates and the Egyptian frontier at Suez, where half a dozen great powers, as highly civilised and organised as Egypt herself, were her neighbours, her sharp-sighted critics, and her constant rivals. How the XIIth Dynasty Pharaohs, great men in their own sphere as they were, might have succeeded had they been faced with the end-lessly complicated situation which confronted their suc-cessors, it is impossible to say; and therefore no true com-parison between the greatness of the two lines, or the prosperity of their periods, is possible.

If, however, the question is merely one of whether the XIIth Dynasty did or did not give the most perfect ex-pression to essentially Egyptian ideals, then the answer must probably be that they did. The imperial expansion of the XVIIIth Dynasty was not in the least a thing natural to the Egyptian genius. The spirit that created it was born partly of the enthusiasm generated by the life and death struggle of the War of Independence, and partly of the desire for revenge for the humiliation which the Hyksos conquest had imposed upon a great nation; and it died down again almost as quickly as it had arisen. There has never been a less military race in the history of the world than the Egyptian, which has always been what it still is to-day, essentially pacific, and content to "cultivate its own garden" if allowed to do so. Therefore the Amenemhats and Senuserts, with their industrious exploitation of the instinct of their people for great constructive work, and their comprehension of the condition of national pros-perity in the utilisation of the Nile, were really more in line with the true destiny of their land than was Thothmes III. with his urging of a spirit which was only temporary and accidental. The greatness of the two periods is in-comparable, because there is no common measure between them. All that can be said is that the earlier Pharaohs were never, fortunately for them, tempted to an adventure which made Egypt the most shining and glorious figure in the ancient world for three centuries, and ruined her in the end.

We have already seen that the Amenemhat I. who founded the new dynasty was probably the same man who, as vizier to the last Mentuhotep of the XIth Dynasty, had obviously climbed to a position which was dangerous to his master's interests and a temptation to himself. The fact is not established; but all the probabilities seem to suggest that he succumbed to the temptation, and either deposed

or otherwise removed his master, or else took advantage of
the latter's natural death to assert his claim to the throne.
One way or another, a new and extraordinarily vigorous
and efficient line begins with the accession of Amenemhat
I., who, though he may have been no more than the vizier
of Mentuhotep V., was also directly related to the Antef
stock from which the XIth Dynasty itself had sprung.
With his accession begins the rise to the chief position in
the Egyptian pantheon of the local god of Thebes, Amen
or Amon, whose name, now enshrined in that of the first
king of the new line, was soon to become supreme among
the names of the Egyptian gods. "A new king of the gods
appeared with the new king of men"; and though the
parvenu god of Thebes had to make a concession to ancient
beliefs and dignities by assimilating the once supreme Ra
of Heliopolis to himself, and becoming Amen-Ra, the
Theban divinity henceforward steadily increased, while
all other gods, with the one exception of Osiris, decreased,
until at last Egyptian religion perished, stifled by the
supremacy of one too powerful priesthood.

Though Amenemhat could impose his local god upon
the nation, he did not find it possible to do the same with
his own native city. The time would come when Thebes
would become the centre of the national life, in spite of its
unfavourable situation; but that time had not yet come,
and the new king speedily realised that to attempt, under
present conditions, to govern the whole land of Egypt from
a point so far removed as Thebes from its centre was a
mistake. The Mentuhoteps had done it; the conquering
kings of the XVIIIth Dynasty would do it again; but all
the same the true centre of gravity of the land was further
north. Consequently Amenemhat swallowed his local
patriotism, and established his seat of government at a
point which was chosen, as its name sufficiently indicates,
for its strategic advantages. Avoiding both Herakleopolis
and Memphis, possibly because of the traditions of former
lines of kings which attached to both towns, he built a
fortress city at a point somewhat north of the Fayum, and
called it Ithttoui, "Controller of the Two Lands"—a title
which suggests that the king did not labour under any

illusions as to his personal popularity with his subjects. He was, as he perfectly well knew, an intruder, who might be personally popular away south in Thebes, but would be regarded as a rank outsider in the more cultured north. His one title to the nation's regard was competency in the task which he had assumed; and the title of his new capital was an advertisement to all and sundry that if they expected the southern barbarian to be a weakling they were going to be disappointed. Controller of the Two Lands he was, and meant to be. The note which he thus struck at the beginning of his reign is one which was maintained, not only throughout his tenure of the kingship, but all through the dynasty. Competency is the distinguishing note of the royal line which he founded, and it is rare to see a line which presents, so far as can be judged, so even a level of efficient administration as does the XIIth Dynasty.

We have already seen that the remarkable piece of literature called the Prophecy of Neferrohu, which professes to predict the advent of King Amenemhat as a saviour of society, is probably to be regarded as a piece of propaganda on behalf of the accomplished fact of his usurpation. When Neferrohu, therefore, predicts that "there shall be built the 'Wall of the Prince', and the Asiatics shall not again be permitted to go down into Egypt," we may safely assume that he is referring to a frontier-wall across the Isthmus which was either built or projected as part of a general policy of restricting those incursions of Asiatics into the Delta which had been so much complained of under previous weak rulers. Mr. Weigall associates this restriction with the somewhat humiliating incident of the expulsion of Abraham from Egypt, as narrated in Genesis xii., which implies a remarkably exact dating of the patriarch's unlucky attempt at fiction. It is, no doubt, pretty certain that Abraham is roughly contemporary with one or other of the XIIth Dynasty kings; but to say that he is exactly contemporary with Amenemhat I., and that his expulsion is a certain event of the reign of that monarch, is to say what cannot be proved, and is, indeed, on other grounds, unlikely. For it is generally accepted that the Amraphel whom Abraham is said to have defeated in his rescue of his nephew Lot, is Hammurabi of Babylon, with whom, therefore, he must have been contemporaneous. But the whole tendency of modern chronology has been in the direction of shifting Hammurabi, and therefore Abraham, to a date later by at least a century than that previously held; and the latest date for the great Babylonian king is now given as 1940 or thereabouts (Sidney Smith, *Early History of Assyria*, 170-71). As Mr. Weigall's absolutely certain date for Amenemhat I. is 2111 B.C., there is therefore a gap of about 170 years between the Abraham who is contemporary with Amenemhat and the Abraham who is contemporary with Hammurabi. The necessity of choosing between two so attractive synchronisms is perhaps merely a warning against the too prompt acceptance of interesting theories or "absolute certainties" of dating in the present state of our knowledge. That Abraham was contemporary with one of the kings of the XIIth Dynasty is perhaps more than likely; that he was contemporary with one of the later kings of the line is perhaps more likely than that he was contemporary with its first king; to say more is to say what is not authorised by the facts at present known.

Amenemhat did not secure his position as Pharaoh without more or less of a struggle. The inscription of Khnumhotep I., the first of the line of powerful barons of Beni-hasan at this period, tells us of an incident which can only be interpreted as having occurred during civil strife. "I went down with His Majesty", he says, "to ——, in twenty ships of cedar which he himself led, coming to ——. He expelled him (the unnamed leader of the opposition party) from the Two Regions. Negroes and Asiatics (mercenaries in the opposition army) fell; he (Amenemhat) seized the lowlands and the highlands in the Two Regions, with the people who had remained in those places." It is possible that this may refer to an attempt on the part of the last Pharaoh of the XIth Dynasty to maintain himself against the usurper; but this is quite uncertain, and the inscription may quite as well refer to another pretender to the throne. In any case, the fighting does not seem to have been on a large scale, to judge by the size of the fleet of river boats employed.

Amenemhat's first task naturally was the re-establishment of order and confidence in his realm. Writing two generations later, Khnumhotep II., grandson of the great baron of the Oryx nome, whose Beni-hasan inscription has just been quoted, says of the king: " . . . At the coming of His Majesty, when he cast out evil, shining like Atum himself, when he restored that which he found ruined; that which a city had taken from its neighbour; while he caused city to know its boundary with city, establishing their landmarks like the heavens, distinguishing their waters according to that which was in the writings, investigating according to that which was of old, because he so greatly loved justice."

A certain proportion of Khnumhotep's praise may, of course, be written off as being merely the customary courtierly adulation of a servant who knew on which side his bread was buttered; but what the nomarch describes is so characteristically Egyptian, and so natural a piece of work to be done by a strong king after a period when royal control had got slack and required to be tightened up, that it may be accepted as in the main a genuine picture of the work of Amenemhat. The mark of the king's strong hand is visible over all the country, and remains of his works can be traced from the edge of the Delta as far south as Korosko, showing that his energy did not belie the name which he had chosen for his capital stronghold. He was indeed Controller of the Two Lands. His building activities were widespread, and one inscription from Wady Hammamat is of interest from the human quality of its conclusion. Its author, Antef, a "hereditary prince and count, wearer of the royal seal, sole companion, royal messenger, superior prophet of Min", had been sent to the valley, as the king himself had been sent in his earlier days, to bring down a great block of stone. Antef evidently began the inscription recording his expedition at the very start of the work, never doubting of its success, and the earlier part of it is finely cut and pompous, as such things usually are. But the job proved a most heart-breaking one, and when at last he had succeeded the weary priest was thankful to squeeze in the hurried account of his fortune anyhow beneath the grandiloquent preface which he had composed before he realised the troubles ahead of him.

"My Lord", he says, "sent me to Hammamat, to bring this august stone; never was brought its like since the time of the god. There was no hunter who knew the marvel of it, none that sought it reached it. I spent eight days searching this highland; I knew not the place wherein it was. I prostrated myself to Min, to Mut, to —— Great-in-Magic, and all the gods of this highland, giving to them incense upon the fire. The land brightened at early morning, I began to go forth to the mountain of Hammamat, my men being behind me, and my people scattered upon the mountains, searching this whole desert. Then I found it, and the workmen were in festivity, the whole army was praising, it rejoiced with obeisance; I gave praise to Montu."

The energies of the king were not confined to his own land. His attempt to restrict Asiatic immigration by the Wall of the Prince was accompanied by more active measures against the Beduin of the eastern desert, as the inscription of Nessumontu, now in the Louvre, shows. Nessumontu was in command of the force which was sent by Amenemhat to raid the Asiatic settlements on the east, and was, like other Egyptian officials, highly pleased with himself and his success in the business. "Respecting every word of this tablet", he says, as men usually do when relating the incredible, "it is truth, which happened by my arm, it is that which I did in reality. There is no deceit, and there is no lie therein. I defeated the Asiatic Cave-dwellers, the Sand-dwellers. I overthrew the strongholds of the nomads, as if they had never been. I coursed through the field, I went forth before those who would have stayed behind their defences, without any equal therein, by command of Montu." Nessumontu's soldiers, it is evident, were by no means so avid of glory as their leader, and preferred security to heroism—an attitude of mind which has remained characteristic of the Egyptian soldier in all ages. He makes, as he made under such leadership as that of Thothmes III., a good and efficient fighting man; but he has no natural warlike instinct, and prefers, like Nessumontu's warriors, to remain "behind his defences".

In Nubia also, Amenemhat made his power felt. He tells us himself, in the "Instruction" which he left to his son, that he warred in Nubia as well as in the east. "I tamed lions and captured crocodiles. I defeated the Wawat, and captured the Matoi. I caused the Sati (Beduin) to go as dogs." A brief inscription on a rock at Korosko proves that this is not merely the common form of a royal boast. "Year 29", it runs, "of the King of Upper and Lower Egypt Se-hotep-ab-ra (Amenemhat I.), living forever. We came to overthrow the Wawat".

Whether Amenemhat was himself in command of this expedition may be doubted, as by this time he must have been advanced in years. Indeed, he had associated his son Senusert I. with himself in the monarchy eight years before the Nubian expedition, setting thereby a precedent which was followed throughout the dynasty, and which obviously made for the stability of a dynasty in the east, where a change of king has always been regarded as a favourable opportunity for revolt and intrigue. There was less possibility of such things when the natural successor had already been crowned, and had been acting for his father in many of the royal functions. The probability is that this course of action was prompted by the conspiracy which culminated in the attempted assassination of the old king—an attempt which was made, as he himself tells us, before he had insured himself against such attacks by associating his son with him. "Behold", he says in the Instruction, "the abominable thing came to pass when I was without thee, when the court had not yet heard that I am resigning (the sovereign power) to thee, when I had not yet sat (on the throne) along with thee". Manifestly such tightening up of the reins as the old king had brought about throughout the land was not likely to make him popular with those who imagined that their interest lay in a laxer administration, and the bitterness with which Amenemhat refers to the ingratitude of the conspirators, while perfectly natural, shows that he was more accomplished as an administrator than as a student of human nature.

The Instruction of King Amenemhat, which he left as his testament to his son Senusert, is a thoroughly human piece of writing, where the irrepressible passion of the man breaks out in fierce and bitter arraignment of the men whom he had benefited, and who had requited his goodness with treachery. The burden of his teaching is the old, sad wisdom of kingship—"a king can have no friend!" "Be on thy guard against subordinates —— approach them not, and be not alone. Trust not a brother, know not a friend, and make not for thyself intimates—that profiteth nothing. If thou sleepest do thou thyself guard thine heart, for in the day of adversity a man hath no adherents. I gave to the poor and nourished the orphan, I caused him that was nothing to reach the goal even as him that was of account." But kindness only bred traitors. "It was he who ate my food that disdained me; it was he to whom I gave my hand that aroused fear therewith (*i.e.* with the power I had given him). They that clothed them in my fine linen looked at me as at a shadow, and they that anointed them with my myrrh poured water (on me)." One is irresistibly reminded of the Psalmist's complaint, "Yea, mine own familiar friend, in whom I trusted, which did eat of my bread, hath lifted up his heel against me".

The conspiracy came to a head during the night. "It was after supper, when night had come; I had taken an hour of repose, and laid me down upon my bed. I was weary, and my heart began to follow after slumber. Then it was as if weapons were brandished, and search was made for me, and I started up like a viper of the desert. I roused me to fight alone, and I marked that it was a hand-to-hand affray of the bodyguard. When I had quickly taken weapons into mine hand, I drave back the rogues." Then the old man adds a pathetic touch, which shows how he felt the need of his son's support: "But there is no strength by night, and one cannot fight alone, and success will not come without thee that protectest me". Plainly, the king suspected that the conspiracy began, where most such things begin in the east, in the harem, and he returns again and again to the bitterness of such an end to all his good work. "Had the women set the battle in array? Had the conflict been fostered within my house? . . . Ill fortune hath not come behind me since my birth, and nought hath happened that might equal my prowess as a doer of valiant deeds"—and yet this is the end of it all!

Then the old man recounts some of his deeds, as we have heard already, and tells of the splendour of the buildings which he reared. No more human outpouring of the heart has survived from the past than this lament of a great man over the malignity which dogs the best intentions, and the ingratitude of human nature. We are dependent for it, curiously enough, upon the bungled work of a schoolboy who had to copy out the story as an exercise in writing about seven centuries later, and he has made sad nonsense of its conclusion, where, no doubt, he grew weary. Yet even the disconnected scraps with which the document closes have a wistful pathos in them, as the disillusioned old hero pours out his pride in the son who shall succeed him, and foresees better things for him than he himself has known —— "King Senusert, thy feet go, Thou art mine own heart, mine eyes gaze upon thee. The children even have an hour of happiness beside the people, when they give thee praise. Behold, I have wrought at the beginning, and thou commandest at the end —— the white crown of the divine seed. There is exultation in the boat of Ra —— Monuments are set up, and thy tomb shall be made splendid."

Senusert's association with his father began in the 21st year of the reign of Amenemhat, probably immediately after the conspiracy had taught the older king the danger which he ran. He lived still for a little more than nine years; but during the later years of his life he apparently entrusted more and more of the royal functions to his son, so that Senusert might have experience, and might be generally recognised as the natural successor when the time came. How completely he had resigned the actual sovereignty is made plain by the inscription on a stele of the priest Her, who ministered to his pyramid, and who dates his stele "Year 9 of Senusert", omitting all references to the corresponding year of Amenemhat, which would have been year 28.

The last important event of the old king's reign was the dispatch of an army to the western frontier to chastise the Libyans and keep them in check. The young king Senusert commanded in person, and the expedition was returning from the border, having completely accomplished its object, when it was met by messengers who had been sent by the chamberlain of the royal palace to inform Senusert that his father had died. The incident is vividly described, along with the sensation and disturbance which it occasioned, in the famous story of Sinuhe, which has been preserved in three manuscripts of the Middle Kingdom, and one papyrus and ten ostraka of the New Empire. Sinuhe's narrative is of great value, not only for its account of historical facts, but also for its incidental descriptions of the life and habits both of the Middle Kingdom Egyptian and of the Syrian tribes with whom the Egyptians were occasionally brought into contact.

The story begins as follows: "The prince and count, administrator of the domains of the sovereign in the lands of the Asiatics, the true acquaintance of the king, whom he loveth, the henchman Sinuhe. He saith: 'I was a henchman who followed his lord, and a servant of the king's harem, waiting on the princess, the greatly praised, the royal consort of Senusert, the royal daughter of Amenemhat in the Pyramid-town of Ka-neferu, even Neferu the revered.'

"In the year 30 (of Amenemhat I.), on the ninth day of the third month of Inundation, the god entered his horizon (the usual euphemism for 'the king died'). King Amenemhat flew away to heaven, and was united with the sun, and the god's body was merged with his creator. The Residence was hushed, hearts were filled with mourning, the Two Great Portals were shut, the courtiers sat head on knees, and the people grieved.

"Now His Majesty had sent forth an army to the land of the Temehu (Libyans), and his eldest son was captain thereof, the good god Senusert; and even now he was returning, having carried away captives of the Tehenu, and all manner of cattle without count. And the Chamberlains of the Royal Palace sent to the Western border to inform the king's son of the event that had befallen at the

Court. And the messengers met him on the road, and reached him at eventide. Not a moment did he tarry; the hawk (the young Senusert) flew away with his henchmen, and did not make it known unto his army. Howbeit, a message had been sent unto the king's children that were with him in the army, and one of them had been summoned!"

Here you have the whole picture of a palace crisis in an ancient Oriental state, with all the intrigue and uncertainty of a doubtful succession, disclosed in a few sentences. Obviously, in spite of Senusert's association with his father, there was a palace plot to supersede him, and to place another son of the royal family upon the throne. The royal chamberlains were loyal to the heir, and advised him of the crisis which demanded his presence without loss of time; but the conspirators had equally good sources of information, and were able to convey the news just as promptly to the prince who was the figure-head of their faction, and who was serving with the army under his brother. Senusert's prompt action in leaving the army at once, and secretly, accompanied by a body of men upon whom he could count, evidently crushed the conspiracy before it had time to materialise, for no more is heard of it; but it had evidently been a serious enough business to make those who had been concerned in it conscious that it was advisable to put as great a distance as possible between themselves and the court before King Senusert got firmly seated in the saddle, and was able to reach out the long arm of authority and secure the persons of his opponents. It is not possible to explain in any other fashion the sudden terror which fell upon Sinuhe when he overheard the conspirators' messengers making their report to the prince-pretender, and which drove him into panic flight from the country which he loved beyond everything, nor the length of time which elapsed before the king allowed him to return from his exile. Sinuhe must have dipped his fingers pretty deeply into the witches' cauldron of palace intrigue before he devastated his whole life and prospects rather than face the new king. Nothing more vivid and picturesque has come down to us from ancient days than his description of his terror-stricken flight.

You imagine the messengers of the disloyal faction whispering under cover of the darkness to the prince whom they had wished to make their tool, and Sinuhe, one of the disloyal lot also, but not of the very innermost circle, cowering in the shadow of a tent and listening breathlessly to their mutterings. He had sense enough to know that a plot which has allowed itself to be anticipated is a plot doomed, and to make himself scarce without more ado. "And lo", he says, "I stood and heard his (the rival prince's) voice as he spake, being a little way off. Then was my heart distraught, mine arms sank, and trembling fell on all my limbs. I betook me thence, leaping, to seek me a hiding-place; I placed me between two bushes, so as to sunder the road from its traveller.

"I set out southward, yet I did not purpose to reach the Residence, for I thought that strife would arise, and I was not minded to live after him. I crossed the waters of Maaty, hard by the Sycamore, and came to the Island of Snefru, and tarried there in a plot of ground. I was afoot early, and when it was day I met a man who stood in my path; he shrank from me, and was afraid. The time of the evening meal came, and I drew nigh to Ox-town. I crossed over in a barge without a rudder, with the aid of the breath of the west wind, and passed on east of the quarry, in the region of the Mistress of the Red Mountain (the local goddess of Kom el-Ahmar). I gave a road to my feet northwards, and attained the Wall of the Prince, which was made to repel the Asiatics. (Built only a few years before by Amenemhat, as we have seen.) I bowed me down in a thicket for fear lest the watcher for the day on the wall should espy me.

"At eventide I passed on, and when day dawned I reached Peten, and halted on the island of Kemwer (in the Bitter Lakes District of the Isthmus of Suez). There it overtook me that I fell down for thirst. I was parched, my throat burned, and I said: 'This is the taste of death.' Then lifted I up mine heart and gathered up my body, for I heard the lowing of cattle and descried Bedouins. The sheikh among them, who had been in Egypt, recognised me. (Sinuhe, therefore, was a prominent figure at the

Egyptian court). He gave me water and cooked milk for me, and I went with him to his tribe, and they entreated me kindly."

So we may for the moment leave Sinuhe, whom we shall meet again later, in the care of his hospitable Arab sheikh. He has given us one of the most vivid and picturesque stories extant of the flight of a political refugee, and one can actually see the panic-stricken courtier lying flat in the thicket, watching the pitiless Egyptian sun glinting on the spear of the sentry on the Wall of the Prince, and cursing the statecraft which had built the wall to cut off his retreat. Nothing quite so perfect in its kind is going to be met with again until we see David Balfour and Alan Breck Stewart lying flat among burdock and butter-bur on the little island where Allan Water falls into the Forth, and listen with them at nightfall to the old woman's stick tapping along as she crosses Stirling Bridge, and turn away sick at heart as the sentry challenges her.

CHAPTER XIV

WHATEVER may have been the strength of the conspiracy against the succession of Senusert, he apparently mastered it completely by the promptitude with which he took action when the news of his father's death reached him; for there is no evidence of any civil strife having followed. Probably the conspirators shrank into obscurity as speedily as they could, and were only too thankful that no notice was taken of them. Sinuhe, at least, shows that one of the conspirators was not of the neck-or-nothing resolution out of which a true conspirator would require to be made. The reign which began amidst such ominous clouds lasted for about forty-five years, including the ten years of co-regency, and was comparatively uneventful, in the sense of being marked by any very great exploits or disasters. At the same time, it was a reign distinguished by great activity in the internal work of the realm, and Senusert occupies a prominent position among the great builder monarchs of Egyptian history.

One of the most important records of his reign which have survived has been preserved to us by the caprice of an Egyptian scribe of five hundred years later, who copied down on a leather roll, for mere practice in writing, the great dedicatory inscription with which Senusert celebrated the completion of his temple to the Sun-god at Heliopolis. The inscription was carved originally on a stone stele which stood in the court of the temple, and our scribe copied it down on the roll where he had already written part of an account of the legal proceedings taken by a sculptor against his own son, and some notes regarding the receipt and issue of lumber. Senusert's stately monument has utterly vanished, along with all but a single obelisk of the temple which it described; but the practice-exercise scribbled in the scribe's commonplace book in such curious company has survived where the more enduring material has perished.

King Senusert's record opens with the picture of his Majesty taking counsel with his advisers over the building of the temple, or rather intimating to them his resolution on the matter. "When the king was crowned with the Double Crown, occurred the sitting in the audience-chamber. One (*i.e.* Pharaoh) asked counsel of his followers, the chamberlains of the palace, and the magistrates, in the place of seclusion. One commanded, while they hearkened. One asked counsel, and caused them to reveal their opinion: 'Behold, My Majesty intendeth a work, and bethinketh him of some good thing for the time to come, that I may erect a monument and set up an abiding memorial tablet for Harakhti. He hath formed me in order to do for him what should be done for him, and to execute that which he commanded to be done. He hath made me the herdsman of this land, for he knew that I would maintain it in order for him. He hath bestowed upon me that which he protecteth, and that which the eye which is in him (the sun) doth illumine. All is done in accordance with his desire.' "

Then follows a lengthy and grandiose description, of a type common in the inscriptions of the Pharaohs, of the glory bestowed upon the king by the favour of the god, and His Majesty goes on: "I establish the food-offerings of the gods, and do a work for my father Atum in the great hall. I cause him to have it as broad as he hath caused me to conquer. I victual his altar on earth. I build mine house in his vicinity. Thus my beauty will be remembered in his house; my name will be the *benben* stone, and my memorial the lake (the sacred lake of the temple). It is to gain eternity, if one doeth for him that which is good, and no king dieth that is mentioned because of his (the god's) possessions —— A name that standeth thereon is . . . mentioned and perisheth not in eternity. What I do is what will be, and what I seek is what is excellent."

To this tirade the counsellors made answer as they were expected to do: "And the chamberlains of the king spake and answered before their god: 'Commanding Utterance is in thy mouth, and Discernment is behind thee. O sovereign, thy designs come to pass. O king, who hast appeared as Uniter of the Two Lands, in order to . . . in thy temple! It is excellent to look upon the morrow —— But mankind together would complete nothing without thee, for Thy Majesty is the eye of all men. Thou art great when thou settest up thy monument in Heliopolis, the dwelling of the gods, before thy father, the lord of the great hall, Atum, the Bull of the Ennead. Erect thine house, and make for it gifts for the stone of oblation, that it may serve its statue, its favourite —— for all eternity.' "

Having thus obtained the unanimous approval of his courtiers for what he meant to do in any case, His Majesty proceeds to give instructions, and the ceremonial connected with what we would call the laying of the foundation-stone of the new temple follows without delay: "The king himself said to the chancellor and first chamberlain, the superintendent of the Two Gold-houses and Silver-houses, him that is over the mysteries of the Two Serpent-diadems: 'It will be thy counsel that causeth the work to be accomplished . . . the coming to pass of that which My Majesty desired. Thou wilt be the director thereof, one that will do according to that which is in my heart —— vigilant, that it may come to pass without languor, and all work that appertains thereto —— They that work are commanded to work according to that which thou wilt ordain.' The king appeared in the diadem and the two feathers, and all the people accompanied him. The chief *kherheb* and scribe of the god's book stretched the cord, and carried out the foundation ceremonies. Then His Majesty caused the royal scribe of the records to go before the people, who stood united together, out of Upper and Lower Egypt ——"

At this point, unfortunately, the record of the scribe's exercise-book ceases, though it is apparent that we have got the gist of the whole business, in which, as is evident, much more attention is paid to the long-winded compliments which the king addresses to himself, and his courtiers address to him, than to the actual work of the founding of the temple.

"My beauty", said Senusert, "will be remembered in his house; my name will be the *benben* stone, and my memorial the lake". If Senusert had depended upon such things for immortality, he would have been apt to come off badly. Of the great temple which was to keep his memory green, precisely three stones are known at the present moment to survive. Of these, one bears the names and titles of the king, and another gives a list of gifts made to various gods by a King Senusert, but does not furnish the details which would enable us to say beyond doubt that the king in question is Senusert I. The third stone, however, is of greater interest, being the great obelisk which now stands, buried deeply in the soil, above the fields of Matariyeh. It is the oldest of surviving Egyptian obelisks, and the foremost of the five which, as modern nations ought to be ashamed to reflect, are all that remain on their original sites in Egypt, all the others having been removed to various European and American cities to gratify a senseless mania, Rome alone possessing nine of over 29 feet in height. This venerable relic of Senusert's temple is 66 feet in height, and is made of a single block of the red granite of Aswan. Each side bears a single line of hieroglyphs which convey the information that the obelisk was made by King Senusert, whom the divine spirits of Heliopolis love, as a memorial of his jubilee. The Arab, Abd el-Latif, writes that when he visited Heliopolis in A.D. 1190 he saw two great obelisks there, one standing, the other prostrate and broken. Originally both obelisks were crowned with caps of burnished copper; but the cap has now vanished from the sole survivor. In 1912, Sir Flinders Petrie and Mr. Engelbach, excavating at the site, discovered fragments of the second obelisk, which have now been arranged round the foot of the standing one; but these showed that the second stone was not erected by Senusert, but by Thothmes III.

Remains of Senusert's building work have been found at Tanis, Bubastis, Begig in the Fayum, Abydos, Koptos, Elephantine, and many other Egyptian sites, while the relics of his activity at Serabit el-Khadim, in the Sinai Peninsula, prove that like almost all the vigorous Pharaohs he gave a good deal of attention to this ancient mining site. Two of the best representations of this energetic Pharaoh were discovered of recent years in a chamber of the tomb of the High-priest of Heliopolis, Imhotep, close to the site of the king's pyramid. They were of cedar-wood, and one of the statues depicts him wearing the Red Crown of Lower Egypt, while in the other case he wears the White Crown of Upper Egypt. It may have been in connection with this pyramid that "The real servant, his favourite, who does all that he praises every day, the revered assistant treasurer, Mery, born of Menkhet", was employed on the commission whose execution he describes with so much enthusiasm on his mortuary stele, now in the Louvre. "I was a zealous servant," he says, "great in character, amiable in love. My lord sent me with a commission, because I was so very zealous, to execute for him an eternal dwelling, greater in name than Restau, and more excellent in appointments than any place, the excellent district of the gods. Its columns pierced heaven; the lake which was dug, it reached the river; the gates, towering heavenward, were of limestone of Turrah. Osiris, First of the Westerners, rejoiced over all the monuments of My Lord; I myself rejoiced, and my heart was glad at that which I had executed." One has often to wish, as here, that, instead of repeating for the hundredth time the conventional hyperboles which were in fashion as descriptions of their public works, these faithful servants of the Pharaohs had simply condescended to give us a few plain and literal details as to the work which they executed for their royal masters.

In warlike affairs, the chief event of the reign was a campaign in Nubia, undertaken with the view of establishing Egyptian influence on a solid basis in the south. Our information with regard to this campaign comes from various sources. First of all, we have a general reference to a campaign in the south, which may possibly be identified with the one in question, on the tomb-inscription of Amenemhat, generally known as Ameny, one of the powerful barons of Beni-hasan, nomarch of the Oryx nome, and successor to his father Khnumhotep, whose inscription has been already quoted. Ameny dates his inscription— "Year 43 under the Majesty of Senusert I., living forever and ever; corresponding to year 25 in the Oryx nome with the hereditary prince and count Amenemhat, justified. Year 43, second month of the first season, day 15." The relevant passage is as follows: "I followed My Lord when he sailed southward to overthrow his enemies among the four barbarians. I sailed southward as the son of a count, wearer of the royal seal, and commander-in-chief of the troops of the Oryx nome, as a man represents his old father (Khnumhotep, therefore, was still living, but of too great age to serve in person), according to his favour in the palace and his love in the court. I passed Kush, sailing southward, I advanced the boundary of the land, I brought all gifts; my praise it reached heaven. Then His Majesty returned in safety, having overthrown his enemies in Kush the vile. I returned, following him, with ready face. There was no loss among my soldiers."

Ameny further records two subsequent expeditions, which, however, were not warlike ones, but were merely intended to procure gold ore, though the character of the country to be traversed made an escort—on the one occasion of 400, on the other of 600 troops—a necessity. If the first expedition commemorated by Ameny is to be identified with the great campaign which carried the Egyptian frontier as far south as Wady Halfa, then we must conclude that, in spite of his own high opinion of his personal merits, Ameny was not in command of the expedition, but only served as a subordinate officer, commanding his own local contingent of militia, and that while the king was nominally in command of the army, the actual operations were conducted, as is not unusual in such a case, by a professional soldier. Mentuhotep, the general who conducted Senusert's southern campaign, has left us an inscription at Wady Halfa, which reveals more than the successful commander ever intended. Mentuhotep, as in duty bound, devoted the first portion of his stele to the glorification of his Pharaoh. Senusert is depicted facing Montu, the war-god of Thebes, who says to him, "I have brought for thee all countries which are in Nubia, beneath thy feet, O Good God". The god leads forward to the king a line of ten bound Nubian captives representing local tribes, each being represented by a head and shoulders above a cartouche which originally bore the name of the tribe in question. Beneath this relief followed a royal inscription of which only a few words survive.

Having thus borne lip-service to his master, however, Mentuhotep evidently considered it safe, in this remote place, to add a little commendation of himself and his achievements. His personal record has suffered almost as greatly as that of the king; but there can still be read a few lines: "Their life is finished, slain —— fire in the tents —— their grain cast into the Nile —— a man in the strength of his *Ka* —— I myself swear, this happened in very truth; I, the general of the army, Amu's son, Mentuhotep". The figure of the victorious general originally appeared in two places, in addition to the verbal references to him in the inscription, once behind the king in the main relief, and once on the left-hand side below the writing. The latter figure has perished, all but the head. The former has been diligently erased by a subsequent sculptor who has rudely carved a hawk-headed figure over that of Senusert's presumptuous general. It is not difficult to read between the lines. Some toady of royalty must have reported to the king that Mentuhotep had actually dared to claim some of the glory of the campaign for himself, and that on the very stele which commemorated the triumph of Senusert himself. The natural result followed, and Mentuhotep paid dearly for his quite natural and pardonable little bit of vanity. The erasure of his figure was no doubt the least unpleasant thing which accompanied his fall from favour.

All the evidence extant from the reign of Senusert points to his having been an active and able administrator, who exercised a strenuous supervision of his subordinates, and secured from them efficient administration in their minor spheres. Ameny's account of his personal bearing in his government of the Oryx nome need not be altogether taken for gospel; but it suggests a sufficiently high ideal of a governor's duties to allow a margin for the inevitable lapses due to human imperfection, and yet leave a fair balance on the side of good government. "I was amiable and greatly beloved, a ruler beloved of his city. Now I passed years as ruler in the Oryx nome. All the imposts of the king's house passed through my hand. The gang-overseers of the Crown possessions of the shepherds of the Oryx nome gave to me 3000 bulls in their yokes. I was praised on account of it in the palace each year of the loan-herds. I carried all their dues to the king's house; there were no arrears against me in any office of his." Evidently Ameny considered his administration as quite satisfactory as regards his loyal service of the king, and we may probably believe him, as the matters in question were open to all in the public records.

He was quite as well pleased with the local aspect of his government, though here we have no means of gauging the truth of his statements. "There was no citizen's daughter whom I misused, there was no widow whom I oppressed, there was no peasant whom I repulsed, there was no shepherd whom I repelled, there was no overseer of serf-labourers whose people I commandeered, there was none wretched in my community, there was none hungry in my time. When years of famine came I ploughed all the fields of the Oryx nome as far as its southern and northern boundary, preserving its people alive and furnishing its food so that there was none hungry therein. I gave to the widow as to her who had a husband; I did not exalt the great above the small in all that I gave. Then came great Niles, possessors of grain and all things; but I did not collect the arrears of the field." It sounds almost too good to be all true; but if even the half of it was fact, the Oryx nome was happy in its nomarch; and the standard of government which Ameny considers as proper is in itself a testimony as to the kind of thing which Senusert expected of his officials.

Senusert's great expedition to the Sudan resulted in a more or less permanent occupation of the land as far south as the Third Cataract, and in the appointment of an Egyptian governor of the occupied region. The governor appointed was a man of considerable importance, and one who had already been well known to students of Egyptian history for some time before the discovery of his great tomb at Kerma in Nubia, a discovery which was made by Dr. G. A. Reisner in 1914–15. He was "the hereditary prince and count, the superior prophet Hepzefi", whose great rock-cut tomb at Siut is the largest known tomb of its kind of Middle Kingdom date. The walls of Hepzefi's tomb bear one of the most important inscriptions of the period, in the shape of the records of the ten separate contracts which the owner of the tomb made with the various priestly bodies of his town for the continual discharge of certain funerary rites at his tomb. These documents are absolutely unique, and furnish us with a priceless mass of information as to the religious festivals of an Egyptian city at the time of the XIIth Dynasty, and the funerary celebrations of private individuals which were combined with the public feasts. The documents, as inscribed on the walls of the tomb, are, as Erman has pointed out, only summaries of the original contracts which were made with the priests, and which were, of course, written on papyrus and sealed; but even as mere abstracts they inspire the reader with a feeling of amazement at the elaboration of legal and religious formality to which the Egyptian community had attained at this early date. Breasted has given a most careful reconstruction of the rites which were performed at the local temples and the tomb of Hepzefi in consequence of his testamentary disposition (*Development of Religion and Thought in Ancient Egypt*, pp. 259-267), and the net result of his study is that "there was not a day in the year when Hepzefi failed to receive the food and drink necessary for his maintenance".

Such was the theory; but it may be questioned if the practice was for long in accordance with the precept. We have already seen how funerary endowments failed to fulfil the object for which they were created, and how one Pharaoh issues a decree declaring that a particular endowment has lapsed, and has ceased to be binding; and one may believe that Hepzefi's elaborate provision for his wellbeing in the other world was no more successful than other attempts to secure immunity from oblivion. For the great man was never buried in his magnificent tomb at Siut, but far away at barbaric Kerma in the Sudan, where the Nubians whom he governed laid him to rest in the midst of a perfect battalion of slaves who were slaughtered to accompany their dead lord through the Underworld. If it was next to impossible to secure the continuance of the funerary rites in the case of men who died and were buried in their own native place, what chance had Hepzefi, dying away in the Sudan, of having his wishes carried out? Dr. Reisner has suggested that it was just the realisation of this fact that brought about the execution of these unique summaries of the funerary contracts. Hepzefi, going to the Sudan, carefully warns his *ka*-priest against the neglect of the rites for which he had contracted, and the priest, whose income depended on the maintenance of the rites, endeavoured to secure that they should not be forgotten, written agreements or no written agreements, by inscribing them on the walls of the tomb.

The instructions which Hepzefi gives to his *ka*-priest, as Reisner suggests, in a letter written from the Sudan shortly before his death, seem to support such an idea. "The hereditary prince, the nomarch, the chief priest Hepzefi, he says to his *ka*-priest: 'See, all these things for which I have contracted with these wa'b priests are under thy oversight; for it is the *ka*-priest of a man who causes his property and his offerings to flourish. See, I have brought to your knowledge these things which I have given to these wa'b priests in return for those things which they have given to me. Guard lest any of them be revoked. Thou shalt speak concerning the things of mine which I have given to them, and thou shalt cause thy son and heir to hear them, he who shall act for me as *ka*-priest. See, I have endowed thee with land, with serfs, with cattle, with gardens, and with everything, like any exalted man of Siut, in order that thou mayest carry out my service with a willing heart, and mayest stand over all my affairs which I have given into thy hand. See, they are before thee in writing. These things shall belong to thy one son whom thou wishest to act as my *ka*-priest from among thy children, as consumer of the revenues, without doing damage, without permitting that he divide it among his children, according to these instructions which I have given thee.' "

Hepzefi, being a priest himself, had, no doubt, good reason for his obvious distrust of "those wa'b priests", over whose conduct he instructed his *ka*-priest to watch so carefully, and believed that his only security was the self-interest of the *ka*-priest whose income depended on the observance of the contract. Doubtless the *ka*-priest attended to his duties for his own sake, if not for Hepzefi's, as long as it was convenient and profitable for him to do so. Hepzefi's tomb would be ablaze with lights, and piled with bread on all the festivals of the gods at Siut, and it would be believed that his spirit travelled from far-off Kerma nightly to animate his statues in the tomb or in the temple, and to partake of the good things which were laid before it. But gradually the diligence with which the rites were performed would decline, as men remembered less and less of the once famous man; until at last we may imagine his carefully guarded endowments going the way of all such things, and being absorbed cither by greedy priests or by a needy Pharaoh, leaving the carven abstracts as his only memorial.

We have seen how Sinuhe, at the beginning of the sole reign of Senusert, fled for his life into Palestine rather than face the new king and the civil strife which he foresaw. It is now time to return to him and his adventures, which are related in a manner which gives us a remarkably vivid picture of Egyptian life and modes of thought at this period, and, incidentally, some interesting glimpses of the Syrian communities of the time. We left Sinuhe in the kindly hands of the Arab sheikh who found him perishing of thirst in the desert. He continues his wanderings in Palestine:

"Land gave me to land. I set forth from Byblos and drew near to Kedemi, and spent half a year there. Nenshi, the son of Amu, the prince of Upper Retenu, took me and said unto me: 'Thou farest well with me, for thou hearest the speech of Egypt'. This said he, for he had become aware of my qualities, and had heard of my wisdom;

Egyptians that dwelt with him had testified concerning me
to him. He said unto me: 'Why art thou come hither? Hath
aught befallen at the Residence?' And I said unto him:
'King Sehetepabra (Amenemhat I.) hath gone to his horizon,
and none knoweth what hath happened in the matter.' And
I said again, dissembling: 'I came from the expedition to
the land of the Temehu, and report was made unto me,
and mine heart trembled and mine heart was no longer in
my body. It carried me away upon the pathways of the
wastes. Yet none had gossiped about me, none had spat in
my face; I had heard no reviling word, and my name had
not been heard in the mouth of the herald (in proclama-
tion as a traitor). I know not what brought me to this land;
it was like the dispensation of God.'

"Then he said unto me: 'How will yon land (Egypt)
fare without him, that beneficent god, the fear of whom
was throughout the lands like that of Sekhmet in a year of
plague?' But I said unto him, answering him: 'Nay, but
his son hath entered into the palace and hath taken the
inheritance of his father, he, the god without peer, whom
none surpasseth, a lord of prudence, excellent in counsel,
efficacious in giving orders. Going out and coming in are
at his command. He it was that subdued the foreign lands,
while his father sat within his palace, that he might report
to him that what had been commanded him had been
done.'" Sinuhe then, like Mr. Silas Wegg, is inspired to
break forth into verse in praise of the young king from
whose face he had found it most convenient to depart, and
expatiates for some time in poetry upon the virtues and
good qualities of Senusert. Obviously the exile was a
model opportunist and a diligent devotee of the cult of the
jumping cat, who saw no sense in clinging to revolutionary
principles which had proved unsuccessful. Senusert was
on the throne, and likely to remain there; therefore it
followed naturally, in Sinuhe's simple creed, that he must
be the best of kings, though in all probability our exile
would have hailed a rival prince just as effusively had he
succeeded in seizing the sceptre.

Nenshi was duly impressed with this outburst of
belated loyalty, and replied with effusion (though he was

unable to soar into verse): "Verily Egypt is happy, for it knoweth that He (Senusert) flourisheth. But see, thou art here and shalt abide with me, and I will entreat thee kindly." Sinuhe thereupon falls heir to the usual good fortune of the hero of romance. He is placed at the head of the chief's own family, and wedded to his eldest daughter. "He made me ruler of a tribe of the best of his country. Bread was made for me for my daily fare, wine for my daily drink, cooked meat and roast fowl, over and above the wild game of the desert; for that men hunted for me and laid it before me, besides the spoils of my hounds." Altogether the wanderer seemed to have fallen on his feet; and we speedily find him becoming the great man of the neighbourhood, just as a civilised European of parts and courage might rise to a position of influence among a semi-barbarous tribe.

The position, however, proved to have its incon-veniences, as well as its advantages. The local bullies, whom Sinuhe had displaced, were naturally disinclined to allow him to carry off the prizes without protest. Their jealousy resulted in a challenge to single combat from "a mighty man of Retenu, a champion without peer, who had subdued the whole of Retenu. He vowed that he would fight with me, he planned to rob me, he plotted to take my cattle as a spoil, by the counsel of his tribe." Sinuhe, who was the man in possession, naturally failed to see why he should be set up as a cock-shy for all the swashbucklers of Syria to aim at. "But", said he, "if that man is a bull and loveth combat, I also am a fighting bull and not afraid to try conclusions with him. If his heart be set on fighting, let him speak his will." Accordingly the day of battle was fixed. "At dawn when Retenu came, it had stirred up its tribes; it had assembled the countries of a half of it, and it had planned this combat. Every heart burned for me; the men's wives jabbered, and every heart was sore for me (Sinuhe surely overrates his popularity as an interloper). They said: 'Is there another mighty man who can fight against him?'"

The combat, of course, ended as such combats always do end when the hero is the story-teller. "I caused his arrows to pass by me, uselessly sped. As one of us approached the other, he charged me, and I shot him, mine arrow sticking in his neck. He cried out, and fell on his nose. I laid him low with his own axe, and raised my shout of victory on his back. Every Asiatic bellowed. I offered praise to Montu (the Theban war-god), and my opponent's following mourned for him. This prince Nenshi, the son of Amu, took me to his embrace. Then I carried off his goods and spoiled his cattle. That which he had devised to do to me I did to him. I seized what was in his tent and plundered his encampment. I became great thereby, wide in my riches, abundant in mine herds."

"And this hath God done", continues our exile, moved now to both piety and poetry, "in order to be gracious to one that had trespassed against him, that had fled away into another land. To-day his heart is again glad—

> Once a fugitive fled in his season—
> Now the report of me is in the Residence.
> Once a laggard lagged because of hunger—
> Now I give bread to my neighbour.
> Once a man left his country because of nakedness—
> Now am I shining in white raiment and linen.
> Once a man sped for lack of one to send—
> Now have I slaves in plenty.
> Fair is my lot, wide my dwelling-place,
> And I am remembered in the palace."

Such triumphs and advantages were all very well; but after all, Sinuhe was an Egyptian, and an Egyptian could no more be permanently happy out of Egypt than a Cockney can imagine life to be worth living out of London. The special form which the exile's home-sickness took is highly typical. Men of other nations would have dwelt on the delights of returning to their own land to live there; Sinuhe, like a true Egyptian, craves to return to Egypt that he may be buried there! Holding the creed that he did, the Egyptian considered it the last and worst misfortune that his death should occur in a land where the due funeral rites could not be rendered to him. All else was of no importance to him compared with the attainment of a decent and complete performance of the ritual over his dead body. Therefore, when Sinuhe has finished his little song of praise, the inmost desire of his heart finds expression:

"O God, whosoever thou art, that didst ordain this flight, be merciful and bring me again to the Residence. Peradventure thou wilt suffer me to see the place wherein mine heart dwelleth. What is a greater matter than that my corpse should be buried in the land wherein I was born? Come to mine aid! May good befall, may God show me mercy —— in order to make good the end of him whom He hath afflicted, His heart being compassionate on him whom He hath compelled to live abroad. Is He in truth appeased to-day? Then may he hearken to the prayer of one that is afar off —— O may the King of Egypt show me mercy, that I may live by his mercy. May I ask the Lady of the Land (the queen) that is in his palace what her will is. May I hear the behests of her children. O may my body grow young again, for now hath old age befallen, and weakness hath overtaken me. Mine eyes are heavy, mine arms are weak, and my legs have ceased to follow. Mine heart is weary, and death draweth nigh unto me. May they bring me to the cities of Eternity. May I serve the Sovereign Lady; O may she speak well to me of her children; may she spend eternity over me."

Sinuhe's lamentations were evidently not merely of personal significance. Like Lord Jeffreys' sobs from the bench, they were meant to be reported at the royal palace, and he no doubt took due precautions that this should be so. Meanwhile, Senusert had been long enough upon the throne to have consolidated his position, and to be able to look back with more or less contemptuous tolerance on the futile efforts of the conspirators who had wished to deprive him of the throne. It seemed a long time now since that night when "the hawk flew away with his henchmen and did not make it known to the army", and when Sinuhe, on the mere whisper of a brother-conspirator, overheard by chance, felt his limbs loosened beneath him and fled for his life. These things were all dead and buried long ago; and Pharaoh, strong and prosperous, felt able to extend a slightly amused and scornful permission to the poor devil away in Syria to come back and taste the joys of civilisation again. Queen Nefert, too, with whose household Sinuhe seems to have been connected in his courtier days, and whose influence seems to have been great with her husband, exercised it in favour of the poor exile; and, accordingly, Sinuhe's heart was gladdened in his Syrian home by the receipt of a rescript from the king's own hand.

Copy of the Decree which was brought to the servant there concerning his return to Egypt.

"Horus, Life-of-Births, Two Crown-Goddessed, Life-of-Births, King of Upper and Lower Egypt, Kheper-ka-Ra, Son of Ra, Senusert, that liveth for ever and ever.

"A royal decree unto the henchman Sinuhe. Behold this decree of the King is brought to thee to instruct thee as here followeth: Thou hast traversed the foreign lands and art come forth from Kedemi to Retenu, and land gave thee to land, by the counsel of thine own heart. What hast thou done that aught should be done against thee? Thou didst not curse, that thy speech should be reproved, and thou didst not so speak in the council of the magistrates, that thine utterances should be thwarted. Only this thought, it carried away thine heart —— But this thine heaven (the queen) that is in the palace, yet abideth and prospereth to-day; she hath her part in the kingdom of the land, and her children are in the council-chamber. Thou wilt long subsist on the good things which they give thee, thou wilt live on their bounty. Come back to Egypt, that thou mayest see the Residence wherein thou didst grow up, that thou mayest kiss the earth at the Two Great Portals, and mingle with the Chamberlains.

"Even to-day thou hast begun to be old, thou hast lost thy manhood, and hast bethought thee of the day of burial, the passing to honour. An evening is devoted to thee with cedar oil and with bandages from the hand of Tait. A funeral procession is made for thee on the day of burial; the mummy-shell is of gold, with head of lapis lazuli; the heaven (the sarcophagus-lid, with its picture of the sky-goddess Nut) is above thee, and thou art placed upon a sledge. Oxen drag thee, and singers go before thee, and the dance of the Muu is performed for thee at the door of thy tomb. The Requirements of the Offering-Table are recited for thee, and victims are slain at thine offering-stones. Thy pillars are wrought of white stone in the midst of the tombs of the royal children. Thus shalt thou not die abroad, nor shall the Asiatics bury thee. Thou shalt not be placed in a sheep-skin —— Wherefore bethink thee of thy corpse and return."

I have given Senusert's letter in full, because of the extraordinary vividness with which it depicts the attitude of mind of an Egyptian with regard to the supreme objects of life. In what other country in the world would a king attempt to lure back a political exile to his native land by depicting to him the details of the first-class funeral which awaited him on his return? In any other land such a procedure would have seemed full of sinister suggestiveness, and the recipient of the letter would have proceeded to put as many more miles as possible between himself and the king who offered him the most exalted burial honours. In Egypt, however, and between Egyptians, Senusert's letter was the most gracious and tactful of invitations, in spite of its slightly contemptuous tone; and Sinuhe received it as the offer of life from the dead. "This decree reached me as I stood in the midst of my tribe. It was read to me, and I threw myself on my belly; I touched the dust and strewed it on my hair. I strode about my encampment rejoicing and saying: 'How should such things be done to a servant, whom his heart led astray to barbarous lands? Yea, good indeed is the Benevolent One that delivereth me from death. Thy *Ka* will suffer me to bring my life to an end in the Residence.'"

Sinuhe's ecstatic response to the royal permission need not detain us. After the usual elaboration of adulation of the Pharaoh, it suggests that evidence as to the writer's *bona fides* should be taken. "Now let Thy Majesty command that Meki be brought from Kedemi, Khentiuiaush from Khentkeshu, and Menus from the lands of the Fenekhu. They are princes and witnesses, that have grown up in love of thee—there is no need for me to mention

Retenu, for that is thine, as it were thy dogs." Then follows a tremulous exposition of the totally involuntary nature of his former flight, which seems to lie open to the objection that Sinuhe "doth protest too much"; and finally the exile intimates his submission to the royal decree. "Whether I am in the Residence or in this place, it is thou that obscurest this horizon, and the sun ariseth at thy pleasure (cf. the French, 'faire la pluie et le beau temps'); the water in the river is drunk when thou willest, and the air in heaven is breathed when thou biddest. The servant there (Sinuhe himself) will hand over my vizier-ship, which the servant there hath exercised in this place. Thereupon men came to the servant there—thy Majesty will do as he pleaseth; men live on thy breath which thou givest. May Ra, Horus, and Hathor love this thine august nose, which Month, Lord of Thebes, willeth shall live for ever."

Having dispatched his letter, Sinuhe proceeded to wind up his affairs in Palestine, where he certainly left his children, and to all appearance his wife also, without the slightest compunction. "I was suffered to spend a day in Yaa, and handed over my substance to my children, so that my eldest son had charge of my tribe, and all my substance was in his hand, my serfs, all my cattle, my fruits, and every pleasant tree of mine." The journey is briefly described, and was apparently mainly by sea. "Every cook was at his task, and I set out and sailed; and men kneaded and brewed beside me, until I reached the town 'Conqueress-of-the-Two-Lands'. (Ithttoui, as al-ready mentioned). And at daybreak, very early, they came to summon me; ten men came and ten men went and con-ducted me to the palace." Sinuhe now proceeds to give an example of the awe with which the presence of Pharaoh was surrounded—an awe which in his case was increased, doubtless, by a lingering uncertainty as to how he would be received after his flight.

"I touched the ground between the sphinxes with my forehead, and the royal children stood in the gateway and received me, and the Chamberlains that conduct to the hall set me on my way to the Privy Chamber. I found His

Majesty on his great throne in the golden gateway. When I had stretched myself on my belly my wits forsook me in his presence, albeit this god addressed me kindly. I was as a man that is carried off in the dusk, my soul fled, my body quaked, mine heart was no longer in my body, and I wist not whether I was alive or dead.

"Then said His Majesty to one of these Chamberlains: 'Raise him up, let him speak to me.' And His Majesty said: 'See, thou art returned, after thou hast trodden the foreign lands —— Eld assaileth thee, and thou hast reached old age. It is no small matter that thy body be laid in the ground, and that the barbarians bury thee not. But be not silent, be not silent; speak, thy name is pronounced.'

"I answered thereto with the answer of one that is afraid: 'What saith My Lord unto me? Would that I might answer it (but I cannot). It is as it were the hand of God, it is a dread; it is in my body, as it were that which once caused that destined flight. Behold, I am in thy presence. Thine is life, and Thy Majesty will do as it pleaseth thee.'"

His Majesty, as it turned out, was pleased to amuse himself with a little chaffing of Sinuhe, whose Asiatic raiment and unshaven chin must have looked excessively funny to a self-respecting and clean-shaven Egyptian, garbed in white linen. "Then the royal children were caused to be ushered in. Said His Majesty to the Queen: 'See, this is Sinuhe, who hath come back as an Asiatic, a creature of the Bedouins'. She uttered an exceeding loud cry, and the royal children shrieked out altogether. They said unto His Majesty: 'It is not he in sooth, O King, my Lord'. His Majesty said: 'It is he in sooth'. Now they had brought with them their necklaces, their rattles, and their sistra. And they held them out to His Majesty: 'Thy hands be on the Beauteous One, O long-living King, on the ornament of the Lady of Heaven. May the Golden One (Hathor) give life to thy nose, and the Mistress of the Stars (Hathor) join herself to thee. May the Upper Egyptian Crown go down-stream and the Lower Egyptian Crown go up-stream, and be joined both together in the mouth of Thy Majesty. May the serpent be set on thy brow. Thou hast delivered the poor from evil. May Ra be gracious unto thee, O Lord of the Two Lands! Hail to thee as to the Mistress of all! Loose thine horn and pull out thine arrow; give breath to him that is stifled, and bestow upon us as our goodly festival-gift this sheikh, the son of the Goddess of the North, this barbarian born in Egypt. He fled through fear of thee; he left the land through dread of thee. But a face that hath seen Thy Majesty shall no more blench, and an eye that hath regarded thee shall not fear.'

"Then said His Majesty: 'He shall not fear, he shall not dread. He shall be a Chamberlain among the magistrates, and be placed in the midst of the courtiers. Get you gone to the Chamber of Adoration, in order to make (his toilet as an Egyptian courtier?)'

"So when I was gone forth from the Privy Chamber, the royal children giving me their hands, we then went to the Two Great Portals. And I was placed in the house of a king's son, in which there was noble equipment, and a bath was therein, and —— Precious things of the Treasury were in it, garments of royal linen, myrrh, and fine oil of the king. Counsellors whom he loveth were in every chamber, and every serving-man was at his task. Years were made to pass away from my body, I was shaved, and my hair was combed. A load of dirt was given back to the desert (from the poor man's neglected body!), and the filthy clothes to the Sand-farers. And I was arrayed in finest linen and anointed with the best oil. I slept on a bed, and gave up the sand to them that be in it, and the oil of wood to him that smeared himself therewith." (Sinuhe seems slightly ungrateful to the Sand-dwellers, of whose help he had been glad enough in his need; but the passage is highly significant of the Egyptian's contempt for other races.)

"And I was given a house such as appertaineth to a Chamberlain. Many artificers built it, and all its wood-work was new appointed. And meals were brought me from the palace, three times and four times a day, over and above that which the royal children gave, without cessation at any time. And there was constructed for me a pyramid of stone, within the precinct of the pyramids. The chief architect began the building of it, the painter designed in it, the master-sculptor carved in it, the master-builders of the necropolis busied themselves with it. All the glistening gear that is placed in a tomb-shaft, the tomb's needs were supplied therefrom. And funerary priests were given me, and there was made for me a sepulchral garden, in which were fields, over against the abode (the tomb?), even as is done for a Chief Chamberlain. And my statue was overlaid with gold, and its apron was of fine gold. It was His Majesty who caused it to be made. There is no humble man for whom the like had been done. And so live I, rewarded by the King, until the day of my death cometh."

So we leave this much-enduring Odysseus of the ancient east happy and satisfied in the contemplation of an orthodox end, and apparently never giving a second thought to the wife and children whom he had left in Palestine. His story has been told almost at full length, and in his own words, because there is no other document which throws such light upon Middle Kingdom Egypt, its ideas and its prejudices. Nothing else in Egyptian literature brings Pharaoh and the royal family so near to us, and lets us see their essential humanity under the official divinity that hedged the Residence, as the extraordinarily finely touched scene wherein the Pharaoh and his family gently make mockery of the Prodigal Son who is going to have the fatted calf killed for him directly. Too much is sometimes made of the official divinity of the Pharaoh, as if there was no coming down at all from the high horse; and it has been asserted that Amenhotep III. of the XVIIIth Dynasty was the first Pharaoh to break through the restrictions of royal etiquette, and appear as a human being. "This lion-hunting, bull-baiting Pharaoh," says Professor Breasted, "who had made a woman of lowly birth his queen, was far indeed from that godlike and unapproachable immobility of his divine ancestors." One looks with suspicion upon theories of "godlike and unapproachable immobility", wherever human beings are concerned; and such a passage as that of the reception of Sinuhe shows conclusively how little importance a Pharaoh, even of one of the greatest of dynasties, could attach to such a thing on occasion, and with what completely human zest he and his queen and family could give themselves *desipere in loco*. The value of its pictures of Egyptian life and modes of thought at this period must be the apology for the length at which Sinuhe's narrative, which, after all, is only the narrative of the adventures of one man, has been dealt with.

King Senusert reigned with conspicuous success for 45 years, and in the 43rd year of his reign, when he might be nearing the seventieth year of his age, he associated his son, Amenemhat II., with himself in the sovereignty. His pyramid was built at Lisht, not far from the capital Ithttoui; and he prepared for the temple of the pyramid ten fine limestone statues of himself. For some obscure reason these ten statues were never set up, either by Senusert or by his son. Instead, they were left lying upon the ground and covered with sand, in which condition they were found in 1894, together with six Osiride figures of Senusert, and thirteen altars dedicated by priestesses of the king. The ten statues, which, with the exception of one which is cracked, are absolutely perfect, are now assembled in the Cairo Museum.

CHAPTER XV

TWO UNDISTINGUISHED REIGNS

THE reigns of Amenemhat I. and Senusert I. may be regarded as having firmly established the XIIth Dynasty on the throne. They were followed by those of another Amenemhat and another Senusert, which do not seem to have been marked by events of the same outstanding importance as those which characterised the reigns of their predecessors, but which, nevertheless, have left us evidence of a steady continuance of national prosperity, and which, in particular, have furnished us with some of our most remarkable evidence as to the high level which the artistic crafts of the Middle Kingdom reached at this period. If the record of the kings themselves is not conspicuously great, the period is marked by several of the most notable of the inscriptions and sculptures of the great local barons; and no other time, save that of Tutankhamen, has provided us with such exquisite examples of Egyptian skill in design and execution of work in the precious metals and in precious stones as is afforded by the two treasures of Dahshur and of Lahun, which belong to these two reigns.

In Egypt itself, Amenemhat II., who took the name of Nub-kau-ra as Reed-and-Hornet king, does not appear to have done any great amount of work on the conspicuous sites; but he was active at Sinai, where the establishment, or re-establishment, of the mining centre of Serabit el-Khadim was due to him. He also revived again the custom of making expeditions to the Land of Punt, a custom which was followed by his son, and which produced one of the best known of Egyptian romantic tales in the Story of the Shipwrecked Sailor. His Sinai adventure is recorded in an inscription cut on the rocks near the great reservoir at

Serabit el-Khadim, which tells us of the opening of a new mine at this place. "Year 24, under the Majesty of the King of Upper and Lower Egypt, Amenemhat II. Mine-chamber which the real king's confidant . . . the captain of sailors, Men, born of Mut, triumphant and revered, excavated"; and Sa-hathor, one of the active officials of the reign, tells us, among other things: "I visited the Mineland (Sinai) as a youth." Nine inscribed tablets and two statuettes of Amenemhat's reign have been found at Sinai, including the lower part of a seated figure of Hathor, "The Lady of Turquoise", and the guardian deity of the miners, which was dedicated by "the chief captain of the ships, Sneferu, born of Maketu".

The reference to the Punt expedition was discovered at Wady Gasus on the Red Sea, and is of interest as having given us the Egyptian name of that harbour, which was used extensively for expeditions both to Sinai and to Punt. The tablet is of one Khentikhetur, and shows us the figure of Amenemhat II. offering libation to Min of Koptos; beneath is the figure of Khentikhetur himself, uplifting his arms in worship. The inscription is as follows: "Giving divine praise and laudation to Horus—to Min of Koptos, by the hereditary prince, count, wearer of the royal seal, the master of the judgment-hall, Khentikhetur, after his arrival in safety from Punt; his army being with him, prosperous and healthy, and his ships having landed at Sewew (Wady Gasus). Year 28."

Sa-hathor, who has already told us of his visit to Sinai, is also responsible for letting us know of the king's activity in Nubia. "I visited the mineland as a youth, and I forced the Nubian chiefs to wash gold. I brought malachite, I reached Nubia of the negroes. I went, overthrowing by the fear of the Lord of the Two Lands. I came to He, I went around its islands, I brought away its produce."

Comparatively little of Amenemhat II.'s work at the temples of Egypt has survived; but it is evident that they were not neglected, and that, if the king was not a great builder, like his father, at all events he saw to it that the existing buildings were kept in good repair. We have direct evidence on this point from the record of an official named

PLATE XVII

W. F. Mansell

GREY GRANITE STATUE OF SENUSERT III. BRITISH MUSEUM. (*p.* 316)

Khentemsemeti, "the king's real favourite servant, master of secret things of the king's Wardrobe", who managed, as he tells us on his stele from Abydos, now in the British Museum, to combine his duty as inspector of temples with his eternal interests, by breaking his journey of inspection at Abydos, and erecting his memorial there. "I came to the front", he says, "in the presence of His Majesty, he had me inspect the divine fathers (priests), to expel evil and to prosper the fashion of their work, in eternal affairs. I commanded to fashion their offering-tables, the electrum was under my seal. I reached Elephantine according to this command; I kissed the earth before the Lord of the Cataract (Khnum). I returned by the way over which I had passed. I drave in the mooring-stake at Abydos. I fixed my name at the place where is the god Osiris, First of the Westerners, lord of eternity, ruler of the West, to which all that is flees, for the sake of the benefit therein, in the midst of the followers of the Lord of Life, that I might eat his loaf, and come forth by day; that my spirit might enjoy the ceremonies of people, kind in heart towards my tomb, and in hand towards my stele. For I have not done (evil); that the god may be favourable to me in judgment when I am 'there'; that I may labour, being a spirit in the necropolis-cliff, the ruler of eternity; that I may handle the rudder, that I may descend into the sacred barque; that I may smell the earth before Upuat. Khentemsemeti, justified, lord of reverence."

When Amenemhat II. had reached the 33rd year of his reign, he associated with himself, according to the custom of his dynasty, his son Senusert II., and the joint reign lasted for between six and seven years before it was interrupted, so Manetho tells us, by a palace conspiracy, in which Amenemhat was slain by his chamberlains—a somewhat senseless business, as it appears to us, seeing that the old king's son was left to succeed him, while he himself, who was probably by this time a man of nearly eighty years, was sacrificed. But our knowledge is too small for us to be able to pronounce upon events so obscure, and of which we have only the evidence of a single doubtful statement.

His pyramid was built at a lonely spot in the desert, about five miles south of Saqqara, and ten miles north

of Lisht, where his father had been buried. Very little
is now left of his tomb; but the royal tombs in its neighbourhood, in which the ladies of the royal house were
buried, have yielded in our time one of the richest stores
of ancient craftsmanship that have ever come to light.
The tombs were those of the queen Kema-nub and the
princesses Ata, Ataurt, Khnumit, and Sathathor-meryt.
Plunderers had been at work on all of them, and the tomb
of the queen had been completely rifled; but a considerable
store of the jewellery of the princesses had escaped the
attention of the robbers, and rewarded the efforts of M. de
Morgan in 1894 and 1895. The treasure of Dahshur is
now one of the most prized possessions of the Cairo
Museum, and not even the amazing wealth of the tomb of
Tutankhamen has yielded anything superior in taste and
in execution to the pectorals, diadems, bracelets, and
necklaces of these XIIth Dynasty princesses. The gems
of the collection, which embraces not only work of the
reign of Amenemhat II., but also later work of the following reigns, down to that of Amenemhat III., are the
diadems of the princess Khnumit, of which the floral
crown is perhaps the most exquisite piece of naturalistic
work which has survived from the ancient world, while
the more formal and conventional diadem with the
Maltese crosses is fully equal to it in its own more stately
and restrained style. But there are other pieces in the
collection which, though not as famous as the two diadems,
are in no way inferior to them in beauty and in the skill
with which they are executed. The next reign will yield us
a similar treasure in the shape of the jewellery of the
princess Sathathor-ant, discovered at Lahun in 1914 by
Sir Flinders Petrie and Mr. Guy Brunton, some of whose
pieces were of even higher quality, if that were possible,
than those of the earlier find.

One thing is evident when we are brought face to face
with work like this; and that is that the Egyptian of the
XIIth Dynasty, nearly four thousand years ago, was, in
some aspects of his life, at all events, quite as highly
civilised as any twentieth-century product of modernism.
Indeed, if the most refined taste, the love of beauty, and

the skill which can gratify that love by the most exquisite combinations of form and colour, are to be regarded as tests of the height of culture to which a nation has attained, then a good deal of our modern culture comes off rather badly in the comparison with the society which demanded such things as the Dahshur jewellery for its gratification, and could find artists and craftsmen equal to the meeting of the demand. Most of our modern jewellery is vulgar and pretentious compared with the best of the ornaments of these XIIth Dynasty princesses. There was, no doubt, a good deal that was barbarous still in Egyptian society. It was not so long ago that the ladies of the royal harem were apparently being slain at the tomb of their royal master; and while that barbarity soon passes away, other barbarisms persist that would make us shudder at the present day, in spite of all our familiarity with the capabilities of the human brute when passion is let loose. But at least the Dahshur jewellery is evidence of a society which was our equal, if not our superior, in artistic taste, and whose conditions of life were cultured, luxurious, and withal elegant and refined, to a degree seldom attained in any other period.

Senusert II., who now succeeded his father, after a joint reign with him of between six and seven years, is distinguished, if Manetho may be believed, as being one of the tallest kings who ever sat upon a throne. His stature, according to the Egyptian historian, was four cubits, three hands, and two fingers, which would make him a trifle over six feet six inches in height. In other respects, however, his reign seems rather to mark a falling off from the high standard of the dynasty, though our material is too scanty to admit a definite statement that this is so. The reign itself was of short duration, compared with the unusually steady average of the dynasty, being of only 19 years, including the six years of joint rule. But the main evidence, scanty enough, it must be admitted, as to a slight declension of power, is in connection with Nubia, where the former kings of the dynasty had advanced the Egyptian frontier to the Third Cataract, and had apparently made some progress in reducing the land thus occupied to a regular Egyptian province. But it would almost appear as if, during the joint-reign of Amenemhat II. and his son, the Egyptian hold upon Nubia had been slackening, and the negro tribes had even been threatening invasion of Egyptian soil.

This is suggested (one can scarcely say more) by the inscription on a tablet found at El-Kab (the Egyptian Nekheb). It is dated in the 44th year of Amenemhat III., the grandson of Senusert II., and reads: "His Majesty ordered the construction of the ramparts which are within the enclosing-walls of Seshemutoui, deceased". Seshemutoui is the Hawk-name of Senusert II., and it is difficult to see why he should have been building enclosing walls at Nekheb, 80 miles north of the First Cataract, in a time when the kingdom was in a state of absolute internal peace and unification, unless there was some threat from the south. Add to this the fact that several great works of fortification in southern Egypt and Lower Nubia appear to date from about this time, and that we have evidence of these fortresses being kept under inspection during the reign, and the possibility becomes apparent of a time of trouble in Nubia, when revolt of the negro tribes may even have threatened the Egyptian frontier.

The inspector of the fortresses under Senusert II. was one Hapu, who has left his record, unfortunately with his title obliterated, on the rocks near Aswan. It bears the names of Amenemhat II., "Beloved of Satet, Mistress of Elephantine", and of Senusert II., "beloved of Khnum, lord of the cataract region", and runs as follows: "Made in the year 3, under the Majesty of Horus: Seshemutoui (Senusert II.), corresponding to the year 35 under the Majesty of Horus: Hekenemmat (Amenemhat II.). The (?) Hapu came, in order to make an inspection of the fortresses of Wawat." Senusert III., the next king, had, as we shall see, to undertake an important expedition against the negro tribes early in his reign; so that, slight as the evidence may be, it is probably the fact that the hold of the Egyptian kings upon their new province had been weakening during the latter years of Amenemhat II. and the reign of Senusert II.

In other respects, however, the usual energy seems to have been displayed. There is evidence of work on various native Egyptian sites, as at Herakleopolis, at Karnak, and at Hierakonpolis, and also within the breccia-quarries at Hammamat. Serabit el-Khadim continued to be the centre of mining activity in the Sinai Peninsula, and an expedition to "God's Land" or Punt, under the "treasurer of the god", Khnumhotep, is recorded on a tablet found at Wady Gasus, and now at Alnwick Castle. The king was married to a lady who was more important than beautiful, if her statue, found at Tanis, does her justice. The inscription on the throne of the statue reads: "The hereditary princess, the great favourite, the greatly praised, the beloved consort of the king, the ruler of all women, the king's daughter of his body, Nefert." Thus the queen had a distinct title to the throne herself, which may account for the unusual title, "ruler of all women" given to her; and Senusert had adopted the custom, so strange to our minds, but so usual and indeed so natural in Egyptian eyes, of marrying his own sister—a proceeding which certainly greatly strengthened his position on the throne, and seems to have had none of the unsatisfactory consequences usually attributed to unions between such close relatives.

The royal pyramid was built at Lahun or Illahun, near the mouth of the Fayum. This province was the subject of especial care and attention on the part of the kings of the XIIth Dynasty; and Senusert showed that he shared in the solicitude with which it was regarded by building his tomb, not actually within the Fayum, but at a spot where the Fayum is visible from the top of the pyramid. The building is a departure from the usual pyramid-practice of the Pharaohs. The core of it is of native rock, which has been isolated from the hill to which it belonged by a deep cutting. The chambers for the accommodation of the king were cut in the solid rock, so that there might be no question of the upper openings which had proved fatal to the security of the older pyramids, and the entrance to them was not within the bounding-walls of the pyramid itself, but was by a shaft whose mouth lay outside of the south face of the building. Over the core of rock, retaining walls of stone, massive and solid, were built, and the spaces between them were filled in with brick, the whole being cased outside with fine limestone. The main shaft of entrance was covered up by the floor of the tomb of one of the royal princesses, as a further precaution against robbers, the secondary shaft being concealed beneath the pavement of the pyramid-court. In spite of all the care of Anpu, the royal architect, however, the tomb had been rifled. The magnificent red granite sarcophagus survives, and is splendidly wrought, "the errors of flatness and straightness being matters of thousandths of an inch". A shrine for the worship of the king stood against the east face of the pyramid, as usual. It had been richly carved and painted; but it was ruthlessly destroyed by the masons of that monumental vandal, Ramses II., whose impertinent cartouche has been left inscribed on one of the blocks of the ruin which they left. About a mile to the east stood another larger temple, probably the public shrine for the royal worship. This also had been remorselessly destroyed, leaving only flakes and chips of basalt statues and shrines and statues of red granite.

By the side of this larger temple stood the town of the workmen who built the pyramid and its accessory temples. It was named Hetep-Senusert, "Contented in Senusert", and it now goes by the name of Kahun. Of course the walls of the houses have been denuded away to a great extent; but the town can still be pretty completely traced on plan, and occupies, as surveyed by Sir Flinders Petrie, an area of about 18 acres, within which over two thousand rooms have been traced. The plans show a complete Egyptian town of the period, with comfortable mansions for the higher officials and rows of little houses for the workmen. Apparently the town almost ceased to be occupied after the completion of the pyramid and temples, the workmen being moved on to another locality; and the folk who remained used the unoccupied houses as rubbish-dumps. The troubles of the Hyksos period completed the desolation of the town, and thus it was left to the slow processes of denudation, almost unaltered in plan from the days of its prosperity.

On the south side of Senusert's pyramid was a group of four tombs belonging to members of the royal family. These had all been plundered; but, in one case, that of the princess Sathathor-ant, a recess in the tomb had been overlooked, and when this was explored in 1914 by Mr. Guy Brunton it was found to contain another treasure of royal jewellery, less in quantity than the Dahshur treasure, but of quality quite equal to the other, and in some instances almost superior. The chief pieces were a princess's crown, or queen's crown, of most refined and exquisite design, perhaps the most satisfying example known of Egyptian skill in this kind of work; pectorals of Senusert II., who was the princess's father, and of Amenemhat III., to whom she was married; girdles, bracelets, anklets, and a silver mirror mounted in obsidian and gold. The pectorals show very clearly the gradual decline of taste between the time of Senusert II. and Amenemhat III. They are both fine, but the execution of the earlier one is much more satisfactory than that of the later piece, which, while it would be considered splendid if seen by itself, looks coarse and hasty alongside of the exquisitely careful work of the Senusert pectoral.

The most interesting inscription of a reign singularly barren in this respect is the famous one of Khnumhotep II., one of the members of the great family which held for several generations the position of nomarchs of the Oryx nome, together with other similar offices. Like the Khety family of Siut during the IXth Dynasty, and the princes of El-Kab during the XVIIIth Dynasty, this great family, whose tombs are at Beni-hasan, was a main pillar of the Egyptian state during the XIIth Dynasty. The rise of the house apparently dates from the reign of Amenemhat I., who appointed Khnumhotep II.'s grandfather, Khnumhotep I., as Count of Menat-Khufu, a district of the Oryx nome, and finally as nomarch of the whole nome. It was this Khnumhotep whom we have seen accompanying Amenemhat I. on his expedition "with twenty ships of cedar". The royal favour was continued by Senusert I., who appointed the two sons of Khnumhotep I., Nakht and Amenemhat, to the charge of Menat-Khufu and the

Oryx nome respectively. Khnumhotep's daughter, Beket, married an official of the court named Nehri, who was nomarch of the Hare nome, immediately south of the family principality. Her son was Khnumhotep II., whom we are now about to hear, and who succeeded to Menat-Khufu on the death of his uncle Nakht, which happened in the 19th year of Amenemhat II. Khnumhotep, who evidently believed in accumulating all the influence he could lay his hands upon, married the lady Kheti, heiress of the nomarch of the Jackal nome, which lay just north of that of the Oryx. His eldest son, Nakht II., thus acquired the office of nomarch of the Jackal nome in his mother's right, while his second son, Khnumhotep III., stepped into his father's position at Menat-Khufu. This notable succession for at least four generations in office and profit reminds one forcibly of the corresponding tradition of our own Whig oligarchy, with which these great barons of Benihasan seem to have had much in common.

Khnumhotep himself is the typical official gentleman who, so long as he continues to hold office, realises that all is for the best in the best of all possible worlds. With admirable unction he tells us the tale of his family's gradual accumulation of offices, beginning with the appointment of his grandfather and namesake. His ancestors, he tells us, obtained their offices because of their surpassing merits, as he obtained his position for similar reasons. His sons have also been successful in the same interesting game of grab, because of their shining qualities. Listen to him as he discourses with eloquence of the virtues and excellences of his younger son, Khnumhotep III.: "Another prince is counsellor, sole companion, great among the sole companions, of numerous gifts to the palace, sole companion. There is not one possessed of his virtues; to whom the officers hearken, the unique mouth, closing other mouths, bringing advantage to its possessor, keeper of the door of the highlands, Khnumhotep, son of Khnumhotep, son of Nehri, who was born of the matron Kheti." Happy must have been the reign of the king who had such paragons as the Khnumhoteps, father and son, for his counsellors!

Khnumhotep's chief achievement, according to himself, was the thoroughly pious and also thoroughly typical one of building the tombs of his fathers, to whom he owed so much that was comfortable and profitable. "I kept alive the name of my fathers, which I found obliterated upon the doorways, making them legible in form, accurate in reading, not putting one in the place of another. Behold it is an excellent son who restores the names of the ancestors; Nehri's son, Khnumhotep, triumphant, revered. (Hear! hear!). My chief nobility was: I executed a cliff-tomb, for a man should imitate that which his father does." And then our good gossip wanders off into a new description of the virtues of his father, which must have been only less than his own. So far as his own testimony goes, the main work which he did for his nome was the glorification of his own family. He makes no mention, as do most of the other nomarchs, of having fed the hungry and clothed the naked, and so forth; but instead, we have the following: "The achievements of the count Khnumhotep: I made a monument in the midst of my city; I built a colonnaded hall which I found in ruin; I erected it with columns anew, inscribed with my own name. (Surely!). I perpetuated the name of my father upon them—I recorded my deeds upon every monument. . . . I was munificent in monuments; I taught every craft which had been neglected in this city, in order that my name might be excellent upon every monument which I made".

So we may leave the excellent Khnumhotep to contemplate his own perfections and those of his family, for whom the world was undoubtedly created. No doubt he was a good enough nomarch, and did as much for his people as others who made more fuss over what they had done; only he was honest enough to tell posterity what others probably believed, but did not tell—that the rest of the human race existed solely for the glory of himself and his house.

Khnumhotep, however, has another title to fame besides the fact that he was "munificent in monuments." Though now cast down from his high estate, he figured for long as one of the infallible proofs of the accuracy of Holy Writ, in the imaginations of such as believe that the value of Scripture depends upon our being able to find a monumental endorsement for every statement made in the Bible. The most famous scene in his tomb depicts the arrival at the nomarch's palace of a party of thirty-seven Beduin, who offer various gifts to Khnumhotep, to whom they are being presented by his scribe Neferhotep. The scribe holds in his hand a papyrus-roll bearing the inscription: "Year six, under the Majesty of Horus, the Guide of the Two Lands, the King of Upper and Lower Egypt, Senusert II. The number of Aamu brought by the son of the *ha*-prince Khnumhotep, on account of the eye-paint, Aamu of Shu, number amounting to 37". The party consists of both men and women, with a couple of children, who are seated in hampers on the back of a donkey. The men are armed with spears and bows, and one of them plays a kind of zither. The women have long dark hair, and wear shoes, not sandals, on their feet. The men are bearded, and offer typically Semitic faces, with the characteristic Hebrew nose. All are dressed in gaily embroidered woollen garments.

The picture was at once seized upon, when discovered, as being a representation of the coming down into Egypt of Jacob and his household, or perhaps of Abraham and his family, for it was not quite certain which patriarch was represented, and the numbers did not tally. Actually, of course, it has no connection with the Biblical incident, save as an illustration of the fact, which nobody doubts, that such visits of Asiatics did occur in the period under question, and that there is, therefore, no inherent improbability in the Bible narrative. The name of the leader of Khnumhotep's Semites is "the *heq*-prince of the deserts Abishai", which, of course, rules out either Abraham or Jacob, but is a good Hebrew name all the same. Though the identification has long ago been given up, the representation has still its own value. Abishai is just such a tribal sheikh as Abraham and Jacob must have been in their day, which cannot have been very far removed, in point of time, from his; and Jacob's family must have looked very much like these 37 desert Aamu, when they came down, with their old father, to find shelter and nourishment under the guardian shield of Pharaoh's

Hebrew vizier, Joseph. They were not uncivilised, judging by Abishai's party, though doubtless Khnumhotep and his little court circle would look with great scorn upon the ragged beards and gaudy woollen garments which made so marked a contrast with their own clean-shaven faces and white linen. Their civilisation was different, perhaps somewhat less refined, than the Egyptian type; but in all the essentials it was not really deficient.

Excavating again in 1920–21 at the pyramid of Senusert II. at Lahun, Sir Flinders Petrie and Mr. Brunton had the singular good fortune to discover the only part of the great royal crown of Egypt which has yet come to light, though representations of the Double Crown are, of course, innumerable. The find was that of the solid golden uraeus which had adorned the front of the crown, and which was found beneath a few inches of rubbish in a rock-cut chamber on the south side of the sepulchre of the pyramid. This unique relic of Egyptian royalty is of solid gold, inlaid with semi-precious stones. The head is cut out of lapis lazuli, with eyes of garnet, set in gold. The hood of the cobra is outlined with lazuli, and the mid-rib of gold is barred in the centre with the same material. For fastening it to the crown two loops of gold are provided at the back; and the inference would seem to be that the uraeus must have been sewn or wired on to the crown, which must therefore have been of some soft material, possibly leather or pleated linen, and must have been rather a mitre than a crown in the ordinary sense of the word. But on this point we must await the much desired discovery of an actual specimen of the most famous of earthly crowns—a discovery which even the treasures of the tomb of Tutankhamen have not yielded.

CHAPTER XVI

THE CULMINATION OF THE MIDDLE KINGDOM

THE two reigns which now follow the comparatively un-distinguished reigns of Amenemhat II. and Senusert II. mark the culmination of the security and power of the Middle Kingdom. Senusert III. and Amenemhat III. were not in any real sense of the word great conquerors. Senusert, indeed, did a considerable amount of fighting in Nubia, where he succeeded in establishing on a firm basis the somewhat shaky fabric of Egyptian domination which had been set up early in the dynasty; while he also made an invasion of Palestine, which, however, seems to have been little more than a raid, and led to no permanent occupation. But these deeds, though they proved sufficient to give him a reputation as one of the great soldier figures of Egyptian history, and indeed have helped him to become at least a part of that famous mythical figure called Sesostris, were really comparatively "small war", not to be mentioned in the same breath with the regular campaigns of Thothmes III., or even with those of Seti I. and Ramses II. The Nubian expeditions were more or less mere punitive raids, which proved sufficient to knock the heart out of the negro effervescence which had apparently been causing some trouble in the preceding reign; and the Palestine expedition, though it involved the siege of one fortified place, was seemingly more a plundering business than anything else, and was not followed up. Amenemhat III. was even less of a military hero than his predecessor, and no record of any war of his has survived.

But the military exploits of Senusert, such as they were, induced a feeling of security in Egypt, which, to judge from the fervour with which it was expressed, had been somewhat lacking before, and gave the king a reputation which, to our minds, seems quite out of proportion to the scale of his achievements; a fact which perhaps merely scrves as a measure of the difficulty of really attaining the point of view of a contemporary of any particular series of events. To this feeling of security, Amenemhat added the consciousness of an abounding prosperity. His excursions beyond the strict frontiers of his own realm were entirely for purposes of trade, as in the case of his dealings with the Sinai Peninsula; while within his land his work was that of a beneficent and far-seeing ruler, who uses his power and his command of the resources of the nation to accomplish for its welfare works which were permanently useful, but which could never have been accomplished by private enterprise. Egypt, under both kings, may have been far from equalling the world-power and reputation which she held under the fighting kings of the XVIIIth Dynasty; but her life was unvexed by external threats, and within her own borders her prosperity was very real. There is nothing very dramatic in the national story of the two reigns; but all the same there can be little doubt that the modern verdict is justified which calls this the true Golden Age of Egyptian history.

Senusert's first work on coming to the throne was the chastisement of the negro tribes in Nubia, which had been getting a little above themselves during the last reign, and had apparently been even a source of anxicty within Egypt itself. The great hindrance to campaigning in the Sudan has always been the interruption of the communications caused by the cataracts of the Nile. To pass an army up-river to the point which the Pharaoh desired to reach required the continuous employment of a numerous fleet, first, for the transport of the men, and then for the maintenance of their supplies. Five hundred years before this, the difficulty had been met by the series of canals which our old friend Una cut for commercial purposes; but during this long interval these had been either destroyed or silted up, and were not available for the present need. Senusert therefore realised that he would have to cut a canal at the First Cataract, which would make the passage navigable. What was contemplated was probably not a complete canal as we understand such a thing, which would serve as a by-pass to evade the cataract altogether, but simply a deepening of the comparatively smooth channel on the east side of the island of Sehel, which would enable boats to be hauled up this passage without much difficulty, instead of having to face the strong current of the western passage.

In any case, the work was done in an early year of the reign, as the inscription at Sehel testifies. It represents Senusert standing before the goddess Anukit, one of the deities of the cataract; while below are the words: "He made it as his monument for Anukit, mistress of Nubia, making for her a canal, whose name is 'Beautiful-are-the-Ways-of-Khakaura (Senusert III.) that he may live forever' ". No date is added to the inscription; but as the passage had to be cleared of silt again in the king's eighth year, it must obviously have been in existence for several years before that. We may imagine the Egyptian army, therefore, passing up the new canal perhaps in the second year of the new king, in blissful unconsciousness that they would have all the work to do over again in another half-dozen years.

The first lesson was not sufficient, apparently, to keep the negro tribes quiet, and when the army was called out again in the eighth year, it was found that the new canal had already been choked with silt to such an extent that it would not allow of the passage of the warships and transports. It was accordingly cleared out again, and the performance was duly recorded on the rocks at Sehel. The king stands, wearing the Double Crown, before the other cataract goddess, Satit, who presents him with "life"; behind him stands the chief treasurer and chief of works, who appears to have been named Ronpetenenkh. The inscription runs thus: "Year 8, under the Majesty of the King of Upper and Lower Egypt; Khakaura (Senusert III.) living forever. His Majesty commanded to make the canal anew, the name of this canal being: 'Beautiful-are-the-Ways-of-Khakaura', living forever, when His Majesty proceeded up-river to overthrow Kush the wretched. Length of this canal, 150 cubits; width,

20; depth, 15." The passage was thus about 250 feet long, 34 feet broad, and 25 feet deep, and was amply sufficient to pass any such boats as would be used for the expedition. The work was well done on this occasion, for the canal was still in use between three and four hundred years later, though it had to be cleared out by both Thothmes I. and Thothmes III., when they went south on an errand similar to that of Senusert.

As he passed southwards, Senusert paid some attention to the fortress of Elephantine, in the direction of improving its access, and one of the local officials has left a record of his accomplishment of the job, which apparently took some time to complete, as it is dated in the following year. "Year 9, third month of the third season under the Majesty of the King of Upper and Lower Egypt, Khakaura, beloved of Satit, Mistress of Elephantine, living forever. Command of His Majesty to the Magnate of the South, Ameni, to make a doorway in the fortress of Elephantine, to make a ―― for the crown possessions of the South—the—people in the region of Elephantine; when my Lord, Life! Prosperity! Health! journeyed to overthrow the wretched Kush."

The expedition resulted in the advance being pushed to a point about 37 miles south of Wady Halfa. This, indeed, was still about 200 miles short of Kerma, where we have seen Hepzefi established as governor in the reign of Senusert I.; but Senusert III. was now determined at least to maintain what he had conquered, which his predecessors had not been able to do. He set up his stele at Semneh, where one of a pair of frontier fortresses was also erected, to secure the new boundary. "Southern boundary, made in the year eight," runs the inscription, "under the Majesty of the King of Upper and Lower Egypt, Khakaura, who is given life forever and ever; in order to prevent that any Negro should cross it, by water or by land, with a ship, or any herds of the Negroes; except a Negro who shall come to do trading in Aken, or with a commission. (In such a case) every good thing shall be done with them (i.e. every facility shall be granted them); but without allowing a ship of the Negroes to pass by Heh going downstream, forever."

In another four years this second campaign in Nubia had to be followed by a third; but the expedition of the twelfth year has left us nothing but a solitary sentence on the rocks at Aswan giving the date, the king's name, and the words: "His Majesty journeyed to overthrow Kush". Kush, however, evidently took a good deal of overthrowing before it finally consented to remain prostrate; for in another four years Senusert was on the war-path once more. On this occasion he set up a second stele at Semneh, whose record we shall hear directly, and he also set up a duplicate of this stele on the island of Uronarti, just below Semneh. The Uronarti stele gives us a piece of valuable information which does not occur upon the Semneh one. After the king's name, it continues: "Stele made in the year 16, third month of the second season, when the fortress: 'Repulse-of-the-Troglodytes' was built".

This inscription, therefore, dates for us the fortress of Uronarti; and as it was part of the system of frontier strongholds, it may be presumed that the other fortresses at this point were erected at the same time. The chief of these is the stronghold of Semneh, or, as it was called, "Semennu-of-the-Realm-of-Khakaura". It was a large and elaborate castle, built of sun-dried brick on a very strong position, whose natural strength was increased by artificial scarping, and it commanded the passage of the river, which is here not more than four hundred yards wide. On the east bank, opposite, a smaller fort, now known as Kummeh, was reared on a natural height, and the cross fire of the two castles must have rendered the passage too difficult to be worth while, unless an invasion in force was contemplated. The ruins of these two castles still survive, and various reconstructions of their probable appearance in the days of their pride have been offered. These, however, though in some cases of singularly imposing appearance, seem to owe more than is advisable to imagination; and it ought to be admitted that we do not actually know what the appearance of the curtains and towers of these ancient castles really was. In each of the strongholds there was a temple, that of Semneh being dedicated to Dedwen, a local god, and to Khnum, the

PLATE XVIII

AN OLD KINGDOM TOMB-CHAPEL   TOMB CHAMBER OF AMENY, BENI HASAN

From Fechheimer's "Die Plastik der Ägypter" (Cassirer)

cataract-god of Aswan and Elephantine, and in these temples a great feast was held in celebration of the victory over the negroes. It was called "Repulse-of-the-Troglodytes", and it was followed by another festival, called "Binding-of-the-Barbarians", at which offerings were made to Senusert's queen, "the great king's wife Merseger". These feasts were remembered long afterwards, and when Thothmes III., three hundred and seventy years later, rebuilt of stone the temple of his great forerunner, he reinstituted them, along with other ceremonies, and associated Senusert III. with the two original deities as a third god of the frontier which he had established—a pious act which was worthy of so great a man as Thothmes, who evidently did not grudge, as Ramses II. did, all honour that was not bestowed upon himself.

The inscription on the second Semneh stele, recording the campaign of the 16th year, is of great importance, not only as fixing the Egyptian frontier of the period in Nubia, but also because it is, as Dr. H. R. Hall says, "couched in unprecedented phraseology, reminding us strangely of the proclamations said by Diodorus to have been inscribed on stelae by the legendary Sesostris to commemorate his conquests". It runs as follows: "Year 16, third month of the second season, His Majesty's making the southern boundary as far as Heh. I have made my boundary beyond that of my fathers; I have increased that which was bequeathed to me. (This was not true, as the boundary of Senusert I. was, as we have seen, at Kerma, 200 miles south of Semneh.) I am a king who speaks and executes; that which my heart conceives is that which is wrought by my hand; eager to possess and strong to succeed; not allowing an affront to sleep in his heart; attacking him who attacks; silent in a matter, or answering a matter according to that which is in it; since, if one is silent after attack, it strengthens the heart of the enemy. Bravery lies in keenness, cowardice in slinking back; he is truly a craven who is repelled upon his own border. Since the Negro is ruled by the word of the mouth, it is a (prompt) answer that drives him back; when one is keen against him he turns his back; when one cowers before him, he begins to be forward. But they are not a people of might; they are poor and broken in heart. My Majesty has seen them; it is not a lie. I captured their women, I carried off their subjects, went forth to their wells, slew their bulls; I reaped their grain, and set fire to the residue thereof. By my own life and my father's life, I have spoken in truth, without any lie coming out of my mouth about it.

"Now as for any son of mine who shall maintain this frontier which My Majesty hath made, he is my son, he is born to My Majesty, a son who is the avenger of his father, who maintains the boundary of him who begat him. But as for him who shall give it up and shall not fight for it, he is not my son; he is not born to me. Now, behold, My Majesty hath caused a statue of My Majesty to be set up at this frontier which My Majesty hath made; in order that ye might be encouraged because of it, and that ye might fight for it." An alternative reading, still adopted by Hall (*Cambridge Ancient History*, i. 308), is "not from any desire that ye should worship it, but that ye should fight for it". Such a reading is obviously desirable, but seems almost too good to be true, and as Dr. Hall himself remarks: "Sarcasm is not usually found in an ancient Egyptian inscription".

These are "prave orts" of Senusert; so brave, in fact, that one feels that the king must have felt that the valour of his subjects needed a good deal of "gingering-up" before they could be trusted to face the Sudanese with any confidence. Plainly, it is the old story of the pacific Egyptian fellah being driven on to fight the naturally pugnacious black Sudanese, and not enjoying the business in the very least—a story which we have heard over again more than once in our own time. In the future, the Egyptian Pharaohs of the Empire were to find that the most reliable battalions of their army were these same negro battalions of which Senusert writes so scornfully. Jeremiah, writing of the army of Necho, which suffered defeat at the hands of Nebuchadrezzar at Carchemish, puts the Ethiopians first of the mercenary troops which made the strength of the Pharaoh's host—"the Ethiopians and the Libyans, that handle the shield; and the Lydians that handle and bend the bow". Altogether it is pretty evident that Egyptian prestige in Ethiopia had been pretty badly shaken during the last two reigns, and that Senusert felt that something drastic had to be said, as well as done, in order to restore it.

The same conclusion is reached when we realise the fuss which was made in later days over the achievement of what, after all, was not such a very heroic task. It seems to us no very splendid achievement for a king leading a well-equipped and disciplined army to raid the territory of a few scattered and ill-provided negro tribes, and to break the strength which had encouraged them to annoy the Egyptian frontier in previous reigns; but Egypt hailed the success of the negro war as the feat of a national hero, from which fact one naturally draws the conclusion that Egypt must have been in a condition of considerable trepidation over the negro menace before the revulsion to a state of security made her so hysterical. Anyhow, one way or another, Senusert reaped from his southern campaigns laurels which seem to us out of all proportion to the scale of his actual accomplishment. Herodotus, in the amazing fairy-tale which he recounts about his Sesostris, tells us: "This king, then, was the only Egyptian who ruled over Ethiopia", which is very far indeed from being the truth, but shows the impression which had been made upon his informants by the success of Senusert. Whether the king actually said that his statue was not to be worshipped or not, his prohibition (if it ever existed) was soon disregarded, and he was at length established as the patron deity of Nubia. We have seen how Thothmes III. associated him with Khnum and Dedwen in the temple within the castle of Semneh; and Taharka, the Ethiopian Pharaoh, nearly twelve hundred years after his conquest, restored the temple and the worship of the conqueror of Nubia.

Herodotus, in his admirable little romance of Sesostris, tells us also how the priests told him "that Sesostris was the first who, setting out in ships of war from the Arabian Gulf, subdued those nations that dwell by the Red Sea; until, sailing onwards, he arrived at a sea which was not navigable on account of the shoals; and afterwards, when he came back to Egypt, according to the report of the priests, he assembled a large army and marched through the continent, subduing every nation that he fell in with; and wherever he met with any who were valiant and who were very ardent in defence of their liberty, he erected columns in their territory, with inscriptions, declaring his own name and country, and how he had conquered them by his power". Further, he says, after having left less seemly memorials in the countries of those who were less valiant, he crossed into Europe, where he subdued the Scythians and Thracians. This, of course, is sheer romancing, for no king of Egypt ever accomplished anything like the feats which are here ascribed to Sesostris; but the erection of the pillars, with their records of the royal opinion as to the valour or cowardice of the foes with whom he had dealt, would seem to be a hazy reminiscence of the stele of Semneh, with its contemptuous references to his negro opponents.

All the same, broken in spirit or not broken, the negroes needed another reminder before Senusert was done with them. He had to make another expedition three years later, as we learn from the inscription of his Master of the Double Cabinet, Sisatet, which was set up at Abydos, and is now in the Museum at Geneva. "He saith: 'I came to Abydos, together with the chief treasurer Ikhernofret, to carve (a statue of) Osiris, lord of Abydos, when the King of Upper and Lower Egypt, Khakaura, living forever, journeyed, while overthrowing the wretched Kush, in the year 19'." It is possible that the date may refer to the completion of the inscription; but more likely that it refers to the event which has just been described in its preceding clause.

Whether that portion of the Sesostris romance of Herodotus which refers to a naval expedition down the Red Sea may have any foundation in an actual feat of Senusert, will depend on the view taken of the fragmentary and undated inscription found by Naville at Bubastis, in which an unnamed king describes an expedition in which negro tribes were defeated, and in which reference is made to some difficulties of navigation "southwards to see the height of Hua, to make known the ways of sailing ——— the north wind was very strong for the coming forth of the height of Hua; the coming forth of this height was in safety, sailing ———." Naville, and apparently Weigall, attribute the inscription to the XIIth Dynasty; but Brcasted has shown reasons for believing that it actually belongs to the XVIIIth, and may refer to the Nubian campaign of Amenhotep III.

On the other hand, the Asiatic triumphs to which Herodotus refers must find their basis, so far as they have any in the work of Senusert, in the solitary Palestine campaign, of which we have the record of Khu-sebek, who on his stele at Abydos has given us an account of his warlike feats under Senusert, which may be compared, *longo intervallo*, to the narratives of Admiral Aahmes and Amenemhab in the days of the Empire. Khu-sebek evidently thought not a little of his achievements in the Syrian campaign, for he begins his story with them, though they must have come pretty well on in his career, and only tells us of his birth and his earlier service at a considerably later point.

"His Majesty proceeded northwards, to overthrow the Mentiu (Asiatics). His Majesty arrived at a district; Sekmem was its name. His Majesty led the good way in proceeding to the palace of Life, Prosperity and Health, when Sekmem had fallen, together with Retenu the wretched, while I was acting as rearguard. Then the civilians of the army (camp-followers) got mixed up in a fight with the Asiatics. Then I captured an Asiatic, and handed his weapons to two civilians of the army, for I did not turn back from the fight, but kept my face to the front, and I did not show my back to the Asiatic. As Senusert lives, I have spoken the truth. Then he (Senusert) gave to me a staff of electrum into my hand, a bow, and a dagger wrought with electrum, together with his (my captive's) weapons."

Khu-sebek then, having recounted the story of the great moment of his career, goes on to tell us of his titles, his birth (under Amenemhat II.), and his first employment as a soldier. "The Majesty of the King of Upper and Lower Egypt, Khakaura (Senusert III.), triumphant, appeared with the Double Diadem upon the Horus-throne of the king. His Majesty caused that I should render service as a warrior, behind and beside His Majesty, with six men of the court. Then I made ready at his side, and His Majesty caused that I be appointed to be an Attendant of the King. I furnished sixty men when His Majesty went southward to overthrow the tribesmen of Nubia. Then I captured a negro in —— alongside the city where I was stationed. Then I proceeded northward, following with six of the court; then He appointed me Commander of the Attendants, and gave to me 100 men as a reward."

The Palestine campaign, little as Khu-sebek tells us of it, is actually the only instance of Egyptian interference in the affairs of Syria during the XIIth Dynasty. At the same time, there is force in what Breasted points out, that the whole atmosphere of Syria in the Sinuhe story is one of deference to the Pharaoh, and of admiration for Egyptian rule and customs. It is quite possible, therefore, that there may have been other campaigns of which no record has survived, though in all probability they, like this Sekmem expedition, were merely plundering raids. The time for serious invasion and occupation of the conquered territory was not yet; and indeed, it was the Asiatic himself who was eventually to provoke it by his invasion and conquest of the Nile Valley under the Hyksos princes. The great Asian victories with which Herodotus credits his Sesostris shrink down to a very small matter, if they are to be regarded as being represented by this solitary *razzia* of Senusert; but indeed, while Senusert may have furnished, so to speak, the framework on which the figure of Sesostris has been built up, a good deal of the flesh and blood with which it is clothed has also been taken from the exploits of later Pharaohs, such as Thothmes III. and Ramses II.

One incident connected with the Nubian wars of Senusert deserves mention, as having preserved for us a record of the various rites connected with the worship of Osiris at this period. During the campaign of the 16th year, Senusert captured a considerable quantity of gold in Nubia, and he resolved to use some of it to adorn the tomb of Osiris at Abydos. This tomb was, as we have seen, actually the tomb of King Zer, of the Ist Dynasty, which had already been confused with that of the God of the Resurrection. This task he entrusted to his Chief Treasurer, Ikhernofret, who had in company with him the Master of the Double Cabinet, Sisatet, whose record we have just heard. The two officials took advantage, apparently, of the fact that Senusert was moving southward again on the expedition of his 19th year, to travel in the royal train, and also, as was to be expected, to leave their own private memorials at the shrine of Osiris, thereby securing, so far as was humanly possible, their eternal destinies. Sisatet's first record (another was erected for him nineteen years later) we have seen. His companion's stele contains much more interesting material. The royal command to Ikhernofret was couched in terms so pleasing to the Chief Treasurer's vanity that he could not forbear to have them carved on his memorial stele, and, accordingly we have, first of all, the royal rescript, and next, the account of its execution.

After the usual flourish at the beginning, it runs as follows: "Royal command to the hereditary prince, count—wearer of the royal seal, sole companion, lord of the Double Gold House, lord of the Double Silver House, Chief Treasurer, Ikhernofret, revered: My Majesty commands that thou shalt be sent up-river to Abydos, to make monuments for my father Osiris, First of the Westerners, to adorn his secret place with gold, which he caused My Majesty to bring from Upper Nubia in victory and triumph. Lo thou shalt do this as an offering, to satisfy my father Osiris, since My Majesty sendeth thee, my heart being sure of thy doing everything according to the desire of My Majesty; thou hast been in the training of My Majesty, and the sole teaching of the palace. My Majesty appointed thee while thou wert a young man of 26 years. My Majesty hath done this, because I have seen thee to be one excellent in character, ready of tongue on coming forth from the body (*i.e.* from birth) and sufficient in speech. My Majesty sendeth thee to do this, since My Majesty has recognised that no one doing it possesses thy good qualities. Quickly go thou, and do thou according to all that My Majesty has commanded."

Next comes the Treasurer's account of his obedience.

"I did according to all that His Majesty commanded, by adorning all that My Lord commanded for his father, Osiris, First of the Westerners, Lord of Abydos, Great, Mighty One residing in Thinis. I acted as 'Son Whom He Loves' (*i.e.* in place of the king) for Osiris, First of the Westerners. I adorned the great (shrine?) forever and ever. I made for him a carrying shrine, the 'Bearer-of-Beauty' of the 'First-of-the-Westerners', of gold, silver, lazuli, fragrant woods, carob wood, and meru wood. I fashioned the gods belonging to his divine ennead, I made their shrines anew. I caused the lay priests to execute their duties, I caused them to know the ritual of every day, the feasts of the beginnings of the seasons. I superintended the work on the sacred barque, I fashioned its chapel. I decked the body of the Lord of Abydos with lazuli and malachite, electrum and every costly stone, among the ornaments (already) upon the limbs of the god. I dressed the god in his regalia by virtue of my office as master of secret things, and of my duty as a priest. I was pure-handed in adorning the god, a priest of clean fingers."

All this is of sufficient interest, as disclosing some of the ritual connected with the worship of one of the great gods. Ikhernofret, however, now proceeds to give us information of a unique character with regard to the celebration of the kind of Passion-play which took place at Abydos in commemoration of the death and resurrection of Osiris. Later, we shall have to discuss the significance of the various incidents which he recounts; in the meantime it is sufficient to record them in his own words. "I celebrated the 'Going-Forth' of Upuat, when he went forth to champion his father. I repelled the foe from the sacred barque; I overthrew the enemies of Osiris. I celebrated 'The Great Going Forth', following the god at his going. I sailed the divine boat of Thoth upon (the sacred lake?). I equipped the barque '*Shining-in-Truth*' of the Lord of Abydos with a chapel. I put on his regalia when he went forth to Peker (the royal necropolis); I led the way of the god to his tomb before Peker; I championed Unnefer (Osiris) at 'That Day of the Great Conflict'; I slew all the enemies upon the canals of Nedyt. I conveyed him into the barque '*The*

Great' when it bore his beauty; I gladdened the heart of the eastern heights; I created rejoicing in the western heights. When they saw the beauty of the sacred barge when it landed at Abydos, they brought Osiris, First of the Westerners, Lord of Abydos, to his palace, and I followed the god into his house, to attend to his ritual when he resumed his abode. I loosed the knot (of the shrine?) in the midst of his attendants, among his courtiers."

One can imagine the worthy Treasurer, mightily uplifted at the thought that he was actually representing Pharaoh at the most sacred of religious ceremonies, throwing himself with the utmost zest into the acts of the Passion-play. No doubt there were many broken heads among the actors who represented the enemies of Osiris as a result of the vigour with which Ikhernofret laid about him on "That Day of the Great Conflict"; but no doubt also a devout Egyptian would count a broken head got in the service of Osiris rather a title to honour than anything else, especially since it had been bestowed by the representative of "the Good God."

The most famous of the local records of the reign of Senusert is the well-known scene from the tomb of Tahuti-hetep, representing the transport of a colossal statue. The statue is that of Tahuti-hetep himself, who was nomarch of the nome of the Hare, whose chief city was Khmunu, the Greek Hermopolis, nearly opposite to El-Bersheh, where the tombs of the nomarch and his family are situated. The scene itself is so familiar as to need no description; attention may be called, however, to the spirit of good-fellowship and eagerness which, according to the inscription accompanying it, pervaded the whole execution of the work. Tahuti-hetep is careful in his inscription to let us know that the erection of such a statue of himself was not a thing of his own imagining, but a mark of royal favour; "their hearts are glad when they see thy favour with the king"; for Senusert was much too powerful and vigilant a monarch to allow to his local magnates the unbounded liberty which had been the ruin of the Old Kingdom.

Apart from this precautionary element in the narrative,

the whole impression which it conveys is one of the gladness of the whole district in the accomplishment of a creditable piece of work, and the willingness of everybody to lend a hand. "Following a statue of 13 cubits (22 feet)", so the inscription runs, "of stone of Hat-nub (alabaster). Lo, the way on which it came was very difficult, beyond everything. Lo, the dragging of the great things upon it was difficult for the heart of the people, because of the difficult stone of the ground, being hard stone. I caused the youth, the young men of the recruits to come, in order to make for the statue a road, together with shifts of necropolis miners and of quarrymen, the foremen and the skilled. The people of strength said: 'We come to bring it'; while my heart was glad; the city was gathered together rejoicing; very good was it to see beyond everything. The old man among them, he leaned upon the child; the strong-armed, together with the tremblers, their courage rose. Their arms grew strong; one of them put forth the strength of a thousand men. . . . Utterance of the recruits of the youth whom their lord mustered, the heir who prospers in the favour of the king, the lord: 'Let us come, let us prosper his children after him! Our hearts are glad at the favour of the king who abides forever'!" One need not take all this at its face value altogether, or imagine that the Hare nome was overjoyed at having to haul a 60-ton colossus for the greater glory of its nomarch; but the comments of Mr. Weigall, who is familiar with the spirit of the modern Egyptian as a labourer, do no more than justice to the truthfulness (in the main) of the old grandee. "We are so inclined to regard these colossal undertakings of the days of the Pharaohs as involving cruel slave-driving and the merciless use of the whip; but actually, as anyone who has employed labour in Egypt will understand, such feats of sheer strength were carried out then, as now, by the mild and good-natured Egyptians with a jollity unknown in the West. The picture of the operation, shown in the tomb, reveals the figure of a man beating time and apparently singing a hauling-song to which the labourers respond; and a knowledge of the customs of the modern Egyptians enables one to reconstruct the scene—the men singing as they work, the foremen jokingly cracking their whips, the laughter at mishaps, the cheering and shouting, and the childlike enthusiasm." No one supposes that hard work in ancient Egypt was heaven, any more than it has ever been in any land or time; but it is as well to remember also that neither was it hell.

Senusert's pyramid is at Dahshur, and near it are the tombs of one of his queens, Neferhent, and the princesses Ment, Sentsenb, Meryt, and Sathathor, from which came part of the great treasure of jewellery already referred to. His secondary tomb was at Abydos, and was of very unusual form with most elaborate provisions to defeat the attacks of plunderers, which had, however, proved as futile as those adopted in every other case. During the last days of his vigorous reign of over 38 years, he associated Amenemhat III. with him on the throne, according to the prudent custom of the kings of his line. The deep impression which his energy and tireless activity made upon his people is witnessed to by the remarkable poem in his honour, which was one of the most precious prizes found among the Kahun papyri. It is, from the point of view of style, perhaps the most perfect example of literary form, the only other poem which approaches it in this respect being the equally famous hymn to Thothmes III.; but still more noteworthy is the testimony which it bears to the character of one whom the Egyptians revered as a new founder of their national prosperity. Later we must deal with the whole poem; a single verse will meanwhile suffice to indicate the spirit in which it regards the achievements of Senusert:

He hath come unto us that he may carry away Upper Egypt;
   the Double Diadem hath rested upon his head.
He hath come unto us and hath united the Two Lands;
   he hath mingled the Reed with the Bee.
He hath come unto us and hath brought the Black Land under his sway;
   he hath apportioned to himself the Red Land.
He hath come unto us and hath taken the Two Lands under his protection;
   he hath given peace unto the Two River-banks.
He hath come unto us and hath made Egypt to live;
   he hath banished its suffering.

He hath come unto us and hath made the people to live;
he hath caused the throat of the subjects to breathe.
He hath come unto us and hath trodden down the foreign countries;
he hath smitten the Troglodytes that knew not the fear of him.
He hath come unto us and hath done battle for his boundaries;
he hath delivered them that were robbed.
He hath come unto us, that we may nurture up our children, and bury
our aged ones.

The long reign of Amenemhat III., who succeeded
Senusert after his brief co-regency, is not marked by any
great feats of war. There are indeed relics of his as far
south as Kerma, where they were found by Dr. G. A.
Reisner. One of these is a stele which records the completion of a building in the construction of which 35,300
bricks were laid. If these things are in their original position, then there must have been a very considerable advance of Egypt into the Sudan, as Kerma marks the furthest
limit of the province over which Hepzefi was governor
under Senusert I., and such an advance could scarcely have
taken place without war; but we have no further record
of any campaign. The fifty years of Amenemhat were as
definitely years of peace as the thirty-eight of Senusert had
been warlike. The two kings were the complement of one
another, and the peaceful Amenemhat consolidated and
maintained what the warlike Senusert had gained.

For the traces of external activity during the reign of
Amenemhat we must turn to Sinai, which was so regularly
exploited under this king as almost to be an Egyptian
province. There are dated records of work, either at Wady
Maghara or at Serabit el-Khadim, of the years 2, 4, 8, 13,
15, 18, 20, 23, 25, 27, 30, 38, 40, 41, 42, 43, 44, and 45, so
that the exploitation of the mines went on with considerable regularity. The only large gap is that between year 30
and year 38, and it is immediately followed by the regular
annual sequence from year 40 to year 45. The earliest of
the inscriptions is that of the Treasurer Khenemsu, who
states that in the second year of Amenemhat he was sent
to Sinai to bring malachite and copper, and that his company included 734 soldiers. His tablet was in the Wady
Maghara; but he also operated at Serabit el-Khadim,
where his officers have left a relief showing the king before

"Hathor, Lady of the Malachite Country". Harnakht, an "official of the Treasury and Chief Fowler", who was evidently attached to the expedition of Khenemsu, has left an inscription on his own account in the Wady Maghara, which tells us that, as we would have anticipated, the journey to Sinai was made at this time by water instead of by the long and toilsome desert route. "The chosen before his subjects, who treads the path of his benefactor, says: 'I crossed over the sea, bearing luxuries, by commission of Horus, Lord of the Palace (The Pharaoh)'." It may be that Harnakht had a special commission to carry these offerings to the shrine of Hathor, and that this independent commission accounts for his putting up of his own personal inscription. One of the very latest inscriptions of Amenemhat's reign, that of Sebek-her-heb, at Serabit, records the opening of a new mine-chamber in the 44th year of the king. "Opening of the mining-chamber successfully; 'Flourish-its-Army-Which-Delivers-That-Which-is-in-It' is its name. . . . Master of the Double Cabinet, Sebek-her-heb; he says: 'I excavated a mine-chamber for my Lord, and my youths returned in full quota, all of them. There was none that fell among them'." The pious Sebek-her-heb duly ascribes his success to the Lady of Turquoise, Hathor, whose favour he had been careful to conciliate. "I brought for her offering-tables of *mesnet* stone, linen —— I presented to her divine offerings —— She led me in by her gracious going to the mine-gallery which I made for her. I swear, I have spoken in truth."

The most interesting of all these mining records, however, is unfortunately undated, and makes no mention of the king in whose reign the expedition which it records took place. The style of the stele, however, is unquestionably of the Middle Kingdom, and its attribution to the reign of Amenemhat III. is generally accepted. Horurra, "Treasurer of the God, Master of the Double Cabinet", who erected it, tells us that he was dispatched to Sinai at a most untoward season. "The Majesty of this God dispatched me to this mining district, and I arrived in this land in the third month of the second season, although it

was not the season for going to this mining district." The
poor man had a sore job to keep up the courage of his
under-officers and workmen under the unfavourable conditions, all the more because in his own heart he agreed
with their objections, and had an uneasy consciousness
that he had been sent on a fool's errand. However, he put
a bold face upon the matter, and records his triumph for
the encouragement of all who may have a similar experience to face.

"This Treasurer of the God saith to the officials who
may have to come to this mine-country at such a season:
'Let not your faces flinch on that account; behold, Hathor
will turn it to profit'. I had to wrestle with myself; for when
I came from Egypt my face flinched, and it was hard for
me, for the desert is hot in summer, and the rocks brand
the skin. When the morning dawns, a man is dismayed
(because of the heat)." Horurra, however, has that courage
which is "feared of a thing, and yet does it", and which, on
Alan Breck Stewart's authority, "makes the prettiest kind
of man", and his attempt to persuade the workmen that
they were unusually favoured in being sent to Sinai at such
a time is delicious; while the workmen's sceptical response
is almost as good as his blarney. "I spoke to the workmen
concerning it, saying: 'How lucky is he who is in this
Mine-land!' They said: 'No doubt there is malachite in
these everlasting hills; but it is foolishness (one imagines
British workmen adding a qualification to the noun) to
seek it at this season. It would be a miracle for us to find
it at this season. It is foolishness to seek for it in this evil
summer season.' "

Horurra was not to be dismayed, even though his own
heart agreed with the scornful comments of his men. He
was inspired by the royal command, and felt a greater
strength than his own; "the soul of the king put it in my
heart. My face flinched not before the work." Fortune as
usual yielded herself to the man who refused to be dis-
couraged by her frowns, and the stout-hearted treasurer
hit on a good vein almost at once, and had his task finished
in record time. "I succeeded in mining good quality (of
malachite), and I finished in the first month of the third

season. I carried away first-rate costly stone (suitable) for luxuries, more of it than anyone else who came hither, and better than if I had come at the accustomed season."

Like a pious man, Horurra gave the credit for his success to the Lady of Turquoise, the local Hathor, and advises others to cultivate her if they wish success. "Make offerings, therefore, to the Lady of Heaven, and propitiate Hathor; if you do this, it will be to your advantage. If ye treat her well, she will make it well with you." Being an Egyptian, however, he could not refrain from adding that his own merits had something to do with his success, as well as the kindness of the goddess. "I led my army very kindly", he says, "and I did not shout at my workmen. I acted (kindly?) before all the army and the recruits, and they had a high opinion of me." Perhaps the man who could keep his temper with hundreds of grumbling workmen in a hot season in Sinai had good reason for putting some of his success down to his own qualities, as well as to divine interposition.

The importance which Amenemhat attached to the mining work at Sinai is evidenced by the work which he did for the miner's temple at Serabit el-Khadim. This temple, where the Lady of Turquoise could be worshipped with such desirable results as Horurra has described, had been in existence since the days of Snefru, relics of whom were found in it by Petrie in 1905; but it was enlarged and furnished with altars and a portico by Amenemhat, whose piety was continued by his successor Amenemhat IV. Inscriptions at Hammamat show that much work was also carried on in the quarries in connection with the great buildings of various sorts which the king executed in Egypt. Of these, one, belonging to an official called Senusert, refers to the getting of "beautiful black stone" (basalt) for "Amenemhat-ankh", the house of Sebek at Crocodilopolis, and states that ten statues of five cubits upon a throne were quarried. These would be seated figures of about eight and a half feet in height, and were probably destined either for the temple which afterwards came to be known as the Labyrinth, or else for the king's own pyramid temple at Hawara, to which the name "Life of

Amenemhat" would seem to refer them. One is reminded of the corresponding group of ten limestone statues which were found at the pyramid of Senusert I. at Lisht. The same expedition is also referred to in another inscription, which gives the numbers of those who were employed in the getting out of the blocks for the statues: "His soldiers of the necropolis (the worker's guard), 20; quarrymen, 30; sailors, 30; a numerous army, 2000". Here it can be seen how small was the proportion of skilled workmen employed upon such work compared with the crowd of unskilled labourers, whose chief function would be to pull and haul under the direction of the quarrymen and the thirty "handy men" from the navy. The quarries at Turrah, which from time immemorial had been the source of the limestone so extensively used for temple-building, were also drawn upon for supplies, as an inscription of the king's 43rd year shows: "Quarry-chambers were opened anew, to quarry fine limestone of Ayan for the temples of this (god?) of millions of years".

But the main monument of Amenemhat's reign, and his chief title to fame, is the colossal work which he did in connection with the eternal problem of ancient Egypt—the regulation of the water of the Inundation. Mr. Weigall, whose ingenuity in identifying well-known Pharaohs with incidents of Bible history seems inexhaustible, has proposed to see in him the Pharaoh whose dreams of the seven fat and lean kine, and seven full and seven blasted ears of corn, led to the deliverance of Joseph from prison and his promotion to the viziership of Egypt; the evidence being the existence of the well-known subsidiary channel known as the *Bahr Yusuf* or "Joseph's Canal", and the fact that a king who was so much concerned with irrigation projects as Amenemhat would naturally be likely to dream such significant dreams! The evidence seems rather a slender foundation on which to rear such an edifice of synchronism, which, incidentally, introduces more difficulties into the question of Biblical chronology than it solves; but at least there can be no question of the great interest which was taken by Amenemhat in a matter which must always have been of vital importance to the Egyptian nation, and the energy with which he set himself to regulate the boon which Nature had bestowed upon his country, and to economise such resources, derived from the Inundation, as were more or less going to waste.

Evidence of the interest which he took in the matter of the Inundation is given by the fact that he caused a record to be kept at Semneh and Kummeh, on the frontier established by Senusert III., of the level reached by the Nile flood in various years. These records still exist, and record the level of high Nile for the years 4, 5, 6, 7, 9, 14, 15, 22, 23, 24, 30, 32, 37, 40, and 41 of the reign. The levels are from 26 to 30 feet higher than the present level of high Nile, and the suggestion has been made that the king may have created a barrage at this point for the purpose of holding up the flood, as is done at present by the great Aswan dam. No trace of such a structure exists, however, and the only possible conclusions seem to be either that the bed of the river in Upper Nubia has been lowered, or that there was a larger discharge of water four thousand years ago than there is at present. If the volcanic disturbance which cut off Lake Tanganyika and other Equatorial sources of supply from the Nile occurred later than this period, the higher level could be explained by the larger discharge of water; but at present this question must be regarded as an unsolved one, though the fact of the levels having been higher seems unquestionable.

There is no question, in any case, about the interest which Amenemhat took in the Fayum, and the great works which he carried out there. The great depression of the Fayum, the bud on the stem of the lily, shooting out westwards, just south of where the stem expands into the flower of the Delta, was probably produced originally by the dislocation of the strata which produced the long cleft of the Nile Valley. Part of it is still occupied by the much shrunken lake which is known as the Birket el-Qurun, whose surface is more than 129 feet below the level of the Mediterranean; but in prehistoric times it is probable that the whole area of the depression was filled with water, making a great lake many miles in diameter, which was fed annually by the water of the Inundation. This expanse of water was called by the early Egyptians "Mour", the Great Water, a name which the Greeks modified into Moeris, thus creating the Lake Moeris familiar from the references of Herodotus. The fenmen who lived around its margin were subdued by Narmer, and their chief figures on the great slate palette of that king. Attempts were made apparently as early as the Vth Dynasty to reclaim some of this area from marsh and lake, and on the area thus acquired, on the eastern side of the lake, there grew up a city named Shedyt, "The Reclaimed". The local god was the Crocodile-god Sebek, about whose sacred crocodiles Herodotus gives us so much gossip, and the Greeks in consequence called the city Crocodilopolis, by which name it is generally known.

Early in the dynasty, Amenemhat I. had conceived the idea of a further reclamation of land, and a fragment of a granite statue of his and a temple lintel show that he must have carried on extensive building work at Crocodilopolis, while the fragment of a great earthen dyke close to the temple may have been part of his scheme. He succeeded in reclaiming a considerable area, as an obelisk of his son Senusert I. lies at Begig, or Ebgig, three or four miles south-west of the temple of Crocodilopolis. The work of Amenemhat III., however, was on a much larger scale. By means of a huge embankment about 20 miles in length, he reclaimed an area of about forty square miles, or about 27,000 acres, which became one of the most fertile parts of the country. On the northern shore of the reclaimed promontory, at a place now known as Biahmu, he raised two massive platforms, on which were placed two seated colossi of himself. They were 39 feet in height, independent of their pedestals, and were carved in hard quartzite. Fragments of these statues were found by Petrie, and are now in the Ashmolean Museum. These were the statues placed on pyramids which Herodotus saw, standing in the midst of the lake, as he imagined, from the fact that he only saw them from a distance across the water.

Important as this reclamation was, it was only secondary to the other part of the scheme, which regulated the inflow and outflow of water from the Inundation, so that the surplus water flowing into the Fayum during high Nile was held up there by means of sluices, and released gradually during the months when the river ran low, thus helping to maintain the level of the river from this point down to the sea, during the time when it would otherwise have been lowest, and so rendering irrigation a much easier matter. It has been estimated that the amount of flood-water thus stored was so great as to be capable of almost doubling the volume of the river during the three months April-June, when it is normally lowest. Thus this enlightened and capable Pharaoh actually appears to have anticipated the methods which have been put into practice on a gigantic scale in our own day; and while his Fayum barrage may seem a small thing compared with the great barrages at Aswan and Assiut, it is probably quite as great a feat of engineering, time and conditions considered, as anything that modern times can show.

Not far from the scene of these great works, Amenemhat erected a building which has some right to be considered the most famous building in the world, were it only for the mystery which has attached to the reason for its creation and the function which it was intended to serve, together with the fact of its total disappearance from the face of the earth. This was the building which Herodotus called the Labyrinth, and which so excited his wonder, though he went far astray in his dating of it, ascribing it to the Saite period, a matter of twelve centuries later than its actual date. "This", says the historian, "I have myself seen, and found it greater than can be described. For if any one should reckon up the buildings and public works of the Greeks, they would be found to have cost less labour and expense than this labyrinth; though the temple in Ephesus is deserving of mention, and also that in Samos. The pyramids likewise were beyond description, and each of them comparable to many of the great Grecian structures. Yet the Labyrinth surpasses even the pyramids. For it has twelve courts enclosed with walls, with doors opposite each other, six facing the north, and six to the south, contiguous to one another; and the same exterior wall encloses them. It contains two kinds of rooms, some

under ground, and some above ground over them, to the
number of three thousand, fifteen hundred of each. The
rooms above ground I myself went through and saw, and
describe from personal inspection. But the underground
rooms I only know from report; for the Egyptians who
have charge of the building would on no account show me
them, saying that they were the sepulchres of the kings
who originally built this labyrinth, and of the sacred
crocodiles. I can therefore only relate what I have heard
from hearsay concerning the lower rooms; but the upper
ones, which surpass all human works, I myself saw; for the
passages through the corridors, and the windings through
the courts, from their great variety, presented a thousand
occasions of wonder, as I passed from a court to the
rooms and from the rooms to halls, and to other corridors
from the halls, and to other courts from the rooms. The
roofs of all these are of stone, as also are the walls; but
the walls are full of sculptured figures. Each court is
surrounded with a colonnade of white stone, closely
fitted. And adjoining the extremity of the Labyrinth is a
pyramid, 40 orgyae (240 feet) in height, on which large
figures are carved, and a way to it has been made underground."

One could wish that Herodotus had not been quite
so ecstatic, and a little more precise in his description; and
the same remark applies to Strabo, though he gives some
very interesting particulars, such as the detail about the
chambers being each roofed with a single slab of stone,
which seems almost too gigantic to be true, and his description of the appearance of the roof—"a stone field, composed thus of these blocks". His suggestion that the
number of chambers was due to the fact that each nome of
Egypt had a separate hall reserved for its meetings and
ritual observances is practically the only light as to the
function of the building which has come down to us from
the classical writers. Pliny gives us a fact as to the destruction of the building which is worth something, though it
would not have needed a wizard to discover it. "With such
solidity is this huge mass of buildings constructed that the
lapse of ages has been totally unable to destroy it, seconded

PLATE XIX

1. STELE OF HOR-UR-RA, SINAI
2. MINERS' WORKINGS AND HUTS, SINAI

From Sir Flinders Petrie's " Researches in Sinai" (John Murray)

as it has been by the people of Herakleopolis, who have marvellously ravaged a work which they have always held in abhorrence." But some features of his description suggest that his dragoman had been experimenting in order to ascertain the capacity of his employer for swallowing fables. "Some of the palaces are so peculiarly constructed that the moment the doors are opened a dreadful sound like that of thunder reverberates within." Just so!

Herakleopolis, whose hostility to the Labyrinth Pliny mentions, worshipped the god Harshefi, whose worshippers were always at feud with those of the Crocodile-god Sebek. On the assumption that the Labyrinth was a temple dedicated to Sebek, therefore, the attempted destruction of it by the Herakleopolites would find a natural explanation. Since Pliny's time, the centuries, and mediaeval and modern vandals, including the workmen who built the Fayum railway in modern times, have been more successful than he anticipated in destroying Egypt's greatest building. When Petrie explored the site in 1889, nothing was left but the foundation-bed of concrete, with immense masses of chips, resulting from the destroying labours of those who had used the place as a quarry. Even so, the scale of the foundations showed that the astonished admiration of the classical writers was not unreasonable. The building covered an area of 1000 feet by 800, "enough to include all the temples of Karnak and of Luqsor". About its purpose, opinion has been divided. The suggestion has been made that it was a kind of administrative centre for the whole country; a kind of County-Council building, in fact, except that it was designed for religious as well as administrative functions; Petrie, however, holds it to have been a temple pure and simple—"a peristyle temple . . . . much like the temple of Abydos", though, of course, much larger.

Like many of his predecessors, Amenemhat III. built two tombs for himself. The most important and the actual place of interment was reared at the entrance to the province of the Fayum, in which so much valuable work was done in this reign. It was of brick, faced with limestone, and was conspicuous for the extraordinary complexity of the internal arrangements by which it was hoped to baffle tomb-robbers. These, however, had proved as futile as all such arrangements have always proved in Egypt, where tomb-robbing has for many centuries been a fine art; and when Petrie entered the sarcophagus chamber in 1888, the royal interments "had been entirely burnt; and only fired grains of diorite and pieces of lazuli inlaying showed the splendour of the decoration of the coffins".

The tomb-chamber itself was one of the most remarkable of Egyptian works. A rectangular cavity was cut into the living rock which rises into the centre of the pyramid mass. Into this cavity a single block of hard yellow quartzite, 26 feet long and 12 feet broad, had been inserted. This was hewn into a chamber, measuring 22 feet by 8 inside, with walls 2 feet thick, and was polished with exquisite skill—the most magnificent death-chamber ever devised for a Pharaoh. Its roof consisted of three huge blocks of the same material, of which one, weighing 45 tons, was dropped into place to close the sepulchre finally when the king had been laid to rest within. The chamber itself weighed about 110 tons, and the cutting and placing of it must have been engineering feats of the highest order. The sarcophagus which occupied this superb resting-place was worthy of its casket, and was hewn out of the same hard and intractable material with extraordinary accuracy. The unique feature of the interment was that the chamber held another sarcophagus, that of Amenemhat's daughter, Ptah-neferu, who had apparently died before her father, but soon after the pyramid was completed, and had been laid by the sorrowing king beside the splendid sarcophagus which was to hold his own remains. An alabaster offering-table in the chamber bore her name, together with representations of the various offerings desired for the princess. The figures of the various beasts and birds in the inscription have been mutilated by the original sculptor of set purpose, so that they should not be able to run off out of the inscription, and so make it unreadable, destroying the princess's chance of abundant provision in the Underworld. Instances of this curious superstition, which regarded the figures in the hieroglyphic writings as living entities, whose activities had to be restricted by the amputation of their means of locomotion, occur elsewhere also.

The other pyramid of Amenemhat was at Dahshur. It contained another magnificent sarcophagus; and the black-granite cap-stone of the pyramid has also survived—a fine piece of work beautifully polished and inscribed. During the last year of his reign, the king associated his son, Amenemhat IV., with him on the throne; but the new king was destined to a reign whose shortness and insignificance present a striking contrast to the length and prosperity of that of his predecessor.

With Amenemhat IV., the long-enduring glories of the XIIth Dynasty "haste to swift decay". The only records of his reign come from beyond the actual limits of the king-dom. There is an inscription from Kummeh recording the height of the Nile there, so that the system of annual records inaugurated by Amenemhat III. was evidently maintained by his successor. Inscriptions of the years 4, 6, 8, and 9 from Wady Maghara and Serabit show that the exploitation of the Sinai mines continued steadily. A few comparatively insignificant objects bearing his name sur-vive, such as the little toilet-box of ebony and ivory which belonged to his "Keeper of the Kitchen Department", a gentleman whose name was Kemen; the plaque of green schist now in the British Museum; and four scarabs. Some of the Kahun papyri are also of this reign. Beyond such trifles, nothing is known of the king or of the events of his reign.

It seems probable that the two ruined pyramids at Mazghuneh, south of Dahshur, belong to him and his sister, Sebek-neferu, who succeeded him. They were never completed, and have no courtier cemetery near them, so that they must belong to royalties whose reigns were brief. The system of internal passages and chambers in both is modelled on the elaborate arrangement of the pyramid of Amenemhat III. at Hawara, so that there is strong likelihood that they belong to the period im-mediately following. Both pyramids lack their casing; but it appears that a burial took place in the southern one of the pair, as a large alabaster dish for offerings was found.

This brief reign of nine years was followed by one still briefer. Amenemhat IV. left no heir, and his sister, Sebek-neferu, mounted the throne. Of her reign, however, we have even scantier knowledge than of that of her brother. Practically all that is known is that her name was found among the ruins of the Labyrinth, and that presumably she may have done some work there in continuation of that of Amenemhat III. One solitary scarab and one cylinder-seal of hers are known, and a sphinx at Khataaneh once bore a cartouche, now mostly obliterated, which may have been hers. Granite architraves at Herakleopolis bear a modified form of her name, which may have been assumed when she succeeded to the throne—Sebek-ka-ra, Sebek-shedti-neferu.

With these pitiful scraps of memorial, the great XIIth Dynasty passes away, to be followed by a time of confusion and internal strife which was interrupted by the greatest humiliation that had ever befallen the land—the Hyksos Conquest. The dynasty had lasted, roughly, for two centuries, which had been fruitful in great work and marked by abounding prosperity. The stability of the national government is very evident in the consistent record of long reigns, the average for the six first reigns, excluding the last two ephemeral ones, being well over thirty years. The kings were manifestly not only physically strong men, but also strong in character, and capable of handling with firmness the unruly elements in the nation which had wrecked the Old Kingdom, and become irreconcilable with the national unity and prosperity. The great local magnate still survives under the Senuserts and Amenemhats; but he sings in a very much more subdued tone, and has plainly been taught to adapt himself to a new condition of things, where he is no longer almost an independent sovereign, but has taken his place as a cog-wheel in the great governmental machine guided by the master of Itht-toui.

Altogether, the parallelism of the course of development and decay followed by the dynasty and the rulers of the Old Kingdom is very remarkable. In both cases the essential organisation and subjugation of disorder and division is accomplished with vigour, not to say roughness, at the very beginning of the period, and is succeeded by a time of comparatively undistinguished consolidation. Thereafter, the nation, having found its feet and realised its strength, enters upon a short period of what may almost be called imperial expansion (in a strictly limited sense). This period is represented for the Old Kingdom by the reign of Pepy I., and for the Middle Kingdom by that of Senusert III. The long reign of Pepy II. is paralleled by that of Amenemhat III., which, however, seems to have been a more brilliant one than that of his longer-lived forerunner; and the extremely rapid collapse which follows in both instances would seem to suggest that too long a period of placid prosperity and external inactivity is an unhealthy condition for a nation in certain stages of its development.

At the same time, there can be no doubt that the XIIth Dynasty represents, in some respects, the highest level which the Egyptian people had yet reached in culture and in mental development—a period when something of the ruggedness of the abundant vigour which had made the Old Kingdom had been, or was in process of being, sloughed off, and when, as yet, there was no such loss of virility as has often accompanied such a change. The period was one of exceptional brilliancy in all departments, and its literature and art alike bear witness to the energy of the race, coupled with a restricting element of taste which prevents some of the crudenesses of the past, while it has not yet paralysed the initiative of the artist. Religion, also, is undergoing modification from the primitive conceptions of the Pyramid Text period. These developments we must attempt to trace in our next chapter.

CHAPTER XVII

THE MIDDLE KINGDOM: SOCIETY, FOREIGN RELATIONS, LITERATURE AND ART

IN some respects the period of the Middle Kingdom is one of the most interesting of the four great flowerings of the Egyptian genius. It is, for instance, the last period in which we shall see that genius comparatively self-determined, and working within almost purely national limits, with national resources, and under national aspirations. That is not to say, of course, that there may not be traced, even at this period, the influence of Egypt's external relationships upon the culture of the land; but that these seem almost negligible in the mass, when the product of Egyptian thought and art at this time is compared with that of the Imperial period, when influences of all sorts were streaming into the Nile Valley from almost every land of the ancient East, and were producing effects which are still perfectly manifest, especially in the art of the New Empire. In the work of the Middle Kingdom there are not as yet the evidences of imperfectly assimilated foreign influence of various sorts which characterise the work of the Empire, seldom to its advantage. Foreign influence did undoubtedly enter the land, but in such comparatively small quantity, and so slowly, that the native genius, one of the most masterful of its kind in all history, was able easily to assimilate it, and work it into its products without any loss of national characteristics or individuality.

The reason for this fact is, of course, that so far Egypt may be considered as having been in the main a self-centred and self-sufficient power. Whatever may have been the scale of the supposed Asiatic invasions which completed the wreck of the Old Kingdom and accentuated the misery

of the First Intermediate Dark period, they did not leave
a permanent mark on the national consciousness, or induce
a new outlook on the world, as was the case with the
Hyksos invasion of the Second Intermediate. The whole
destiny of the Egyptian people was profoundly modified
by the new knowledge and the new attitude of mind which
the Hyksos invasion brought in and created. Probably
some such modification would have come in the natural
course of human development in any case; but that it came
when it did, and assumed the form that it did, was the
result of the wholesale shattering of old conceptions, and
the creation of new enmities, which the conquest by the
desert princes brought about. The world, it may be said,
was ripe for an Imperial experiment when the XVIIIth
Dynasty started on its career of conquest in Asia; but it
was the shock which the old state of things had received in
Egypt under the Hyksos domination, and the thirst for
revenge for a great humiliation, which set the experiment
in motion.

No such results had been produced by the earlier
Asiatic invasions which are now believed to have contributed to the downfall of the Old Kingdom and to the
state of chaos and wretchedness which followed that event.
The Egypt which slowly emerged under the fostering care,
first of the Antefs and Mentuhoteps of the XIth Dynasty,
then of the Amenemhats and Senuserts of the XIIth, was
not a new Egypt, as was the Egypt of the XVIIIth Dynasty.
It was the old nation, with its old ideals comparatively
unchanged, and with its relations to the rest of the world
scarcely modified from those of its forefathers in the Old
Kingdom. Egypt was still sufficient unto herself, and
content, in a sense, to live and die unto herself, as she
never was again in her history. She knew, of course, that
there were other kingdoms beyond her own borders, and
even beyond the usual limits of her trading expeditions
and forays, with whom it was even conceivable that she
might find it to her advantage to enter into trading
relationships in the future, and therein she differed from
the strictly Chinese attitude which is often ascribed to her.
It ought not to be forgotten that the mental attitude of the

kingdoms of that ancient world, so far as it can be discerned, was not in the least one of stupid incuriosity as to what existed and was being done outside of one's own water-tight compartment, but, on the contrary, one of lively curiosity as to these things. The popular Egyptian literature of this period is in itself sufficient witness to this fact, and the Story of Sinuhe, for example, reveals an amount of coming and going between the nations which is quite incompatible with the "cloistered nation" theory.

But, at the same time, it is just as obvious that the native Egyptian looked down on the other peoples of his little world from a position of ineffable superiority, in spite of the fact that they might occasionally be useful to him. Senusert I. evidently regards it as the finest of jokes to see Sinuhe, who had once been a respectable clean-shaven courtier of the Residence, dressed in Syrian clothes and wearing a beard like one of those inferior creatures, the Asiatics. He must needs call the whole royal family in to share his merriment over this delicate piece of humour. "Then the royal children were caused to be ushered in. Said His Majesty to the Queen: 'See, this is Sinuhe, who has come back as an Asiatic, a creature of the Bedouin kind'. She uttered an exceeding loud cry, and the royal children shrieked out all together. They said unto His Majesty: 'It can never really be he, O King, Our Lord'. His Majesty said: 'Verily it is he!'" And Sinuhe himself, who had lived long enough among his kind friends in Syria to know better, evidently thought His Majesty's merriment quite natural, and was quite disgusted at the figure he cut as an Asiatic in the midst of the superior beings who had never left Egypt. Syrians were good enough to help one in a strait; but the moment there was a chance of becoming an Egyptian again it was to be snatched at, quite regardless of the feelings of his late hosts. "I slept on a bed," remarks the ungrateful Sinuhe, "and gave up the sand to them that be in it, and wood oil to him that smeareth himself therewith." The Aamu who come to the nomarch Khnumhotep "about the business of the eye-paint", seem to our plebeian eyes quite respectable and civilised members of society, with their embroidered

PLATE XX

Cairo Museum

STATUE OF AMENEMHAT III

robes, their musical instruments, and their carefully-dressed beards; but the XIIth Dynasty Egyptian obviously regarded them as a schoolboy to-day might regard the fat woman or the bearded lady in a travelling show. They were interesting—as freaks.

In short, while the XIIth Dynasty Egyptian was not by any means so ignorant as he was once believed to be of the fact that there were other people in the world besides himself, he held the highly comfortable belief that he was pretty much the only person who really counted. The others were useful in their own way, no doubt—when you happened to want cedar-wood for a bark of the gods, or a big sea-going ship, or when gold-dust and ivory had to be brought up from the Sudan; but it was difficult to see for what other purpose they had been created. There were many planes in the world besides the one on which he lived and moved and had his being; but his plane was exalted beyond all comparison above that of any other race. The time will come when we shall find Pharaoh of Egypt recognising the other kings of the eastern world as more or less of the same nature as himself, his brothers, though, of course, rather poor relations; but that time was not yet due, and one imagines that Senusert III., for instance, would have had a somewhat rude answer for any eastern royalty who addressed him as Tushratta of Mitanni used to address his dear brother-in-law Amenhotep III. when he was wanting some gold out of that good-natured hedonist.

With the qualification which we have already noted, Dr. H. R. Hall's summing up of the Egyptian attitude of the period is probably pretty near the truth. "We may compare the Pharaohs of the XIIth Dynasty, in relation to the outer-world of Babylon, of Elam, or of the Hittites, the world of Hammurabi and his predecessors, with the great Chinese emperors of the eighteenth century, with K'ang-hsi and Chien-lung, in their relation to the outer-world of England, France, and Holland, before the catastrophe of the wars of the nineteenth century proved to China, as the Hyksos conquest had to Egypt so many thousand years before, that there were other people in the world besides herself." We are not to imagine, as I have pointed out, that Egypt had absolutely ignored this fact, nor are we to take the comparison *au pied de la lettre*, and imagine that the difference in knowledge and efficiency between Egypt and the rest of her eastern world was anything like that between eighteenth century China and the Western nations. In knowledge, Egypt of the XIIth Dynasty was at least the equal of anything else in the world of the time; in art, she was manifestly superior; only in one application of knowledge to warlike purposes had she lagged behind: but in other respects the illustration is quite apt, and the awakening which the Egyptian nation was destined to get at the rough hands of the desert princes was doubtless quite as unpleasant as that which China experienced from the "outer barbarians", who did their best to vindicate the title by which she had called them by burning the summer palace of her emperors. The awakening, when it came, produced results quite the opposite to those which were produced in China, and the reaction from it made Egypt for several generations a conquering power, instead of a helpless prey, as in the Chinese instance; but it may be questioned if the permanent results of the process were any more profitable for the Nile Valley than they have proved for China so far.

We must realise, therefore, that the Egypt of the Middle Kingdom, on which we are now looking, is an Egypt not in any vital sense differing from the Egypt of the Old Kingdom which had preceded it. There are changes, as we shall see, in many respects, in the social organisation of the land, and in the administration, in the language, in the religion, and in the art of the country; but these, while neither few nor unimportant, are yet all changes produced, not by outside influences to any extent, but by natural processes of internal development. Though Egypt is moving forward, she is still moving within her own natural limits, and the result of her movement is still purely Egyptian. The land is still self-centred and self-sufficient, though this is the last of the periods of her history of which this is true. And therefore all that has survived from this period in art, in literature, in religious teaching, and in evidence of the state of administration is of peculiar interest to the student of ancient Egypt, because for the last time you are in a position to see what may be called pure Egypt in all these respects, and to see the very best that this great original culture was capable of before it became subjected to the vital changes induced by outside influences.

In the social organisation of the country, we are conscious of several important changes from the state of things prevailing in the later days of the Old Kingdom and the troubled days of the First Intermediate period; but some of these, though not all, are more of the nature of a reversion to the condition of things which prevailed in the heyday of the Old Kingdom than actual novelties. The most manifest is the absolute supremacy of the Pharaoh. The man who sits in Ithttoui is no longer a royal figurehead who is supported or exploited on the one hand by over-powerful subjects who find him useful for their own purposes, and flouted on the other by other local magnates who want nothing of what a king should have but the name. He is master of the whole land, and not a finger can be moved or a voice raised without his permission. It is quite impossible, for instance, to imagine one of the Amenemhats or Senuserts submitting to be trailed about in the train of a local prince, as Khety was in the train of Prince Khety of Siut during his wars with the rising princes of Thebes. Even the least vigorous of the XIIth Dynasty Pharaohs would very speedily have taught the prince of Siut his proper place, while getting out of him all service which was necessary to the welfare of the state. During the miserable days of anarchy, it was possible for a local princelet even to resist successfully with armed force the will of his nominal king. Two of the earlier princes of El Bersheh, who ruled the Hare nome from the famous city of Hermopolis, state: "I rescued my city in the day of violence from the terrors of the royal house", a boast which, however satisfactory to the pride of him who made it, points to a state of things which was by no means conducive to the good government and happiness of the whole land.

The strong hand of the Pharaohs of the XIth and XIIth Dynasties succeeded in putting an end to this impossible state of affairs. Two great changes were made which must have notably diminished the power of the local magnate for harm, and equally increased the peace and happiness of his hereditary estate. The first was the forbidding of private war, which these powerful and turbulent barons had been in the habit of waging with something of the freedom of the European Feudal Age; and the second was the abolishing of unrestricted hereditary jurisdiction. The first of these changes must have been an almost unmixed boon to the country people; the second, while it may have meant occasionally a lack of local sympathy in the administration, as compared with that of the ideal nomarch, who was probably a pretty rare bird at any time, must, on the whole, have operated in the direction of securing impartiality, so far as this can ever be secured in the East. The local lord, if he had local knowledge and sympathy to guide him in his administration, had also local prejudices and grudges which did not conduce to the distribution of even-handed justice; the official appointed by the central administration, if he had not the advantage of the one, was presumably free from the temptations of the other.

The great barons of the kingdom, however, were by no means suppressed, though their claws were cut. Centralisation was by no means carried to such a point as to involve either the disappearance of the nobility or their reduction to a position of merely ornamental *fainéance*. The local baron was still a great power in his own district. He maintained his own little court, which was a miniature of that of his sovereign, with treasurers, courts of justice, scribes, and other officials. He was responsible for the collection of the revenue of his district, was nominally high-priest of the local temple or temples, and had at his command the militia of the neighbourhood, though it was no longer at his disposal for the purpose of gratifying his own private spites or avenging his own private wrongs. He could even build great public buildings, as in the case of Khnumhotep II. of Beni-hasan, or erect a colossal statue of himself, as in the case of Tahutihetep of the Hare nome. But in such cases the work was not a sign of any claim to independence, and Tahutihetep is careful to tell us that he had express permission from the king for the execution of his colossus. "Their heart is in festivity when they see their lord, the son of their lord, making his monument as a favour from the king." In short, the Pharaohs of the XIIth Dynasty seem to have been in the happy position of being able to get the maximum of good work out of their territorial aristocracy without incurring the dangers which the existence of so powerful a body of nobles has often created and, indeed, did create in the latter days of the Old Kingdom in Egypt.

The reasons for their notable success in this respect seem to have been mainly two. In the first place, the Pharaoh had ceased to be entirely dependent, for the execution of his will or the maintenance of his authority, on the feudal militia of the great lords. Just as the first step towards the establishment of a standing army in England, a step viewed with extreme jealousy by the nation, was the organisation of the King's Guards, a comparatively small body of soldiers specially attached to the King's person, so the first step to a similar end in Egypt was taken by the Pharaohs of the XIIth Dynasty in the form of the organisation of a body of "followers of His Majesty"—a force which was kept on a permanent footing, and seems to have been largely recruited from the warlike Sudanese tribes. Such a body of troops, who had no local sympathies, but were bound by strong ties to the royal master on whose favour their career depended, and who were in a state of constant training and efficiency, must have given the Pharaoh an obvious advantage as compared with his predecessors who had to rely on the imperfectly trained local levies, whose hearts were often more with the nomarch who commanded them than with the Pharaoh of whose throne they were the somewhat shaky prop. A small body of trained troops, who could be relied upon to carry out the king's orders, and no one else's, and who were so distributed as to secure the main strategic positions in the Nile Valley, enabled the king to regard the territorial forces of the great lords with perfect equanimity, as he

would know that he could at once crush any local movement before it had time to gather momentum. We shall
find this dependence upon a permanent body of royal
guards becoming a lasting feature of Egyptian army
organisation from this time onwards, the regiments being
recruited from various foreign nations, as the Ægean
races (the famous "Sherden"), the Libyans, and the
Sudanese, the last named remaining throughout the most
important element in the army.

The other bridle by whose means the Pharaoh was able
to maintain a check upon his great lords was afforded by
the matter of succession. The great baron of the kingdom
did not hold his possessions by an absolutely unqualified
title. He held two different kinds of estate, of which one,
his "paternal estate", passed naturally in his line from
generation to generation, and could not be alienated; and
in this respect he was practically independent of his king,
who had to observe the laws of succession like any other
man. But he held also another type of landed property,
which was, strictly speaking, a royal fief, and to which his
succession had to be confirmed by the king in order to
secure its validity. Normally, no doubt, the confirmation
was more or less a matter of course; but the form had to be
observed, even in the case of such loyal and useful servants
as the members of the Khnumhotep family of the Oryx
nome, and Khnumhotep II. records it as a special favour of
the king that his uncle Nakht was appointed to the "count's
fief" of Menat - Khufu. "He appointed . . . Nakht,
triumphant, revered, to the rule of his inheritance in
Menat-Khufu, as a great favour of the king, by the
command which issued from the mouth of the Majesty of
King Senusert I., who is given life, stability, satisfaction
like Ra, forever." Khnumhotep II. himself had to undergo
the same investiture before succeeding to the same
count's fief. "The King Amenemhat II. . . . . brought me,
being the son of a count, into the inheritance of the
governorship of my mother's father, because he so loved
justice. . . . He appointed me to be count in the year 19,
in Menat-Khufu."

Thus we see that while it was the usual thing to

continue a family in the tenure of its "count's fiefs" as well
as in its hereditary estates, the rule that royal confirmation
was necessary was by no means a dead letter during the
rule of the XIIth Dynasty Pharaohs; and while the Beni-
hasan house (model territorial magnates, if their own
testimony is to be believed) found no difficulty in getting
their titles confirmed, it does not follow that less satisfactory nobles did the same. Pharaoh had the whip-hand of
his nobles under such a system; always provided, of course,
that he was strong and courageous enough to use the
advantage given him by this double tenure. There was no
question of either the strength or the courage of the
Pharaohs of the Middle Kingdom, and consequently the
great nobles quietly subsided from the position in which
they had been as much a danger as a buttress to the state
into one in which their activities were in general useful,
and, if not that, were at least harmless, thus following
what appears to be the normal progress of territorial
aristocracies.

This development was, doubtless, both helped and
hastened by the rapid rise of another form of aristocracy
which was destined to occupy a growingly important place
in the social organisation of the kingdom, and whose influence was by no means always for good. It is quite possible that we are liable to overestimate somewhat the extent to which Egyptian life was dominated by the bureaucracy and its somewhat objectionable instrument the
scribe, seeing that, just because he was the scribe, this
gentleman has had a quite undue advantage in respect of
the prominence which he occupies in the written records
of the kingdom. If we were in a position in which we could
hear the story as it appeared to the other classes of society,
to the soldier, for example, it is more than likely that the
scribe would not bulk anything so large as he does in narratives where he had the whole business in his own hands,
and could make himself out as important as he liked. But
at the same time, there can be no doubt that the scribe,
the man of learning, and literally of letters, occupied in
ancient Egypt a position such as he has occupied in few
other countries, and that it was largely during this period

that he began to attain it, and to assert himself with all the insufferable self-sufficiency and arrogance of his kind. The parallel with China at once suggests itself again, and if we may believe the scribe's own account of things (a rather large "if" be it remembered), the one passport to advancement and favour in Middle Kingdom Egypt, as in China, was the possession of a scribal education.

However this may have been (and we shall have the opportunity of seeing with what smug self-sufficiency and contempt of all other callings the scribe maintained that it was as he claimed), there is no doubt of the existence and universal activity of a huge official class. In the old days, the administration had been locally almost entirely in the hands of the nomarchs, with their local staffs. To a certain extent this custom of local administration still continued; but side by side with it there had now been established a system of officials who were responsible directly to the vizier and, through him, to the Pharaoh. In every nome there was a royal deputy, and overseers of all Crown property, and also representatives of the central authority in each division of the nome. These were called "corner men", the first instance of the use of that time-dishonoured phrase; and they reported directly to the vizier, who was thus kept *au courant* with all that was happening in the nome, and was thus able to give His Majesty first-hand information as to the conduct of each nomarch in the realm, and, if necessary, to forestall any attempt on the part of a disloyal nomarch to make trouble. Thus there was a double system of administration, in which the local authorities, while nominally responsible for the welfare of their own district, were in reality liable to be overruled at any moment by the central authority, acting on the reports of its corner men. It does not sound like a pleasant or even an efficient method, and it must obviously have tended to produce some of the worst features of officialdom, in the shape of petty jealousies and spyings; but it doubtless served one purpose, that of keeping the local authorities from gathering too much power into their hands, as they had done under previous governments.

Its effect upon the official class was notable. They came to regard themselves as indispensable to the state, and in fact as the one and only class in the state which really counted; and their arrogance and self-conceit is reflected in a score of compositions which to us at the present seem merely insufferable, but doubtless to the scribe and all his class seemed only the natural reflection of his own inestimable qualities. One of the most striking examples of the scribal outlook upon life is afforded us by a famous document, "The Instruction of Duauf", which, though only surviving in the shape of two papyri and a few ostraka of the New Empire, when the book was used for schoolboys' exercises, really dates originally from the period of the Middle Kingdom. The view of the author is exactly that of the old official class of China—that the one matter that really counts in the world is books and the knowledge of them; and his conviction that every profession or trade, save that of letters, is simply contemptible, and that the scribe alone has the *Open Sesame* to success in life, is almost pathetic in its intensity and its blindness to the hard facts.

"Instruction which a man named Duauf, the son of Khety, composed for his son named Pepi, when he voyaged up to the Residence to put him in the School of Books, among the children of the magistrates." You see the worthy father leading his promising son to the boarding school where, in company with other young shoots of bureaucracy, he was to learn how to become a snob like his father and his companions. As he goes, the honest man descants on the supreme advantages of learning, chiefly as a means of escaping from hard work. To the Egyptian, or rather to the Egyptian scribe, learning had no charms in itself; it was to be pursued solely because of the advantages and rewards in position and pudding which it brought, and, above all, because in a land whose fame rests upon its sound and splendid workmanship it enabled its possessor to be an unproductive parasite. "He said unto him: I have seen him that is beaten, him that is beaten; thou art to set thine heart on books. I have beheld him that is set free from forced labour; behold nothing surpasseth books. . . .

Would that I might make thee love books more than thy mother, would that I might bring their beauty before thy face. It is greater than any calling. If the scholar has begun to succeed, even though he is yet a child, men kow-tow to him. He is sent to carry out important behests, and he cometh not home to put on the workman's apron."

Mr. Worldly Wiseman then proceeds to depreciate the callings whose fruits have been the glory of Egypt: "Never have I seen a sculptor sent on an embassy, nor a goldsmith bearing dispatches. But I have seen the smith at his task at the mouth of his furnace. His fingers were like crocodile skin, and he stank more than fish-guts. Every artisan that wieldeth the chisel has a wearier time than if he were a delver; his field is of wood, and his hoe is his chisel. In the night when he should be free, he worketh overtime beyond his strength; in the night he lights a light (to see how to work). The builder seeketh for work in all manner of hard stone. When he hath finished it, his arms are destroyed and he is weary. When such an one sitteth down at dusk, his thighs and his back are broken." And so on through all the honourable callings which were making Egypt great forever in the eyes of the world. They were all contemptible in the purblind eye of the scribe, and his own calling alone was honourable, because it enabled him to squat at his ease in his office and accumulate adipose tissue, like his representative the Sitting Scribe of the Louvre. "Mesekhent (the Goddess of Birth) hath vouch-safed success to the scribe; at the head of the officials is he set, and his father and mother thank God for it —— Behold, this it is that I set before thee and thy children's children." Such was the scribe's view, in the spacious times of the XIIth Dynasty, of the purpose for which his great and glorious country existed; briefly, that God made Egypt for the scribe to exploit it. "The fly sat upon the axle of the chariot, and said, 'What a dust I do raise!'"

Later we shall see that this Duauf spirit, as we may call it from its first exemplar, persisted right down through Egypt's history, and that in the time of the New Empire the Duauf of the period was as contemptuous of the soldiers who were conquering Palestine and Naharina for him to batten upon as his ancestor of the Middle Kingdom had been of the makers of colossi and the builders of temples. This base outlook is one of the disagreeable features of Egyptian life, and it has been worth lingering upon, because it was one of the elements which contributed in the end to the strangulation and death of all originality and vitality in Egyptian thought and art.

In the other great branch of the royal service, the army, the chief change was the introduction, which has already been noticed, of the nucleus of a standing army in the shape of the royal guards or "Followers of His Majesty". The equipment of the troops remained almost exactly as it had been under the Old Kingdom, and consisted of the bow, with arrows still tipped with flint, the broad-bladed spear, the bill, and the small hatchet, somewhat inefficiently attached to its haft. No true sword was used, but a short hanger or rather long dagger was common, until the introduction of the curiously shaped and seemingly cumbrous scimitar which afterwards became so popular, and generally figures as the Pharaoh's special weapon in his battle scenes. Stone weapons, except in the case of arrow-heads, were going out of use—notably the stone-headed mace of the Old Kingdom. Their place was taken by copper, though towards the end of the period bronze is beginning to appear. But, on the whole, the Egyptians were somewhat backward in the invention and adoption of new types of warlike weapons, a sluggishness for which they suffered in the succeeding period. The chariot and war-horse, of course, were unknown to them until they learned their value by sad experience at the hands of the Hyksos; and for this ignorance they need not be blamed, as it was apparently one which they shared with all the resident nations of the ancient eastern world, to which the introduction of this formidable engine of warfare by Indo-European invaders came as a complete surprise. But they were curiously backward in other matters of this kind also, and the hafting of their battle-axes, for instance, is greatly inferior to that of the corresponding implements which are being unearthed at Ur of the Chaldees from graves of a much earlier period. This backwardness is all the more striking when the easy supremacy of the Egyptian craftsman in other respects is considered. But the Egyptians were never a warlike people, and not even the vigour and initiative of Senusert III. could make them what Nature had not made them.

They were by no means backward, however, in naval matters, where, on the contrary, they led the world. We know of nothing to compare even remotely with the design and manifest efficiency of the Egyptian ship of the period, which was capable not only of river work, but of genuine sea-going voyages. Such voyages had now been carried out by Egyptian sailors for a period of at least a thousand years; and the tradition of Snefru's time was well maintained by the sailors of the Middle Kingdom. The local inscriptions of the Red Sea coast show that traffic with Punt was pretty constant, though it seemingly fell off during the troubled times which followed. That the romance of the sea and its adventures appealed to the Egyptian mind is evident from such a story as that of the Shipwrecked Sailor, which belongs to this period, and is of interest as being the first extant example of an innumerable host of such tales. This Middle Kingdom *Robinson Crusoe* is by no means devoid of merit as a literary performance; but, apart from its romantic interest, it also affords us hints as to the scale on which Egyptian shipbuilding construction was being carried on at the time of its invention. The figures which the Shipwrecked Sailor gives as to his ship are perhaps not to be taken literally, any more than his description of the wonderful talking serpent, with his beard and eyebrows of true lapis lazuli and his body overlaid with gold; but at least they represent what the public mind of the time was prepared to accept as a description of a reasonable ship, such as might be expected to be engaged in the Red Sea navigation. The ship is of 120 cubits in length (150 according to another version), and 40 cubits in breadth, or, in other words, she measures 180 feet by 60 according to the smaller estimate, and 225 feet by 60 on the larger. We need not imagine that this implies such a tonnage as would be involved in a modern ship of such dimensions. The length of the larger ship is at least twenty feet greater than that of

the biggest battleship built for our Navy before the advent
of steam; but it is not to be supposed that the Shipwrecked Sailor's galley measured anything like the four
thousand odd tons of the *Queen*. Yet the fact that she
carried a crew of 120 (or 150) men is sufficient evidence
that she was of respectable size.

The fact is that the Egyptian sailor has never had the
credit given to him which is undoubtedly his due. It has
been customary to depreciate his achievements in favour of
those of his successor, the Phoenician, who undoubtedly
accomplished more, but who came later to the adventure,
and had the advantage of all the experience of his predecessors; but in no estimate of our debt to the world's
seamen can the contribution of the world's first navigators
be neglected. If their voyages were only such as we should
call mere coasting cruises to-day, we have to remember
that they were made on an almost unknown element, and
in face of all the mystery of the uncomprehended ocean;
and perhaps, viewed in that light, the voyage to Somaliland
was as great a piece of heroism as any of the cruises of our
merchant adventurers. A well-known authority on the
sailing ship has told us that the modern racing cutter
descends by direct filiation from the Egyptian galley with
her long overhang, and that an old Egyptian designer, if
you could bring him to Cowes to see the last word in naval
architecture there, would tell you that *White Heather* and
Shamrock were based on the designs which he drew for his
masters of the XIIth Dynasty. Egyptian sailors fought well
in two of the most famous of naval battles, Salamis and
Navarino, and formed not the least efficient contingents
in the defeated fleet on either occasion. Altogether both
naval architecture and navigation owe more to the pioneering spirit of the ancient Egyptian than has ever been
acknowledged.

The period of the Middle Kingdom was evidently
regarded by the Egyptians themselves as that in which
their literature reached its culminating point—so far at
least as regards its style. Up to this point, the language had
been gradually taking shape and form, and ridding itself
of the crudities and barbarisms which characterised its

earlier developments; but it now attains what the succeeding ages evidently regarded as the perfection of its style, from which the deviations of the future could only be error and loss. Classical Egyptian style in writing is the Egyptian of the Middle Kingdom. That this is so is seen in the fact that the specimens of the literature of this period which have survived have done so largely because they were used in the schools of the land at a later time as examples of correct style, much as the masterpieces of our own literature are used for the forming of a correct style among scholars of the present day. We should know nothing of quite a number of the masterpieces of Egyptian literature were it not for the fact that they were copied on writing-boards, papyri, and ostraka by weary schoolboys, who doubtless wished that they had never been written, as they toiled over their often very inaccurate copies, perhaps reminded now and again in a very practical manner of the Egyptian belief that "a boy's ears are on his back and he hears when he is beaten". A somewhat pathetic touch is added to the gratitude which we owe to these old exercise books by the fact that they have been mostly derived from tombs, where they had been buried by sorrowing parents whose boys never reached an age when they could put into practice the lessons of good style which they had so laboriously, and, it must be allowed, with so little success, struggled to learn. It would seem that scarcely sufficient allowance has been made for this fact in the estimates which have been formed of the merits of the writings which have come down to us under such unfavourable conditions. It seems probable that our opinion of the merits even of our own most famous poets might be somewhat less favourable if the only copies of their works which we possessed were in the shape of impositions written by schoolboys in atonement of their lapses, or exercises set to them for the purpose of training them in handwriting and in the elements of a correct style. Yet this is literally the condition under which some of the most famous masterpieces of Egyptian Middle Kingdom literature present themselves to us.

We owe perhaps to this scholastic medium the feature

of the literature which is most obvious and least attractive to our minds. Classical Egyptian delights in what Mrs. Malaprop aptly calls "a fine derangement of epitaphs", and is stiff with choice and far-fetched expressions. The fact cannot be questioned; but it is permissible to question whether the originals from which our copies were derived were so overloaded with "correct" phrases, and so enamoured of euphuisms as might be supposed from the evidence which we possess. Again, what might our own masterpieces look like were the devastating hand of the schoolmaster allowed free course with them, and permitted to substitute correct phrases for all the felicities of personal expression which make their charm to all but the scholastic eye and ear?

Chief among the departments of Middle Kingdom literature is undoubtedly that store of more or less pessimistic utterances of which we have already had specimens in the dialogue of A-Man-Weary-of-Life with his Soul, the Admonitions of Ipuwer, and the Prophecy of Neferrohu. It is obviously the product of an age which had witnessed the downfall of all the hopes which had been based upon the splendid attainments of the great men of the Old Kingdom, and which, though it had lasted long enough to see the dawn of better things after the misery and iniquity of the Intermediate period, was deeply sceptical of the permanent endurance of good conditions in an imperfect and ever-changing world. Some of the utterances, as we have seen, so vividly depict the wretched conditions of which they complain as to make it fairly certain that they are contemporary with what they describe; while others again, unless we are prepared to admit a genuinely predictive element in them, must belong to a date when the disturbed conditions were already beginning to pass away under the firm rule of the Middle Kingdom Pharaohs. But even the most hopeful of them have a tang of bitterness, and a sense of the vanity of all human effort and the lack of endurance of the best and greatest of human works.

Perhaps the most poignant expression of this pessimistic attitude towards all human attainment is given us in the Banqueting Song of the Middle Kingdom which has come down to us under the title of "The Song from the House (*i.e.* the Tomb) of King Antef, Written in front of the Harper". It was such singing at the funerary banquets wherewith the memory of the dead was honoured that doubtless gave rise to the melancholy story which Herodotus narrates of the carrying around of a model coffin and mummy at each feast, with the words, "Look upon this, then drink and enjoy yourself; for when dead you will be like this".

Well is it with this good prince, the goodly destiny is accomplished!
Men pass away, and others come in their place, since the time of the ancestors.
The Gods (*i.e.* the Pharaohs) that were aforetime rest in their pyramids, and likewise the noble and the glorified they rest entombed.
They who build houses, their dwellings are no more. What hath been done with them?
I have heard the words of Imhotep and Hordadef, whose wise sayings are in everyone's mouth:
What are their dwellings now? Their walls are destroyed, their habitations are no more, as if they had never existed.
None cometh from thence that he may tell us how they fare, that he may tell us what they need,
That he may satisfy our heart, until we also depart to the place whither they have gone.
Be glad now, that thou mayest cause thine heart to forget that men will one day pay thee also thy funeral honours.
Follow thy desire, so long as thou livest. Put myrrh on thine head, clothe thee in fine linen,
And anoint thee with the genuine marvels of the things of the god.
Add yet more to the delights which thou hast, and let not thine heart be denied. Follow thy desire, and do good to thyself.
Do what thou wishest on earth, and vex not thine heart—until that day of lamentation cometh unto thee.
Yet He-with-the-Quiet-Heart (Osiris) heareth not their lamentations; and cries deliver no man from the Underworld.
Spend the day happily, neither weary thereof; for lo, no man taketh his goods with him, Yea, none that hath departed can return again.

Even to us, who read this fragment of vain protest against merciless death after so many centuries, its poignancy can scarcely fail to make appeal. How much more must it have appealed to the men of that time, who, in spite of their emergence from the miserable anarchy in which their fathers had lived and died, still had under their eyes the grim evidence of how little human strength and wisdom avail to secure immunity from the common lot, and how vain are the most colossal efforts to defy destroying time. Imhotep and Hordadef are the typical Wise Men of the past whom the singer chooses to point his moral— Imhotep, who planned the first Pyramid, Hordadef, the wise man of the next age, and son of him who built the greatest of the Pyramids. Everybody, says the singer, knows them, and their wise saws are in everybody's mouth; and what good has all their wisdom done them? "What are their dwellings now? Their walls are destroyed, their habitations are no more, as if they had never existed." It is an impressive appeal even now. It must have been almost intolerably impressive when the singer had but to wave his arm to point out the melancholy wrecks of past greatness of which he sang.

"There they stretched," says Professor Breasted, "like a line of silent outposts on the frontiers of death. It was a thousand years since the first of them had been built, and five hundred years had elapsed since the architects had rolled up their papyrus drawings of the latest, and the last group of workmen had gathered up their tools and departed. The priesthoods too, left without support, had long forsaken the sumptuous temples and monumental approaches that rose on the valley side. The sixty-mile pyramid cemetery lay in silent desolation, deeply encumbered with sand half hiding the ruins of massive architecture, of fallen architraves and prostrate colonnades, a solitary waste where only the slinking figure of the vanishing jackal suggested the futile protection of the old mortuary gods of the desert. . . . On the minds of the men of the Feudal Age the Pyramid cemetery made a profound impression. If already in the Pyramid Age there had been some relaxation in the conviction that by sheer material force man might make conquest of immortality, the spectacle of these colossal ruins now quickened such doubts into open scepticism."

Along with this development of scepticism as to the means on which former ages had relied for securing immortality went a faint dawning, which we can do no more than mention in passing, of the idea that well-being in the world after death might depend, not on earthly rank, state, or power, but on moral qualities, and that before the eternal Judge a man might receive according to what he had done in the body, whether it was good or bad. This conception, entirely novel to Egyptian thought hitherto, was apparently one result of the time of anarchy when neither earthly rank or power or virtue availed to secure any man against the assaults of ill-fortune or the fury of wicked men. There must be justice beyond, since there was none on earth! The thought comes out very remarkably in a single passage from that Instruction for King Merykara, which, as we have seen, is probably to be regarded as the work, or at least as being attributed to the hand, of that unlucky King Khety of the IXth Dynasty who had such a poor time of it during his troubled reign: "The judges who judge the oppressed, thou knowest that they are not lenient on that day of judging the miserable, in the hour of carrying out the decision. Ill fareth it when the accuser is the Wise One (Thoth, the God of Wisdom, who keeps the record in the trial before Osiris)!—Put not thy trust in length of years; they regard a lifetime as an hour. A man remaineth over after death and his deeds are placed beside him in heaps. But it is for eternity that one is there, and he is a fool that maketh light of them (the judges). But he that cometh unto them without wrong-doing, he shall continue yonder like a god, stepping boldly forward like the Lords of Eternity!"

The same conception emerges obscurely and briefly in the concluding verses of the dialogue with His Soul of A-Man-Weary-of-his-Life, where, after his commendation of death the writer turns to contemplate the life beyond, and finds it one where earthly standards are ignored and earthly judgments reversed:

He that is yonder shall be
  One that shall seize the sinner as a living god,
And shall inflict punishment for sin upon him that doeth it.
He that is yonder shall be
  One that standeth in the barque of the Sun,
And shall assign the choicest things therein unto the temples.

He who is yonder shall be
  A man of knowledge, and he is not hindered (in his approach to God)
And he prayeth to Ra when he speaketh.

The just man may have a poor time in this life; but
hereafter his goodness shall be justified. He shall himself
judge the men who mocked at his righteousness in life; he .
shall journey with the Sun-god in his daily voyage across
the heavens, see his god, and be able to secure that the
offerings are no longer wasted on corrupt officials, but
reach their rightful destination. Finally, he shall have free
access to the presence of God, and a ready hearing for his
petitions, instead of being thrust out of the presence by
proud priests as heretofore. With due allowance for the
differences of country and race, this is remarkably like the
solution which Job finds, centuries later, for his problem
of why the good man should often have to suffer in this
life. Not even the stilted style of what the succeeding ages
in Egypt considered the fine writing of this period can
altogether disguise the real human interest of such grop-
ings of the human spirit after the meaning which lies behind the appearances of human existence.

A more practical approach to the problems of justice
and injustice in daily life is offered to us by a document
which was evidently considered by the Egyptians to be one
of the most perfect models of literary style. This treasure-
house of elegant expression is known either as "The
Eloquent Peasant", or the "Complaints of the Peasant",
and describes at intolerable length and with insufferable profusion of far-fetched conceits, the adventures
of a peasant whose property is seized on a trumped-up
complaint by a minor official. The peasant makes appeal
to the official's superior, who is Grand Steward of
Pharaoh himself, and the Grand Steward is so charmed
with the eloquence of the ill-used man that he reports
the whole matter to Pharaoh. The king enters into the
game with delight, and the poor peasant is kept hanging
on with his wrong unrighted until he has made nine
several appeals to the Grand Steward, each more eloquent
than the one which went before it. Finally, when the
joke has been carried on sufficiently long, the wrong-doer

is punished and the wrong is righted. As the long delay in his case had brought the poor peasant to the point where he wished death rather than life, it seems that the jest did not appeal to him quite so much as it did to the high Steward and the Pharaoh; but apparently the Egyptian mind was quite satisfied with the poetic justice administered at last.

"Then the high steward Rensi, the son of Meru, caused the apparitors to go and bring Khunanup back. And this peasant was afraid and thought that it was being done to punish him for this speech which he had spoken. And this peasant said: 'As the thirsty man draweth near to water, as the mouth of the suckling reacheth after milk, so I long to see how death cometh'. The high steward Rensi, the son of Meru, said: 'Fear not, peasant. Behold thou shalt dwell with me'. Then this peasant swore, saying: 'I will forever eat of thy bread and drink of thy beer'. And the high steward said: 'Well, come this way, that thou mayest hear thy petitions'. And he caused them to be read out from a new papyrus roll, every petition according to its content. And the high steward Rensi, the son of Meru, caused it to be sent in to the Majesty of King Nebkaura, justified. And it pleased the king more than anything that was in the entire land." If so, all that one can say is that His Majesty was easily pleased, for to a modern reader the intolerable eloquence of the injured man almost seems to justify the injustice which had been done to him; but perhaps this makes the book all the more valuable as an example of how the tastes of different lands and ages may differ from one another. "Indeed," says Erman, "the book is primarily an example of that rhetoric which is entirely given up to elegant expressions. . . . That in these speeches right is praised and the baseness of officials condemned, is almost forgotten by us in face of the flood of far-fetched expressions. Monotonous, obscure, and farfetched as these nine speeches may appear to us to-day, they really may not have sounded so to an Egyptian. He was sensible of much in them that was elegant and witty, which quite escapes us who only understand the book very incompletely."

PLATE XXI

1. HAND-MIRROR IN SILVER, OBSIDIAN, AND GOLD.   LAHUN
2. CANOPIC JARS OF PRINCESS SAT-HATHOR-ANT.   LAHUN
By permission of Sir Flinders Petrie

The straining after eloquence and brilliancy which makes the book repulsive to us, ought not, in any case, to blind us to the ideals of social justice which are set forth, albeit, with such wearisome prolixity, in the book. Breasted has assigned to it, in this respect, a very high position: "The high ideal of justice to the poor and oppressed set forth in this tale is but a breath of that wholesome moral atmosphere which pervades the social thinking of the official class. It is remarkable, indeed, to find these aristocrats of the Pharaoh's court four thousand years ago sufficiently concerned for the welfare of the lower classes to have given themselves the trouble to issue what are evidently propaganda for a regime of justice and kindness toward the poor. They were pamphleteers in a crusade for social justice." One may suspect that Professor Breasted is here, to some extent, committing the fatal error of "making pictures for himself" of a state of things which never really existed in Egyptian officialdom, and that the unquenchable thirst for social justice which he attributes to the officials of the Middle Kingdom only exists in his own generous imagination. The bulk of our evidence on the point goes to show that "a crusade for social justice" would have been the very last thing of which an Egyptian scribe of any period would have dreamed, and that the average official cared no more for what happened to the average peasant than the high steward Rensi cared for the sufferings of the wretched man whom he kept wriggling on the hook for the amusement of himself and the king. But it must be admitted that the lofty ideals maintained by poor Khunanup, when dressed up in a sufficiently gaudy garment of rhetoric, did commend themselves, at least, to the taste of the cultured class in the Egypt of the Middle Kingdom, though it may have been a case of *video meliora proboque, deteriora sequor*, and though in the peasant's eloquence the solid nucleus of social justice among the frothy rhetoric may appear no more than the "one halfpennyworth of bread to this intolerable deal of sack" of Falstaff's tavern bill.

Moral and social treatises, however, such as these, are far from being the only output of Middle Kingdom literature. It is to this period that we have to attribute the first

Egyptian essays in a class of writing which has since grown to proportions which make the contrast between the full-grown tree and the diminutive seed all the more remarkable. The world must always owe to the Egyptian a very considerable debt because it was he who first essayed to travel into the realms of fiction, and to set down in writing the romantic stories which had delighted him as they were told, that they might also delight others in future generations. The Story of the Shipwrecked Sailor, simple though its elements may be, is by no means an unworthy beginning for the long series of wonder tales of adventure which number among them some of the masterpieces of the world's literature; the Story of Sinuhe, though it has its own historical value, must be regarded mainly as an historical romance, the first of its kind, and not the least pleasing; while the Tales of King Khufu and the Magicians, though probably they were originally told at an even earlier date, owe their present form to the late Middle Kingdom or the Second Intermediate Dark period.

It is to this fruitful era also that we owe the first regularly formed verse in Egyptian literature. Much of such early writing as the Pyramid Texts is rudely poetical in form as well as in substance; but it is during the Middle Kingdom that we begin to find poetry definitely emerging in ordered verse form. Singing has always been a characteristic feature of Egyptian labour in all ages, as it is at the present day. "Whoever is closely acquainted with modern Egypt", says Erman, "will carry about with him a recollection of the singing of the *fellahin* and boatmen, whose monotonous songs resound continually over the green fields and over the yellow Nile. I do not know if the peculiar nasal drawl of this singing, which strikes us as so peculiar, is to be claimed as an inheritance from ancient times, but the joy in singing certainly is. The peasant and craftsman of ancient Egypt also accompanied their work with their unpretentious singing, which so obviously formed part of the task in hand that the sculptor, when depicting this, also added the song to the representation." A fact which in itself suggests that the Egyptian workman was not the down-trodden slave, whose blood and tears stained the gigantic works of the Pharaohs with an eternal shame, but a cheery fellow who had his own joy in the work which he did so well. We have already seen Miss Murray's happy rendering into modern verse of the Song of the Shepherds from the Old Kingdom. Such songs were common in all periods. But the foremost example of Egyptian poetry from this the classical period of the literature is the famous Hymn to Senusert III., which was apparently sung on the occasion of his formal crowning in one of the cities of Upper Egypt. It is, as Breasted has said, "the earliest known example of poetry exhibiting rigid strophic structure and all the conscious artificialities of literary art", and as such would be worthy of attention even apart from any intrinsic merits which it might possess. But these are by no means negligible, and the picture of the might of Senusert, illustrated with so many characteristically Egyptian instances, makes a real impression on the imagination of the reader, in spite of the stiff and stilted form of the verse and the sometimes difficult line of thought. One of its strophes has already been quoted; it will suffice if we give another, which exhibits the typically Egyptian character of its selection of emblems by which to depict the might of the Pharaoh:

How great is the Lord for his city: he alone is a million, little are other men.

How great is the Lord for his city: he is like a dyke that keepeth back the river in its water-floods.

How great is the Lord for his city: he is like a cool lodge that letteth a man sleep unto daylight.

.   .   .   .

How great is the Lord for his city: he is like a bulwark that delivereth the fearful from his enemy.

How great is the Lord for his city: he is like the shade of the season of Inundation for cooling in summer.

How great is the Lord for his city: he is like a corner warm and dry in time of winter.

How great is the Lord for his city: he is like a mountain, that keepeth back the storm-blast, when the sky is in riot.

How great is the Lord for his city: he is like Sekhmet unto foes that overstep his boundaries.

Later we shall meet with another hymn of similar type,

though of somewhat different structure, to the great soldier of the New Empire, Thothmes III.; but interesting and effective though the later composition may be, it has not the stateliness of the verses which celebrate the greatness of the conqueror of the Sudan.

In considering the art of the Middle Kingdom, we are handicapped to a certain extent by the fact that of the great architectural masterpieces of the period practically nothing is left. How great is our loss in this respect must be judged from the opinion which a careful observer like Herodotus formed of the merits of the outstanding building of the time—the Labyrinth of Amenemhat III. A building which surpassed, in his opinion, even the Pyramids, and was more noteworthy than all the great buildings of Greece put together, must have been a work of unusual magnitude and quality, even for Egypt. Unfortunately its destruction has been so complete that not even the slightest idea of its appearance can be formed, and the various theories which have been put forward as to the interpretation of the somewhat confused description of Herodotus agree only in demonstrating that practically nothing is really known about the building or its purpose. All that is certainly known is that the Labyrinth was of such a size as to be unique even in this land of gigantic structures. Whatever its architectural merits, or demerits, which we shall never know, a building which could have included within its limits all the existing structures of Karnak and Luxor put together must have been a phenomenal piece of work. The one fragment remaining of the temple which Senusert I. founded at Heliopolis is of interest, not only in itself, but as indicating that Egyptian temple architecture at this period had already developed some of the features which are most characteristic of its later stages. At Karnak the XIIth Dynasty remains are not sufficient to enable us to judge of the scale or appearance of the Amen temple of the time; but the fortunate survival of so much of the Mentuhotep funerary temple of the XIth Dynasty at Der el-Bahri shows that the Middle Kingdom architects were not lacking in originality or in the sense of fitness. The skilful adaptation of his ramps and colonnades to the de-

mands of a most exacting site, where any attempt to rival
the soaring lines of the great cliffs behind would have been
absolute folly, shows that the architect of the temple, who
may have been the Mertisen who has left us an eulogy of
his own skill in his art characterised by the usual shrinking
modesty of the Egyptian official, understood and appreciated the problem set him as well as any modern architect.
The one blot upon his design, as reconstructed by modern
investigators, is the presence of the small and ugly pyramid
in its centre, which breaks the general horizontality of the
plan, and achieves nothing in the way of dignity, owing to
its small scale. It is only fair to him, however, to say, on the
one hand, that if the pyramid was there, it was doubtless
because tradition demanded its presence, regardless of
artistic considerations, and, on the other, that competent
judges, such as Sir Flinders Petrie, are very doubtful as
to the actual existence of any pyramid in the completed
temple.

Though pyramid-building still went on, and was still
considered the right form for the royal tomb to take, the
day for such gigantic structures as the pyramids of the
Gizeh group had passed, and the pyramids of the Middle
Kingdom are remarkable, not for their size, but for the
complexity of the design of their internal passages, and the
ingenuity with which these had been planned so as to
weary out and defeat the tomb-robbers. The robbers,
however, proved themselves still more ingenious than the
royal architects, or perhaps more patient than they were
given credit for being, and not a single pyramid of the
period has escaped desecration by ancient plunderers.
The striking architectural development of the time is not
that of the royal tombs, but that of the rock-hewn tomb
affected by the local magnates of this Feudal Age. These
tombs of the Middle Kingdom nomarchs are of a type
quite distinct from the later rock tombs of the Valley of
the Kings, and are in some instances of outstanding architectural merit. "The tomb of Ameni at Beni-hasan", says
Dr. H. R. Hall, "is a revelation to those whose knowledge
of Egyptian art is derived chiefly from the gigantic
abominations of Karnak or Abu Simbel. Nothing so fine

as the perfectly proportioned tomb-hall of Ameni, with its beautiful pillars, was ever excavated in an Egyptian cliff in later days. . . . Nor are other tombs of this period far behind it in beauty."

The most striking feature of the surviving architecture of the time, as seen at Der el-Bahri and in the rock tombs of Beni-hasan, is the extensive use made of the polygonal column, sometimes octagonal, sometimes sixteen-sided, and sometimes, as in the case of the tomb of Ameni, fluted to a slight depth down all the sixteen sides save one, which is left flat for an inscription. These columns have been called proto-Doric, which is perhaps making too great a demand on our belief in the continuity and transmission of an architectural form whose invention in different localities at widely different times does not seem to present insuperable difficulties; but it is difficult to understand why most architects should foam at the mouth when the possibility of the derivation of the Doric column from the Egyptian polygonal column of Beni-hasan is suggested.

The art of the sculptor had evidently suffered eclipse during the disastrous Intermediate period. A country which was in the anarchic condition of the Egypt of this time was not likely to produce monumental works in this kind on any scale or in any number. The conditions which had fostered the art being removed for the time, the art itself naturally declined. By the time when conditions were beginning to improve with the rise of the XIth Dynasty at Thebes, the technical skill which produced the great masterpieces of the Old Kingdom had been largely lost, though the traditional forms had survived; and the early work of the XIth Dynasty sculptors is extraordinarily poor and barbarous. The sculptor knows what he should aim at; but he simply has not the skill to produce anything better than a caricature of his models. Gradually, however, an improvement appears and grows, possibly when the unification of the kingdom under the new Theban line allowed of the importation to Upper Egypt of workmen from Memphis who had not altogether lost the tradition of the superb workmanship of the great Memphite school of the Old Kingdom. In this connection an extraordinary interest attaches to the relief sculpture of the shrines of the six priestesses of Mentuhotep II., which, as we have seen, were incorporated into the later temple of Mentuhotep III. at Der el-Bahri. The work on these beautiful shrines has still a certain stiffness and angularity which seem to indicate an art which had not quite found its full confidence as yet; but it is also of remarkable freshness and charm, and perhaps the touch of timidity and the almost childlike stiffness of it only add to the attractiveness of the whole.

Soon, however, this archaic touch is left behind, and we have the Middle Kingdom artist in the full sweep of his power. Mertisen, the royal architect and sculptor of Mentuhotep III., has already told us how admirably qualified he and his son were in all the mysteries of their profession. Possibly the very insistence with which he lays before us the details of his competence may be regarded as showing that such competence was somewhat of a novelty in his day, and a thing to be very proud of indeed; but if it is Mertisen who was responsible for the decoration of his king's funerary temple, as is more than likely, he had no need to be ashamed of his work. Complete recovery is not attained until the fulness of the XIIth Dynasty; but by the time that the great line of the Senuserts and Amenemhats had completed their consolidation of the united Egypt which the Mentuhoteps had handed down to them, Egyptian sculpture had attained to a mastery quite fairly comparable with that of the best of the Old Kingdom artists.

There will always be many to whom

the season
Of art's spring-birth, so fresh and dewy,

will be more attractive than the accomplished product of a period of maturity, and to whom the majesty of the great diorite Khafra, and the straightforward and vigorous life-likeness of the Rahotep and Nefert, will make a greater appeal than anything that can be shown them of the work of the sculptors who have left us portraits of the strong men of the Middle Kingdom in their habit as they lived; but no one can possibly question the power and the interpretative skill of the best work of the time.

There is a difference; but it is certainly not in the direction which Professor Breasted has suggested when he says that the figures of the Middle Kingdom sculptors "rarely possess the striking vivacity and the strong individuality which are so characteristic of the Old Kingdom sculpture". Such an incomprehensible judgment may be balanced by the exactly contradictory verdict of Dr. Hall: "The great reliefs and statues of the kings (of the Middle Kingdom) . . . show us portraits of a power which the artists of the IVth Dynasty cannot rival. The fidelity of these portraits we cannot question." The fact is that the difference is not one of the possession or lack of vivacity and individuality at all. Neither the Old Kingdom artist nor his brother of the Middle Kingdom was lacking in these points (that is when we take the best examples of his art, as we are bound to do); and it would be impossible to say that the one was superior or inferior to the other. The real difference is one which it is perfectly natural to expect, and which is perfectly manifest to one who looks at the great portraits of the two periods with understanding eyes.

It is simply this, that the artists are dealing with different periods, and with men who are the products of their periods. The Old Kingdom sculptor comes to his work in the fresh morning of the world, conscious of his own power to represent what he sees. What he sees is a monarch who is as conscious of his own power as is the artist who is to represent him, and who has not yet learned what succeeding ages would teach his successors only too surely—that even power, like everything else, is only vanity and vexation of spirit. So we have in the resultant portrait the expression of confident and unharassed majesty which is so manifest in the crowning masterpiece of the time, the great Khafra, but is also felt in greater or less degree in all this Old Kingdom work. The sculptor of the later age has a different outlook, and a model to work from who also has a different outlook. Both have learned that the world is not their oyster as it seemed to their confident predecessors, and the knowledge of the possibility, nay, the certainty of disappointments and even disasters has left its unmistakable mark on the face which is recorded, and on the spirit with which its characteristics have been seen and transmitted.

The Senuserts and Amenemhats, successful in the main as they had been, had behind them the memories of a past through which the Pyramid-builders had never had to pass, and knew all the bitterness of that time of shame and anarchy which Ipuwer has depicted with such monotonous iteration in his Admonitions. The colossal head of Senusert III. in granite, from Karnak, and perhaps even more the similar granite colossus from Abydos (though the battered condition of the latter makes comparison difficult), shows not only the consciousness of power, but also the sense of the weariness and vanity of it; and the same spirit of bitterness seems to breathe from the series of magnificent statues in grey granite which were found at Der el-Bahri, three of which are now in the British Museum. Even more striking is the growth of the same spirit as it can be seen in the remarkable series of portrait heads of Amenemhat III. It may not be possible to claim with certainty that some of the heads which are attributed to this great Pharaoh actually represent him, in view of the absence of inscriptional evidence. This uncertainty affects particularly such an amazing piece of workmanship and character study as the little obsidian head which was formerly in the MacGregor Collection, and which, to whatever period it may finally be dated, is an absolute miracle of mastery over the most intractable of materials; but there remain enough portraits of Amenemhat whose title is unquestioned to enable us to trace the deepening of the lines and the embittering of the expression in the face of the great Pharaoh, from the smooth and care-free beauty of the youthful Hawara statue now in the Cairo Museum, through the maturer majesty and dignity of the superb grey granite colossal head from Bubastis, in the British Museum, and the harsher and fiercer strength of the fine Berlin granite life-size figure, to the weariness of the head which was, and perhaps still is, in the Hermitage at Leningrad. The obsidian head must not be relied upon, in view of the questions as to its date; but it is hard to accept a late date for this masterpiece when one compares its astonishing rendering of worn and tired majesty with the other assured Amenemhat portraits.

The relief work of the period begins with work of a very crude and clumsy type, as may be seen from the limestone stele of Antef, an XIth Dynasty official, in the British Museum. From that, however, it quickly passes to such attractive work as that on the sarcophagi from the shrines of the priestesses at Der el-Bahri, which is charming in its slight stiffness and angularity, reminding one of the work of the Italian primitives. Early in the XIIth Dynasty, it has become capable of such accomplished pieces of relief portraiture as the Senusert I. from the Koptos slab, representing the king dancing before the god Min.

The tomb-painting of the period fairly maintains the Old Kingdom standard in its better examples. Breasted, whose estimate of the art of the Middle Kingdom is incomprehensibly low, asserts that the tomb-paintings of the nomarchs of the XIIth Dynasty "are for the most part distinctly inferior to the earlier work". Against this niggardly estimate may be set the enthusiastic verdict of Dr. Hall: "The naturalism of the multitudinous groups of wrestling men which are painted on the walls around the entrance to the inner chamber (of Ameni's tomb at Benihasan) is paralleled only by that of the Greek vase-paintings of the best period: the decoration of this wall . . . reminds us of nothing so much as of the decoration of a Clazomenian sarcophagus". Over-enthusiastic though such an opinion may seem to some critics, there can be little question that it comes much nearer to the truth than the grudging judgment of Professor Breasted.

After all, however, the aspect of Middle Kingdom art which has made most appeal to the modern world is not that of the sculptor's or the painter's work, but rather the "small art", which, in spite of the loss of what we must assume to have been a far greater quantity of fine specimens than those which have survived, still offers to the student of ancient art a wealth of beauty and of delicate skill in workmanship which is paralleled by no other period of Egyptian history, and therefore by no other period in the history of any country of the world. The tomb of Tutankhamen has, no doubt, revealed a greater mass of beautiful work in the minor arts and crafts than has been found in any other instance or country; but the XIIth Dynasty work from the tombs of the princesses at Dahshur and Lahun, though far less in quantity, more than holds its own, as regards quality, with the best that has ever come out of the Valley of the Kings. As an example of naturalistic work, in which the goldsmith has allowed himself to play with the precious metal, and with the colours of beautiful stones, in playful rivalry with the profusion of nature, the floral diadem of the princess Khnumit is unsurpassed and unsurpassable; though many will prefer the more formal dignity of the other coronet belonging to the same great lady in which the leading motive of the design is the Maltese Cross. Nothing has ever surpassed the simple dignity and beauty of the exquisite queen's crown of the Lahun treasure, with its severe band of burnished gold, decorated only with inlaid rosettes, its streamers of thin gold ribbon, its tall plume of golden feathers behind, which must have quivered with every movement of the wearer, and the uraeus, in gold and cloisonné inlay, rearing his brilliant crest upon the brow. The diadem from Tutankhamen's tomb is a fine and satisfying piece of design and workmanship; but the Lahun crown surpasses it; and all our modern diadems, it is almost needless to say, look vulgar and overloaded beside this masterpiece of four thousand years ago.

One point that is suggested by these diadems when viewed in connection with the remarkable finds of royal jewellery at Ur can only be mentioned in passing. No one can fail to be struck with the extraordinary similarity in style, allowing for the more dilapidated condition of the Mesopotamian jewellery, between the XIIth Dynasty diadems of the Egyptian princesses and the jewellery of Queen Shub-ad of Ur. Mr. Woolley's description of the two head-dresses of the Mesopotamian queen reads almost like that of the floral diadem of the princess Khnumit; while the Sumerian head-dress was of a size which meant that it could only have been worn over a wig, precisely as in the case of the Lahun crown. One of the main arguments for the shorter dating of the Egyptian dynasties before 1580 B.C., which involves the placing of the XIIth Dynasty round about 2000 B.C. is that there is no such difference between the art of the XVIIIth Dynasty and that of the XIIth as would account. for the extra 1460 years which Sir Flinders Petrie's dating demands. But the jewellery of Ur is dated by its discoverer about 3500-3200 B.C., and no one seems to have suggested a lower date for it than 3200 B.C. Yet, so far as can be judged from the evidence presented at the present time, there seems to be as great a similarity between the art of the Mesopotamian treasure and that of Dahshur and Lahun as there can possibly be between the XIIth Dynasty and the XVIIIth Dynasty Egyptian work. Are we therefore to assume that either the jewellery from Ur must be brought down to a date within reasonable distance of the Egyptian treasure, or the date of the Egyptian work carried forward to match the Mesopotamian head-dresses? If the latter assumption were to be made, the curious thing is that it would bring the dates of the XIIth Dynasty to almost exactly the position at which Petrie's dating has placed them. Perhaps, however, the only really satisfactory conclusion that can be derived from such a consideration is that comparisons of style are not by any means such a certain ground for the fixing of dates as has sometimes been assumed.

Some of the other articles of the various finds of this period are quite as fine in design and workmanship, though not so splendid, as the diadems of the princesses. The pectorals, both of the Dahshur and the Lahun treasure, are masterpieces of an art in which the Egyptian goldsmith was unrivalled—that of cloisonné inlay. It is curious to see, at the same time, how, even within so short a period as that which divides the earliest of these beautiful ornaments from the latest, there has been a decided falling off in both taste and skill. The later pectorals, which date from the reign of Amenemhat III., are by no means such satisfactory pieces of design as the earlier from the reign of Senusert II.; and the execution of the work shows a corresponding deficiency in thoroughness and finish. Amenemhat may have been by far the greater king of the two; but he had not at his command the same sure artistic skill as the earlier and less important Pharaoh. Such a falling-off has often marked the later years of a great period, when material power seems still to be at its zenith, but the spiritual element which was the real secret of the period's greatness is beginning to wane; and it is often the first indication of the coming downfall. So it was in this case.

All the same, the triumphs of the Middle Kingdom craftsman are so great that even his second-rate work seems surprisingly good until his best has been seen. Dr. Hall's summing up of the period does its quality no more than justice. "Under the XIIth Dynasty Egyptian art reached its apogee of delicacy, taste, and proportion. Nothing more beautiful in its own *genre* was ever produced in Egypt than the jewellery of gold and cloisonné stones, carnelian, lapis, felspar and amethyst, which has been found in the pyramids of kings of this dynasty at Dahshur and Lahun. Hardly anything more beautiful of its kind has ever been produced anywhere. And the same feeling for combinations of beautiful colours and textures, for proportion and appropriateness of decoration, characterises all the art of this particular period, both great and small." There are few surer tests of the presence of one aspect, and that not the least important, of a high degree of civilisation in a race than its love for really beautiful things, and its sureness of taste in what is really beautiful; judged by such a standard, the Egyptian of the Middle Kingdom was more highly civilised than most of the human race to-day. The ladies who demanded for the gratification of their artistic sense such things as the diadems and pectorals of Dahshur and Lahun, and the workmen who designed and wrought them, had a far higher sense of the beautiful than ninety-nine out of every hundred educated Europeans or Americans of our own day.

Another of the interesting survivals of the period shows us that the Egyptian of this time was becoming civilised in another aspect of his nature, where he had continued a barbarous and primitive practice for a surprisingly long time. We have seen that the mortality among the priestesses of the XIth Dynasty at the temple of Der el-Bahri was such as to suggest that not natural death, but ritual sacrifice at the grave of their dead king, was in question, and also that such sacrifice is absolutely certain in the case of the slaves of Hepzefi of Siut at Kerma in Nubia in this same period. But the passing away of this barbarous custom is growingly indicated, as the time goes on, by the corresponding growth in the habit of burying in the grave of the dead person sets of models of all the servants and animals on whom he had depended for his comfort and sustenance in his earthly life, and on whom he would presumably still depend in the Underworld. These models obviously were meant to take the place of the servants and animals who were formerly slaughtered at the tomb, and they are therefore welcome as indications of the growing disgust of the Egyptian at such barbarity. In other respects they are of great value, as they preserve for us contemporary representations of almost every occupation of Egyptian life, from the leisured ease of the great man who watches his cattle being driven before him as he sits under his verandah, to the toil of the humblest of his labourers. In artistic merit, these models of course differ among themselves to an extreme degree. Some of them are as crude and clumsy as such things could be, without losing all semblance of likeness to what they were meant for. Others are really works of art, and are characterised by an astonishing vivacity and dash. But, from the crudest specimens to the most highly finished, their value is not to be judged only by their artistic qualities or their lack of any such quality, but by the fact that they are the best of all historical documents for the life of ancient Egypt of the Middle Kingdom.

CHAPTER XVIII

THE SECOND INTERMEDIATE PERIOD AND THE
HYKSOS DOMINATION

THE Second Intermediate Dark period, which so suddenly
succeeds to what seemed the enduring stability and prosperity of the XIIth Dynasty, is one of those periods which
seem destined to be the despair of the historian, so utterly
impossible is it, not only to weave an interesting narrative
out of the hopeless tangle of thrums with which we are
presented by way of the facts of the time, but even to find
any single distinct clue which will carry us through more
than a year or two before it leaves us at a loose end.

"The darkness which followed", says Professor
Breasted, "is only the more obscure by contrast. The
country was broken up into petty kingdoms. . . . Without
any dynastic division which can be discerned, we find here
the remains of at least one hundred and eighteen names of
kings, whose ceaseless struggles to gain or to hold the throne
of the Pharaohs make up the obscure history of this dark
century and a half since the fall of the Twelfth Dynasty."

Mr. Weigall, indeed, says that it is not so: "The Thir-
teenth Dynasty presents an epoch which, in spite of the
usual statement to the contrary, is not at all obscure in its
general structure". It must be confessed, however, that
Mr. Weigall does not succeed in imparting his own confidence to the average reader of the seventy-five pages of
jig-saw puzzle work and squeezing of the figures of
Manetho with which he presents us as the history of the
period. A well-known Biblical critic once remarked of the
latter part of the prophecies of Zechariah: "Here one
enters into an impenetrable mist, from which at intervals
proceed the sounds of heavy firing". This is emphatically

the case with the period which begins with the first Pharaoh of the XIIIth Dynasty, and ends, more or less, with the rise of the XVIIth Dynasty.

It is not that there is any lack of kings to fill in the space; rather that there are far too many kings, about almost all of whom we know little or nothing. Manetho states that there were sixty kings of the XIIIth Dynasty and seventy-six of the XIVth, and Petrie has collected all the scraps of material which have survived from the reigns of scores of these. But to call the most of these so-called Pharaohs shadow-kings would be to do them far too much honour; nothing about them has enough solidity to cast even the most insignificant of shadows. A scarab here, a cylinder there, perhaps the occurrence of a cartouche on a private monument of the period, a fragment of a statue or a building block, with a broken line of inscription; such are the more solid materials surviving for the identifiable reigns, while for many of the royal names there is not even so much. One unusually well-furnished king has left us five scarabs; but on the other hand we know absolutely nothing else about him, and the only distinction between him and another king of the same name is that his scarabs are coarser, so that he is presumably to be placed later, when art had declined from earlier standards. To talk about writing the history of such monarchs, who, so far as we are concerned, are literally nonentities, is utterly to misuse terms. History, in any real sense of the word, is impossible under such conditions. A catalogue of royal names might be more or less possible; but of what use is such a catalogue to anybody?

So far as it is possible to make out anything clearly through the confusion of the period, it would seem that the general order of things was something like the following. When the direct line of the XIIth Dynasty came to a close with Amenemhat IV. and Queen Sebekneferura, the succession passed, quite legally, to the king who is known as Khutauira Ugaf, and who ranks as the first Pharaoh of the XIIIth Dynasty. His name, Ugaf, shows that he was not of the royal line. He may have been a noble, or a high court-official of commoner birth; such rises from the ranks became increasingly common with the great development

PLATE XXII

STATUE OF SEKHEM-SUAZ-TAUIRA ($p.$ 387)

From Sir Wallis Budge's "Egyptian Sculptures in the British Museum"

of the bureaucracy which has been already noticed. The legitimacy of his accession doubtless depended on his marriage to one of the royal princesses, who carried with them a more valid title than that of any prince except the chosen and associated heir. Whatever the basis of Ugaf's title may have been, he apparently found no difficulty in asserting his position, and his short reign was apparently carried out from the same centre, Itht-toui, which had been the seat of government during the XIIth Dynasty. Before long, however, Thebes, which had doubtless sub-mitted to see its princes transferring the seat of govern-ment to the north only because of its pride in the splendid line which it had bred, refused to acknowledge the right of this new line to rule all Egypt from Itht-toui. Very probably the Thebans had a junior prince of the royal line among them, and him they set up as Pharaoh of Upper Egypt, just as the Theban princes in the earlier dark period had asserted themselves against the weak Herakleopolitan Pharaohs. Several monarchs of this southern line of Pharaohs reigned at Thebes while the legitimate line was reigning at Itht-toui, among them a Senusert IV. and several Mentuhoteps; the persistence of the family names seeming to indicate that these sovereigns were genuine descendants of the princes of the XIth and XIIth Dynasties.

Meanwhile the line of Ugaf had been carrying on, seemingly not without its own difficulties, in the north. Ugaf had three successors, and then there occurs in the list a name, Aufni, or Yufni, which is as innocent of royal connection as that of the founder of the line himself. Yufni may therefore have been an usurper, or he may only have been another instance of a plebeian succeeding in virtue of his wife's royal descent. The favourite royal name among his successors is Sebekhetep, which means "Sebek is satis-fied", Sebek being the crocodile-god of the Fayum; and hence we can see that the royal connection with the Fayum which had been begun by the Pharaohs of the XIIth Dynasty was now maintained and emphasised, probably with results of doubtful value as regards the unity of the realm. The Theban Pharaohs continued to maintain themselves, and erected their statues as if they had been legitimate kings; but they were not so regarded by the makers of the royal lists, who only acknowledge the line of Itht-toui.

Thus Egypt had drifted back again into a state of division similar to that which prevailed under the Herakleopolitan Pharaohs—another example of that tendency to which the long straggling nature of the land always exposed her. For a short time, unity was restored by a vigorous king of the Itht-toui line, Sebekhetep I. (or II.?), otherwise known as Sekhemkhutauira. Sebekhetep apparently ruled over the whole land, from the Delta to the limits of Egyptian empire in Nubia; for he has left remains of his building work at Bubastis in the north-eastern Delta, and several inscriptions recording the height of the flood-Nile at Semneh, in continuation of the series of records which Amenemhat III. had begun at that Nubian frontier fortress. Sebekhetep's Semneh records are the last of the flood records at this place, and therefore the most complete specimen of them may be quoted—it is also the only extant historical inscription of his reign: "Height of the Nile of the year 3, under the Majesty of King Sekhemkhutauira, living forever; when the wearer of the royal seal, the commander of the army, Rensenb, was commanding in the fortress 'Mighty-is-Khakaura' (Senusert III.)".

This unification, however, depended, as such things have mostly depended in the east at all times, simply on the force of character of the ruling monarch, and after the interlude of Sebekhetep we seemingly drift back into the old state of disunion again, as there appear at Thebes three kings named Sebekemsaf, of whom one was destined to a strange and grim destiny some six centuries later. Indications of confusion and probably of forcible usurpation of the throne appear in such unusual Pharaonic names as those of Mermeshau, whose name means "Commander of the Army", and who may be assumed to have been a military usurper; Nehesi "The Negro", who was in all probability a commander of the Sudanese royal guards who used his position to climb to the throne; and Khenzer, whose name suggests a Babylonian origin. Another of the numerous Sebekheteps of the period, probably the third of the name, and known also by his Reed-and-Hornet name of Sekhem-suaz-tauira, seems to have exercised some sort of sovereignty over the whole of Egypt, as work of his has been found at Luxor and Karnak, at Koptos, north of Thebes, and at Gebelen and El Kab, south of Thebes; while his granite statue, now in the British Museum, was found at Bubastis, in the north-eastern Delta. It is by no means a contemptible piece of work, even for a time of decadence, and shows that the Egyptian sculptor of this troubled period could still command at least a good deal of the technical skill which had marked his predecessors of the XIIth Dynasty; but it shows a smallness of conception, with its pinched waist and over-small head, which puts it far below the superb work of the earlier period.

Another usurper, who bears the more seemly Egyptian name of Neferhotep, has no scruples whatsoever in informing us that he was of plebeian origin, and tells us quite plainly, on a tablet cut on the rocks at Aswan, that he was the son of a priest, and that not of a high rank, "the Divine Father Haenkhef". Of him we shall hear again directly, as he has left us a little more to tell us of his doings than most of his shadowy companions. He also appears to have held rule over the whole land; at least he has left traces as far south as Wady Halfa, while he has evidently complete command at Abydos, and is represented by cartouches or steles at Silsileh, Sehel, and Konosso, near the First Cataract. His black basalt statuette, now in the Bologna Museum, shows the continuation of the Fayum tradition, as it presents the adoration of the crocodile-god Sebek. The work of the statuette is again, as in the case of Sekhem-suaz-tauira's larger statue, of quite respectable quality, so far as technique goes; but the conception of the monarch is feeble in the extreme. Neferhotep had a brother, Menuazra, who also reigned, and one of the Sebekheteps seems to have been a third of the same family; so that the Divine Father Haenkhef, though his rank in the priesthood was never very high, managed to place his sons well. Their names are almost the last among the kings who have any claim to a rule over united Egypt. At Thebes, the old family name of the Antefs reappears for a while, and several Antefs ruled at Thebes, either at this time or towards the end of the Hyksos period, over a seemingly fairly prosperous Upper Egypt. The north was evidently a prey to civil war. A shadowy line of Delta Pharaohs ruled part of the country from Xois, and is reckoned by Manetho his XIVth Dynasty. One of the names on the list of these Xoite kings is that of Thetumra, who may just possibly be the king Timaios or Toutimaios, whose evil luck it was to have to meet the first inrush of the great invasion from the north-east which we know by the name of the Hyksos Conquest. And with that event or series of events, we begin to get not quite within sight of land historically, but at all events to a position where we can see rocks ahead for Egypt. But before we attempt to deal with the Hyksos, we have still to gather up the few scanty fragments of fact relating to the less shadowy of the many shadow-Pharaohs whom we have been passing in brief review.

The earliest of these who comes before us is the young king Fuabra Her-uat, whose tomb was discovered by de Morgan at Dahshur. The tomb had been rifled in ancient days, and everything in precious metal had been carried off; but there remained a number of sticks and sceptres, with insignia in gilded wood together with canopic jars. The most interesting part of the find, however, was the beautiful wooden statue of the *ka* of the king. He is represented as a young man absolutely naked; the eyes are inlaid, and the carving is fine and delicate. The figure is represented with the attributes of a god, and while the inscriptions in the other parts of the tomb give the king his personal name Her-uat, which means "The Wayfarer", on the shrine which contained the *ka* statue this name was omitted, and in its place was the name Hor, or Horus, within the royal cartouche, implying the identity of his *ka* with the divine son of Osiris. Nothing else is known of this young Pharaoh, who, if his statue may be trusted, was a young man of delicate and almost effeminate beauty. Even his place in the roll of Pharaohs is quite uncertain, and it has even been supposed that he may have been a son of

PLATE XXIII

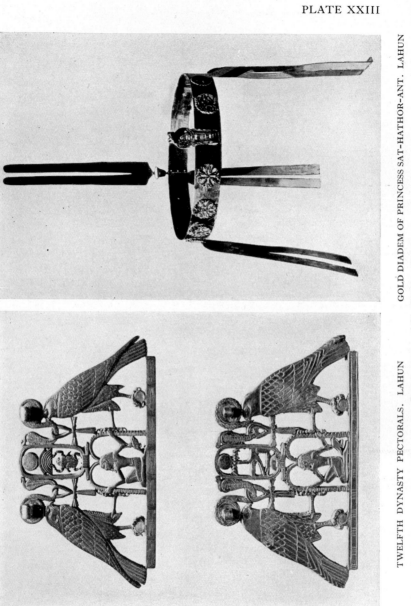

TWELFTH DYNASTY PECTORALS. LAHUN   GOLD DIADEM OF PRINCESS SAT-HATHOR-ANT. LAHUN

By permission of Sir Flinders Petrie

Amenemhat III.; but the style of his statue is quite incon-sistent with such a supposition. It shows none of the virility and power of XIIth Dynasty work, but is much more in keeping with other statues of the XIIIth. Besides, it is almost inconceivable that in a period so well known as that of the XIIth Dynasty no mention should be made of such a king, who, however short his life may have been, did actually reign.

The plebeian usurper, Neferhotep, has left us an inter-esting memorial of himself in the shape of a large stele from Abydos. Elsewhere, as we have seen, he tells us that he was the son of a priest, "the divine father Haenkhef", and the record on his stele shows that he inherited a pro-fessional zeal for the worship of the gods, coupled with the thoroughly priestly desire to secure that everything con-nected with the divine worship should be carried out ex-actly as in ancient days. His zeal in this respect led him to make a personal voyage to Abydos, where, by his special request, the image of Osiris was brought out on the river to meet him, and king and god returned together to the temple, enacting in the procession the Passion-play of the Death and Resurrection of Osiris, at which we have already seen Ikhernofret assisting in earlier days. The record of the whole investigation and journey is given with some detail as follows:

"His Majesty appeared upon the throne of Horus in the palace 'Bearer-of-Beauty'. His Majesty spake to the nobles and companions who were of his suite, the real scribes of the hieroglyphs, the masters of all secrets, say-ing: 'My heart hath desired to see the ancient writings of Atum; open ye for me a great investigation; let the god know concerning his creation, and concerning the fashion-ing of the gods, their offerings and their oblations .... let me know the god in his form, that I may fashion him as he was formerly, when they (*i.e.* the gods) made the statues in their council, in order to establish their monuments upon earth. They have given to me the inheritance of Ra as far as the circuit of the sun. I will add to what I find, and their love to me shall increase according to my obedience to their commands'.

"These companions said: 'That which thy *ka* hath commanded is that which happens, O King and Lord. Let Thy Majesty proceed to the libraries, and let Thy Majesty see every hieroglyph'.

"His Majesty proceeded to the library. His Majesty opened the rolls together with these companions. Lo His Majesty found the rolls of the House of Osiris, First of the Westerners, Lord of Abydos. His Majesty said to these companions: 'My Majesty hails my father, Osiris, First of the Westerners, Lord of Abydos. I will fashion him, his limbs, his face, his fingers, according to that which My Majesty has seen in the rolls (showing) his form as King of Upper and Lower Egypt, at his coming forth from the body of Nut'.

"His Majesty had the king's confidant, who was in His Majesty's following, called to him; His Majesty said to him: 'Betake thyself southward, with troops and marines. Sleep not, night nor day, until thou arrivest at Abydos; cause the First of the Westerners to proceed forth. May I make his monuments according to what was in the beginning.'

"These companions said: 'That which thou commandest happens, O King, our Lord; thou doest all in Abydos for thy father, First of the Westerners'.

"This official betook himself southward to do that which His Majesty commanded him. He arrived at Abydos. The majesty of this god came to the sacred barge of the Lord of Eternity; the banks of the river were flooded with the odours of Punt. . . . One came to inform His Majesty, saying, 'This god hath proceeded in peace'. His Majesty proceeded in the sacred ship together with this god, causing that sacred offerings be presented to his father, the First of the Westerners: myrrh . . . and sacred things for Osiris, First of the Westerners, in all his names . . . the opponents of the sacred barge were overthrown (part of the Passion-play was a mock battle with the priests who enacted the enemies of Osiris). Lo the majesty of this god appeared in procession, his ennead united with him; Upuat was before him, he opened the ways. Lo His Majesty caused that this god should proceed to his abode, that he should rest upon his throne in the Golden House; in order to fashion the beauty of his majesty and his ennead, and his offering-tables of every splendid costly stone of God's Land. Behold the king himself led the work upon them in gold; His Majesty was pure with the purity of a god."

Having accomplished his task with all the vigour of a President of an Ecclesiological Society, His Majesty delivered a concluding oration to the priests of Abydos: "Be ye watchful for the temple, look to the monuments which I have made. I put the eternal plan before me, I sought that which was useful for the future by putting this example in your hearts . . . because of my desire to establish my monuments in his temple, to perpetuate my contracts (for the upkeep of the services) in his house. His Majesty (Osiris) loves that which I have done for him. He rejoices over that which I have decreed to do; triumph has been given to him. I am his son, his protector, he giveth to me the inheritance of the earth. I am the king, great in strength, excellent in commandment. He shall not live who is hostile to me; he shall not breathe the air who revolts against me; his name shall not be among the living; his *ka* shall be seized before the officials; he shall be cast out from this god, he who shall disregard the command of My Majesty and those who shall not do according to this command of My Majesty, who shall not exalt me to this august god, who shall not honour that which I have done concerning his offerings, and give to me praise at every feast of this temple, of the entire priesthood of the sanctuary of this temple, and every office of Abydos. Behold My Majesty has made these monuments for my father Osiris, First of the Westerners, Lord of Abydos, because I so much loved him, more than all gods; that he might give to me a reward for this which I have done, consisting of millions of years. . . ."

So ends this curious record of this royal ecclesiastical antiquary of three and a half millenniums ago. He has left us another elaborate piece of futility in the shape of a decree forbidding all public access to a particularly sacred part of the cemetery of Abydos: "As for him whom anyone shall find within these stelai, whether he be a craftsman or a priest upon his business, he shall be branded. As for any official who shall have a tomb made for himself within this cemetery, he shall be reported, and the law shall be executed upon him, and on the necropolis custodian from this day onwards."

Neferhotep's records are not only of remarkable interest as witnessing to the early appearance of a well-known and usually quite harmless type—that of the ecclesiastical enthusiast to whom everything that is merely old is of supreme importance because of its age, whether it have any other merits or no, but also because he reveals to us the spirit which, in the end, was the destruction alike of Egyptian religion and Egyptian art. The blind worshippers of the past, whether in religion or in art, never seem to be able to understand that religion and art, if they are to remain living, must be perpetually growing away from the past, though they have their roots in it, and that to condemn them to exist merely as copyists of things which once were good and beautiful is to doom them to present barrenness and eventual death. It was because Egypt had too many Neferhoteps that her religion became the stiff and rigid corpse which not even the living breath of Atenism could do more than galvanise into a semblance of life for a few years, and which relapsed at once upon Akhenaten's death into its helpless round of barren ritual; it was because her artists had to depend upon so many Neferhoteps for their living, that her art, which had once such possibilities of living greatness, ended as the mere repetition of the cast-iron conventions which the pious king so industriously sought out and perpetuated.

Neferhotep would doubtless have made an admirable Anglo-Catholic had he lived in our own time; living when and as he did, he was a mistake, and a somewhat costly one for Egypt. He went back to Heliopolis, doubtless well pleased with himself, and equally without doubt the priests of Abydos did as they pleased with regard to his instructions; while the tomb-robbers of the necropolis no doubt rested their swag upon his boundary steles, and blessed him for having provided so convenient aids to their time-dishonoured trade. And the country which the king was doing his best to force back into blind adoration of its past was rapidly getting ready for the reception of a stock which was more alive to the conditions of the present. It seems almost incredible, at first sight, that the nation which had stood so strong and prosperous under the great kings of the XIIth Dynasty should have fallen so softly before the Hyksos invaders; but when one reads Neferhotep's record, the thing is more intelligible. A few Neferhoteps on the throne would take the heart out of any nation, as they have, under other conditions, taken the heart out of so many faiths and so many arts.

It is curious that it should be another usurper, bearing the Babylonian-sounding name of Khenzer, in whose reign we get another glimpse of the temple of Osiris at Abydos, where poor Neferhotep had, as he imagined, put everything right for all coming time. Apparently his efforts had not had the lasting effect which he had hoped for from them, for the record tells us of the need of the temple for cleansing and restoration, and, worst of all, Neferhotep's reforms are not so much as mentioned, the record going back to the work of Senusert I. as though our amiable royal ecclesiastic had never existed. The official concerned is the priest Amenisenb, "son of Emku, born of the matron Nebetyotef", whose stele is now in the Louvre. He has given us gossipy details of his commission, and of the rewards which came to him for his fidelity in the discharge of it. "The scribe of the vizier Senb, the son of the vizier, came to call me, by order of the vizier. So I went with him, and found the vizier Enkhu in his hall. Then this official laid upon me a command, saying: 'Behold it is commanded that thou cleanse this temple of Abydos. Artificers shall be given to thee for the contract thereof, together with the lay priesthood of the districts of the storehouse of offerings!'

"Then I cleansed it in the lower house and the upper house, on its walls, behind and within; and the painters filled up with colour and with paste, restoring that which the King of Upper and Lower Egypt, Kheperkara (Senusert I.), triumphant, made. Then came The-Protector-of-the-Oil-Tree to assume his place in this temple, while the deputy of the Chief Treasurer, Sionouris, followed him. (The cultus image with its guardian priest had evidently been removed from the temple while this spring-cleaning was going on). Then he thanked me greatly, beyond every-thing, saying: 'How prosperous is he who has done this for his god!' Then he gave to me a heap (of money) of 10 deben weight, and supplied me with dates and half an ox. Then came the official of —— downstream; then these works were seen; then was rejoicing thereat exceedingly, beyond everything."

Fortunately Amenisenb has seen fit to preserve for us the royal rescript in which his services on this occasion are commended, and in which he is rewarded with the post of permanent inspector of the temple of Abydos, and it is from this second stele that the name of the Pharaoh under whom he served is known. The inscription is in the follow-ing terms: "The Good God, Lord of the Two Lands, Lord of Offerings, King of Upper and Lower Egypt, Nebmaatra-Nebkhara, who is given life forever; Bodily Son of Ra, Khenzer, who is given life, stability, satisfaction forever. It was commanded to charge the chief of a priestly clan of Abydos, Amenisenb, triumphant, saying: 'Behold these works which thou hast done have been seen; the king praises thee, his *ka* praises thee. Spend thy good old age in this temple of thy god'. Then it was commanded to give to me the hind quarters of an ox, and it was commanded to charge me, saying: 'Conduct every inspection which takes place in this temple'. I did according to all that was commanded; I had every shrine of every god who is in this temple restored, their altars renewed with cedar, and the great offering-table which was in the presence. I executed my desire, it pleased my god; the king praised me."

So the worthy inspector of Abydos goes on his way, and we see him no more. We may hope that, as his king wished for him, he spent his "good old age" in the temple which he had tidied up, and that he passed into the closer keeping of Osiris before the evil days came which were lying ahead. He has given us one of the very few authentic glimpses of what was actually happening in this dark time; and it is somewhat surprising to see that in spite of what is evidently a disturbed succession, things go on much as usual in the internal administration, and that Pharaoh, however outlandish his name may be, is still able to send his servants on his errands unquestioned, and still claims the full title of Lord of the Two Lands. But that outlandish name seems ominous, and though we have no ground for connecting it with the coming of the Hyksos, it seems strange that a king whose name sounds of Babylon, and certainly not of Egypt, should be attending to the needs of the great sanctuary of the most Egyptian of gods.

Our next glimpse seems to bring us actually into touch with the hated invaders who humiliated Egypt in a manner never undergone before, and destined to leave a permanent mark on the consciousness of the nation, and even, for a while, to change its whole outlook towards the other peoples of the ancient world. It is not quite certain where we are to place the king Nebkheperura Antef, whose name is associated with the decree of Koptos, which is the document in question. Obviously he was of the ancient stock which had founded the Middle Kingdom in the days of the early XIth Dynasty; equally obviously his decree refers to a traitor within the Egyptian camp: but whether the traitor be a mere rebel, one of the many who found their allegiance sit lightly upon their shoulders in these days of usurpation, and had attempted a treachery to his Theban overlord which failed, or whether his guilt was even darker, and he had entered into treacherous dealings with the Hyksos invaders, it is impossible to say. It seems, however, that the probability lies on the latter side, and that we are to place the reign of this Antef of Thebes during the time when the Hyksos were gradually bringing the land under their sway, after the first rush of conquest had placed them in command of Lower Egypt. In this case, the danger must have been coming very near, as Koptos is only thirty miles north of Thebes, so that treachery like this, at his very door, must have hit the native Egyptian king very hard. The decree is a very remarkable one, absolutely unique in Egyptian history, and noteworthy almost as much for the penalties it does not proclaim as for those it does.

"The third year, month Phamenoth, day 25, of His Majesty the King of Upper and Lower Egypt, Nubkheperura, Son of Ra, Antef, who is given life, like Ra, forever. Decree of the king to the chancellor, prince of Koptos, Minemhat, the king's son, administrator of Koptos, Ka-nen, the chancellor Menkh-Min, the scribe of the temple Neferhetepur, all the garrison of Koptos, and all the officials of the temple,—Behold ye, this decree has been brought to you that ye may know that My Majesty has sent the scribe and divine chancellor of Amen, Amense, and the *semsu-hayt* Amen-user, to make inquisition in the temple of Min:—Whereas the officials of the temple of my father Min came to My Majesty to say that an evil thing is come to pass in this temple, even a harbouring of enemies by Teta, son of Minhotep (blasted be his name!):— Therefore let him be cast out upon the ground from the temple of my father Min, let him be driven from his office of the temple to the son of his son, and the heir of his heir; may they be cast abroad upon the earth, let his loaves and his sacred meat be seized, let his name not be remembered in this temple, as is done to one like him who has transgressed in the matter of an enemy to his god; let his writings (titles) in the temple of Min be destroyed, and in the government office on every roll likewise:—And every king and puissant ruler who shall forgive him, may he not receive the White Crown, or support the Red Crown, or sit upon the throne of the living Horus; let not the Two Diadems grant him favours as beloved of him; and every administrator or prince who shall approach the Lord to forgive him, let his people, his possessions, and his lands be given to the endowment of my father Min of Koptos; also let not any man of his circle, of the relations of his father or of his mother be raised to this office:—also let this office be given to the chancellor overseer in the palace, Minemhat, and let there be given to him its bread and its sacred meat, established unto him in writings in the temple of my father Min of Koptos, to the son of his son, and the heir of his heir."

It is a thousand pities that we have no certainty as to the occasion which called forth this extraordinary edict; but though certainty be unattainable, or at least unattained, the Hyksos application seems to be more suitable than any other. The document shows a considerable

PLATE XXIV

Cairo Museum

1. CORONET OF PRINCESS KHNUMIT
2. PECTORAL OF AMENEMHAT III, DAHSHUR
3. PECTORAL OF SENUSERT II, DAHSHUR

facility in cursing, and covers the ground with tolerable
thoroughness; but not the least remarkable feature about
it is the comparative lenity of the punishments which it
imposes. Whether the guilt involved was that of internal
rebellion, or the still deeper turpitude of dealing with
foreign enemies, the offence was high treason. One can
imagine how such a crime would have been dealt with by
certain other countries of the ancient east, in which death
would have been the least of the penalties meted out to the
traitor, and one does not need to imagine how he would
have been handled in our own land, say in Tudor times, or
even later. In Egypt, he is excommunicated, certainly, and
loses his rank and the emoluments of his office, the loss
extending "unto the third and fourth generation"; but
there is no hint of any bodily penalty, still less of the
ghastly horrors which were common in the near east, and
which our ancestors did not shrink from inflicting on the
traitor only three centuries ago, and even less. But then the
Egyptians were a civilised nation!

The Antef who was responsible for this excommunica-
tion of the traitor Teta has left a few more traces of his
existence than most of the shadow kings of this period. A
statuette shows him triumphing over Asiatics and negroes,
in the traditional manner of a more fortunate age; but
this is merely in accordance with tradition, and one may
suspect, in view of the Hyksos conquest, that his triumphs
in either kind were strictly limited. His tomb at Thebes
was once adorned with two small obelisks, $11\frac{1}{2}$ feet high,
bearing all his names and titles; these are now lying somewhere in the Nile, and it is unlikely that they will ever be
recovered. He had also the somewhat unusual luck, for a
Pharaoh, of lying undisturbed in his tomb for at least five
hundred years. In the great investigation of the royal
tombs at Thebes, made in the reign of Ramses IX., his
tomb was visited by the royal inspectors, and their report
showed that while he had not escaped an attempt upon his
rest, the robbers had come short of complete success.
"The monument of King Nubkheperura, Son of the Sun,
Antuf, was found to have been pierced by the hands of the
thieves, who had made a hole of two and a half cubits in its

surrounding wall, and a hole of one cubit in the great outer chamber of the sepulchre of the chief of the transport of offerings, Auri of Pa-amen, which is in ruins. The royal tomb was in good condition, the thieves not having been able to penetrate into it.

Our Antef's immunity was shared by his namesake and predecessor (presumable) Ra-seshes-up-maat Antef, whose tomb was thus reported upon by the Ramesside inspectors: "The monument of King Ra-seshesem-upu-ma, Son of the Sun, Antuf-aa. It was found to have been pierced by the hands of the thieves at the spot where the tablet of the monument is fixed. Examined on that day, it was found entire, the thieves not having been able to penetrate into it." What the thieves of three thousand years ago could not accomplish has been done, though in more seemly fashion, in modern days, and the gilded coffin of the king lies now in the British Museum, along with a pyramidion which bears his name, and which may have been the capstone of the pyramid which defeated the robbers; while the funeral box for holding his canopic jars is in the Louvre.

Other Pharaohs of the same period were not so lucky as the Antefs in escaping the gentle attentions of the Ramesside rascals, and one of the Sebekemsafs, who reigned at Thebes probably somewhat before the later Antefs, has furnished, together with his wife, the classical example of the way in which the Egyptian tomb-robber dealt with the remains of "the Good God" when he was lucky enough to come upon them. The sad fate of King Sebekemsaf and his wife Nubkhas, however, must be told not here, but when we come to the drama of the Royal Tombs in the Ramesside age.

Across all the welter of ephemeral and inadequate kings which had now been cursing Egypt for so long came a yet greater curse—the Hyksos invasion and conquest. It was an event which the Egyptians never forgot and never forgave to the descendants of the Asiatic invaders who had brought so great a humiliation upon the ancient glories of the Nile Valley. Moreover it was an event which filled the Egyptian mind with almost as much surprise as shame. That the worm should have turned and proved a destroy-

ing serpent—that the despised Sand-dwellers, over whose
barbaric appearance and customs Senusert I. and his
family had shrieked with amusement when they saw the
returned exile Sinuhe, should have trodden the ancient
civilisation of Egypt, with its immemorial refinements,
under their brutal feet: all this filled the Egyptian mind,
even centuries after the event, with a bewildered amazement which could only ascribe the disaster to the anger of
a hostile God. Manetho's precious fragment, preserved for
us by Josephus, has been perhaps oftener quoted than any
other piece of ancient history; but it must always be quoted
again in dealing with the events which it describes, and it
expresses perfectly, even after so many centuries, the per-
plexed astonishment, mixed with indignation, which was
the habitual attitude of the Egyptians towards the greatest
disaster of their history.

"We had once a king", says the Ptolemaic historian,
"whose name was Timaios. In his time it came to pass, I
know not how, that God was adverse to us, and there came
out of the East in an extraordinary manner men of ignoble
race, who had the temerity to invade our country, and
easily subdued it by force without a battle. And when they
had our rulers in their power, they burnt our cities and
demolished the temples of the gods, and used the inhabitants after a most barbarous manner, slaying some, and
leading the wives and children of others into captivity. At
length they made one of themselves king, whose name was
Salatis; he lived at Memphis, and made both the Upper
and Lower Countries tributary, and stationed garrisons
in the places best adapted for them. He chiefly aimed to
secure the eastern frontier, for he regarded with misgiving
the great power of the Assyrians, who, he foresaw, would
one day invade the kingdom. And, finding in the Saite
nome to the east of the Bubastite channel a city well
adapted for his purpose, which was called from some
ancient mythological reference, Avaris, he rebuilt it and
made it very strong with walls, and garrisoned it with a
force of two hundred and forty thousand men completely
armed. Thither Salatis repaired in summer, to collect his
tribute and pay his troops, and to exercise them so as to

strike terror into the foreigners. And when this man had reigned nineteen years, after him reigned another, called Bnon, for forty-four years; after him another, called Apakhnas, thirty-six years and seven months; after him Apophis, who reigned sixty-one years; and then Ianias, fifty years and one month. After all these reigned Assis forty-nine years and two months. These six were the first rulers among them, and during the whole period of their power they made war upon the Egyptians, being desirous of destroying them utterly."

For the moment we are not so much concerned with the matter of this most valuable statement as with the manner of it. "Men of ignoble race, who had the temerity to invade our country." "Goodness only knows how it happened", grumbles poor Manetho, as his forefathers had been grumbling for twelve hundred years. "God must have been angry with us." "I purified the temples", says Prince Mentuemhat of Thebes after the Assyrian conquest a thousand years after the Hyksos, "after there had been an invasion of unclean foreigners in the Southland." "Unclean foreigner" as a description of the magnificent Ashurbani-pal strikes one as scarcely adequate; perhaps "men of ignoble race" was scarcely more adequate as a description of the Desert princes. But just so would a cultured Chinaman of the mid-nineteenth century have described the foreign devils who had presumed to capture Peking and loot the Summer Palace.

What seemed so inexplicable to Manetho, however, has become less so to us to-day, in consequence of the new knowledge which has been accumulating of other great movements of the nations at this time. Perhaps God was adverse to the tumultuous Egypt of the time; He generally is adverse to a nation which cannot keep its house in order, until it has learned sense out of its disasters. But actually the great humiliation which befell Egypt was the repercussion of events which had been taking place for a long time now, and far enough away from the Nile Valley. Briefly, the invasion of Egypt was a consequence of the first appearance on the stage of the ancient East of the Indo-European race. A little before the time when the

XIIth Dynasty began its great work in Egypt, and Hammurabi his in Babylon, the Aryan intruders began to come down from Central Asia, and to press through Media upon the frontiers of Babylonia. In the time of Hammurabi's descendant, Samsu-ditana, Babylon was sacked and her power weakened by an astonishing feat of raiding on the part of the Hittites from Anatolia. Nothing could have better suited the game of the advancing Aryans, who forthwith pounced upon the wreck which the Hittites had left, and founded the Kassite dynasty of Babylonia, which lasted for six centuries of comparative uselessness. Other Aryan waves swept over Mesopotamia, and resulted in the formation of the anomalous kingdom of Mitanni, which played so important and unfortunate a part in the history of the eastern world six hundred years later. Nothing in the subsequent history of the Kassites in Babylon, or the Aryan barons in Mitanni, suggests that they conquered because of any inherent superiority which they possessed in the arts of either war or government, for their record, after the first impetus had passed, is singularly barren in both respects. But they had one inestimable advantage on the field of battle, which secured their triumph until the nations which they defeated had learned to copy their practice. They brought with them from Central Asia the weapon of warfare which was henceforth for nearly four thousand years to be one of the supreme deciding factors in warfare, until in our own time he appears to have been permanently superseded by mechanical substitutes—the war-horse. The appearance of "the ass from the east", with the swift war-chariot yoked to it, and the consequent facility of movement which was given to a striking force on the battlefield, decided the supremacy of the invaders almost at once. Such a displacement of peoples as was created by this great incursion of the Aryans could not possibly be without far-reaching consequences. The whole of the already fairly highly civilised region of Northern Syria (the Egyptian Naharina) was taken from its tenants, who were perforce obliged to find for themselves homes further south. They pressed down into Palestine, bringing with them the knowledge and use of the new weapon of warfare which had brought about their own expatriation, and quite possibly accompanied by some of the more ad-venturous of the Aryan invaders. Palestine could not hold them, and the desert can only support a limited number of nomads. Their only hope was to go further, since they had gone so far; and beyond the Isthmus of Suez lay the richest land of the ancient east, well-known already to many of the Sand-dwellers whom the advancing tide of invasion was carrying along with it.

The Egyptians, in their comparative seclusion, had learned nothing of the terrible new weapon which was now to be employed against them; in all probability, though they had been among the earliest of nations, if not the earliest, to use copper, they had no knowledge as yet of how to harden copper by alloying it with tin so as to make bronze; and the invaders, with bronze swords and spears, had therefore another signal advantage over the native Egyptian troops. Even so, it might have been possible for a united nation, under a great Pharaoh such as Senusert III., to have worn down the attack in the end. But Egypt was no longer united; and the three factors of her own dis-union, the use of the war-chariot and that of the bronze weapon against the copper proved swiftly decisive. Man-etho's "without a battle" need not be interpreted literally; but one can understand how little chance there was of the local levies of the various rival claimants to the proud title of Pharaoh looking their formidable opponents in the face once they had learned how heavily the dice were loaded against them.

The Delta and the lower part of the Nile Valley must have been speedily overrun. The upper valley would be a somewhat more difficult proposition, and it would seem as if the Theban princes of the old house of Antef held out against the invaders for some time; but the decree of ex-communication against the traitor Teta of Koptos shows that the conquerors were gaining a footing within thirty miles of Thebes itself. It does not appear that Thebes was ever absolutely overrun by them; but at least the situation, when the War of Independence began under Seqenenra III., was such that the Hyksos king in the north claimed suzerainty over the Theban in the south, and that the latter shook in his shoes whenever his overlord sent a truculent message to him, and could scarcely pluck up courage to defy him even when his requests were manifestly designed to provoke a quarrel.

The Egyptians called their conquerors *Hiqu-Khasut*, "Princes of the Deserts". This was already the standard title for the Beduin chiefs who were in the habit of visiting Egypt. Abishai, the leader of the thirty-seven Aamu who visited the nomarch Khnumhotep in the reign of Senusert II., is so named in the inscription at Beni-hasan. In later days the word *Khasut* was probably pronounced something like *Shos*, and Manetho, whose knowledge of the Beduin was not so much of the warlike horse-breeder and raider as of the tamer shepherd type which lives on the border of civilisation, mixed the older appellation with the general term for Beduin, *Shasu*. As the Shasu who were known to his time were mainly shepherds, the old Desert Princes of the Invasion became transformed into the Shepherd Princes of the Manethonian tradition.

As for the rest of Manetho's account of the invader, we may take it as genuinely historical, with the exception of his reference to the Assyrians as the enemies against whom the first Hyksos king provided his fortified camp. There Manetho was writing with the knowledge which comes after the event, and after Egypt had indeed known what it meant to be invaded by a race of warriors as much more terrible than the Hyksos as they were more terrible than any enemy whom the Egyptians had ever met; but if Salatis foresaw the rise of Assyrian power at his time of day, his remarkable gifts as a warrior must have been quite overshadowed by his endowments as a prophet. Otherwise, however, the statement seems quite reasonable. Nothing was more natural than that the Hyksos chiefs should hold the conquered country down by means of fortified posts such as the historian describes, and a place somewhere in the Delta was obviously the natural position for the central stronghold of the conquerors. Whether Avaris is to be identified with Pelusium, as some modern authorities consider probable, or with Tell el-Yehudiyeh, is still uncertain. The Egyptian equivalent for Avaris is *Het-uart*, "The House of the Leg", a curious name which points to the place having been the place of burial of one of the legs of Osiris after his dismemberment by Set; and this fact may lead in the end to certainty on the matter, should traces of such a sacred spot be found associated with any of the claimants to the name. Certainly there was a fortified camp of the kind described by Manetho, and belonging to this period, at Tell el-Yehudiyeh, which is otherwise in a position quite suited to the uses for which Avaris was created. The number which the historian assigns to its garrison is, of course, preposterous, and merely the customary way of indicating a large garrison. Salatis no more gathered 240,000 men in permanent garrison at Avaris than Aahmes gathered 400,000 to drive the Hyksos out; and, generally speaking, the huge estimates of the sizes of armies offered to us by ancient historians should be received with more than a little scepticism. Where the actual size of an Egyptian army is approximately known, as in the very important case of the battle of Kadesh, we find that it is a very different thing from the unmanageable numbers which the fertile imagination of the ancient chronicler has conjured up.

The barbarities to which Manetho refers were doubtless real enough, at least in the earlier days of the Hyksos domination. Had it not been so, it would be difficult to account for the extreme bitterness of feeling with which the Egyptians always regarded this period of shame and misery. Probably the conquerors were no more brutal than the average conqueror of ancient warfare, who was never in the habit of considering the feelings of the vanquished, except as they might heighten his pleasure in his conquest. One can imagine to some extent the shock it must have been to the representatives of an ancient and highly-developed civilisation, the culmination of whose prosperity was still comparatively recent, to see their land overrun by a fierce race of men who, to an Egyptian's eyes, must have seemed outer barbarians in dress, speech, and manners; their immemorial customs overthrown and scorned; their temples demolished or desecrated; and outlandish gods installed in place of Ra and Osiris. Even apart from exceptional cruelty, though cruelty was doubtless not lacking, such insults to national and religious feeling are the things which a proud people never forgets or forgives. That there was such destruction of sacred things on the part of the Hyksos is manifest from practically contemporary evidence, in the shape of the well-known inscription of Queen Hatshepsut at Speos Artemidos. "I have restored that which was ruins," says the great queen; "I have raised up that which was unfinished since the Aamu were in the midst of Avaris of the Northland, and the barbarians were in the midst of them, overthrowing that which was made, while they ruled in ignorance of Ra".

The conquest once complete, however, it may be presumed that the barbarities gradually ceased, as the Hyksos rulers became subdued to what they worked in. There is scarcely anything more remarkable or more constant in human history than the way in which the ancient native culture of a land gradually and insensibly imposes itself upon an alien race which has conquered the native inhabitants. The conquerors may be of a type widely distinct from the conquered race; they may have a well-established culture of their own: in the end the land and its traditions will wear down all such distinctions, and the conquerors, if not driven out again before the process of assimilation is complete, will finally become almost more native than the aboriginals over whom they have ruled. Such a process could not fail to produce its natural results in the case of a land so unique, and a culture so ancient, so imposing, and so rich as the Egyptian. It was not allowed to produce its final effects in the complete Egyptianising of one of the branches of the great Semitic stock, for the reaction of Egypt against the tyranny of the conquerors drove them out before the process was very far advanced; but there is evidence that it had definitely begun where it was natural that it should begin, on the throne, and that the later kings of the Hyksos were tending as nearly as they could to the adoption of Egyptian forms and practices.

The six Hyksos Pharaohs of Manetho's XVth Dynasty

are Salatis, Bnon or Beon, Apakhnas, Apophis, Iannias and Assis. Innumerable attempts have been made to identify these with some of the obscure Pharaohs of whom more or less insignificant relics actually survive; but on the whole each attempt has proved satisfactory only to its author, and has been promptly disowned by the next interpreter, who has proceeded to construct a quite different set of identifications. It seems pretty certain that Manetho's Apophis represents a name really borne by several Hyksos Pharaohs, of whom three Apepas or Apopis can be identified with more or less assurance. His Iannias may possibly be Khyan, who seems, as we shall see, to have been the most powerful and widely known of the Hyksos kings; but this identification is doubtful. Several kings bear names of obviously Semitic character, such as Yekeb-hal, "Jacob is God", Yekeb-ba'al, "Jacob is Lord", and Ant-hal, "Anath is God", though the meaning of these suggestive names is quite obscure, unless on the supposition of the existence of an otherwise unknown Semitic god, Jacob. Manetho's Assis may possibly be the king Shesha of whom scarabs exist; but this also is quite uncertain. Indeed it cannot be too clearly understood that identifications, in the present state of knowledge, are next to valueless, and are liable to be upset at any time by the emergence of new facts. In these circumstances, it seems better to make no further attempt of such a kind, but simply to content ourselves with the recital of the facts which are certainly known with regard to a few of the Hyksos sovereigns.

Even here, however, one is met at once with an element of uncertainty. It seems moderately certain that there were three Apepas or Apopis; but authorities disagree as to the order in which these should be placed. One of them must be the Apepa III. who was contemporary with the Theban vassal-king Seqenenra III., as the War of Independence began with the famous quarrel about the noise of the Theban hippopotami, which Apepa wished his Theban vassal to silence. But the Apepa III. of Petrie is Neb-khepesh-Ra, "Lord of the Scimitar of Ra", and it is to his Apepa II., Oa-qenen-ra, that he refers the quarrel with

Seqenenra. Petrie's Apepa III., the Lord of the Scimitar, is Hall's Apepa I., while Petrie's Apepa I., Oa-user-ra, is Hall's Apepa II. In the face of such division of opinion, which might be exemplified to a much greater extent, it is perhaps wisest merely to insist upon the salient fact that, however one may shuffle the Apepas in the pack, they are all clad in Egyptian garments and conform, with limitations, to Egyptian customs. One or other of them erected at Bubastis, in the Delta, "many columns and a gate of brass to this god", and left an inscription on red granite to that effect. It is to this Pharaoh's reign also that the famous Rhind Mathematical Papyrus belongs; while a lintel found at Gebelen also bears his name, Oa-user-ra. The fact that he conforms to Egyptian custom in dedicating temple work at Bubastis and Gebelen, together with the fact of a scientific papyrus being dated in his reign, would seem to suggest a place for this king late in the Hyksos period, when Egyptian customs had dominated the conquerors; but, on the other hand, the fact that he was able to do work at Gebelen, south of Thebes, rather suggests a position for him among the earlier Hyksos kings, who were masters of the whole land, than one among the later sovereigns, whose dominion was becoming more restricted. Accordingly, while Hall places our religious and scientific Apepa second among the three of the name, and late in the period, Petrie places him first, as we have seen, and is followed in this by Weigall. The fact of the assimilation of Egyptian ideas and practices remains, however the kings responsible for it may be placed. That the foreign kings still remained devoted, if not to alien gods, at least to gods who could be assimilated to one or other of their foreign deities, is witnessed to by the fine black granite altar of Apepa Oa-qenen-ra, which is dedicated to "the god Set, Lord of Avaris". At Tanis this same Apepa usurped the grey granite statue of a former usurping Pharaoh, the Mer-meshau, whose name, as we saw, means simply Commander of the Soldiers. The inscription which Apepa added to the soldier's statue runs: "Good God, Aa-qenen-ra, Son of the Sun, Apepa, giving life, beloved of Set". His devotion to Set, therefore, is a fixed fact about him, and as the Egyptian

Set was identified with the Semitic god Sutekh, this would seem to indicate that this Apepa Oa-qenen-ra is the Apepa III. who began the quarrel with the Theban line of Seqenenra. For the beginning of the famous folk-tale in the Sallier Papyrus tells us that "King Apepa took to him Sutekh for lord, and served not any god that was in the whole land, save only Sutekh. He built him a temple in good everlasting work. He had offerings made daily to Sutekh, and the councillors of the king stood there with flowers, even as is done for the temple of Ra-Harakhti."

By far the most impressive among the little known Hyksos Pharaohs is Khyan, of whom a number of relics survive, including the lower part of a black granite statue of fine workmanship from Bubastis, an inscribed block from Gebelen, various scarabs, and a gold ring, which is now at Leyden. It is noteworthy that, although he habitu-ally uses the regular titles of Egyptian royalty, he also sometimes calls himself *hiq-khasut*, or "prince of the deserts", showing that he had not forgotten "the hole of the pit from which he was digged". More interesting still is the Horus name which he uses. It is "Ank-adebu", or "Embracer of Territories", a title which may mean little or much according to the imagination of the person who reads it, and which, in this case, has been so interpreted as to mean a very great deal. The lid of an alabaster ointment box found at Knossos bears his name, and so also does a small stone lion found at Baghdad. These two finds, of course, do not in the least necessarily mean that Khyan held power over either Crete or Baghdad, and either sup-position is in the highest degree improbable. Yet at least the existence of such inscribed articles at points so far dis-tant from one another is evidence of trade communica-tions over a very wide stretch of country, and points to the probability of this king's position in Egypt being thoroughly consolidated.

Together with the unusual Horus-name of the king, it has inspired Professor Breasted with "the vision of a vanished empire which once stretched from the Euphrates to the first cataract of the Nile, an empire of which all other evidence has perished, for the reason that Avaris, the capital of its rulers, was in the Delta, where, like so many other Delta cities, it suffered a destruction so complete that we cannot even locate the spot on which it once stood". The suggestion is a fascinating one; but it ought to be said that there is absolutely no evidence in its favour beyond what has been stated already. It is true that the Hyksos, when expelled from Egypt, retreated into Palestine; they had nowhere else to retreat to; true also that they were able to maintain themselves against the victorious Egyptians there for several years. But this is no evidence that they were merely falling back upon the Asiatic portion of their imaginary empire, but merely of the fact that, fighting in a friendly country and among men of their own race, they provided the Egyptians, as yet unskilled in siege warfare, and never at their best masters of it, as the Assyrians were, with a tough nut to crack. Nothing was more natural in the circumstances. Khyan was no doubt a powerful and prosperous king; but the kings of the east, and perhaps especially those of the race to which he belonged, were too generous to themselves in the use of ample titles for us to be able to concede to him this vast unknown empire on the strength of the fact that he called himself "Embracer of Territories", and that two articles bearing his name eventually reached Knossos and Baghdad in the ordinary course of trade circulation.

Nothing has been said so far of the much canvassed connection between the Hyksos domination of Egypt and the Hebrew residence and subsequent oppression in the land and their Exodus from it. Nor will much be said now, for the simple reason that to the present writer it does not seem that the materials for forming any definite conclusions on the points in dispute are really available. Up to the year 1896, when Petrie excavated the funerary temple of Merenptah at Thebes, and found the black granite stele with the long-looked-for mention of the Children of Israel, there was a moderately comfortable acceptance of the theory that the Hebrews entered Egypt at Joseph's invitation under one of the later Hyksos Pharaohs, which would account for their favourable reception as Semites, and for other points in the Biblical narrative, that their oppression culminated under Ramses II., the most grandiose of Egyptian builder Pharaohs, and that their Exodus took place during the reign of his son and successor, Merenptah. Petrie's discovery, which showed us Israelites unmistakably in Palestine and established there in Merenptah's time, gave a severe blow to this view, which at once shook the confidence of many in it. As the Tell el-Amarna tablets came to be more closely studied, the resemblance between the Hebrew conquest of Palestine and the advance of the Habiru, as described in the Amarna correspondence, was insisted upon with more and more confidence, until at last it became the dominating view that the Habiru actually represent the conquering Hebrews, and that the Exodus must therefore have taken place about the reign of Amenhotep II., or at least two centuries earlier than the previously accepted date.

Within recent years the general acceptance of this date, round about 1420, has been on the wane. The discoveries at Beth-shean have revealed the thoroughness of the Egyptian hold upon Palestine up to a period far later than that of the Exodus as fixed in the early XVIIIth Dynasty, and have rendered it increasingly difficult to accept the Habiru as anything like adequate representatives of the Hebrew conquerors; and new views have been emerging which, if accepted, would be destructive of both of the older theories. Thus Dr. H. R. Hall still maintains the view which he stated in 1913, that the Exodus and the expulsion of the Hyksos are the same event, viewed from the Hebrew and the Egyptian standpoints respectively; while Dr. Stanley Cook carries this process of identification a stage further back, and suggests that it is possible that "the descent of Jacob or Israel into Egypt . . . represents the Biblical writers' idea of the Hyksos invasion". A further element of confusion is introduced by Mr. Weigall's theory that the Exodus took place in the reign of Tutankhamen, or 1346 B.C.

What is to be made out of this welter of mutually contradictory views? Not much more, I think, than Professor Macalister has said in his summary of the problem: "To sum up, we have three possible correlations of the Exodus story with historical events which excavation in Egypt has revealed to us; but all three are involved in difficulties, through which without further light it is impossible to see our way. If we take the Hyksos expulsion as representing the Exodus, we shall find it impossible to explain the condition of things which exists in the Tell-el-Amarna period with any conservation of the Biblical story whatsoever. If we choose the Amarna period as being the time of the Exodus, the details will be found quite irreconcilable, although the broad outlines are not dissimilar. If we return to the old theory of Ramessu II. and Merneptah, we must explain the 'Israel' stele of Merneptah in some more satisfactory way than has yet been discovered, and we must also explain how the Israelites hoped to get away from the sway of an oppressor who maintained a great fortress in the middle of the land to which they were fleeing."

To add any further discrepant theories to the already more than sufficient number extant would be both vain and useless. May it not be that we have been making the mistake of attempting to treat as a single event, occurring at a definite date in history, something which was in reality not an event, but a process, which went on at intervals during a very considerable period of time, and of which the event which the Hebrews knew as the Exodus was but the culmination? It cannot for a moment be supposed that the Hebrew scriptures give us the whole history of the race; and it is quite evident from other sources that a vast deal happened to men of the Hebrew stock in Palestine, long before the time of Moses and Joshua, of which the Biblical documents have left us no account. For the correlation of the Biblical narrative with the facts as exploration has gradually been revealing them to us in Palestine and Egypt we must wait until so much more has been revealed as will clear up the apparent discrepancies between the two sources. The one thing which seems reasonably certain is that no single one of the present theories contains more than a part of the truth.

The later part of the Hyksos period, which embraced Manetho's XVIth Dynasty, the six great early Hyksos princes having constituted his XVth, appears to have been, on the whole, marked by the gradual decline of the oppressors' power from the high-water mark which it had reached under great kings like Khyan. Apepa II. still possessed sufficient power to undertake important work at Gebelen, and to make the Theban Pharaoh, Seqenenra, tremulously apologetic when the Hyksos showed signs of wishing to pick a quarrel with him; but it is evident that the oppressors made the mistake of deferring the quarrel too long, and that they found, when at last they had forced the native princes into war, that it was too late to do what they might have done with comparative ease at an earlier date. Even as it was, the struggle was a long and desperate one, in which at least one of the Theban princes met his death, and the doubtful nature of the strife shows that Seqenenra had reason for his hesitation in taking up Apepa's challenge; but from the nature of the case the struggle was one in which, if the Hyksos did not succeed speedily, they could not hope to succeed at all. Their resources, as an alien tyranny within a populous and hostile state, were bound to diminish as the contest dragged along; while those of their opponents naturally increased. The struggle may have lasted for half a century, with greater or less intensity; but at last it was brought to a close with the capture of Avaris, and the hated yoke was broken from the necks of the Egyptians. The story of the contest, however, must be left for another chapter.

CHAPTER XIX

THE WAR OF INDEPENDENCE

FOR our account of the events which finally led to the expulsion of the Hyksos overlords of Egypt, we are indebted to a schoolboy's exercise written some three hundred and fifty years later than the incidents which it professes to describe. The fragment of Papyrus Sallier i. 1-3, now in the British Museum, which preserves the story, is in the condition which so often exasperates the student of ancient records. There are long gaps in the surviving part of the narrative; even where it is fairly intact "it has been sadly corrupted by the ignorant schoolboy who had to copy it out", and it breaks off suddenly in the most interesting part of the story with that instinct for an exciting situation which so often characterises the breaks in our papyri, and which has survived so notably among the editors of such magazines as run serial stories. Notwithstanding all these defects, the narrative of Papyrus Sallier i. is of supreme interest, as giving us the folk-tale which was current among the Egyptians themselves with regard to the manner in which the final rupture came about between their tyrants and the native prince of Thebes, who was the protagonist in the struggle for independence. It is not history, but it embodies, if not the literal truth about what happened, at least the spirit of the series of events which led to the outbreak of war.

Here, at all events, is what the Egyptians of the time of Merenptah of the XIXth Dynasty (1230 B.C.) believed to have happened in the time of Seqenenra, the native prince of Thebes, who was ruling as vassal to the Hyksos Pharaoh Apepa, somewhere about 1595 B.C. It may be prefaced by a few words of explanation, as the lacunae in the text leave

413

the course of events somewhat obscure here and there. What is obvious is that the Hyksos Pharaoh had begun to feel his position somewhat uncomfortable. The Theban prince, though he still paid his tribute, and was very deferential to his overlord, was becoming too strong for Apepa's peace of mind, and it was advisable to teach him his place, and put upon him a humiliation which would destroy his prestige in the eyes of the nation for the time being. Accordingly, after taking council with his wise men, Apepa sends to Thebes a request so ridiculous that it could only be viewed as being a pretext for the beginning of a quarrel. If Seqenenra tried to take any steps to meet the request he would only succeed in making himself look like a fool, for the request was manifestly an impossible one. If, on the other hand, he dismissed the complaint, Apepa had gained his point and succeeded in establishing a *casus belli*.

"Now it came to pass", says the papyrus, "that the land of Egypt was in distress and there was no supreme king. —— As for King Seqenenra, he was ruler in the Southern City (Thebes)——Apepa was in Avaris, and the whole land paid him tribute and dues. The south paid tribute to him, likewise the north, with all the goodly products of the Delta.

"Now King Apepa took to himself Sutekh (an Asiatic variant of the Egyptian god Set) as lord, and served not any god that was in the whole land save only Sutekh. He built for him a temple in good everlasting work. Offerings were made daily to Sutekh, and the councillors of the king came with flowers, even as is done for the temple of Ra-Harakhti."

The details of the next part of the story are much interrupted and confused. We have evidently the calling of a council by Apepa, at which his wise men advise him to make a complaint about the noise of the hippopotami in the pool at Thebes, which was robbing him of sleep. They also remark, however, that King Seqenenra of Thebes has Amen on his side; so that there is manifestly a rivalry, not only between the two kings, but also between the two gods. "Amen with him as protector," the papyrus goes on, "he relieth not on any god that is in the whole land, saving only

Amen-Ra, King of Gods." Apepa takes the advice of his councillors, and the narrative proceeds without undue interruption from this point to the disastrous break which cuts us off just where the interest is culminating:

"Now, many days after this, King Apepa sent to the Prince of the Southern City concerning the accusation which his scribes and wise men had spoken about him. And the messenger of King Apepa reached the Prince of the Southern City, and they took him into the presence of the Prince of the Southern City. And One (*i.e.* Seqenenra, the usual Egyptian phrase for royalty) said to the messenger of King Apepa: 'What is thy message to the Southern City; how didst thou venture to make this journey?' And the messenger said unto him: 'King Apepa sends to thee to say: "Give orders that the hippopotamus-pool which is in the flowing spring of the city be abandoned; for they do not allow sleep to come to me either by day or by night; but their noise is in mine ear"'.

"Then the Prince of the Southern City remained silent and wept a long time, for he did not know how to return answer to the messenger of King Apepa. And the Prince of the Southern City said unto him: 'How did thy lord come to hear of the pool which is in the flowing spring of the Southern City?' And the messenger said unto him —— 'the matter concerning which he sent unto thee?' And the Prince of the Southern City caused the messenger of King Apepa to be tended with all kinds of good things, meat, cakes —— And the Prince of the Southern City said unto him: 'Return thou to King Apepa thy lord —— whatsoever thou sayest unto him, I will do it, when thou comest' —— And the messenger of King Apepa set out on his journey to the place where his lord was.

"Then the Prince of the Southern City caused to be summoned his great officers, and likewise all the chief soldiers that he had, and he repeated to them the accusation concerning which King Apepa had sent unto him. They were silent for a long time with one accord, neither knew they how to answer him, whether good or bad. And King Apepa sent to——"

Here, unfortunately, our exasperating papyrus breaks

off. The schoolmaster summoned his scholar to the copying of some model letters, "a style of composition", to use the words of Battiscombe Gunn and Alan Gardiner, "doubtless more educationally profitable, but to the modern reader considerably less interesting", and we are left with the picture of poor King Seqenenra and his great men sitting in dumb distress gazing into vacancy, conscious that King Apepa was making them look very foolish; conscious also of the fact that he had succeeded in putting them into a very awkward hole, and that the only way out was by fighting, but uncommonly unwilling to begin.

Of course, as we have seen, all this is not history; one can only wish that history were half as picturesque as this. "The preposterous *casus belli*," says Breasted, "the complaint of Apophis in the Delta that he was disturbed by the noise of the Theban hippopotami, is folk-history, a wave mark among the people, left by the tide which the Hyksos war set in motion." In fact, the story belongs to the same category as the challenge which the King of the Ethiopians sent to the Pharaoh Usimares in the second story of Setna-Khaemuast, and which was met by the success of the young Senosiris in divining the contents of the sealed letter, or (with a still greater degree of resemblance) the riddle which the Pharaoh Nectanebo sent to Lycerus, King of Babylon, about the Egyptian mares which conceived at the neighing of the horses in Babylon, and which was solved, or rather evaded, by the ready wit of Aesop the Phrygian.

At the same time, there can be little doubt that the old folk-tale has actually preserved for us the true spirit of the situation. The details which it gives are doubtless quite imaginary, as well as preposterous; but the reality which lies behind them is that the situation, as between the Hyksos king and his vassal of Thebes, had gradually been growing more and more strained, that Apepa felt the need of bringing things to a head, and that he was not too scrupulous in the means which he employed with a view to the accomplishment of his end. A policy of pin-pricks has not infrequently been adopted by a power which wished to force a rival into war; and such a policy is obviously what is suggested by the romance of the splashing of the hippopotami. One way or another the Hyksos king felt that he must provoke his vassal into a premature rebellion, so that he might have an opportunity of crushing him before it was too late. Unfortunately for Apepa, he found that he had delayed too long, and that the Thebans, almost ludicrously unwilling as they were to begin the strife, were too hard for him once they had entered upon it.

For the details of the outbreak of war, and of the earlier campaigns, we are left entirely without evidence. The one fact which may conceivably indicate to us something of the bitter nature of the struggle is the condition of the mummy of Seqenenra, which was one of those found in the great *cache* at Der el-Bahri in 1881. The patriot king obviously met with a violent death—in fact, the actual manner in which he was stricken down and in which his wounds were inflicted can be reconstituted by the examination of his body. Maspero's summary may be quoted: "Two or three men, whether assassins or soldiers, must have surrounded and despatched him before help was available. A blow from an axe must have severed part of his left cheek, exposed the teeth, fractured the jaw, and sent him senseless to the ground; another blow must have seriously injured the skull, and a dagger or javelin has cut open the forehead on the right side, a little above the eye. His body must have remained lying where it fell for some time. When found, decomposition had set in, and the embalming had to be hastily performed as best it might." Altogether, the mummy is one of the grimmest sights of a somewhat gruesome gathering which has now wisely been withdrawn from public view. The question as to whether the king's death was due to assassination or to battle is undetermined and indeterminable; but the probabilities seem to point in the direction of the more honourable alternative. There appears to be no reason whatever to invoke the otherwise quite unvouched-for existence of a palace plot, when we know already of a quite adequate reason for the violent death of the king in the shape of his strife with the hereditary enemies of his people. The very fact of the hasty and imperfect wrapping of the corpse, which has been used as an argument in favour of the assassination theory, actually points in the other direction. The fortunes of a stubbornly contested battlefield may well have made it impossible to attend to the due rites of sepulture until the decomposition which Maspero notes had set in, as it would speedily do in a hot climate; and the hasty wrapping is just what might have been expected under the conditions of a strenuous conflict.

It would thus appear that poor Seqenenra's hesitation as to meeting the provocation of his overlord was justified, though we need not suppose that the Hyksos arms were victorious in the first encounters. The fact that the king's body was rescued and preserved at all, however rudely, rather suggests that the Egyptian troops had at least remained masters of the field of battle. But it is also plain that the struggle was of an obstinate and long-drawn-out character, and that for a considerable period there was comparatively little sign, on the Egyptian part, of the triumphant success which ultimately fell to the champions of national independence. At all events we have evidence that in the reign of the next king, Kames, who succeeded to the throne and the quarrel of Seqenenra, the position of the native Egyptian sovereign was such as to be felt by him as deeply humiliating, and to drive him on, much against the will of his councillors, to make a further attempt to free himself from the irksome conditions which the fortunes of war had so far imposed upon him.

Our information on this point we owe, once more, to the writing-board of an Egyptian schoolboy, which was discovered during the excavations of the late Earl of Carnarvon in 1908, among the rubbish near the mouth of a plundered tomb not far from the entrance to the Der el-Bahri valley. But though it be merely a scholastic exercise, this document stands on a very different footing from the narrative of the splashing of the hippopotami in Papyrus Sallier i. It is in all probability a direct copy from a stele of victory set up by King Kames himself, and may have been written within fifty years of the events which it commemorates. It is thus, to all appearance, an historical document of the first class, and its intrinsic interest is heightened by the vigorous and unconventional language which is used by the king in his account of his council, and of the war which followed it. It is therefore presented here in full in a version which makes use of that of Gardiner and that of Erman, as the one or the other seems best to express the sense.

"Year III., Horus 'Manifest-on-His-Throne', Two Goddesses 'Repeating-Monuments', Horus of Gold 'Making-Content-the-Two-Lands', King of Upper and Lower Egypt Uazkheperra, Son of Ra, Kames, given life for ever and ever; beloved of Amenra, Lord of Karnak.

"The strong king in Thebes, Kames, given life for ever, was an excellent king, and Ra caused him to be king in very deed, and handed over power to him in very sooth. Now His Majesty spake thus in his palace to the council of his grandees who were of his following: 'I should like to know what use my power is to me, when there is one prince sitting in Avaris and another in Kush, while I sit cheek by jowl with an Asiatic and a Nigger! Each hath his slice of Egypt, and divides the land with me—as far as Memphis, on the water of Egypt. Behold he (*i.e.* the Hyksos enemy) holdeth Shmun (Hermopolis), and no man standeth against him, being wasted by the imposts of the Beduin. I will grapple with him and rip open his belly; for my desire is to deliver Egypt and to smite the Asiatics.'

"But the great men of his council said thus: 'Behold, even if it is true that the Asiatics have advanced as far as Cusae, and have put out their tongues all together at us, yet we are in quietness, holding our own part of Egypt. Elephantine is strong, and the midlands are with us as far as Cusae. Men till for us the finest of their land; our cattle are in the papyrus marshes; spelt is trodden out for our swine, and our oxen are not taken away. He (the Hyksos king) hath the land of the Asiatics and we have Egypt. But if any man cometh up-river and attacketh us, him we will oppose.'

"And they were displeasing to the heart of His Majesty: 'As to this counsel of yours, it is wrong, and I will fight with these Asiatics, for the whole land weepeth —— Men shall hail me as the mighty ruler in Thebes, Kames, the Protector of Egypt.'"

Kames now gives us his own personal narrative of the fighting which followed upon his bold decision: "Then sailed I downstream as a champion to overthrow the Asiatics by the command of Amen, wise of counsel. My brave army marched before me like a blast of fire; troops of Mazoi were our vanguard in order to spy out the Beduin and to destroy their lairs. East and West brought fat and wine, and the host abounded in victuals everywhere. I sent on a strong troop of Mazoi in advance, and I abode on guard in order to coop up Teta, the son of Pepy, within Nefrusi (a city a few miles north of Hermopolis). I was not going to allow him to escape, and I held off the Asiatics——

"I passed the night in my ship with gladsome heart. When day dawned I was on him like an hawk. When the time of perfuming the mouth came (breakfast-time: poor Teta was evidently surprised at his morning meal) I over-threw him, I destroyed his wall, I slew his folk. His wife I caused to go down to the river-bank (as a captive). My soldiers were like lions over their prey, with slaves, herds, fat and honey, dividing up the possessions (of the enemy) with joyful hearts. The district of Nefrusi yielded; it was no great business for us to break its spirit. The —— Pershak was in a panic when I reached it; their horses had fled within. The garrison—— "

Here the narrative suddenly breaks off, leaving us uncertain as to the extent of the triumph of Kames, and whether he at once attacked Memphis, or left it for a future campaign. It is tempting to recall, in connection with the discomfiture of "Teta, son of Pepy", the treachery of Teta, son of Minhotep, in the reign of Khenzer; but there can be no real connection between the two enemies of Egypt, and the probability is that Teta, son of Pepy, was a son of the Hyksos king Apepa, who may by now have been wishing that he had not sent that message about the splashing of the hippopotami. On the whole, it seems likely that the work of Kames in delivering his country from the oppression of the Hyksos was successful to the extent that Middle Egypt passed into the hands of the

Theban prince almost entirely. The fact that no capture of
Memphis is mentioned in the autobiography of Aahmes of
El-Kab, to which we have now to turn, and that the old
soldier mentions that the name of one of his ships was
"Shining-in-Memphis", or "Manifestation-in-Memphis",
would seem to suggest that the great city may have been
captured by Kames before the time of which the veteran
is writing; but this is quite uncertain, and no other materials
which might settle the question are known to exist. The
reign of Kames, whether it was more or less successful,
can only have been a short one; and when his early death
(whether in battle or otherwise is not known) placed the
sceptre in the hands of his son (?) Aahmes I., the young
king succeeded also to the long and strenuous task of
completing the expulsion of the national enemy.

Nor were the troubles of Aahmes confined to his
northern frontier. We have already seen from the blunt
speech of Kames to his council that there was trouble also
in Nubia, where a powerful native prince claimed equality
with the Theban Pharaoh. "I sit cheek by jowl with an
Asiatic and a Nigger. Each hath his slice of Egypt." This
undesirable condition of things, with an enemy on both of
his frontiers, continued during all the struggle of Aahmes
with the Hyksos, and it was only after the completion of
his triumph over his northern enemy by the capture of
Sharuhen in Palestine that he was able to deal with the
southern pretender to sovereignty, whom he defeated
"with great slaughter". He had also to deal with more than
one rebellion within his own borders before the land finally
settled down to liberty and prosperity under his leadership. For all these facts, our chief and, indeed, almost our
sole informant is the old Admiral Aahmes, son of Baba and
the lady Abana of El-Kab, who has left us his autobiography on the walls of his rock-tomb in his native city,
some fifty miles south of Thebes. His story is as follows:

"The Chief of the Sailors, Aahmes, son of Abana,
justified (Aahmes, as usual, mentions his mother first of
his parents). He says: 'I speak to you, all men; I will cause
you to know the honours which have come to me. I have
been rewarded with the Gold (the technical phrase for the

reward of valour) seven times in the sight of the whole land, and with men slaves and women slaves in like manner, and how I have been endowed with many fields (sixty-seven acres, as Gunn and Gardiner reckon; so that the old sailor's endowments were pretty modest after all). For the fame of a valiant man lies in what he has done; it shall not perish in this land forever.'

"Thus he speaks: 'I was brought up in the town of Nekheb (El-Kab), my father being a soldier of the King of Upper and Lower Egypt, Seqenenra, justified, whose name was Baba, son of Royenet. I began to serve as soldier in his stead, in the ship, "The Wild Bull", in the time of the Lord of the Two Lands, Nebpehtira (Aahmes I.), justified, when I was a youngster, and had not taken a wife, but was sleeping in a sailor's net hammock. Now, when I had set up a household I was appointed to the ship "Northern" because I was valiant (or perhaps "to the northern fleet" to serve against the Hyksos, his previous service having been on the upper river); and I used to accompany His Majesty on foot when he rode abroad in his chariot. One sat down before the city of Avaris; I showed valour on foot in His Majesty's presence; whereupon I was promoted to the ship "Shining-in-Memphis".

"Fighting followed on the water in the canal Pazedku of Avaris; I made a capture, and brought away (also) a hand. It was reported to the King's Remembrancer, and the Gold of Valour was given to me. Once more there was fighting in this place; I made a second capture there and brought away a hand. And the Gold of Valour was given to me for the second time.

"Now, when they fought in this Egypt, south of this town (Avaris), I brought off a male living prisoner. I went down into the water—he was taken prisoner on the city side—and I carried him over the water with me. It was reported to the King's Remembrancer, and thereupon, behold I was rewarded with the Gold afresh.

"One (Pharaoh) captured Avaris; I took captive there one man, three women; total, four heads. His Majesty gave them to me for slaves. One besieged Sharuhen for three years, and when His Majesty spoiled it I carried away spoil thence: two women and a hand. One gave me the Gold of Valour, and behold my spoil was given to me for slaves."

So far the old sailor of El-Kab, who has now brought his narrative down to the point at which the Hyksos had finally been driven out of Egypt, and were even worried out of their last stronghold in Palestine. Later we shall have to follow him as he traces the fortunes of his Pharaoh in Nubia, and in dealing with internal rebellion; meanwhile he has carried us to where the Hyksos disappear from history as an organised unit. They were not, of course, exterminated, and no doubt many of them and of their descendants were among the enemies who made Palestine and Syria uncomfortable for the conquering Pharaohs of the XVIIIth Dynasty; but as a ruling race they vanish with the captures of Avaris and Sharuhen. It is perhaps unfortunate that we have no more complete account of this disappearance of a race whose triumphs and overthrows have for long constituted one of the enigmas and romances of ancient history than the narrative of a tarry old sailor, sitting in his old age before his cottage at El-Kab, watching the crops ripen on the sixty-seven acres which he had so hardly won, and counting on his battered old fingers the number of captives he had taken, and the number of times he had won the Egyptian Victoria Cross; but there is actually a savour of reality and verisimilitude about the veteran's unvarnished tale that is often lacking in much more pretentious historical documents, and one has the feeling that when Aahmes, son of Abana, says that such and such things happened so, he is telling the plain truth, so far as it came under his observation. Egyptian history is fortunate in having more than one of such simple narratives of events by men who were eye-witnesses and participants in what they narrate; the only pity is that it has not a great many more of them.

Thus Egypt was delivered at last from the stranglehold of the Old Man of the Sea who had sat upon her shoulders for so long. The war which ended in the expulsion of the Hyksos probably lasted, doubtless with more or less peaceful intervals due to the exhaustion of the combatants, for forty-five or fifty years. Manetho's version of the great event would seem to indicate that the siege of Avaris was ended by a compromise, under which the Hyksos king and his people had permission to withdraw upon the terms of a capitulation from their last stronghold into Palestine. The narrative of Admiral Aahmes, however, seems to indicate quite plainly that the place was captured by storm, and the fact that the fleeing Hyksos were pursued by King Aahmes into Palestine, where their fortress of Sharuhen was reduced after a lengthy siege, points in the same direction. If there had been an evacuation of Egypt on agreed terms, it is difficult to see how the raid into Palestine and the siege of Sharuhen should have taken place; but they fall into place quite naturally as the conclusion of a victorious campaign, and indeed may be regarded as natural measures for the young Pharaoh to take for the protection of the new-won liberties of his land.

One result of the long struggle was natural enough, though probably it was foreseen by no one. The native Egyptian was by no means naturally a soldier, as were some of his rival races of the ancient East. He had indeed reason, adequate or inadequate, to do a good deal of more or less desultory fighting in all ages, and the attempt to picture him as an early pacifist, who accomplished wonders of development intellectually and materially because he was left in peace to do his work, and left other peoples in peace to do theirs is a ludicrous misrepresentation of the facts of the case, as he himself has recorded them. But, at the same time, he was never of the type which delights in fighting for fighting's sake, and his predatory instincts were mostly gratified in places and on peoples where there was not likely to be any very strong resistance. The long struggle with the Hyksos, however, wrought a change for a time. A generation grew up which had never known anything but a condition of warfare, and which actually found that war was an exciting, and, under victorious conditions, even a profitable form of amusement, and which, besides, carried with it into warfare the convenient consciousness that it was avenging ancient national wrongs by the invasion of the countries from which the hated Hyksos tyrants had come. It was this generation which began the process that resulted in the appearance of Egypt on the stage of the ancient East as a great world-conquering power—a role for which the race was probably the least well-fitted of all the races which have aspired to play it, and whose playing ended in the disastrous diversion of the Egyptian genius for several generations from its true function of leading the world in the useful arts and crafts. The progress of this diversion, with the temporary blaze of glory and prosperity which accompanied it, we shall have to trace in the next volume.

SUPPLEMENTARY NOTE ON THE HYKSOS RULE

After this volume had passed through the press, a communication was received from Sir Flinders Petrie with regard to the results of his work at Beth-Peleth in Southern Palestine during the season 1928–29. Its bearing on the question of the duration and extent of the Hyksos domination is so manifest that it is here quoted as received.

"We cleared about two dozen tombs of Hyksos age, mostly with scarabs, the gradual decline and changes in which serve to show the relative order of the tombs. At the beginning of the series comes a new Hyksos name, Maot-neb-ra, and just below the well-known Maot-ab-ra. These are certainly XVIth dynasty. At the middle of the series, that is at the latter part of the XVIth, or perhaps in the XVIIth, there comes a scarab of the well-known vizier Har or Hal, of whom over twenty scarabs are known from Egypt, but this one has three signs made differently from the Egyptian form, and is therefore Palestinian. The implication of this is therefore that late in the XVIIth there was still a unified Hyksos rule over Egypt and Palestine. This gives a longer importance to the Hyksos that I had anticipated, and still more does it make impossible the ignoring or telescoping of their rule to fit Berlin requirements."

It is obvious that though there is here only the addition of one more name of a Hyksos king to those already known, together with the evidence of Hyksos rule in Palestine as well as in Egypt up to a late period in the XVIth dynasty or the beginning of the XVIIth, the possibility is opened up of further additions which may make the reconciling of known facts with the extremely short period allotted by some historians to the Hyksos rule an exceedingly difficult process. "The Manethonian tradition", writes Professor Breasted, "in which we find three dynasties of Shepherds or Hyksos (the XVth to XVIIth) is totally without support from the contemporary monuments in the matter of the duration of the Hyksos supremacy in Egypt. A hundred years is ample for the whole period."

Already the facts have made this single-century estimate an impossibility, and, for instance, the *Cambridge Ancient History* now allows (with marks of interrogation) 220 years for a period which Professor Breasted declared to be amply provided for with less than half that time; it seems not impossible that even the reluctantly extended estimates which have recently been conceded will have to be stretched still further.

END OF VOL. I

Printed in Great Britain by R. & R. CLARK, LIMITED, *Edinburgh.*

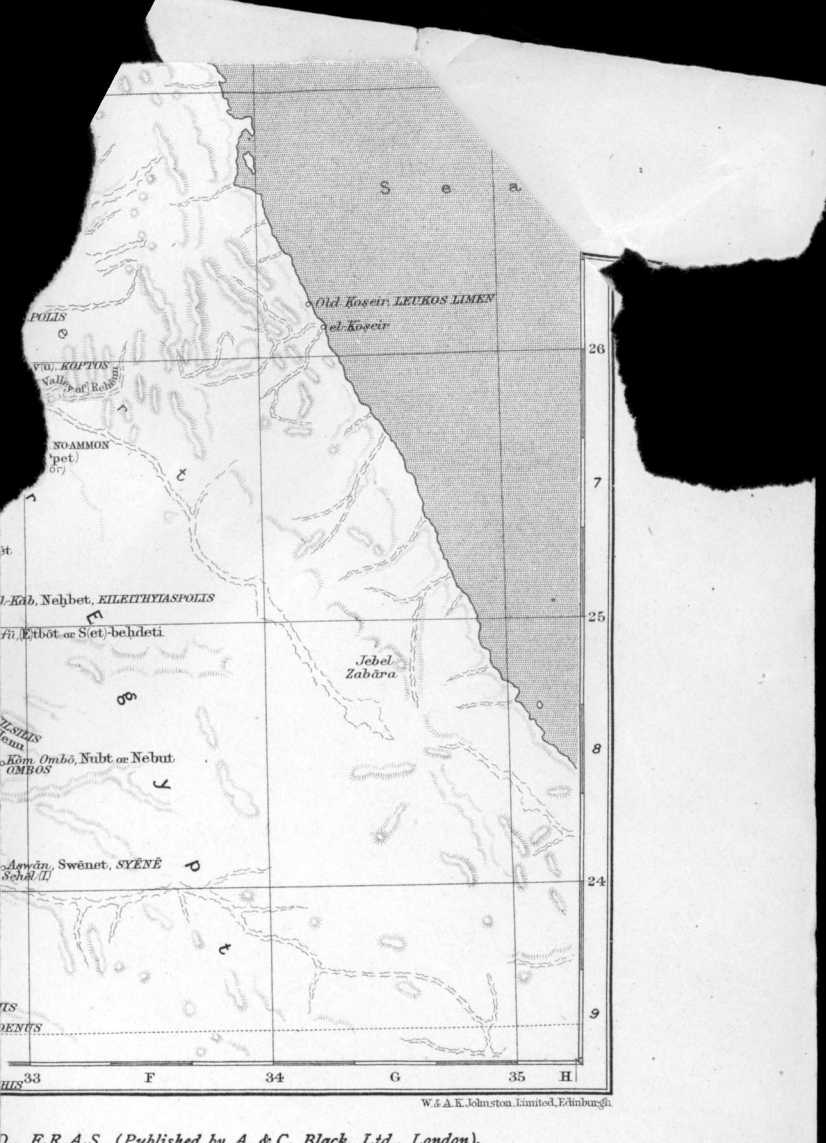

W. & A.K. Johnston, Limited, Edinburgh.

D., F.R.A.S. (Published by A. & C. Black, Ltd., London).

EGYPT

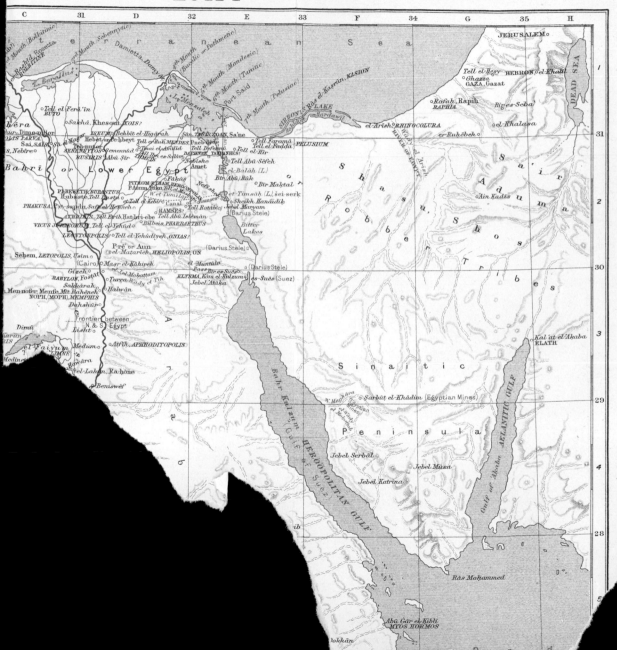

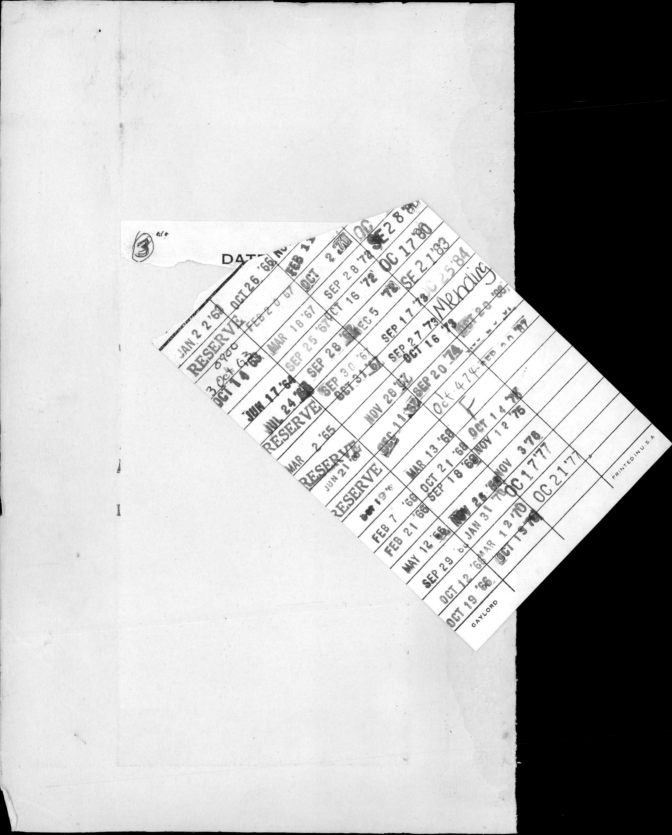